THE TRIAL AND
DEATH OF JESUS

THE TRIAL AND DEATH OF JESUS

by Haim Cohn

KTAV PUBLISHING HOUSE, INC.

NEW YORK

1977

Grateful acknowledgment is made for permisssion to reprint from *New Testament Apocrypha,* Volume One, edited by Edgar Hennecke and Wilhelm Schneemelcher. English translation edited by R. McL. Wilson. Published in the U.S.A. by The Westminster Press, 1963. Copyright © 1959, J. C. B. Mohr (Paul Siebeck), Tübingen. English translation © 1963, Lutterworth Press.

Library of Congress Cataloging in Publication Data

Cohn, Haim Hermann, 1911-
  The trial and death of Jesus.

  Bibliography: p.
  Includes index.
  1. Jesus Christ—Trial. 2. Jesus Christ—Crucifixion. I. Title.
[BT440.C65 1977]   232.96′2   77-3434
ISBN 0-87068-443-4

Manufactured in the United States of America

CONTENTS

viii | CONTENTS

ACKNOWLEDGMENTS

The thesis expounded in this book was first enunciated as the Annual Moshe Smoira Memorial Lecture for 1966 at the Hebrew University of Jerusalem. A paper in English based on that lecture was published in the *Israel Law Review,* Volume 2 (1967), under the title, "Reflections on the Trial and Death of Jesus." A much enlarged version in Hebrew was published in book form in 1968 by the Dvir Publishing Company of Tel-Aviv under the title, *Mishpato u-Moto shel Yeishu ha-Notzri.* I am very grateful to the Israel Law Review Association and to the Dvir Publishing Company for allowing me the fullest liberty to draw on those previous publications for the present book, many passages of which are, indeed, but repetitions of what I had written there.

I could not have hoped to produce a book palatable to the English-reading public were it not for the unfailing help graciously extended to me by that great master of English, Max Nurock, of Jerusalem. His sovereign command of the language, the perfection of his style, and his expert knowledge of ancient history and classical literature combined to bestow quite undeserved benefits on my humble effort—and if this book has any literary merit, the merit is his and not mine.

I must also acknowledge my indebtedness to the writings of the late Dr. Paul Winter, of London, whose untimely death last year has deprived New Testament scholarship of one of its outstanding legal exponents.

Finally, I should like to express my gratitude to my good friend, Leo Guzik, of New York, who relieved me of the business matters connected with the publication of this book, and without whose optimistic encouragement I would hardly have ventured on this ambitious undertaking.

INTRODUCTION

Of the sixty thousand-odd books said to have been written on the life of Jesus in the last century alone,[1] not many paid particular attention to his trial, as if the story of it were not really part of the story of his life.[2] Nor were many books written on the trial itself, and of those concerned with investigation and description of the judicial proceedings against Jesus, only a few were written by lawyers and legalistically. This is indeed surprising. No trial in the history of mankind has had such momentous consequences. None has given rise to such far-reaching, authoritative, and persistent assertions of a grave miscarriage of justice. None has had repercussions which have lost nothing of their impact or actuality even after the lapse of almost two millennia. And none has been so widely and yet so inconclusively and unsatisfactorily reported. That all the reports, such as they are, expressly or by necessary implication insinuate that the trial was but a travesty of justice and the crucifixion a judicial murder should have put conscientious legal observers on the alert, rather than dazzle them, with the rest of Christianity, into a belief that no legal argument could shake. It is a belief still so strong and apparently so changeless that the largest concession which even the great liberals among the hierarchy of the Catholic Church would nowadays be prepared to make would be to absolve the Jewish people as a whole, and the Jews of later generations, from a guilt which—they hold—attaches irrevocably to the Jews whom the Gospels accuse of an active part in the trial.

The fact that legal research into the trial and its historical and political background had been undertaken, in the most impressive and thorough manner, by nonlawyers, by theologians and historians may have led jurist students of legal history to believe that nothing was left to be done. It is true that we owe a great debt of gratitude to scholars like Mommsen or Schuerer, who painstakingly and, as a rule, conscientiously collected legal background material from Jewish and Roman sources and made ample use of it for their own purposes; no successor could, or can, do without the foundation that they laid. But, to the lawyer working on this material, it soon becomes evident that what it provides is, indeed, foundation only, raw stuff which must be sifted, analyzed, and appraised to arrive at valid conclusions. Any such process of research presupposes, of course, a readiness in principle to approach the sources critically, with no preconceptions as to their conclusiveness.

That, however, is not the approach to be found in all the books by lawyers on the trial. Even a modern lawyer, brought up in the common law tradition of fairness and caution in evaluating evidence, will ordinarily be unable, if he be a faithful son of the Church, to emancipate himself from the dogma of the "Gospel truth," and will find "legal" ways and means to invest the Gospel reports with evidentiary import and reliability. Thus, in his introduction to a book on the trial, an English judge writes that he shares the traditional Christian belief "that there is weighty historical and other evidence to justify a belief beyond reasonable doubt that the writers of the Gospels had personal knowledge and information of the matters about which they wrote; that their original writings were read and treasured in the Apostolic Churches; that when the original writings disappeared, authentic copies continued in use; that the greater part of the New Testament was in writing before the fall of Jerusalem in A.D. 70 and that the remainder came into existence soon after that event."[3] We shall try to show that the factual premises given by the learned judge as to the nature and dating of the Gospel reports are mistaken; but at least he grants that the premises, which he takes for his starting point, are, for him, a matter of "traditional Christian belief" and, therefore, for him again, unassailable.

Another distinguished jurist, a former Chief Justice of Ontario, says, in the preface to his recent book on the trial, that "the record as contained in the four Gospels is accepted as fact. Where the authors are at variance with one another, their differences are considered just as those found in the evidence of honest witnesses. All evidence is affected by the capacity of the witness to observe, his powers of accurate recollection, his gift of expression and, where his evidence depends on the word of others, the accuracy of the information communicated to him. It is for biblical scholars to debate the authenticity of the Gospel records and how far one version of the same event is to be preferred to another. The approach of the layman is to accept what he finds and in doing so to treat the respective accounts as supplementing one another. This I have done."[4] Here we have a very proper reservation with respect to the experts in purely exegetic and text-critical analysis of the Scriptures; but the implied admission that the texts stand in need of such analysis, presupposing, as it should, some natural caution in assessing them, is straightway thrown to the winds, and they are accepted as they are, as if they were the recorded testimony of credible and trustworthy eyewitnesses. In accepting "what he finds," the author deliberately blinds himself to the fact that what he has found and accepted may well, on specialist scrutiny, be proven unauthentic and, therefore, unreliable. The potential unauthenticity and the manifest inconsistency of the Gospel reports must, then, give the legal historian cause and justification to reject narratives which cannot be supported by law or reason, and accept only what is reasonable or corroborated by legal customs and practices of the time.

It is now no longer seriously disputed that there was not available to the authors of the Gospels any testimony of eyewitnesses who were present at any of the stages of the arrest, trial, or crucifixion of Jesus and gave a direct account of it.[5] There is a vague reference to such in the first verses of the Gospel of Luke: his oral tradition, which he now seeks to preserve in writing, has for its ultimate, but not direct, source what the "eyewitnesses and ministers of the word" had "delivered unto us . . . from the beginning" (1:1–4).[6] A second reference is in the Gospel According to John, saying that he who saw the crucifixion "bare record, and his record is true, and he knoweth that he saith true, that ye might believe" (19:35), again an assurance that the tradition is well founded, but—if only because of the undisclosed identity of the witness—too imprecise to be of any evidentiary value.[7] Theories propounded time and again that the fourth evangelist himself, or Joseph of Arimathaea, may have attended the meeting of the Sanhedrin lack support even in the Gospels. And Peter rendered himself unavailable as an eyewitness by his reported denials (Mark 14:66–72; Matt. 26:69–75; Luke 22:55–62; John 18:16–17). No minutes were taken at the proceedings, and if any documents were indited in connection with the trial, none was preserved.[8] There is not only no resemblance at all between the Gospel accounts and the testimony of witnesses, but they cannot even lay claim to such credit as would normally be accorded nowadays to a reporter's version of proceedings which he had attended.

This rejection of the Gospel reports as dependable evidence is not to be stigmatized as the presumptuous arrogance of lawyers notoriously preoccupied with technicalities. In this respect, lawyers find themselves in the numerous company of theologians and historians who have concluded that the Gospel texts are not, nor were meant to be, historical records of the events which they describe. "The Gospels were not written for the purpose of guiding historians," pronounced a recent book on the trial;[9] "the use which their authors intended for the Gospels was religious, not historical. When the evangelists wrote down their account of Jesus' trial, they did so not with a view to preserving a record for historical research, but in order to convey a religious message." And a great contemporary theologian warns the readers of his biography of Jesus of Nazareth[10] that if they wanted to learn from the Gospel records what really happened, was said and done then and there, they would be disappointed: "If we were to accept uncritically all the traditions recorded in the Gospels as if they were historical accounts, we would submit the Gospels to an examination which is alien to their nature, and would presuppose a historical understanding which they did not pretend to have." But, he continues, it would be quite wrong to assume that, with all their "historical carelessness," the Gospels forbade an independent investigation into what really happened. On the contrary, the theological issues which they raise and determine make one almost compulsory: the independent investigator finds himself challenged by innumerable problems for whose solution the Gospels provide questions but not answers, and "there is no keeping back the stream, however many of its waters may have been channeled into erroneous courses: it is for us then to build true dams and make those waters disappear, and the solid land spread before our eyes."[11] In short, the Gospel traditions are "messages of faith and not historiography":[12] any historical material in their hands the authors used "to add detail and graphic quality," but, on the whole, they freely exercised their fantasy "in presenting, and in meaning to present, not history but theology."[13]

It is submitted—and on good authority—that they had in mind not only this theological purpose but also an apologetic one. The earliest Gospel, of Mark, was written between A.D. 70 and 72, some forty years after the trial and crucifixion;[14] the Gospel of Luke was next, written about 85;[15] the Gospel of Matthew is commonly dated about 90, and that of John about 110.[16] Over the span of the second half of the first and the beginning of the second century, the Christians were a small community, struggling desperately for some measure of tolerance from their Roman overlords, who regarded Christian refusal to worship the deified emperor, Christian insistence on worshiping God and His Messiah, the Christ, as a capital offense.[17] It was bad enough to deny the imperial divinity and pray to an invisible God, as the Jews did; but it was unforgivable, on top of that, to worship "a malefactor crucified by the government of Rome and declared to have an authority exceeding that of the emperor of Rome." Infuriated by the "inflexible obstinacy" of the Christians, by their "adherence to a depraved superstition,"[18] the Romans persecuted them cruelly: surely, from any "public relations" point of view, there can have been no more urgent or important concern for the tormented Christians than to try to enhance their prestige, and better the image of their religion and of Christ, in the eyes of the Roman government and public alike, whereas to admit that Christ had been crucified by Roman authority for a criminal offense, or, a fortiori, to level the slightest criticism or reproach at the Romans for having tried and crucified him, would have been likely to heap fuel on the flames of oppression. It was, therefore, in the vital interest of the Christians, at the time, to represent the contemporary Roman powers-that-be as favorably inclined to the Christ, his activities and teachings, and with no hand at all in his trial and its sequel: if it could be made out that the Roman governor in Jerusalem had been satisfied of the legitimacy and harmlessness of Jesus' works and doctrines, there would be no sense or justice in persecuting Christians in Rome for adopting and following them. This, we hold, is the motive which prompted the evangelists to depict the passion story in a manner calculated to discharge the Roman governor of any responsibility for the crucifixion, placing it squarely upon the shoulders of the Jews, who were anyway an object of intense and equal hatred to Romans and Christians.[19]

It has been suggested that while Jewish Christians must have seen the glory of martyrdom in the Christ precisely because he had been sentenced and crucified by the abhorred Roman governor, the Gentile Christians living in Rome, "who were now acutely conscious that many thousands of Jewish rebels had died similar deaths for contesting Rome's rights to dominion over their land," could never have associated the crucifixion of a rebel or other criminal by the procurator of an overseas province with the alleged divine act of salvation.[20] Thus it was for the sake of Gentile Christianity, no less than for official and outside consumption, that the Roman governor had to be thoroughly whitewashed and a belief in the Christ, his innocence and integrity shown to be entirely compatible with loyalty to Rome and confidence in Roman justice.

Seen in this light, all the "fantasies" and "historical carelessness" of the Gospel authors assume new qualities: in the given situation, they would have done the greatest disservice to their faith- indeed, they might have been persuaded that they would jeopardize its very survival—by reporting the truth that Jesus had been found guilty of the capital *crimen maiestatis* and duly tried and crucified in accordance with Roman law. Even if they had been aware of that truth, they would not, and could not, admit and broadcast it; they felt called upon, not to serve as law reporters or neutral chroniclers, but rather to do their utmost to promote their faith and save it from perdition. Even without taking into account the physical danger in which every Christian found himself, and his licit and fully understandable resolve to guard life and liberty, the purely religious issue was burning enough to warrant emergency action. It was not the first time, or —alas!—the only one, in the history of religions, that, for the glory of God and the victory of the true faith, all otherwise poignant inhibitions would be shed, justice be suppressed, and truth trampled underfoot. In comparison with crimes and atrocities committed in later centuries for those twin causes, falsifications of historical fact, such as those in which the evangelists may have indulged, might, to the outside observer, appear harmless enough.[21] Not only were there misrepresentations dictated by necessity, but nobody really knows to what extent they—or some of them—did not *bona fide* accept the veracity of the stories which they had been told or—albeit not without deviations—had copied from earlier texts.

Another circumstance that impugns the historicity and reliability of the Gospel accounts is a natural tendency of the authors, who, it must be remembered, were not, and did not profess to be, trained historians, to transplant situations of their own experience, and personalities of their own knowledge, into that comparatively distant past in which the events which they describe had taken place. For them, it was self-evident that "rabbis," "scribes," or "elders" in Jerusalem at the time of Jesus were the counterparts of those whom they themselves encountered in the current Jewish communities in Rome or Alexandria, two or three generations afterward. And their cardinal mistake was to assume that the attitude of contemporary rabbis toward Christianity and its founder must have been identical with that of their Jerusalem precursors toward Jesus. They failed to take into consideration that Christianity, as a competing creed, had not come into existence until long after Jesus' death, and that the attitude of Judaism toward its apostatical, traitorous, and ever more popular rival must now have been altogether different from what it was toward an individual preacher and prophet from its own midst. The more numerously the Christian faith took root and the wider the incompatibility became between Jewish tenets and Christian—mainly Pauline—theology, the greater would be the scorn and outspokenness of orthodox Jewish reaction, and, if, as the Gospels were being written, Christians were seemingly harassed by the Romans much more than were Jews, that only sharpened Jewish disdain and disappointment at their heresy.

So the Gospel authors were accustomed to rabbis and scribes and elders who—true enough—were devoured by venom and hatred toward Christians,[22] and the Jerusalem council of priests and elders and scribes (Mark 14:53) could be surmised to have been not otherwise. This is why we find the evangelists portraying councils and crowds of Jews as they knew them from their own local observation, little caring or inquiring whether there was, in fact, any similarity, as far as the attitude to the Christ was concerned, between them and their Jerusalem forebears. Small wonder that the Jews of Jerusalem at the trial of Jesus were supposed by the evangelists to have lived up to their imagined character, and that the conduct of the council of priests and elders was patterned after the open hostility that the evangelists had encountered from rabbis of their own day.[23]

Taking for granted, then, the questionability of the Gospel reports in the light of their purpose and orientation, we must still ask whether the evangelists could not, and did not, rely on valid oral or written traditions for some, at least, of the events which they narrated, and if so, whether it would not be possible to identify them, establish their validity, and single them out for special reliance. The quest for such traditions has occupied scholars for more than a century now, with the upshot that it appears "quite certain" that the Gospels were "preceded by some written accounts, more or less fragmentary, of the Gospel tradition."[24] Luke testifies that "many have taken in hand to set forth in order a declaration of those things which are most surely believed among us" (1:1), but, of the manifold settings-forth, only those of the four evangelists have been preserved, and we do not know whether the others anteceded them and provided them with source material. It is generally assumed that a collection of the sayings of Jesus (the so-called *Logia*) had been in existence and available at least to Luke and Matthew, and its reconstruction was attempted,[25] but sayings in it could bear no relation to the accounts of Jesus' trial and crucifixion. As to the events with which we are concerned, the existence and contents of any literature earlier than the year 70 are matters of pure speculation. In the last analysis, it comes down

to this: the traditions were presumably oral, of the first generation of Jesus' disciples; but it has truly been said that they were
handed down in "separate pieces, passed round independently,
and put together by collectors who adopt a standpoint altogether
foreign to the material itself."[26] In the judgment of a second-
century historian, Papias, "Mark was quite justified in writing
down some things just as he remembered them," without caring
much about their authenticity; and Papias himself, "unlike most
people," "felt at home not with those who had a great deal to
say," but with those who sifted their material and, in the event,
"taught the truth." We owe this information to Eusebius (260–
340), who comments that "Papias got these notions by misinter-
preting the apostolic accounts and failing to grasp what they had
said in mystic and symbolic language. For he seems to have been a
man of very small intelligence, to judge from his books."[27] It is
illuminating that the sources and methods of the evangelists and
apostles should in those earliest centuries have already given rise
to doubts and discussions, and it is hardly surprising that this
dubiety has persisted until today.[28]

Even if we must despair of the possibility of validating any
given tradition on the strength of external evidence, we should
perhaps not abandon the possibility of doing so by other means.
One test, for instance, could be that the tradition is common to
all the evangelists: if each repeated and adopted it, one might
presume that they had a satisfactory and conclusive source.
Another could be that it is objectively reasonable that the events
could indeed, in the given and known circumstances, have happened in the way and the setting described.[29] Either test may be
expressed negatively. A tradition reported in an earlier Gospel,
which the later evangelists, or any of them, saw fit to dismiss, by
contradiction or exclusion, as untrue or unreliable may well be
viewed with suspicion. Or events which could not, in the given
and known circumstances, actually have happened in fact in the
way and the setting described may safely be ascribed to fancy
rather than to sober tradition.

It is by no means an easy task to determine which of the traditions that found expression in the Gospels has the fiat of all the
evangelists: the discrepancies are many and multiple, and at times
concern issues so fundamental that, at first glance, one might

think that they spoke of totally different events and personalities. It looks as if Jesus in Mark were not the same person as Jesus in John: "They speak differently, act differently, die differently."[30] For our purpose, there is nothing so relevant as the traditions surrounding the events that led up to the crucifixion, but it is just in that context that the Gospels are full of contradictions, and many of the incongruities do not lend themselves to reconciliation. We are faced with the choices of a night trial before the Sanhedrin (Mark 14:55–64 and Matt. 26:59–66), an early morning trial (Luke 22:66–71), and no sanhedrial trial at all (John 18:19–21), and there are several variants as to the details of the proceedings before Pilate. The dilemma could be made less tractable only if, as has been suggested, we were to read into one Gospel accounts coming from another:[31] that would, indeed, not be legitimate, and would cause confusion rather than clarification. Bible exegetes and text critics claim that they can sift the reliable from the not, or the more from the less, accepting one version as original and authentic, discarding the other as corruption and interpolation—a method not open to, or envied by, the unbiased lay reader, who is, a priori, entirely ready to give every version that he meets the like credit and an even chance of authenticity. Nor can he be greatly encouraged by the results of the critical exegesis, seeing that, to the original inconsistencies in the Gospel accounts, there are added those which stem from the all too often irreconcilable differences of opinion among the exegetes. Rather than rely on this or the other exegetic theory, we shall invoke the benefit of laity and endeavor to consider each version on its merits, disregarding none, however much it may be rebutted.

There are, to be sure, a good many traditions which have mustered the consensus of all evangelists and thus pass our first test. Of those which directly concern us, the following enjoy that unanimity: Jesus was arrested at night; some Jews were present at the arrest and took part in it; after arrest, he was brought into the house of the high priest; the next morning, the Jews brought him before Pontius Pilate; to Pilate's question "Art thou the King of the Jews?" he replied, "Thou sayest it" (or: "Thou sayest that I am a king"); Pilate "delivered" him to be crucified; he was crucified, together with two other convicts, by Roman soldiers; and a "title" was put on the cross with the words "King of the Jews."

Our inquiry will show that these traditions satisfy also our second test: what they tell is objectively reasonable because, in the circumstances and under the prevailing conditions as we know them, it could, in fact, have happened. In this respect, they differ from other traditions on which, also, the evangelists are unanimous: it will be shown that the episodes of Judas Iscariot and of Barabbas, for instance, could not have so happened, and, therefore, cannot be accepted as "objectively reasonable."

We shall start, then, from the premise that events described by all the evangelists in substantially the same manner which, in the circumstances and under the prevailing conditions as we know them from independent and indubitable sources, could conceivably have taken place in that manner did, indeed, so happen. The framework thus fashioned will have to be engrossed with such further detail as the source material available to us may warrant.

The fact that, in the circumstances as we know them, any such reported event could conceivably have happened does not necessarily mean that it did in fact happen. We are concerned not so much with the historicity of the events as with the evidentiary worth of the tradition. Once accepted as potentially valid testimony, each tradition will be the starting point from which the further inquiry may proceed, the nucleus around which the potentially true story will have to be retold. For example, that Jesus was arrested, if accepted as a practically uncontested starting point, will at once invite the questions by whom, on whose orders, and for what purpose. Or, that he was brought into the high priest's house, though an accepted fact, is, in itself, inconclusive until one knows why, and what actually happened, or might have happened, there before he was delivered into the hands of the Roman governor.

It is as well to avoid involvement in the centuries-old argument as to the historicity or nonhistoricity of Jesus himself, his ministry, or any particular episodes of his life, or, for that matter, the life of Pontius Pilate and his governorship of Judaea. Jewish advocates of nonhistoricity have, at times, tried to set aside not only Christian eschatology, but Christology as a whole, by the simple expedient of denying that Jesus had ever lived or been crucified. Non-Jewish protagonists of the theory have cited the inherent uncertainty of the Gospel tradition and the absence of all external evidence.[32] But Rousseau gave early warning that denial of the historicity of Jesus is nothing more than reluctance to grapple with the difficulties presented by the Gospel inconsistencies, not a solution of them; moreover, "things like that are not just invented."[33] We may go along with a great contemporary Protestant scholar who lamented that "we cannot know the character of Jesus, his life, or his personality; none of his words can be regarded as purely authentic,"[34] and confessed that, in his opinion, "we can sum up what we know of the life and personality of Jesus as simply nothing,"[35] yet asserted unequivocally that "there is no ground at all for any doubt of the actual existence of Jesus; indeed, the idea of his historicity need not be defended."[36] Belief in the historicity of Jesus is not at odds with acceptance of the shortcomings and even valuelessness of much of the source material, any more than belief in his nonhistoricity is a necessary or inescapable consequence of conceding that the sources to hand are unauthentic and unreliable. It will transpire that, however critical and skeptical the approach to the sources may be, what emerges from the analysis of such traditions as are found objectively probable and thus potentially valid is amply sufficient to make Jesus appear—even to those without emotional or religious predilections—as a personality very much alive, and very much to be admired.

We shall be constrained to pass upon the historicity of certain events in negative mood, by showing that they could never have happened as reported. In our test of "objective reasonableness" is implied a negation of the objectively unreasonable, and hence unbelievable: if it can be determined that the description or interpretation of a certain event is at variance or discordant with facts satisfactorily established, or with the natural and logical trend of contemporaneous reasoning, or with known data of contemporaneous religious or political expediencies and necessities, it ought not, in reason and fairness, to be assumed that, though so pictured in the Gospel reports, people did in actuality behave abnormally and unnaturally and against their better interest. If we start from the premise that the reports are biased and tendentious, it is only by testing every detail against the background of conditions of life at the time, including laws and customs as we know them from independent sources, that we may succeed in winnowing the reliable from the uncertain, the acceptable from the inadmissible.[37] It is true that this examination and the consequent rejection of a particular report may entail, at one and the same time, acceptance of traditions found potentially valid and rejection of apparently authentic interpretations of them as unreasonable: while, for instance, accepting the tradition that Jesus, after arrest, was brought into the house of the high priest, we may have to reject the Gospel report as to why he was brought there. But, insofar as concerns motives and intentions behind overt acts, interpretations by reporters—including trained historians—are always open to doubt and revision, and are, in fact, always approached questioningly by critics possessing their own means of information; and where a reporter is known to have written with some tendentious purpose, those interpretations of his are highly suspicious in any case, however exact his reportage of the outward events. If that applies to contemporary history, it must apply all the more to events described after the lapse of half a century; and if it applies to history written in our own days, with all the modern apparatus of research at the reporter's disposal, it must apply all the more to "history" written two thousand years ago. Even where any interpretation of intention or motive was itself based on some tradition, that is to say, even where the evangelists had a tradition to rely upon not only for the occurrence of an event but also for what had prompted the actors in it to act as they did, the interpretative element of the tradition may legitimately be jettisoned even though the factual element is not. Aside from personal views and conclusions, traditions, too, may have their origin in preconceived ideas, in prejudices, in slanted orientations. To discover and comprehend the true meaning and import of events described, and the considerations and aims behind them, we will do better to look at the actors rather than at the reporters. We pride ourselves on knowing today a good deal more about the actors than the reporters did: we have neutral and credible evidence of their laws and customs,[38] their way of thinking and reacting, their internal strife, their political aspirations and frustrations, their religious and scholarly involvements. It is in the light of this knowledge that we shall try to understand their conduct and bare their motives, and so arrive at a reconstruction of the events as, in the circumstances and with these particular dramatis personae, they could well have happened. This may, of course, amount to a finding that, since they could have happened only in a certain way, they could not have happened in any other, that, if they did happen, it was thus alone.

It is the lawyer's privilege never to take the reported fact for granted: rightly or wrongly, he feels called upon to delve into the evidence, ascertain its source and validity, and make sure of its credibility before conceding the fact as established to his satisfaction.[39] Neither the reputation of illustrious and ancient historians and scholars nor the authority and sacrosanctity of Scripture can deflect him from his task of weighing and appraising every piece of evidence on its merits. There is no shred of disrespect in an investigation of this kind: even the greatest genius, even the holiest of men, by undertaking to interpret reported facts, implicitly invites a critical assessment of his views; it was only by later canonizers that some such books were elevated to the rank of untouchability and indisputability. True scholarship—including true theological scholarship—always held itself entitled, and in duty bound, to explore the factual background of scriptural tradition, undismayed by the possibility that its conclusions might conflict with biblical texts. This is, indeed, the stand which modern Christian theology has taken in respect of the life and death of Jesus as reported in the Gospels; and it is not least the courage and imagination displayed by some of the eminent theologians of our time toward a revision of inveterate errors and prejudices that sprang from misconceived Gospel interpretations that heartened me to embark, from the lawyer's point of view and with a lawyer's tools, on an inquiry into those aspects of that life and death which have made legal history.

PART ONE

Dramatis Personae

1   THE ROMANS

Jesus was a small child when King Herod, sometimes called the Great, died (4 B.C.). Whether or not, shortly before, he had ordered all the children "from two years old and under" in Bethlehem to be killed (Matt. 2:16), and whether or not Jesus' parents had to flee to Egypt to escape his wrath and cruelty (2:13-14), the fact is undisputed that his death, as he had himself anticipated,[1] was an occasion of immense joy and relief for the people.[2] Herod had been an absolute monarch of uninhibited viciousness, whose persecutions and murders were not confined to his real or imaginary political enemies but extended to all who were suspected of disliking or disobeying him, his own next of kin not excepted. What the Jews had resented perhaps more than his wanton savagery was his flagrant transgression of law and tradition, and his trespasses upon the competence of Jewish courts and established institutions.[3] With his passing, the Jews could breathe freely again, and fugitives came back with new hopes (Matt. 2:19-21).

But a bitter disappointment was in store. Herod, though of Idumean descent, had been a Jew and a Jewish king—albeit by the grace of the Roman emperor who was suzerain of Judaea. It was one thing to be ruled by a Jewish king, even though one knew

3

perfectly well, and was reminded all too often, that he owed tribute to Rome and was its vassal, and quite another to be ruled by a heathen, an alien enemy, a ruthless foreign captor. When a quarrel for the succession erupted among Herod's sons, the emperor decided to placate each with territory to the north and east, but to Judaea itself he sent a Roman procurator, an imperial agent or commissioner, fully empowered to administer the province and governing in lieu of the emperor in person.

The province of Judaea in general and the city of Jerusalem in particular were notorious in Rome as hotbeds of insurrection and revolt. There was probably no place in the vast empire where the Romans were so deeply hated and so implacably despised as in Jerusalem. It has rightly been observed that these feelings were not based solely upon patriotic motivation: their real roots were religious.[4] For the Jews, this was their holy land, and Jerusalem holier still, and the temple in Jerusalem the holiest of all: the presence and government there of the abominable pagan were a pollution and a defilement, an unforgivable insult to the invisible but ever present God Who had chosen that temple for His own sanctuary. The Jews never made any secret of their affronted susceptibilities, and the emperors well knew with what kind of people they had to deal, a people who, so far from being amenable to recognition of the emperor as a god incarnate, or at least to belief in the long-standing and incontestable pantheon of Rome, clung to this invisible and illusory phantom of a God with a loyalty and persistence exclusive of even minimal allegiance to their rightful Roman lords.

When, after Herod's death, the emperor left a Roman commander in charge of the garrison in Jerusalem, the Jews thought that the time had come, with no new ruler yet appointed, "to recover the freedom of their fathers."[5] They rose up against the commander, and were so desperate and bold in battle that they were on the brink of overwhelming the garrison and expelling it when some of its officers set fire to the temple; in the conflagration thousands died and the rest were forced to surrender.[6] Varus, governor of Syria, brought down reinforcements to suppress further uprisings; he is reported to have ordered the crucifixion of two thousand of the instigators of the rebellion.[7]

Wholesale massacres of that kind were not likely to heighten local esteem of the Roman occupation forces, or of Roman rule. The people were hopeless and embittered, and the emperor could be sure that revolt might recur any day. Being vitally interested—and not only for reasons of imperial prestige—in keeping Judaea under Roman governance, and having, apparently, been unable to find, either among Herod's sons or elsewhere, a Jewish choice for a puppet kingship whom he could trust to maintain peace and order and to support and promote Roman interests, he naturally looked among his generals and administrators for a strong man to whom the control of this pernicious people could safely be assigned.

During the next thirty years, governors came and went. However long or brief their tenure, all saw it their paramount duty ruthlessly to smother any possible opposition to Rome, and, more particularly, any manifestation of violent resistance or revolt. And they had one other important, if private, purpose in common: to extract from their stay in Judaea as much wealth as they possibly could.[8] It is true that, in this respect, Judaea presumably did not differ from other Roman provinces, and that the gubernatorial appetite for enrichment was everywhere the same; but then the people in Judaea might have been somewhat less affluent, and hence much more sensitive to extortions. Taxation does not generally endear authority to the populace; but taxation by an alien occupier, which gives the taxpayer no tangible consideration beyond oppression and contempt, is the best way of filling him with enduring rancor. Nor were the methods of Roman taxation such as to mitigate the evil: a man could not know beforehand what he would have to pay, because there was no law or decree to determine it; if he at least knew to what use his money was going to be put, he might perhaps have taken the taxation as a normal and unavoidable incidence of government, be it ever so dictatorial and detestable. Many of the Roman governors of Judaea levied taxes in indeterminate amounts,[9] and "taxation" assumed confiscatory proportions. Roman and Roman-appointed tax collectors often neglected to differentiate between the imperial fisc and their private pockets,[10] exacting more "than which is appointed them" (Luke 3:13). Citizens from whom all their money had already been squeezed found themselves sued and jailed as defaulting debtors. Tax collector deservedly became synonymous with thief and blackmailer:[11] no criminal wrongdoer could have been more dangerous or contemptible than these official robbers, who, enjoying governmental power and immunity, would take double and threefold revenge on their victims for hating and despising them as they did.

The Jewish attitude to tax collectors for the Romans is symptomatic. We have it on the authority of both Talmud and New Testament that they were regarded as "sinners" with whom self-respecting Jews like Pharisees would not sit at table or in any other way communicate; they are the "publicans" of whom Jesus said that they are "sick" (Matt. 9:12). A Jew who would collaborate with the Romans, for instance by gathering taxes for them, would be deemed a malefactor and an outcast, excluded from Jewish society (the "sitting at table together"), disqualified as witness in court;[12] even the members of his family would be suspect if they failed to prevent him from so degrading himself as to become a lackey of Rome.[13]

This kind of ostracism was enforced not only for Jewish collaborators but also, and much more rigorously, for the Romans themselves. The story in the Gospel According to John that the Jews would not enter the palace of the Roman governor lest they defile themselves (18:28), even if, as will appear, irrelevant in the context, throws light on the prevalent Jewish aversion from entering a Roman dwelling. Elsewhere, we are told that Peter entered the home of Cornelius, a Roman captain, and though Cornelius is described as "a devout man, and one that feared God with all his house, which gave much alms to the people, and prayed to God alway" (Acts 10:2), yet Peter said, "Ye know how that it is an unlawful thing for a man that is a Jew to keep company, or come unto one of another nation" (10:28), and felt it necessary to explain why he thought fit to break the law. It is not only that the Roman is "unclean"—the detailed and intricate laws of purification being unknown and unintelligible to him; it is that he is the living incarnation of idolatry and debauchery, of materialism and sensuality, of might and tyranny—in short, of everything repugnant to what Judaism stands for. Not only would the Jew not enter the Roman's dwelling, he would not even touch him, let alone shake hands with him. The remark of Tacitus that the Jews "confront the rest of the world with the hatred reserved for enemies"[14] correctly reflects their attitude to Romans; and when he goes on to say that "to the Jews all things are profane that we hold sacred,"[15] he is expressing with precision the exactly converse feeling of Jews in respect of things Roman. When Tacitus wrote, all Jewish resistance had been finally overcome and nothing was left of Jewish statehood; and while their deportment toward the victors was far from friendly or conciliatory, Jews overseas would certainly hold aloof from Romans as best they could; yet all this was negligible compared with the open revulsion with which they confronted the enemy in their own land.

It is not a simple or pleasant situation when a Roman dignitary, representing the empire in an occupied country, finds himself not only detested and despised but shunned and avoided as if stricken by a foul or contagious sickness. Officers like Cornelius, God-fearing and benevolent, must have been rare exceptions; but even to them the "law" applied that forbade all fraternizing. Cornelius seems to have accepted the ban with a good grace; but in that respect, too, he must have been unique. From what we know of the Roman governors in Judaea in general, and of Pontius Pilate in particular, it must be inferred that they reacted to the insulting and offensive impertinence of barbarous natives with blind fury. And things were made worse by their awareness that this Jewish hatred and contempt was not a spontaneous retort of the vanquished to the presence and provocation of the oppressor, but a matter of law and policy, its source in an insolent superiority complex, and systematically nurtured as a requisite of true religion and personal purity. A Roman governor who could look upon this behavior with detachment would scarcely have been human, and it cannot be said of that cadre in Judaea that it was distinguished for its magnanimity.

Pontius Pilate became governor of Judaea in the year 25. The first thing that he did was, in the words of Josephus, "to demonstrate his contempt of the Jewish laws."[16] It is a fundamental precept of the Decalogue that "thou shall not make unto thee any graven image or any likeness of any thing that is in heaven above or that is in the earth beneath" (Exod. 20:4; Deut. 5:8), but ancient Roman custom was to display the image of the deified emperor, graven or sculptured or limned, on monuments and buildings, on military standards and insignia. The contemptuous Pilate accordingly had the emperor's image mounted on all standards and brought into the holy city of Jerusalem. He was fully conscious of the hazard—a predictable Jewish rejoinder to a provocation so gross, and maybe it was anticipations of that contingency that had restrained his predecessors. But Pilate was guileful: he would not lay his troops open to violence from an enraged populace: the images would be introduced clandestinely at night and mounted in the streets, so that, at morn, vainglorious Jews would find their sacred capital bedecked with the profane imperial likeness, willy-nilly, and his soldiers would be safely back in barracks.[17] Apart from the spitefulness of his maneuver, he might have thought that it was timely to teach these stubborn people a lesson. What was good and self-understood for the plethora of nations subject to Roman rule, which—no less than the Jews—had deities and loyalties of their own but still *nolentes volentes* had accepted the imperial insignia in their—no less holy—cities,[18] was good and should be self-understood for the Jews. He would stand no nonsense from them. He would face them with a *fait accompli* which would bring home to them what the new kind of order was that would reign in their cities, and who the exalted ruler was that they would be well advised to honor and obey.

We may take it that the legionaries, back in barracks, were on the alert for a dawn outbreak. Whether it was because the Jews, realizing that the troops were ready to strike mercilessly, desired to avoid bloodshed, or whether it was because Pilate was a new governor, as yet unknown, and they wanted to give him a chance and remonstrate first before breaking off relations—the fact is that, however chagrined and outraged they were, no disorder took place. Josephus recounts that great throngs, from Jerusalem and the surrounding countryside, marched to Caesarea where the governor lived. The journey must have taken several days, and there can be little doubt that, from the towns and villages on the way, hundreds more joined the march, so that the multitudes were such in the end that room could be found for them only in the large stadium of Caesarea, and that is where, by Pilate's orders, they were herded. We are told that they implored Pilate to have the imperial insignia taken out of Jerusalem, but he refused, "because that would be an insult to the emperor." They would not take no for an answer, and for six days and six nights lay upon the ground, unmoving. On the seventh day, "Pilate ordered his troops to arm themselves and hide behind (or beneath) the platform of the stadium, and then suddenly commanded them to encircle the Jews. He then threatened the Jews that they would all be mowed down unless they departed at once. Whereupon they threw themselves down, bared their throats, and declared that they would rather die than have their wise and just laws violated."[19] In another version, Pilate asked them not to depart at once, but willingly to accept the emperor's images in their cities; and they, baring their throats, cried out that "rather would they let themselves be killed than break their laws."[20] The two versions seem complementary: the Jews would not depart, and would not agree to the mounting of the insignia in their cities. Though they were unarmed, and Pilate had nothing to fear from them for himself or his troops, or possibly because of that, he gave no order to carry out his threat, but bade his troops withdraw. Josephus reports that "Pilate could not but admire such constancy in the observance of law, and he gave orders for the standards to be brought back from Jerusalem to Caesarea."[21]

It has with good reason been noted that this passage in Josephus is much obscured by apologetics: he sought to place both the Roman governor and his own—the Jewish—people in the most favorable light before his Roman readers.[22] It is surprising that the Jews, who would not normally refrain from violent and spontaneous outbursts if their religious feelings were hurt, should deliberately organize a well-marshaled and well-behaved mass demonstration, and that myriads should march to faraway Caesarea in peaceful protest and to parley with the governor. And no less surprising that Pilate, having gone the lengths of planning a nocturnal intrusion of the insignia and dispatching standards and soldiery to Jerusalem, and after seeing his plan succeed, should suddenly be overwhelmed by a spectacle of "the constancy" in observance of Jewish law and give in lamely to the Jews' demands: it was this very "constancy," dubbed "stubborn obstinacy," which had first prompted him to teach them a lesson. It could be nothing new to him now; and it does not stand to reason that he should, all of a sudden, be so charitably impressed by it. It may well be that Josephus did not give us the full story: perhaps there were disturbances in Jerusalem and the Roman troops fared badly;

perhaps, reporting to Rome and asking for instructions, Pilate was told not, for the time being, to let clashes with the natives over their ancestral religion go to extremes. At all events, the fact that the first real encounter between the new governor and the Jews ended with his defeat and their victory could only have exacerbated Pilate's aversion to them, with dislike now deepened by a sense of frustration and fury.

As far as the Jews were concerned, the organizers of the march to Caesarea would certainly have known that it might entail grave dangers and even be regarded as outright and officially sponsored rebellion. In the issue, they were proven sound in their surmise that in the first months of his governorship Pilate would probably not involve himself in embarrassing massacres of peaceful demonstrators or would get instructions from Rome to curb himself. One may guess that the demonstrators were no less astonished at the swift, fortuitous turn of events than their leaders in Jerusalem, and the success is likely to have inspired the adoption of similar methods in a comparable predicament fifteen years later,[23] again with eventual effect. That the Jews found themselves in this kind of trouble under subsequent governors only shows that Pilate's individual failure did not deter his successors from trying again, not only with the imperial insignia mounted in the streets or on the walls of the city, but even with the emperor's bust in the very temple.[24] Some ancient Christian sources aver that Pilate himself had placed a bust of Caesar in the temple,[25] but the statements are uncorroborated and evidently based on "inaccurate reminiscence."[26]

When Pilate decided to provide Jerusalem with an extra supply of water and looked about for its financing, he turned, as a matter of course, to the temple treasury—not by negotiating with the wardens of it for voluntary or quasi-voluntary contributions or votes, but by peremptory sequester. Needless to say, the Jews rebelled—or, in the delicate language of Josephus, were somewhat "displeased"; and "thousands of people ran together and, loudly shouting, demanded that he should abstain." Pilate thereupon "sent a strong detachment of soldiers, disguised as Jews, with clubs hidden beneath their clothes, to a place where they could easily encircle the Jews." When the Jews refused to disperse and piled abuse on the Romans, Pilate "gave the soldiers a prearranged sign, and they descended upon peaceful citizens as well as upon insurgents, much more savagely than Pilate had intended. But the Jews would not give up their stubbornness, and as they were unarmed, they could not defend themselves against the armed soldiers, and many of them were killed, many others were carried away wounded. Thus this rebellion was suppressed.''[27] Josephus reports that "the shock at the horrible fate of the casualties brought the people to silence.''[28]

Josephus does not enlighten us on why Pilate chose that his soldiers mingle in disguise with the people, not suppress the rising openly and straightforwardly. There is the hint that he had not intended such savage manhandling, and the theory has been propounded that by arming the troops with clubs, not swords, he may have intended police rather than army action and wished no bloodletting.[29] I am inclined to think that his plan was purely strategic: in an open encounter with a crowd of thousands, a much larger repressive force would be required than if there was surprise from within, and the sequel proved him right. It is noteworthy that he had to garb his men as Jews: for a Roman, as such, to mix among the Jews was perilous indeed. But even that subterfuge, shameful though it was for a Roman procurator, was a welcome means in his eyes, if thereby he might only achieve his purpose of putting down the rebellion firmly and finally, and suffer no Roman losses.

Of a third major clash between Pilate and the Jews, also linked with the temple, we have some scant evidence in the Gospels. When Jesus was in Jerusalem, "there were present at that season some that told him of the Galilaeans, whose blood Pilate had mingled with their sacrifices" (Luke 13:1). It appears that Pilate had decreed a slaughter of Galileans who had come to Jerusalem for the festival offerings; but there is no indication what his reason was. It would be logical to assume that these Galileans were rebellious zealots, and, indeed, in later Christian sources we find "Galilean" as a synonym for zealot:[30] there may have been an uprising in Jerusalem during the festival, which Pilate decided to quell by surprising the worshipers at their prayers in the temple and massacring them on the spot.[31]

In the same context, Jesus speaks of "those eighteen, upon whom the tower in Siloam fell, and slew them" (Luke 13:4), enigmatic words which have been taken to refer to the construction of the aqueduct for the water supply, when such an accident may have happened;[32] it has even been contended that the incident is identical with the rebellion reported in Josephus over that project,[33] but the theory appears untenable in view not only of the enormous disparity in the numbers of the victims but also of the difference of localities. Nor is there ground enough to dismiss the Gospel account as having mistaken Pilate for another governor in whose time there may have been a similar accident.[34] It is much more plausible that the words, read in their context, refer to another brutal attack by orders of Pilate in which, again, innocent people were wantonly killed.[35]

Finally, Pilate and the Jews seem to have collided on a minor scale when on the former palace of Herod in Jerusalem he set up "some guilded shields," bearing no image of the emperor but only a brief inscription recording his name and that of the person who had vowed the shields to him. One might have supposed that such objects would be deemed innocuous even by the most pedantic of Jewish legalists. But apparently it was not so, and a Jewish delegation, led by four Herodian princes, petitioned Pilate to remove them, on the plea that they infringed native customs which other kings and emperors had respected. When Pilate is obdurate, the Jews are represented

as torn between their loyalty to the emperor and obedience to their religion. They call on Pilate not to cause a revolt, nor break the peace, nor use Tiberius as an excuse for insulting their nation. They challenge Pilate to produce the authority for his action, and threaten to appeal to the emperor, whom they significantly call their master. This threat is stated to have disturbed Pilate most profoundly, because he feared that his maladministration would thus become known to Tiberius, who would not tolerate such action.[36]

In contradistinction to his alleged indulgence in the matter of the imperial insignia, Pilate is said not to have yielded. The Jews did complain to the emperor, and Tiberius is described as "moved by excessive anger" on receipt of their complaint, and to have written to Pilate condemning him "for his rash innovation in the most uncompromising manner."[37] It is highly improbable that the emperor would thus interfere with his provincial governor's dis-

cretion in a matter of such unimportance, and the whole story—
said to have been told in a letter from the Jewish prince Agrippa
to the Emperor Gaius—appears to have been transmitted for the
sake of the concluding remark: "that in this signal manner the
traditional [Roman] policy towards Jerusalem had been maintained."[38] Gaius was the adopted son and successor of Tiberius,
and it would only be natural for a vassal-prince to pen flattery
of that emperor to him; and Agrippa was, of course, interested in
establishing that "the traditional Roman policy toward Jerusalem"
was generous and indulgent, however implacable and oppressive
this or the other governor may have been. Not that Roman policy
was as generous and indulgent as all that; but neither did Pilate's
conduct in this particular affair show any unusual or insulting
highhandedness. The Herodian palace in Jerusalem was a secular
building, with no religious association at all; after Herod's death
it served the Roman governors as their Jerusalem residence, and
there was no ostensible reason why a governor should not exhibit
such harmless, though typically Roman, embellishments on it. As
a matter of fact, the objection would not, and cannot, have come
either from Jewish religious authorities or from the Jewish public:
neither could have been pained by the setting up of the shields
any more than by the governor's residence as such. That the
"delegation" to Pilate was "headed by four Herodian princes"
suggests the clue: it was the Herodian clan which must have resented the interference with the beautiful façade of its palace, and,
to induce the governor to leave it intact, resorted to arguments
of Jewish laws and customs: to such, or so the clan thought, the
governor must be amenable, and besides, he would be unable to
check their accuracy. What the governor did know was that, of all
the Jews, it was only the Herodian princes who had access to, and
influence in, the emperor's court; if, nevertheless, he refused their
petition, he must have had a healthy dislike for them, as is, indeed,
borne out by the "enmity" reported in Luke 23:12.

That Roman policy toward Jerusalem during the reign of
Tiberius was anything but generous or tolerant, and that there
was no love lost between the emperor and the Jews, we know from
Roman sources. Tiberius abolished "the Jewish cult," and forced
all citizens embracing this "superstitious faith" to burn their religious vestments and other accessories. "Jews of military age were

removed to unhealthy regions, on the pretext of drafting them into the army; those too old or too young to serve were expelled from the city and threatened with slavery if they defied the order."[39] How this squared with the emperor's character and general thinking is evidenced by the pronouncement of the same or similar decrees against other foreign cults and against astrologers; the Jews were in no wise singled out. A complaint to Tiberius of the governor's disregard of Jewish customs by parading Roman decorations on his official residence, so far from moving Tiberius to "excessive anger" against Pilate, would probably have ended in his confiscating the Herodian palace for the governor and divesting the complainants of their title. For that is how "leading Spanish, Gallic, Syrian and Greek provincials" fared when they offered him the slightest pretext, the "most trivial and absurd" cause, to enrich himself by seizing their properties.[40] If Tiberius was conspicuous in any one branch of law enforcement, it was *crimen laesae maiestatis,* where his own honor was involved: "for criticizing anything the emperor had ever said or done," a man would be put to death; to wear robes resembling the emperor's was also a capital offense; to carry a ring or coin bearing his image "into a privy or a brothel," likewise; and "the climax came when a man died merely for letting an honor be voted to him by his native town council on the same day that honors had once been voted" to the emperor.[41] His motto was: Let them hate me, so long as they fear me![42] and he succeeded amazingly well in his twin objectives.

Pontius Pilate was a loyal servant of his emperor, and the imperial policies were no secret to him. We have it on the authority of Philo, as reported by Eusebius, that Sejanus, the all-powerful minister at the emperor's court, had taken "energetic steps to exterminate the whole Jewish race":[43] it is assumed that, with this purpose in mind, he had prevailed upon Tiberius, or his predecessor, to send Pilate as governor to Judaea[44]—he was strong-minded, ruthless, and dependable enough to be entrusted with a mission of that nature. Quite apart from the imperial policy toward the Jews and Judaism, Pilate faithfully pursued the policy of Tiberius respecting *crimen maiestatis;* if we have no records of legal absurdities as extravagant as are reported of his master in person, it may safely be assumed that Pilate would in no case and in no circumstances make light of a charge smacking of contempt of him or of actual or planned rebellion against him. There was ample precedent, express and implied sanction, to give the relevant statutes the widest possible interpretation;[45] and if the emperor in Rome saw fit, and considered it necessary, to enforce the law of *crimen maiestatis* with the utmost rigor and severity, his agent in a faraway province, with inhabitants notoriously defiant of Roman rule and contemptuous of the emperor, must have all the more reason, and feel all the more constrained, to proceed remorselessly against provincials suspected of that effrontery.

For this kind of job Pilate was eminently right. Philo makes Agrippa, in the letter to Gaius, portray Pilate's character thus: he was "naturally inflexible and stubbornly relentless"; he committed "acts of corruption, insults, rapine, outrages on the people, arrogance, repeated murders of innocent victims, and constant and most galling savagery.[46] We may accept the view that "Philo's testimony as to Pilate's character is the most trustworthy we possess. In the first place, as a contemporary of Pilate, Philo was in a better position than any of the latter writers to come to an accurate assessment; in the second place, Philo's judgment was not in any way influenced by the part Pilate played in the condemnation of Jesus—indeed, he does not seem to have been aware of the existence of Jesus."[47] We have, then, the arrogant and ruthless emperor represented in Judaea by a governor no less ruthless and arrogant: each excelled in "outrages on the people" and "constant and most galling savagery," and the emperor's aversion to the Jewish cult as well as to its followers was shared by Pilate to the full. If ever there was a dedicated servant carrying out his master's instructions in the spirit in which they were given, performing his odious duties in the fashion in which his master would wish them performed, it was Pontius Pilate; and the corruption, rapine, and murders of innocents, of which Pilate is said to have been guilty, were also wholly in the style and true to the form of his emperor and employer.

Our premise, then, is that Pilate was chosen for the procuratorship of Judaea, presumably by Sejanus, because of his character qualifications. But there are those who think—and there is no evidence to the contrary—that he acquired his evil ways only after he came to Judaea. He was certainly not an ideal governor, Eduard

Meyer writes, "but if even their own rulers could never cope with the Jews, and each measure they took provoked immediate criticism and fanatical resistance—a normal Roman officer must have been driven by them to utter despair. . . . Add thereto the never ending acts of violence of the bandits, always covered up by religio-political motives. That the governors then occasionally grew wild and attacked blindly, ought only too well to be understood."[48] The immense difficulty of governing Jews against their will should not be underrated, but it is submitted that his wild wrath and insensate onslaughts afford an illustration of Pilate's character rather than of his Jewish victims: and this is in the knowledge that there always are—and particularly where persecution of Jews is concerned there always were—men only too eager and willing to incriminate not the murderer but the murdered. In truth, there may have been, here, an interplay of cause and effect: the more oppressive the Roman governor, the more mutinous and unyielding the Jews; the more stiff-necked and insurgent the Jews, the less scruple and mercy in the governor. At the time of which we write, Pilate had been in Judaea for five years, amply long enough to become thoroughly acquainted with the kind of people whom he had to govern, and all his evil ways presumably had been afforded frequent opportunity to develop and emerge.

His last act as governor of Judaea, so Josephus tells, was to intercept with cavalry and foot soldiers a procession of Samaritans to their holy place, the Mount of Gerizim, killing many, taking many prisoners, putting the rest to flight.[49] Of the prisoners, all of influence and eminence were put to death. Whereupon the "high council of the Samaritans" complained to the governor of Syria, protesting loyalty to Rome but charging Pilate with injustice and cruelty. The governor of Syria sent another procurator to Judaea and instructed Pilate to return to Rome and answer before the emperor to the charges. Pilate "did not dare to disobey the instruction received," Judaea being regarded, within the empire, as part of Syria, but by the time that he reached Rome, Tiberius was alive no longer.[50] It seems that with the demise of his erstwhile sponsor and great model—and Sejanus had been liquidated six years earlier for his part in a conspiracy against the throne[51]—Pilate fell into disgrace, and there are pointers that he did not die a natural death.[52]

It has been said that Pilate would always refuse what the Jews desired of him, and always do what they implored him not to.[53] This generalization is plainly disproved by the Gospel reports that the crucifixion of Jesus was but a concession which he made to the Jews, however reluctantly he is depicted as making it. The Johannine version that the Jews threatened Pilate, "If thou let this man go, thou art not Caesar's friend" (John 19:12), is possibly an attempt at reconciling an original rejection of the Jewish demand with an eventual compliance; but all that we know of Pilate and his emperor attests the certainty that any Jew who dared to remind the governor of his duty toward the emperor, or to hint at more fervid patriotism and stouter loyalty to the emperor than of the governor himself, would not be let live another hour. Not only would the governor rightly regard such insolence as a gross contempt of himself and his court, but considering the notorious hostility of the Jews to Rome and its emperor, and their persistent flouting of Roman rule and suzerainty, for them to remind the governor of his duties as a Roman imperial officer and judge surely amounted to contempt of the emperor, too, and, as such, meant the death penalty. The last thing that a Jew would venture, or need, to do would be gratuitously to counsel a Roman governor that it was incumbent upon him to punish "whosoever . . . speaketh against Caesar" (John 19:12). All Jews spoke against Caesar—that was well known and undeniable—so that any such innuendo would be a clear invitation to have themselves punished, too, and in the first place. It is sometimes argued that the Jews who were present and active at the trial of Jesus were collaborators with Rome; but such Jews were exceedingly rare, a very small minority ostracized and shunned by the Jewish community at large, whereas the Gospels paint the Jews at the trial as most representative "multitudes," with priests, elders, and scribes among them. The Synoptic Gospels do not place this species of "patriotic" argument on Jewish lips, and that the author of the Gospel of John finds it meet to do so points as well to his embarrassment at the unexplained contradiction between Pilate's alleged intentions and his eventual action as to his ingenuousness in ignoring the practical impossibility of subject people thus addressing their accredited governor or complaining of him to the emperor.[54]

The only other Gospel reference to the Jewish attitude to the Romans is to be found, perhaps, in the interchange of question and answer on the payment of tribute. Certain "Pharisees and Herodians" are said to have been sent to Jesus, "to catch him in his words." To trap him, they asked him: "Is it lawful to give tribute to Caesar or not? Shall we give, or shall we not give?" And Jesus, shown the coin with Caesar's image and superscription, gave his celebrated answer: "Render to Caesar the things that are Caesar's, and to God the things that are God's" (Mark 12:13–17; similarly Matt. 22:15–22; Luke 20:22–26). If we disregard for a moment the alleged motivation of the questioning, it appears that it was not a matter of course, and by no means so self-understood as to preclude all doubts, that the Jews ought to comply with Roman tax laws. It was not merely a political but also a religious issue. The resistance fighters "upbraided the people as cowards for consenting to pay tribute to Rome and tolerate mortal masters, after having God for their lord,"[55] and seemingly not without success: many joined the zealots and, to escape the Roman tax collectors, hid in caves;[56] many went to live abroad.[57] The question whether one ought to pay taxes or not was, therefore, neither unreasonable nor untimely, and it might have been asked in perfectly good faith of Jesus, that master and rabbi who was true and cared for no man (Mark 12:14). But let us take it that the question was put with fraudulent intent, to beguile Jesus into furnishing his interlocutors with evidence of his disloyalty to Rome. That would only mean that they expected him, with good reason, to affirm what everybody wanted to hear, that a good and God-fearing Jew would not pay taxes to the Romans. Only if the answer were as they anticipated that it would be could it justify his allegedly desired denunciation to the Romans. They "marvelled" at his answer (Mark 12:17): it was as simple and straightforward as it was harmless and incontestable. It could supply no evidence of disloyalty to Rome; there was no vestige in it of disavowal of the Jewish anti-Roman attitude. In fact, it left open the further question, what was God's and what was Caesar's; and it could well be interpreted as endorsing the zealots' proclamation, and as meaning that, since everything was God's, nothing could be Caesar's.[58] But even if construed to signify: "Better pay your taxes to the Romans; anyway you only give them their own coins back," it would be good practical advice, and we find it tendered not by Jesus alone, but also by talmudic scholars.[59] For that reason, apart from others, the theory cannot be sustained that it was this pro-Roman opinion of his which thenceforth cost Jesus Jewish popular support:[60] opinions appear to have been divided, and his was as good as the next. What his answer does bring out clearly is the antithesis between God and Caesar: Roman belief in the divinity of Caesar is implicitly but unmistakably rejected. And the positive injunction plainly entails the negative: Do not render unto Caesar what is God's; and nothing that you render unto Caesar can discharge you from your duty toward God.

There is, then, nothing in the Gospels to show that Jesus' attitude to the Romans differed from that of the Jewish generality. Indeed, his messianic prophecies of the kingdom of God were only an answer to the sighs and yearnings of a long-suffering people, under the yoke of enemy occupation and colonial oppression. There was no sight so revolting as that of Roman officers, Roman soldiers, Roman tax collectors;[61] and the way in which Roman governors rode persistently roughshod over Jewish customs and traditions and privileges "goaded the people to absolute frenzy."[62] This testimony of the fourth-century Christian historian truly delineates the frame of mind of the Jews in Jerusalem at that time: it was not just righteous anger, not just indignation at never-ceasing affronts and indignities, but such a tremulous and ireful agitation, such an "absolute frenzy," as would render any cooperation with the detested rulers well nigh inconceivable. Add to this the disgust and disdain which the Jews aroused in the Roman governor and his entourage, and the picture of absolute mutual rejection and dissociation will be complete.

Even the provision of public utilities, such as the water aqueduct, could do nothing to reconcile the Jews with their Roman tormentors. A talmudic story goes that God asked the Romans: What did you do during your administration of My Land? And the Romans replied: Master of the World, we established market places, we built many bathhouses, we multiplied gold and silver, and everything we did, we did for the sake of Israel, that they may be free to study their law. Said God Almighty: Imbeciles! Everything that you did, you did only for your own good. You established market places to have your brothels, you built bathhouses to give pleasure to your bodies, and the gold and silver you stole from Me, for so it is written, the silver is Mine and the gold is Mine, saith the Lord of hosts (Hag. 2:8). Whereupon the Romans went away dumfounded. . . .[63]

In an apocryphal Jewish book known as the Sybilline Oracles, written perhaps a generation or two before Jesus' time, we find an elaborate prayer for the destruction of Rome, which reflects the contemporaneous Jewish thought: "A holy king will come and reign over all the world—and then his wrath will fall on the people of Latium, and Rome will be destroyed to the ground. O God, send a stream of fire from heaven, and let the Romans perish, each in his own house! O poor and desolate me! When will the day come, the judgment day of the eternal God, of the great king?"[64]

2 CHIEF PRIESTS, ELDERS, SCRIBES, AND ALL THE COUNCIL

It is Jewish law that the high priest is appointed for life,[1] but the Roman governors had introduced the innovation that the appointment would be made and unmade by them at pleasure.[2] It was, also under Jewish law, the Great Sanhedrin of Seventy-one which had the prerogative of appointing and impeaching incumbents,[3] but the Roman governors imagined that, by arrogating the power to appoint and remove, by seeing to it that their choices were always Romanophile and trustworthy, they could effectively control the Jews.[4] The high priesthood was the symbol of Jewish national pride and aspirations, of Jewish religious superiority. National and religious life centered in the temple at Jerusalem, of which the high priest was exalted guardian and supreme commander. The temple police was the only Jewish armed force officially tolerated. By striking at the autonomy and independence of the high priest, the Romans struck at the nerve ganglion of Jewish autonomy and independence. "Josephus tells nothing of the reaction of his people to this shocking degradation of the high priesthood. His silence is surely eloquent, for that reaction, even if it did not find active expression, must have been very bitter."[5] That the Jews were likely to lose confidence in Roman nominees to the sacred office is one thing; but every expression of anger that the sacrosanct right of the Great Sanhedrin was being usurped and profaned would only magnify the hatred that the Romans felt for them.

Kaiaphas, the high priest, had been appointed by Pilate's predecessor, Valerius Gratius, and held office for eighteen years, from 18 to 36, a much longer spell than Pilate's as governor of Judaea.[6] It has been said that the very fact that Pilate allowed Kaiaphas to abide undisturbedly throughout his own term speaks for great amity and close understanding between the two.[7] It has also been suggested that Pilate's successor got rid of Kaiaphas as a friendly gesture of conciliation toward the Jews, who destested the high priest for what he had done to Jesus.[8] The true reason for Kaiaphas' retention in office by Pilate may well be that he had paid the price of it in good money: we know that the high-priestly appointment had developed into a lucrative source of private income for the governors—if an incumbent could or would not pay the price, he would be unseated, and one more forthcoming would replace him.[9] But if a governor could earn as much by letting the incumbent be, why go to the trouble of deposition and a new appointment?

In Roman times the high priesthood was confined to a few families: identical names recur again and again. It was not that qualified candidates could not be found in other circles, but that these were the only Jerusalem clans that could afford the costs involved. How rich the popular imagination made them out to be is shown by a talmudic tradition that their elders used only and always vessels of silver and gold.[10] All the families belonged to the Sadducean aristocracy, so that the mass of the people found itself faced by an apparent alliance between the hateful alien overlord and the rich and wealthy Jews: the natural and social aversion to the prosperous and mighty was joined, and intensified, by the natural and patriotic aversion to the enemy oppressor, of which the high priests—and the rich in general—were, of course, well aware. They knew not only how intensely the Romans were hated, but also that their own collaboration with the Romans and their dependence on them were popularly viewed with scorn and disgust. And the fact that it was by their wealth alone that the high priests had qualified for the holy office, and had procured and went on holding it, did nothing to enhance their standing or give them added goodwill.

But however little he was liked, however odious the form and incidents of his appointment and tenure, the high priest was always in supreme command of the temple administration, the temple police included, and responsible, without reserve, for all temple services.[11] And from the point of view of external relations, he would be regarded—especially, but not exclusively, by the Roman governor—as chief and spokesman of the nation, not only because the Romans would not recognize any but their own nominees as accreditable negotiators,[12] but also because the Jews would rather that any unavoidable contact with the enemy be made by his own puppet. It was a curious and ambivalent situation: on the one hand, the Jews despised the high priests as Roman quislings; on the other, they had to, and did, use the sacerdotal good offices in mediacy with the authorities. It is, perhaps, no less strange that a similar ambivalence prevailed internally: on the one hand, the Jews despised the high priest for his Sadducean affiliations and his moral and professional flaws; on the other, they had to, and did, duly recognize him as the lawful holder of the highest national and religious post. A modern politician might be in the like predicament when his party adversary, at whose qualifications he scoffs and whose opinions he vehemently scouts, has been elected to high office: while never forsaking his own views or betraying his own ideals, he will—at least outwardly—spare no conscious effort at loyal cooperation with him.

When, however, we come to details of the high priest's competences, we shall find it not at all easy to grope our way through the tangle of disputatious scholarship. For instance, on the first question that springs to mind in connection with the trial of Jesus, the scholars are hopelessly divided. Did the high priest preside over the Sanhedrin or did he not? Was he, or was he not, competent to convene it? Scores of theories have been developed on this issue,[13] ranging from the assertion that he presided and convened at will[14] to the denial that he ever presided or had the right to preside or convene,[15] with intermediate assertions and denials.[16] None of the Gospels says expressly that it was the high priest who presided over the meeting in the matter of Jesus, and for our specific purpose, we might leave it at that and take no stand in the controversy. It is only the possible bearing, on the question of ultimate "responsibility," of our adopting or rejecting this or the other theory that requires us clearly to decide on the position that we are going to take.

The dignity, fame, and sacrosanctity of the high-priestly office were such that it would, I think, be virtually inconceivable for its holder to attend any session of the Sanhedrin or council in which he would not, as a matter of course and tradition, preside. He was the only man chosen and qualified to enter the Holy of Holies in the temple once a year (Lev. 16:32) : he who was nearest to God, at least physically, and anointed to represent the people before God, would certainly be the first among men and entitled to preside over them.

Nothing much is known of Kaiaphas in particular. We have it on the authority of the Fourth Gospel that he was the son-in-law of a former high priest, Annas (John 18:13) : Annas functioned between the years 6 and 15, which means his displacement fifteen years before our events.[17] Whether it was because of the comparative lack of standing or importance of the three intervening incumbents, or because they were no longer alive, we find both Annas and Kaiaphas described as high priests during the governorship of Pilate (Luke 3:2), and, in another context, Annas as the only high priest and Kaiaphas as just one of his kindred (Acts 4:6). It would seem that Annas' official reputation lasted longer than Kaiaphas': notwithstanding the role ascribed to Kaiaphas in the Passion story, it is the name of Annas that loomed large in later traditions. But only in the Fourth Gospel is any part in the questioning of Jesus attributed to Annas (John 18:19–23); the remarkable omission of all mention of the high priest's name in the trial accounts of Mark and Luke may predicate a lack of interest in his identity, and it has, indeed, been said to lend "considerable force to the argument that the hierarch's actual part in the proceedings against Jesus was far from being as commanding as the evangelists suggest."[18]

A high priest by the name of Elionai son of Kaiaph,[19] mentioned in the Jewish sources, has been taken to be a son of our Kaiaphas.[20] He has also been identified with a high priest of whom Josephus speaks, Elionaeus son of Kantheras.[21] The Greek name Kantheras was understood by Jewish traditional lexicographers to mean donkey, and the Hebrew or Aramaic Kaiaph to mean monkey,[22] both, ostensibly, regarded as fit zoological descriptions to serve our Kaiaphas as sobriquets of abuse or ridicule. Whether this interpretation is warranted, whether Kaiaph was not just an innocent and meaningless surname, cannot now be ascertained. A possible sense of Kaiaph might be fortuneteller,[23] but the theory that Pilate conferred on the high priest the name or title of Kaiaphas as meaning inquisitor or accuser[24] has no historical or etymological support.

It was Kaiaphas, then, possibly with the high priest emeritus Annas at his side, who presided over the council. What was this council, how was it composed, what were its functions?

It has been suggested that there were several such "councils" in Jerusalem at the time, all mistakenly and indiscriminately referred to in the Jewish sources as "Sanhedrin" and in the Gospels as the "whole council" (Mark 15:1) of chief priests, elders, and scribes. Only one of them, it is said, and that a political or a priestly one, would be controlled and presided over by the high priest, and his Sadducean intimates would form its membership.[25] Confining the high priest to the presidency of a purely political body, directed by him and constituted at his pleasure, not unlike the family or privy councils reported to have been called together time and again by King Herod[26] for specific consultations, would, of course, answer the purpose, intended or not, of freeing the true and real Great Sanhedrin of Israel of all responsibility for whatever had happened in the case of Jesus, and placing it, as far as the Jews were concerned, squarely on the shoulders of the high priest whom the Romans had appointed and his personal clique. According to this theory, the high priest and his council were charged by the Roman governor not only with sacerdotal matters, but also, perhaps mainly, with "native affairs,"[27] that is, with inquiry into local anti-Roman activities and their denunciation, and it was in that capacity that they "delivered" Jesus into his hands.

I see no reason to decry the character of "the whole council" of which the evangelists tell us. There is no case for regarding the assembly that night in the high priest's home as some high-priestly *ad hoc* council in which the great majority of chief priests, elders, and scribes was unrepresented. On the contrary, I shall assume that what the Gospels call "the chief priests and elders and all the council" (Matt. 25:59), or "all the chief priests and the elders and the scribes" (Mark 14:53; similarly Luke 22:66), was indeed the Great Sanhedrin of Seventy-one "from which the Torah went out to all Israel,"[28] and that no more august, representative, or authoritative body could have foregathered there that night. That it had, indeed, been convened by the high priest and that it had been invited into his home are circumstances which will claim our attention in due course.

In listing chief priests, elders, and scribes as making up the membership of the—then—Sanhedrin, the authors of the Gospels may have disregarded technical terminology, but, in essence, they were not far from giving an accurate picture of its three main groups: first, the leading priests and Levites,[29] representing the sacerdotal authorities; second, "senators," as they would say in Rome, men of ancient lineage or aristocrats, into whose families even officiating priests were allowed to marry without question;[30] and last, members co-opted from time to time from among the scholars entitled to attend sessions.[31] Not only the moral, professional, and political impact of the third group, but also its numerical strength, had risen progressively with the rise of scholars in reputation and popularity, and the corresponding decline of many of the priests and aristocrats in moral stature and professional qualification. So far from boycotting the council in which sat so many factions adverse to them, the scholars (called "sages") advisedly took part: just

as the holiness of the temple was not impaired in the estimation of the sages by the high priests who were unworthy of officiating, so it never entered their minds to repudiate the institution of the Sanhedrin, or to set up a rival to it in the form of a competing court, even if they did not approve of its composition, and even if they opposed the high priest and his entourage. They endeavoured rather to exercise their influence and to introduce their rulings and views even into the ritual of the temple service and into the Sanhedrin's methods of operation.[32]

These scholars were Pharisees, whereas among the chief priests and elders many were Sadducees; and we have the testimony of Josephus that the Sadducees would always vote with the Pharisees, "because the people would not have it otherwise,"[33] a remarkable index of the practical influence which public opinion exerted on the decisions of the Sanhedrin, and of the sensitivity of priests and elders to *vox populi* and popular sentiment. There can be no doubt that public opinion in Judaea and Jerusalem was as anti-Roman as it was pro-Pharisaic, and that with the growth of Pharisaic popularity the Sadducees lost more and more of their positions. Not that the masses had the capacity, or interest, to assess the respective merits or demerits of Pharisaic and Sadducean doctrine, for if they had, they would, in all probability, have preferred the simple and straightforward Sadducean conception of strict and exclusive adherence to the written word of Scripture to the vagaries and complications of the Pharisaic oral law, about whose scope and content the scholars were endlessly disputing among themselves, and often in diametrical opposition to one another. If the generality followed the Pharisees and accepted Pharisaic teachings, it was because the Pharisaic scholars were men after their own hearts: we have the evidence of such an un-Pharisaic witness as Josephus that they were poor and did not aspire to worldy affluence; that they were prudent and always acted after careful deliberation and to the best of their knowledge; that they were humble and showed respect to their elders; and that they were pious and believed that a merciful God would requite all good and righteous men in a better world to come for the misery suffered on earth.[34] But, most important of all, the Pharisees held popular sympathy because, true Jewish patriots that they were,[35] they could safely be relied upon, in the counsels of state, to provide the required counterbalance to potential or actual collaborators with Rome. It cannot be gainsaid that among the Pharisaic scholars themselves there were differences of approach and opinion in respect of Roman politics: even from the purely theological standpoint, some, inevitably, would bow to foreign dominion as a God-sent calamity which must be taken to be merited and accepted with love and humility and an unswerving faith in divine justice. Others may have seen in heathen rule an affront to God and His chosen people and His holy land, which could not, at any cost, be endured.[36] However manifest these doctrinal discords may have been, what distinguished the Pharisaic scholars from other groups would be that in making their decisions they would be actuated only by Jewish concerns: they would not direct their minds to any considerations other than those reflecting what they knew to be in the best general Jewish interest. In this respect, they differed from the well-to-do and well-established, whose primary solicitude would always be for their own vested interests; and, needless to say, from those who—like the high priest—depended on Roman goodwill for continuation in office or status or had to render to the Romans account of their conduct. Popular mistrust of all sorts of collaborators, and of all ideologies underlying collaboration, was deeply entrenched—the spectacle of the "moral and spiritual decadence of the once exalted family" of the Hasmonaeans, who had become "pure assimilationists," was still vivid enough in the consciousness of the people to "strengthen the morale and increase the numbers of the Pharisaic opposition."[37] As oppression by the Roman occupying power mounted, it was equally inevitable that, in the course of time, the strengthened Pharisaic opposition and its scholarly spokesmen should come to be regarded and revered, in the public mind, as the embodiment of genuine Jewish patriotism.

But the popular pro-Pharisaic sentiment gives only one side of the picture. No public opinion can avail, unless the powers-that-be are awake and sensitive to it. The Roman governor of Judaea, for instance, was entirely impervious, not because he may not have been familiar with the more elementary features of democracy, but because he in person, and the duty that he had to perform, and all that he represented and stood for were so incompatible and out of tune with the "native" and—to him—wholly barbarous ideas and aspirations, and *Weltanschauung* by and large, of a deplorably "retarded," indigenous folk that to give ear to its uncivilized babble would be so much waste of time and effort. It seems, however, that the position was totally different with the high priest and, probably, also with the Sadducean nobility. The high priest could be under no illusion as to the opprobrium that he and his predecessors had earned among the people by craving Roman appointments and purchasing them. He had firsthand intelligence of the wrath and wild fury of the people against the Romans and their garrisons, and I do not think that he could have entertained any hopes that this attitude might change: at any rate, he knew that it was not he who could alter it. Our knowledge of individual high priests is not enough to judge whether they collaborated with the Romans, if at all, by inclination rather than out of what they regarded as necessity: we should, I submit, give them the benefit of the doubt and assume, as the Pharisaic scholars apparently did, that in collaborating they acted in good faith in what they believed were the best interests of their people. But the fact remains that his Roman nomination would not advantage the high priest a great deal unless he could reckon with some measure of cooperation from the Sanhedrin and from the public at large. From the internal angle, any resistance of scholars or priests to his authority would necessarily render his appointment nugatory: it would do him little good to be recognized as high priest by the Roman governor if he were not accepted as such by his own Jews. He might, of course, always ask for troops to crush resistance by force; but from recent, and not so recent, experiences he could predict what the outcome would be: not only would the desired moral authority still be to seek, but martyrs would be made in the cause against him, and his last remnant of sympathy and prestige be lost. There is no high priest on record who would—or, for that matter, had to—resort to Roman military aid to render his office workable: the price that he would have to pay would have stultified the whole endeavor.

That he was a Roman nominee, ultimately responsible to the Roman governor and removable by him, must have stimulated rather than diminished the high priest's natural aspiration to manage the internal affairs of the Jews so smoothly and efficiently that there would never be any ground for Roman interference. By relying on him, who, of course, enjoyed some measure of their confidence, the Romans were to be satisfied at all times that the administration of those affairs was in safe and proficient hands. It was a no less instinctive ambition of the high priest to secure for himself, and for the organs under his control, as much power and discretion as possible: negative success in preventing Roman interference must be complemented by positive success in the recognition and reinforcement of the autonomy and jurisdiction of the Jewish authorities. Any failure of his and of those directive organs to uphold internal peace and order and good government might result, if not in peremptory Roman intervention, at least in curtailment of the powers and competences previously enjoyed and exercised; peaceful and proper functioning would prove their capacity and might even tempt the Romans to strengthen their autonomy and enlarge it.

To succeed, then, the high priest patently depended on the smooth working of the Sanhedrin and of the temple establishment, that is to say, on the nature and extent of the cooperation which he contrived to enlist from the members of the council and from the priesthood. It must have been vital to him to gain the support and goodwill of anyone with a seat and a voice in the counsels of state, and it was axiomatic for him that his surest technique was to pursue policies which would meet their wishes. As it was, he must by law pursue the policies of the majority, for all decisions had to be passed by its vote; but where its views ran counter to his own inclinations, he would rather yield to it, that being the standard and safest way for men in authority to win popular support and trust. But even where numerical predominance in the Sanhedrin might be Sadducean, the high priest, though himself one by birth and persuasion, and probably or potentially Romanophile, would prefer to side with the Pharisees and let them carry the day, not because he thought that they were necessarily right, but because he knew that they enjoyed the affection and confidence of the great bulk of the population; and the Sadducean votes in the Sanhedrin could, presumably, always be swung by him. Nor would he deviate in the slightest from the traditional temple ritual: not that he would not perhaps have liked at times to humor this or the other Roman caprice, but, as a matter of deliberate internal policy, he would choose to bow to the piety and orthodoxy of most of the priests.

He was thus in the unenviable position of a suitor for the regard and respect of a Jewry which feared, suspected, and somehow despised him. In simple psychology as well as prudent policy, he would go about his task by attempting to enlist, first and foremost, the cooperation of the Pharisaic members of the Sanhedrin; and the best means to that end was to raise their numerical strength and voting power. It was through the Pharisees that he sought to reach the people. Any action or conduct on his part that might estrange the Pharisees would be likely to wreck the over-all policy to which he must have been committed.

There was one fundamental issue on which there certainly was a general consensus among Pharisees and Sadducees—priests and elders and scribes: preservation of the powers of the Sanhedrin and prevention of further Roman encroachments upon them. What these powers actually were is, again, multitudinously controversial. There is no serious doubt as to the autonomy of the council in purely religious matters of the native Jews: the Romans allowed them to exercise their religion and would not normally interfere with the manner of its exercise; their several attempts to do so, particularly with the emperor's image, apparently failed. "Religious matters" included everything connected with the temple establishment, including the temple police, and, for the purposes of our inquiry, we may postulate that there was no Roman interference with the high priest's command of that constabulary.

But on the question with which we are primarily concerned, that is, the power of the Sanhedrin to try criminal cases and carry out capital punishment, there is no end to disputes among the scholars, ancient and modern. In the Gospel According to John, Jews are credited with saying: "It is not lawful for us to put any man to death" (18:31). It will be shown that this could not, in fact, have been said by any Jews in authority and that it is, plainly and simply, untrue,[38] yet it has been taken as sufficient evidence that the Jews had been deprived by the Romans either of all capital jurisdiction [39] or at least of the power to carry out their capital sentences.[40] It is because of this passage in the Gospel of John that much scholarly attention and effort have been devoted to inquiry into the scope and particulars of sanhedrial criminal jurisdiction. It has, however, already been convincingly pronounced that, as far as Jewish responsibility for the death of Jesus is in question, such inquiry is largely irrelevant:[41] if the capital jurisdiction of the Sanhedrin was unimpaired, it does not follow that, in this particular case, the council exercised it; and if it had been wholly or partly withdrawn, it would not follow that the council could not have taken some action outside its formal powers or within the limits of the restrictions set upon it. We shall, therefore, relinquish the jurisdictional theories[42] to the handling of legal historians, and start from the premise that the Sanhedrin had retained all the capital jurisdiction that it had ever possessed under Jewish law, and that there was no jurisdictional obstacle to its proceeding against Jesus for any offense under, and in any manner compatible with, that law. But the fact is that there is not enough historical or other material available—notwithstanding talmudic traditions to the contrary[43]—to warrant a conclusion that the Sanhedrin had been deprived by the Roman authorities, or by Roman statute, of any part of its jurisdiction under Jewish law.[44]

While the Great Sanhedrin of Seventy-one was regarded as the ultimate fount of all jurisdiction, civil, criminal, administrative, and advisory, it did not itself exercise civil or criminal jurisdiction except in a very few well-defined cases, as, for instance, when the high priest was criminally indicted.[45] General criminal jurisdiction, including that in capital cases, was exercised by the so-called Small Sanhedrin of twenty-three judges.[46] Josephus records the establishment of such Small Sanhedrins in five different towns in about 60 B.C.,[47] and at the time which concerns us, Small Sanhedrins sat in all major towns throughout Judaea and Galilee.

The Great Sanhedrin was, in essence, a legislative body. In periods of war and enemy occupation it would, of course, like any legislature, be mainly preoccupied with the political issues on which national and religious survival would hinge. Indeed, that such preoccupation, even as a matter of law, came within its purview may be inferred from the rule that no warlike operations might be commenced except by virtue of its resolution.[48] And it was a preoccupation all the more reasonable and necessary inasmuch as the Jews, on the one hand, were divided among themselves in questions that touched on Roman and general politics, but, on the other, agreed that, as toward the Romans, it was wiser to present a united front. There were, to be sure, the zealots or underground fighters who deprecated any "diplomatic" relations whatsoever with the enemy: while they mustered recruits and sympathizers from all classes of the population and were certainly countenanced, if not actively encouraged, by the prevailing opinion in the Sanhedrin, the independent policy which they pursued toward the Romans was one with which the Sanhedrin could not very well officially associate itself.

We shall see that if the Great Sanhedrin did meet in the case of Jesus, it did so as the council in charge of political affairs. It was not just a Small Sanhedrin, which could have exercised jurisdiction in a criminal or capital case, but the Great Sanhedrin, which would not exercise such jurisdiction at all even if possibly competent to, if only for the reason that it was much too much taken up at the time with current and pressing political issues.

Respecting general criminal jurisdiction, two further points must be noted. One is that no Sanhedrin could ever have exercised any jurisdiction at all save in accordance with Jewish law: it could take cognizance only of offenses known to and defined in that law and could adopt only such criminal procedures as that law allowed. And the other is that, with the advent of Rome, there was established in Judaea a second—the Roman—criminal jurisdiction, which means that the Jewish courts no longer monopolized it. The two points are closely interconnected, because what actually transpired was that the Jewish courts exercised exclusive criminal jurisdiction in respect of acts which were offenses only against Jewish law, and the Roman governor's court exercised exclusive criminal jurisdiction in respect of acts which were offenses only against Roman law. For example, the offense of desecrating the Sabbath, or of idolatry, either an offense solely by Jewish law, would be within the exclusive jurisdiction of the Jewish courts, and the Roman governor would never claim jurisdiction over it; he could not, because Roman law did not regard either act as a criminal offense. On the other hand, sedition against the Roman government, or contempt of the Roman emperor, would be an offense within the exclusive jurisdiction of the governor; Jewish law did not regard such acts as criminal offenses, and no Jewish court would ever have punished anybody for what, from the Jewish viewpoint, must have been regarded as harmless or even laudable.

Some difficulty may have arisen in conflict situations, in which an offense was common to Roman and Jewish law. Murder and robbery, for instance, were offenses punishable under both systems, and the Roman governor and the Jewish courts might each have claimed jurisdiction. Conflicts such as these may have been solved according to the identity of the accused: we know from the story of Paul that a Roman citizen could demand trial by a Roman court for any offense which was not one purely of Jewish law (Acts 23:27–29). Conversely, a non-Roman native would presumably have been entitled to trial by a Jewish court, even if the offense charged was recognized as such in Roman law also. It is, however, not unlikely that the Roman governor could in such a case require the surrender of the accused to him, and it is probable that on his part he would never surrender to native Jewish courts an offender already in his own custody, for instance, a robber caught by Roman troops *in flagrante delicto*. All power being virtually concentrated in his hands, he could dictate to the Jewish courts when to exercise jurisdiction in any such case and when not.

It would come to this, then: the Small Sanhedrin could try any Jew for any offense under Jewish law, and sentence him to death, and carry out the death penalty, and the Roman governor would not interfere in any way, for all that he had the physical and political power to. On the other hand, we must assume that the Romans would not carry out the capital sentence of a Jewish or other non-Roman court, but only put to judicial death offenders tried and convicted by a Roman court for offenses against Roman law.

Legal assumptions and considerations of this kind have encountered marked impatience, mainly from certain theologians: it is all very well to argue the law, they would say, when you talk of people who may reasonably be assumed to abide by it; but the people with whom we are here concerned are criminals, corrupt high priests, "unrighteous scribes," and unscrupulous elders, accustomed and determined to break every ordinance for the attainment of their ugly purpose, and the law would be as relevant in their regard as it would be to clinch that a thief could not have stolen because it was unlawful to. The same priests and elders who would, without the flicker of an eyelash, suborn Judas with thirty silver coins to betray his master (Matt. 26:15) would never be deterred from using any illegal means, bribery not excepted, to get the Roman governor to do their bidding, or from contravening and disregarding their own statutes and procedures.

Several "authorities" are instanced for the proposition that the priests and elders of the Jews at the time were not much better than common criminals. First, of course, there are Jesus' own diatribes against the scribes and Pharisees; and to these we will revert in the next chapter. Then a report in Josephus that "high priests went so far in their boldness and wickedness that they did not even recoil from sending their slaves to the threshing-floors and have them take away the tithes due to the priests, with the result that the poorer priests starved to death."[49] But this was in a period thirty years after ours; and the high priests mentioned were not even Roman appointees but nominees of King Agrippa. The situation in Judaea in the year 60 was entirely different from what it had been under the governorship of Pilate. Furthermore, this passage in Josephus has with good reason been interpreted as misrepresenting action taken by pro-Roman high priests and a sacerdotal aristocracy, backed by the king, against lower orders of the priesthood which had joined forces with the zealots. Seen in this light, the seizure of the tithes was no common larceny, but, however morally unjustified, a disciplinary measure; and the strife between the factions was no quarrel of rival gangsters, but the fresh outbreak of an inveterate dispute between violent and non-violent resisters to Rome, or between resisters and collaborators.[50] The dispute was as old as the Roman conquest, but it had apparently not exploded grievously until about the year 60; and, as events have shown, it led to disastrous consequences, once it burst the bounds of domestic altercation and the outwardly united front could hold no longer. Indeed, once internal feuding was allowed to erupt tumultuously, it was only natural that the less inhibited elements, of whatever partisanship, should give free rein to their maleficent inclinations, a phenomenon common to all civil commotions.[51]

Another much-quoted authority for the alleged criminality of the high priests is what has been called "a popular squib preserved in the Talmud," said to be aimed "against the principal high pries   them were looting and ruining the natior   ts the clubs and fists, the pens and whisp   priests named in it, and their henchmer   Not only certain of the priestly names rec   s of the narrators, suggest that the tirade   quent period. The tale is told by Abba   lived about the year 80, and Abba Sha   t twenty years before him; and of the h   t were appointed after Jesus' death.[54]   es well with Josephus' later reports of]   ness and the force used against the zealot   ot impossible that the narrators were the zealots and had themselves ached from the clubs and rods of pro-Roman factionists. The talmudic context tends to show

that what was really at issue were the causes given for the destruction of the temple and the ultimate overthrow of Judaea: it was
this misbehavior by those succeeding high priests and their clans
that brought divine wrath down upon the temple, for the "squib"
is instantly followed by a saying that it was destroyed because they
"loved money and hated each other."[55]

It is not our intention to embark on apologetics of Kaiaphas:
we know little of him, and he may conceivably have deserved a
better testimonial than the "squib" implies. Considering the disdain in which the Roman-appointed and all high priests thereafter were held by the people, no factual conclusions ought to
be drawn against them from their disparagement in a popular
lampoon; and in the absence of any circumstantial data to rebut
it, I think that even high priests should be entitled to the benefit
of the presumption of innocence.

Finally, there is the suggestion that, as in all countries under
enemy occupation, at all periods of history, so in Judaea at that
time there were traitors and collaborators who served Rome's interests, though occupying high office in the local administration.
It is said, in their justification, that unless they agreed to act as
informers, they jeopardized their lives, and to save themselves,
they had to sacrifice others.[56] But there is not a scrap of evidence
for the charge that Kaiaphas was a traitor of that kind, or that
any of the Jews said to have played a part in the Passion story
were agents of Rome; there is, indeed, some indication to the contrary in the Gospel reports (*cf.* John 11:48), and neither there nor
anywhere else any hint of treasonable Jewish activity.[57] Knowing
what we do of the prevailing spirit of the Jewish rank and file, the
ever greater popularity of the zealots, and the role assumed by
Pharisaic scholars in the leadership or organization of armed uprisings,[58] it is, I submit, unthinkable that informers and quislings
—be they even high priests—would have been let live in continuing
treachery. They might not have been lynched, but they would be
conscious that their fate was at the mercy of enraged and implacable zealot coreligionists, and rather than perish shamefully
as contemptible turncoats, they would, we may guess, prefer to
run the risk of Roman disfavor. We know that if an "unofficed"
individual betrayed a fellow Jew, he would not ordinarily be able
to live on. There is the illuminating example of Judas, who is

said to have hanged himself after betrayal of his master (Matt. 27:5) : had he not taken his own life, or not been lynched by an infuriated populace, he would still have suffered a violent and ignominious death (Acts 1:18), soon to be known "unto all dwellers of Jerusalem" (1:19).

We do not know, and shall not maintain, that Kaiaphas was a man of strong character or personal integrity. But neither shall we assume that he was devoid of common honesty and decency, or prompted in action and decision by criminal or insincere urgings.[59] Rather we shall place him and those who acted with him in the perspective of their political circumambience, and take it for granted that—from deliberate prudence as from natural instincts of self-preservation—they conducted themselves in such manner as they thought best in the Jewish national and religious interest. We have seen what this interest was in the eyes of the high priest on the one hand and of the Pharisees on the other, and how, notwithstanding fundamental doctrinal differences, the two could, and would, act in concord inside the Great Sanhedrin, more particularly where Jewish national or religious concerns, and Jewish autonomy, had to be defended and upheld against the Roman governor. Applying the standards of the reasonably circumspect politician and of the reasonably fair judge, it ought not be too difficult for us to reconstruct the state of things in which the high priest and the Sanhedrin, and Jesus, confronted each other. But before we come to that confrontation, we must look upon Jesus.

3 JESUS

It is not within the purview of this inquiry to portray Jesus. His life, his personality, and his teachings are subjects of long-raging and never-ending theological and historical controversies. Many of the questions in dispute are essentially questions of faith and of orientation, and we shall take no stand on them. Our purpose is to show that neither Pharisees nor Sadducees, neither priests nor elders, neither scribes nor any Jews, had any reasonable cause to seek the death of Jesus or his removal. Without such, it will be submitted, the reports that they sought to destroy him (Matt. 12:14; Luke 19:47) or that they counseled together "for to put him to death" (John 11:53; Luke 22:2; Mark 14:1) are stripped of all plausibility.

The "Pharisees" were singled out by the evangelists as the veritable archenemies of Jesus. Their somewhat exotic name, especially in Gentile ears, furnishes an obscurity behind which a clearly perceptible but wholly unexplained hostility seems to lurk. Jesus is represented in the Gospels as harboring no illusions about their hateful character and implacable enmity; and, indeed, to judge from Gospel reports, no group could be more hypocritical, cunning, selfish, proud, opinionated, intolerant, and un-scrupulous. What is at first sight remarkable, though it does not appear to have bothered the theologians overmuch,[1] is that in some of his speeches, and in his general attitude to the "Phari-sees," Jesus seems to have abandoned his own teaching that you must love your enemies and pray for them that despitefully perse-cute you (Matt. 5:44) : even assuming that Jesus thought that he was being hounded by them and that they were his foes, not only did he not pray for them, but, if the Gospel is to be believed, he cursed and reviled them with no least restraint.

The picture is not, however, always painted as black as all that. According to the Gospels of Matthew and Luke, Jesus once or twice accepted an invitation to the home of a Jewish tax collector, a "publican," who, as we have said, by entering into Roman serv-ice had, in the eyes of the people, forfeited the right to mix in good Jewish society: no Jew would sit at table with him. As dis-tinguished from the disqualification of such men as witnesses,[2] this was not a rule of Pharisaic law, but a widespread custom which may have grown out of an instinctive rejection and boycott of Roman hirelings. The "Pharisees" (Matt. 9:11), who in the other Gospels are joined by "scribes" (Mark 2:16; Luke 5:30) , are said to have "murmured" and asked Jesus' disciples, "How is it that he eateth and drinketh with publicans and sinners?" (Mark 2:16) . Jesus heard the question and gave the answer: "They that are whole have no need of the physician, but they that are sick: I came not to call the righteous, but sinners to repentance" (Mark 2:17; similarly Matt. 9:12–13; Luke 5:31–32) . From this answer it would appear, first, that Jesus agreed with the "Pharisees" that these publicans were in the category of sinners (compare Luke 18:9–14) ; second, that Jesus knew of the popular avoidance of sitting at table with them, and had nothing against those that practiced it; third, that the "Pharisees" would take it for granted that Jesus, as a matter of course, would observe all their own ways; fourth, that he conceded the necessity to justify his nonob-servance of any such way by some special reason; and fifth, and most important of all, that he had nevertheless sat down and eaten with "publicans," not in spite but because of their being sinners: the righteous, the "Pharisees," with whom everybody might dine, did not need his medicine. It is significant that none of the Gospels puts any reply in the mouths of the "Pharisees," who, then, seem to accept Jesus' explanation as wholly satisfactory.

Upon the episode with the publican there follows another exchange of question and answer between the "Pharisees," with or without "scribes," and Jesus. Why, it is asked, do not Jesus' disciples, like those of the Pharisees and of John the Baptist, fast (Matt. 9:14; Mark 2:18) and make prayers, but rather eat and drink (Luke 5:33)? The normal thing, we are allowed to infer, would have been for Jesus and his disciples to behave and conduct themselves as all Pharisees did, including Jesus' teacher, John the Baptist; if they swerved from Pharisaic mode, surely there must be some cogent reason. And, indeed, already in the Sermon on the Mount we find very clear indication that Jesus and his disciples did fast (Matt. 6:16–18).[3] Fasting was not only a favorite Pharisaic exercise in asceticism, but also, throughout Jewish history, a sign of mourning and an accompaniment to prayers in national calamity;[4] but it is the Pharisaic rule that there be no fasting on festive days.[5] Jesus' answer that his disciples are like "the children of the bridechamber" who "have the bridegroom with them" (Mark 2:19; Matt. 9:15; Luke 5:34) is a perfect adaptation of the Pharisaic rule. Again, the "Pharisees" do not react: if your disciples are so exuberantly merry and joyous, then they should not fast. (The theory has been propounded that the Gospels refer here to the days of fast commemorating the destruction of the temple,[6] which would be turned into days of "joy and gladness and cheerful feasts" [Zech. 8:19] on the advent of the Messiah, the "bridegroom"; but while the evangelists may, of course, have had some such afterthoughts and theological purpose, we must be entitled to take the story at its face value, referring as it does to fasting generally as an element of ascetic life and piety, and not necessarily to commemorative fasting only.)

Not only did Jesus move and feel at home in the company of Pharisees from early childhood (Luke 2:46), but he continued to teach before "Pharisees and doctors of the law . . . which were come out of every town of Galilee, and Judaea, and Jerusalem" (Luke 5:17), presumably to hear him and to study under him. He took his meals on the Sabbath in the homes of Pharisees and readily accepted their invitations (Luke 7:36; 11:37; 14:1).[7]

The tendentiousness of the evangelist is betrayed in his report of what happened at one such Sabbath meal: first it is said that the Pharisees, who were Jesus' hosts, "watched him" (Luke 14:1), insinuating that, as a matter of course, they were out to trap him in some misfeasance. Then and there, very obligingly, there appeared a man "which had the dropsy," and Jesus asked the "lawyers and Pharisees" present whether it would be lawful to heal a man on the Sabbath (Luke 14:2–3). His question appears to be entirely rhetorical: Jesus and the evangelist each knew the answer, and that, whatever the answer, Jesus would proceed to heal the man, for have we not, in the preceding chapter of the same Gospel, heard Jesus' rebuke to a "ruler of the synagogue" who had ventured the opinion that healing on the Sabbath was forbidden (Luke 13:14–16)? And in an earlier chapter we were told of a man "whose right hand was withered" and whom Jesus healed on the Sabbath, in the very synagogue where "scribes and Pharisees" were present and "watched him, whether he would heal on the sabbath day; that they might find an accusation against him" (Luke 6:6–7). On that previous occasion, Jesus had asked of the "scribes and Pharisees" the self-same question, and there it had admittedly and manifestly been rhetorical: "I will ask you one thing: Is it lawful on the sabbath days to do good, or to do evil? to save life, or to destroy it?" (Luke 6:9). This episode is reported also in the Gospels of Mark and Matthew; in Mark the words of Jesus are similar to those quoted from Luke (Mark 3:4); but in Matthew he is said to have asked the "Pharisees": "What man shall there be among you, that shall have one sheep, and if it fall into a pit on the sabbath day, will he not lay hold on it, and lift it out? How much then is a man better than a sheep? Wherefore it is lawful to do well on the sabbath days" (12:11–12). This, curiously enough, is the answer that Luke puts into the mouth of Jesus at the Sabbath meal with the Pharisees: "Which of you shall have an ass or an ox fallen into a pit, and will not straightway pull him out on a sabbath day?" (14:5). We have thus two sets of answers: one in which the "Pharisees" are directly counseled that, just as you save your beasts on the Sabbath, so must you be allowed to save human lives as well; and the other in which the counsel is that it cannot be lawful to do evil on the Sabbath, but must be lawful to do good. The two have this in common: they clearly hint that the "Pharisees" would not, as a matter of course, and maybe also of law, do evil on the Sabbath—it was only that they would not do good; or that "Pharisees" would, again as a matter of course, and maybe also of law, save their own property on a Sabbath—it was only that they would not save human lives. This kind of reflection on sabbatical evildoers, killers, and skin-flints is, as far as Jesus is concerned, quite uncalled for, and can only serve the biased purpose of the evangelists. The natural—and true—answer to give, or, rather, the fair and simple way of for-mulating the answer which Jesus did give, would have been this: of course it is lawful to do good and save life on the Sabbath day!

None of the Gospels alleges that the "Pharisees," with or with-out "scribes," maintained that it was unlawful to heal on the Sabbath: they only "watched," and once they specifically asked Jesus whether it was lawful, so "that they might accuse him" (Matt. 12:10). But having seen Jesus at his healing, and heard his reasons, they once more "held their peace" (Luke 14:4), for "they could not answer him again to these things" (Luke 14:6), not because they were dumfounded or outwitted or offended, but because they could not dispute Jesus' ruling or in any wise chal-lenge his conduct: healing on the Sabbath, as Jesus had healed, was perfectly licit under Pharisaic law, even where there was no instant danger to life.[8]

The image of the Pharisees which the evangelists had, or in-vented, was one of stubborn and inflexible legalists: perhaps not-ing, with horror, the punctilious observance of absolute sabbati-cal rest by their orthodox Jewish contemporaries, they simply could not conceive that healing would not fall under the ban like-wise. Undoubtedly, they possessed many traditions of Jesus' acts of healing, and they set some of those acts on the Sabbath, to form the arena in which a clash between Jesus and "Pharisees" might conveniently be staged. The clash is now duly *mise en scène,* with more than a sufficiency of taunts, put impolitely into the mouth of Jesus, thrown in for good measure, and the result, premeditated as it is, can no longer surprise: the "Pharisees" were "filled with madness; and communed one with another what they might do to Jesus" (Luke 6:11); or they "went out, and held a council against him, how they might destroy him" (Matt. 12:14). Ac-cording to Mark, the "Pharisees" even "straightway took counsel

with the Herodians against him, how they might destroy him"
(3:6), as if the Herodians, of all people, could be shocked by the
news that a sick man was healed on the Sabbath day.

Not that it is inconceivable that at the time of the ministry of
Jesus the question of the permissibility of sabbatical healing was
still unresolved. It could well be that this was one of the countless
legal-religious issues yet to be discussed or determined, and that
the Pharisaic law which has been preserved belongs to a subsequent period. It could then happen that if a sick man came
forward on a Sabbath demanding treatment and remedy instan-
taneously, a scholar might inquire whether the law allowed it. In
any ensuing disputation, contradictory views might be aired, and
there could always be among the scholars a man of practicality
who would first of all help the sufferer and only then contribute his
share to the academic discussion, vindicating his action. Nobody
could reproach such a one for breaking the law: the law was not
yet settled, and his conception of what it was, or ought to be,
would be as valid, and carry as much force, as that of the next
man. In an indeterminate legal situation such as this, the Pharisaic rule is that each may act as he thinks right;[9] and in the formation of Jewish law a particular rule is crystallized time and again
by virtue of a scholar's behaving in practice as if it were already
operative.[10] There could, therefore, have been no objection or
protest on the part of Pharisees to Jesus' healing the sick on the
Sabbath, even if the rule making it lawful had not yet been codified; there could have been legitimate differences of opinion, but
no rancorous exception could have been taken to one divergent
opinion among several being propounded and demonstrated.

Healing was not the only alleged desecration of the Sabbath
which afforded the evangelists a cause and a theater of friction between Jesus and "Pharisees." It is reported of his disciples that
as they went with Jesus "through the corn fields on a sabbath
day," with—or so it seems—the "Pharisees" again conveniently
present, they began "to pluck the ears of corn" (Mark 2:23) and
eat them (Matt. 12:1), "rubbing them in their hands" (Luke
6:1). The "Pharisees" said to Jesus, "Behold, thy disciples do that
which is not lawful to do upon the sabbath day" (Matt. 12:2;
and in the form of a question: Mark 2:24; Luke 6:2). Before we
look at Jesus' reply, let us consider the Pharisaic law: you may

gather corn on a Sabbath for your own consumption on the spot; what you may not do is gather it by way of reaping and harvesting,[11] probably with a tool, such as sickle or spade.[12] The disciples apparently picked only the ear of the corn with the grain in it and left the stalk intact, which would not amount to reaping within the meaning of the embargo.[13] It is to be observed that, in this instance, it was not Jesus who garnered; in distinction from the case of healing, where he deliberately took personal action to make his doctrinal point, here the disciples plucked the ears of corn innocently and instinctively, as if it were the commonest and most natural thing to do; and they would presumably not have done so had the law forbade the doing on the Sabbath. It was not they who were the great reformers of the law, and there is no sign in the Gospels that Jesus had already lifted any of the sabbatical bans for them. But Jesus' retort to the "Pharisees" was not that the doing of the disciples was perfectly lawful: perhaps he himself thought that it was not, or that it was doubtful; or perhaps he did not desire to enter into any discussion of the technicalities of sabbatical ordinances. What he said, in effect, was that the disciples had been hungry, for he quoted the precedent of "what David did, when he was an hungred . . . how he entered into the house of God, and did eat the shewbread, which was not lawful for him to eat" (Matt. 12:3–4; Mark 2:25–26; Luke 6:3–4) : as David thought it right to transgress the law in relief of hunger and need, so do I, Jesus, think it right to break the Sabbath if there are hunger and need to be stilled; "and he said unto them, The sabbath was made for man, and not man for the sabbath" (Mark 2:27) .

Again, there is no record that the "Pharisees" had any rejoinder: Jesus' words conclude the Gospel reports of the episode. Nor would they have any rejoinder: it is true enough that David compelled the high priest to deliver the sacred shewbread into his hands, and though the chronicler does not enlighten us as to the reason for David's demand (except that he falsely pretended to act on the king's orders) , it is equally true that Jewish tradition is that he must have been pathologically and ravenously famished.[14] The high priest, however, seems to have been altogether unaware of his starving condition and to have obeyed only the behest of a distant monarch (I Sam. 21:1–6) . What is interesting, at all events, is that Jesus gave the "Pharisees" the traditional Pharisaic interpretation of David's misdeed, and so, in good Pharisaic manner, adduced it as a precedent for his own indulgence. That the precedent, as lawyers would say, is not on all fours with the case under advisement is made abundantly clear by Jesus himself: for while nobody, not even "Pharisees," can deny that the Sabbath was made for man, and not man for the Sabbath,[15] everybody will agree that the sacred shewbread was made for God and might be consumed, against replacement, by priests alone (Lev. 24:9). It is possible that the reference to David and his unlawful appropriation of the shewbread was but an overture to Jesus' concluding declaration that "the Son of man is Lord also of the sabbath" (Luke 6:5; Mark 2:28; Matt. 12:8), meaning that, like David, anointed of God, so the "Son of man" is sovereign in the interpretation and application of God's laws. This construction would perhaps solve the patent difficulty that, notwithstanding that sovereignty, Jesus gave Pharisaic legal reasons for the lawfulness of his disciples' behavior.[16] For our purpose, it suffices to remark that in the disquisition between Jesus and the "Pharisees" provoked by the incident of the ears of corn Jesus again took up any challenge that there may have been and satisfied his interlocutors by arguments representing the best Pharisaic dialectics.

Similar considerations apply to all other reported doctrinal encounters between Jesus and "Pharisees," with or without "scribes," and we shall consider several illustratively. There is the washing of hands: it is told that "Pharisees" came to Jesus and asked him, "Why do thy disciples transgress the tradition of the elders? for they wash not their hands when they eat bread" (Matt. 15:1-2). In the Gospel According to Mark, the phrasing is that when the "Pharisees" saw "some of his disciples eat bread with defiled, that is to say, with unwashen, hands, they found fault" (7:2). Mark then gives a discursive explanation: "For the Pharisees, and all the Jews, except they wash their hands oft, eat not, holding the tradition of the elders. And when they come from the market, except they wash, they eat not. And many other things there be, which they have received to hold, as the washing of cups, and pots, brasen vessels, and of tables. Then the Pharisees and scribes asked him, Why walk not thy disciples according to the tradition of the elders, but eat bread with unwashen hands?" (7:3-5). The story

in Luke is different: here it is not the disciples who neglect wash-
ing before meals, but Jesus himself, and the incredulous question
is not asked by unidentified "Pharisees" and "scribes," but by the
Pharisee at whose table Jesus had been invited to sup (11:37–38).
Now it will be marked that nowhere in the words ascribed to the
"Pharisees" is there any breach of the law charged: what they
complain of is nonobservance of a "tradition" common to "the
Pharisees and all the Jews."

The fact is that the washing of hands before meals was first
set down as a rule of law by El'azar ben Arakh, who taught more
than fifty years after Jesus' death,[17] and we still find scholars long
afterward in disagreement whether or not it is obligatory.[18] This
"tradition" of washing one's hands may, then, fairly be compared
to present-day norms of civilized deportment: you would not
punish a man for being unwashed, or for joining you at dinner
without having washed his hands, but—especially if he is a great
teacher and popular leader—you might be somewhat taken aback
by his conduct and ask him why it was that he eschewed the rite.
That is exactly what the "Pharisees" are said to have done. In a
Jewish home where, according to Luke, Jesus had been invited to
eat, all the other guests and the host would, automatically, and as
"all the Jews" always did, wash their hands before sitting down;
if Jesus would not join them, but demonstratively refused to wash,
surely that must have given rise to comment and question. And
there is not necessarily any censure in the question; on the contrary, it may have been addressed in a truly academic spirit, as
such questions are put in talmudic discussions. Could it be—a
guest might ask—that our tradition of washing before meals, and
of washing cups, pots, platters, and tables, is wrong, involving, as
it does, the consumption of great amounts of water, a commodity
which in the Jerusalem of those days was in very short supply and
costly? Perhaps you abstain from washing for some valid reason,
and we ought to follow your example and amend our tradition.
But, again, the question may never have been asked at all. It is
possible that Jesus, or his disciples, were misrepresented altogether, and that the whole incident was invented for the sake of
Jesus' answer: "Now do ye Pharisees make clean the outside of
the cup and the platter; but your inward part is full of ravening
and wickedness" (Luke 11:39), a rather discourteous animadver-

sion, by the way, where his Pharisaic host was concerned. Or: "laying aside the commandment of God, ye hold the tradition of men, as the washing of pots and cups, and many other such like things ye do" (Mark 7:8). But this kind of reply does not answer the question at all: understandably, Jesus insisted, for himself and his disciples, that they should not content themselves with being clean on the outside, but always be as pure within; which does not mean that, to be pure within, they must needs be unclean and impure without.

The dictum of Jesus, that you do not serve God by honoring him with your lips, but only by worshiping Him in your heart (Matt. 15:8), and that what you outwardly do is of no use and avail if it does not come from the heart, is nothing new, either, to "Pharisees." As Jesus himself told them, he was only affirming what the prophet Isaiah had said long before (Mark 7:6; Matt. 15:7) and in even stronger terms.[19]

If Jesus saw in the washing of hands an empty gesture, he had good authority of long standing to denounce it, as, indeed, he did, with this and similar ritualistic camouflage, in no unmistakable terms: "Ye devour widows' houses, and for a pretence make long prayer" (Matt. 23:14); "Ye pay tithe of mint and anise and cummin, and have omitted the weightier matters of the law, judgment, mercy, and faith: these ought ye to have done, and not to leave the other undone" (23:23); "Ye make clean the outside of the cup and of the platter, but within they are full of extortion and excess. Thou blind Pharisee, cleanse first that which is within the cup and platter, that the outside of them may be clean also" (23:25–26); "Ye are like unto whited sepulchres, which indeed appear beautiful outward, but are within full of dead men's bones, and of all uncleanness. Even so ye also outwardly appear righteous unto men, but within ye are full of hypocrisy and iniquity" (23:27–28).

I have advisedly omitted from those quotations the invectives which the evangelist makes Jesus utter, such as vipers, serpents, fools, or blind guides, and for a moment I disregard the fact that this series of exhortations is said to be addressed to the "scribes and Pharisees." In fact, it did not have to be so intended, but might very well, and very properly, have been meant for the people at large. I doubt whether, even in the time of Jesus, the

"scribes and Pharisees," whoever they were, monopolized hypocrisy or empty ritualism: there must have been hypocrites and
specious ritualists among the Sadducees and the unschooled, too.
As exhortations to the whole nation, all of Jesus' complaints and
demands are perfectly justified, and every true Pharisee would subscribe to them wholeheartedly. If a preacher addresses the totality
of his congregation at large, reproaching them with sin and evil-
doing and hypocrisy, not even the most pious and sincerest con-
gregant could be offended; he would assume, or might know, that
there were men in the congregation for whom the reproaches were
destined, and in his heart would ally himself unreservedly with the
preacher and all his words. But if a preacher were to single out
a certain group, identify them by name or distinctive feature, and
then bombard them with public rebukes, hurling insult and in-
vective at them, he might find himself called upon to furnish
proof of the veracity of each rebuke and in respect of each identifiable member of the group. Jesus was not so compelled, because
he would never have uttered such insults, and because he never
singled out "the scribes and Pharisees" as particular targets of his
remonstrances; and the evangelists who set all this obloquy on his
tongue, and who ought, therefore, to have been so compelled,
would never have been able to offer the tiniest item of evidence.
Not that there were no hypocrites and sinners among "scribes and
Pharisees" also. There certainly were, but as a group, as scribes
and as Pharisees, they were not worse, but very much better, than
the average citizen.

In this context, it should be noted that the term "hypocrite"
is not reserved in the Gospels for "scribes and Pharisees" exclusively: we find the general public so styled (Luke 6:42; Matt.
7:5), and in his reference to the prophesies of Isaiah, Jesus said
that they were addressed to "you hypocrites" (Mark 7:6). Jesus'
use of the term in addressing his audiences of actual or potential
sinners may have been an original tradition, such supplementary
terms as "scribes and Pharisees" being superadded by the evangelists. As we shall see, in the much later Gospel According to
John, a great deal of what in the Synoptic Gospels had been
ascribed to "scribes" or "Pharisees" or both is now attributed to
"the Jews"; but the object appears to be a better and broader
placing of responsibility rather than a whitewashing of "scribes"

or "Pharisees." In the doctrinal altercation reported in John, again, it is chiefly the "Pharisees" who figure as Jesus' disputants (8:3, 13; 19:13, 15, 16, 40), and we find "many of the Jews" telling the "Pharisees" "what things Jesus had done" (11:45-46).

Luke writes that straightway upon Jesus' outburst against the hypocritical "Pharisees," words were exchanged between him and the "lawyers"—in the Greek original *nomikoi,* persons learned in the laws *(nomoi)* —apparently non-Pharisees who, together with Jesus, had been invited to dine at the Pharisee's table. They said to him, "Master [or, rather, Rabbi], thus saying thou reproachest us also" (11:45), probably meaning that they, too, and not only the "Pharisees," loved "the uppermost seats in the synagogues and greetings in the market" (11:43; similarly Matt. 12:38-39), and washed their hands regularly, and saw to it that their cups and tables were clean. This voluntary and seemingly innocent plea of guilty from the "lawyers" is said to have brought down Jesus' wrath upon them as well: "Woe unto you also, ye lawyers!" And he reproached them not only with burdening men "with burdens grievous to be borne, and ye yourselves touch not the burdens with one of your fingers," but also with building "the sepulchres of the prophets" whom their fathers had killed (11:46-48). While the first indictment appears to be one directed specifically against lawyers and legislators, whose office is to lay burdens on others rather than on themselves, the second is decidedly one to be leveled at the people as a whole, including "Pharisees," the more so as it is really an introduction to the announcement that follows of the "prophets and apostles" to come, who will also be slain and persecuted as were the prophets of old (11:49), but surely not by lawyers necessarily. The conclusion seems warranted, if not inevitable, that many of Jesus' sayings, recorded by the evangelists as spoken to "scribes" or "Pharisees" or "lawyers," were—or were to be—in actuality spoken to all the Jews.

Similarly, the long harangue in Matthew, with the sevenfold refrain, "Woe unto you, scribes and Pharisees!" (23:13-29), is but a prelude to the ultimate prophecy: "Wherefore ye be witnesses unto yourselves, that ye are the children of them that killed the prophets. Fill ye up then the measure of your fathers. Ye serpents, ye generation of vipers, how can ye escape the damnation of hell? Wherefore, behold, I send unto you prophets, and wise men, and scribes: and some of them ye shall kill and crucify; and some of them shall ye scourge in your synagogues, and persecute them from city to city: That upon you may come all the righteous blood shed upon the earth, from the blood of righteous Abel unto the blood of Zacharias[20] son of Barachias, whom ye slew between the temple and the altar. Verily I say unto you, All these things shall come upon this generation" (23:31–36). It will be observed that before the prophecy of the killing and crucifying of some of the "prophets, and wise men, and scribes" who are to come, the evangelist switches from the "scribes and Pharisees" of his previous arraigning to the "serpents, generation of vipers." The term "generation" occurs several times in the Gospel reports of Jesus' speeches with different attributes: adulterous and sinful generation (Mark 8:38), evil generation (Luke 11:29), faithless and perverse generation (Matt. 17:17; Luke 9:41), and the like, but the specific form of address, "generation," is not confined to "Pharisees" or to any other given group. The entire nation, not just the "Pharisees," are the "children of them that killed the prophets," and it is upon them, who will themselves be, or will produce, the killers and crucifiers of the prophets to come, that all the righteous blood spilled in bygone generations will descend.

That Jesus did, verily, preach to the evil and sinful and faithless generation may be taken for granted without demur: no preacher or prophet in any age ever did otherwise. In the Gospel According to Mark (7:21–23), Jesus is said to have preached of and to "all men." The prefacing of his prophecies and preachings by recurring vilification of "scribes" and "Pharisees"—and this must have been what the evangelists purposed—creates the impression that these same "scribes" and "Pharisees" will be the killers and crucifiers in the end, sprung from forefathers that ever and always rioted in the wholesale letting of righteous blood. These hypocrites, you are led to believe, wash outwardly just to hide an inner impurity; they bid you to eat at their board only to kill you "by subtilty" (Matt. 26:4), by snatching at a casual word of yours that might bolster a capital charge against you (Luke 11:54). They have nothing in mind but "extortion and excess" (Matt. 23:25), and all their professed piety is but a cunningly devised cover for the "hypocrisy and iniquity" which fill them (23:28). Need we marvel, then, that shedding righteous and innocent

blood means nothing to them? They will cloak it with some ceremonial or other, and wash their hands as before. From hearts such
as theirs nothing flows but "evil thoughts, murders, adulteries,
fornications, thefts, perjuries, blasphemies" (Matt. 15:19), and
they defile themselves with all the crimes on earth, not just—as is
our case who rail against them—with the peccadillo of neglecting
to wash before partaking of food (15:20). You have, here, the
perfect character-building of the villains who, at the end of the
story, will engineer all the horrors. If, indeed, Jesus did heap
upon the "scribes" and "Pharisees" even a fraction of the frightful
maledictions which the evangelists ascribe to him, it is hardly
surprising that the disciples, as we are told, felt impelled to warn
him that the "Pharisees" felt somewhat insulted: "Knowest thou
that the Pharisees were offended, after they heard this saying?"
(15:12).

We learn that the "chief priests and scribes" were "sore displeased" with Jesus when they saw "the wonderful things" that
he had done and were apprised of the ovations that he had received (Matt. 21:15); he had, indeed, done "wonderful things,"
healing the blind and the halt (21:14). In two earlier instances,
his feats of healing had already provoked adverse comment. When
he healed a man "sick of palsy," having first forgiven him his sins,
"certain of the scribes" had "said within themselves, This man
blasphemeth" (Matt. 9:2–3), because nobody but God can so forgive (Mark 2:7); in the Gospel According to Luke, the "scribes"
are joined by "Pharisees" (5:21). At another time, there "was
brought unto him one possessed with a devil, blind, and dumb:
and he healed him, insomuch that the blind and dumb both
spake and saw. And all the people were amazed, and said, Is not
this the son of David? But when the Pharisees heard it, they
said, This fellow doth not cast out devils, but by Beelzebub the
prince of the devils" (Matt. 12:22–24). Luke replaces the "Pharisees" by the "people," who "wondered and said, He casteth out
devils through Beelzebub the chief of the devils" (11:14–15).

There are, then, three variations on the one theme: Jesus
miraculous successes as a healer displeased the "scribes," with or
without "Pharisees," first, that they were covetous (Luke 16:14)
and envied him his applause; second, that they saw in his pretensions a usurpation of divine prerogatives; and, third, that they

suspected him of diabolic machinations in casting out devils. Now it is intrinsically probable that many "scribes" and "Pharisees" may have envied Jesus his healing powers: it is only human to be jealous at the sight of a fellow's exceptional achievements. At that time, therapeutic processes and methods were not the monopoly of any medical profession or school of thought. People believed a disease or a disability to be God's punishment for either one's own sin or one's ancestors', or a sinister, hellish mischief. Certain ancient sources seem to suggest that physical ailment would be due to divine intervention, mental to satanic. Therapy, of course, had to be adapted to the nature and origin of the complaint. Casting out devils was a different process from winning God's mercy and forgiveness. We know from the Talmud that "whispering," for instance, was a recognized mode of treatment,[21] but there was a dissentient view that no whispering ought to be allowed "in respect of demons," which seems to imply that for demoniac states other cures were prescribed, and that whispering was good only for natural, that is, divinely sent, illnesses. That healing was essayed by touching the sick part of the body, or by the laying on of hands or by massage, or by rubbing spittle on it, is likewise vouched for in the Talmud;[22] and, needless to say, prayers would always be the best and last resort (Num. 12:13). What all these techniques have in common, of course, is that they require no mechanical or chemical contrivances: rather than medical knowledge or surgical skill, their success depends on divine grace and condescension. Pharisaic scholars, who may with justice have considered themselves eminently qualified to pray to God and invoke His help and mercy, must have undergone abysmal frustration at their helplessness to heal or even assuage the pain of the sick man whom Jesus set to rights by a few words or by the touch of his hand. And those who—as everybody did—believed in demons may well have thought that supernatural powers were aiding Jesus, more particularly where the malady was one commonly attributed to demonic evil.

As for sicknesses inflicted as God's punishment, every Jew believed in God's omnipotence, and His unfathomable choice of the instrument to carry out His will and of the objects of His grace would never be challenged. Envy there could be of the divine choice falling on one's neighbor, who might, in human judgment, be deemed unworthy, but there would never be any demonstration or activation of the "displeasure" aroused by it. Nor could the manifest divine acceptance of Jesus' healing stir any charge of blasphemy: on the contrary, what might be blasphemous would be denial of God's manifestation in the miraculous healing of the apparently incurable. That these people were cured was a fact amounting to conclusive proof that their sins had been forgiven, else God would not have remitted the punishment which He had seen fit to lay on them. Jesus' words, "Son, thy sins be forgiven thee" (Mark 2:5; Matt. 9:2), may be read as expressive of a forgiving by God and not necessarily of a forgiving by Jesus in independence of Him. Bible and Talmud are full of authoritative pronouncements by mortal men that God has forgiven, or will forgive, sins in general or particular transgressions. Never has it entered anybody's mind to regard such pronouncements as blasphemy, or as in any way trespassing on God's own prerogative. There is no escaping the suspicion that the allegation of blasphemy, out of place as it is in this context, was inserted only to prepare the way, and the mind, for the charge of "blasphemy" that is to reappear at a much later and more critical stage.

It is told that priests and scribes were even more sorely put out by what Jesus did in the temple and said about it. Indeed, his assertion that "There shall not be left here one stone upon another that shall not be thrown down" (Matt. 24:2; Mark 13:2) was likely—and was meant—to sadden and alarm: it was a prophecy of impending doom, of divine retribution soon to be exacted. Like the forebodings of Jeremiah to exactly the same effect centuries earlier, so must Jesus' prediction have filled Jewish hearts with fright and dismay. But there was nothing offensive or unlawful about it: that God visited His people at times with dire calamity was borne out only too convincingly by the Roman oppression and the loss of freedom and independence. That, notwithstanding such unmistakable portents of God's wrath, men did not mend their ways but persisted in sinfulness, none knew better, or deplored more bitterly, than priests and Pharisees. And that God's blazing fury might soon ignite another, more horrendous, conflagration was a timely warning, and it did not take much originality to sound it. Nor was Jesus alone in this: from Josephus we learn of at least two others who trumpeted the same anticipa-

tions of disaster,[23] and there must have been not a few unchronicled. There is nothing in the Gospels to show that it was this
kind of prophecy that spurred priests or scribes or Pharisees to
action or to indignation, nor was there anything in it to warrant
any such impulse, so long as it had not conclusively been proved
false (Deut. 18:21–22). Another utterance attributed to Jesus, that
he would himself destroy the temple and rebuild it in three days
(John 2:19), was chosen by Mark (14:58) and Matthew (26:61)
as the matter of his indictment before the Sanhedrin; and we shall
revert to that in due course and in greater detail.

But while the words of Jesus about the imminent destruction of
the temple can be explained, and accepted, as neutral and inof-
fensive prophesying for the wholly laudable purpose of exhorting
the folk to mend their ways, it is claimed that his acts in the
temple were bound to inflame the priests and elders in authority
to such incandescent anger that drastic steps against him were
inescapable. This is the famous story: "And Jesus went into the
temple of God, and cast out all them that sold and bought in the
temple, and overthrew the tables of the moneychangers, and the
seats of them that sold doves. And said unto them, It is written,
My house shall be called the house of prayer; but ye have made
it a den of thieves" (Matt. 21:12–13). When the "scribes and
chief priests heard it," they "sought how they might destroy him:
for they feared him, because all the people was astonished at his
doctrine" (Mark 11:18). It is not without significance that only
Mark and Luke report this reaction on the part of chief priests
and scribes; Matthew records none at all; in John the Jews merely
ask Jesus for his authority to do these things (2:18); and Luke
very meaningfully reports, following his account of the cleansing,
that Jesus "taught daily in the temple. But the chief priests and
the scribes and the chief of the people sought to destroy him"
(19:47). If, indeed, as has often been argued, Jesus' "attack on the
temple" endangered the whole trading system and "constituted a
most radical challenge to the authority of the sacerdotal aristocracy," and if, indeed, it was "taken by the sacerdotal aristocracy
as a declaration of war against them by Jesus,"[24] it is difficult to
understand why the temple authorities did not proceed instantly
against him. They had the armed temple police at their disposal
and could easily have had Jesus arrested there and then. That

Jesus enjoyed popular backing and may even—as is surmised[25]—have done the cleansing with the aid of "an excited crowd of his supporters," would afford all the more reason for prompt and energetic police intervention to restore order and prevent violence and plunder. Not only do the authorities not interfere, but they apparently welcome Jesus to the temple and let him teach there every day. Even if they did not have him taken into custody by temple police, the least they would do would be to eject him and deny him any facility to teach in the temple. But, instead, they let him eject the buyers and sellers and moneychangers.

The incongruity of the story has not escaped the author of the Gospel of Mark, who feels that he has to give some reason why the "scribes and chief priests" did not proceed at once against Jesus. So he informs us that "they feared him, because all the people was astonished at his doctrine" (11:18), meaning, to be sure, that they resented not only what he did and taught, but, more particularly, his immense popularity: only the day before, the citizens of Jerusalem had accorded him a rousing reception (11:8–10). If they desired to rob him of the popular loyalty, what better opportunity could there be than to catch him out *in flagrante delicto* and apprehend him for desecration of the temple grounds and usurpation of temple authority? The burgesses were not likely to stomach a desecration of the temple, and the keeping of peace and order in the sacred precincts was a police duty, whose due discharge would surely command public support and aid. And if Jesus' followers had resisted his arrest, and their resistance had been successful, the authorities would then have had a perfectly lawful and reasonable cause to prosecute him whenever they could lay their hands on him; and it is just that, we are told, that they so badly wanted to do!

The simple fact is that Jesus' act of "cleansing" was no offense at all: our data are an indication that it must—at least tacitly—have had the approval of the temple authorities.

Let us, first of all, look at the milieu where it could have taken place. The Gospel translations, which render it as "the temple," are inaccurate: the locality mentioned in the Gospels is the Mount of the Temple,[26] an area which comprised not only the temple proper but also administrative buildings, stores, stables, and bazaars. The area outside the temple on the Mount was accessible to everybody, including the impure and unwashed: there was no restriction of movement in it, or any limitation, restriction, or supervision of trading. It is true that, for their business, all the traders speculated on the needs of temple visitors: moneychangers converted the coins brought by the pilgrims from their districts into the shekel (or half-shekel), the only currency circulating as the prescribed temple gift (Exod. 21:13–16), and three weeks before the festivals, when the great pilgrimages to the temple started, the moneychangers had already to be at their counters.[27] There is an ancient report that on the Mount there stood two large cypresses: under one were four booths for the sale of pure sacrificial animals, under the other so many dovecotes that, from the birds bred in them, not only all temple requirements but the markets all over Israel could be supplied.[28] Doves were in especial demand, being the sacrificial offering of the proletariat which could not afford costlier victims (Lev. 5:7). There were, no doubt, also booths for the sale of frankincense, wine, oil, and fine flour—all of them concomitants of sacrifice (Lev. 2:5–7, 15; 7:12).

It has been suggested that all these creatures and commodities had to be "officially inspected" so as to exclude "any doubt of ritual purity"; that the pilgrims had no choice but to pay well and even exorbitantly for the certainty that their offerings would not be rejected for some flaw; and that the priests, to whom inspection fees went, were so interested in their "perquisite" that they must have fumed against any meddling with the traders and moneychangers as a brazen trespass on their own revenue.[29] There is no authority whatever for this suggestion. Any animal not "without blemish" (Lev. 3:1, 6) could not be sacrified, and would, admittedly, be set aside by the priest, but the vendor must take it back and return the purchase money, it being of the essence of any sale concluded there that it be "without blemish" and fit for the altar. The insinuation that because of their financial interest in getting a commission on sales the priests were so corrupt as to sacrifice flawed animals is not only unsupported by any evidence, but also intrinsically unreasonable: there were always hundreds of priests and Levites on duty in the temple, and scores of persons learned in the law present, so that any least departure by an officiating priest from elementary sacrificial rules would have been detected by a dozen sharp eyes and at once stopped. If, on the other hand, the creatures and commodities sold were "without blemish" and fit for sacrifice, a condition easily ascertainable by outward inspection, why should the vendors, or, for that matter, the buyers, the public, have agreed to pay commission to any priest? It advantaged the priests to keep the prices of sacrificial animals at the lowest possible level, so that more could afford to buy, because whatever was left after sacrificing belonged to the priests (Lev. 7:8 *et al.*) : the costlier the animals, the more the people would protest that they could not spare the money and content themselves with sacrificing doves, of which nothing would be left over for the priests. In short, there is no reason, and no testimony, for the assumption that priests or elders or any other persons in authority had any financial or other personal interest in the trade on the Mount of the Temple.[30]

While, then, priests and elders and other persons in authority may be acquitted of any part in illicit dealings, the traders and moneychangers have no such presumption to rely upon. There were no bars, either of law or of known custom, on setting oneself up as a trader in sacrificial stock; there was no licensing system under which one must show any moral or professional qualification. It was, thus, practically unavoidable that there should at all times be among the traders and moneychangers men below what one would expect temple standards to be: hard bargainers, unscrupulous profiteers, unfair competitors, uninhibited canvassers, and all sorts of busybodies soliciting business and volunteering advice and guidance. The spectacle is familiar to every visitor of Eastern bazaars or the market places in front of the great churches and mosques in Mediterranean lands.

It is not improbable that Jesus came upon a trader or moneychanger in the act of cheating or profiteering, or found hucksters brawling over a customer or a deal, or witnessed a disturbance of the peace in the market. Many others would, perhaps, not have cared, but Jesus was deeply upset by the desecration of the temple precincts: that the place destined to be the house of prayer for all the nations (Isa. 56:7) should give thieves a chance to make their den there (Mark 11:17; Matt. 21:13; Luke 19:46) was more than he could in silence bear. Again, his outburst is an echo of Jeremiah's thundering, "Is this house, which is called by my name, become a den of robbers in your eyes?" (7:11), and there was nothing in Jesus' words which was not familiar to every listener. Some authors[31] regard the incident as proof of his zealotic inclinations or association; but he need have been neither zealot nor fanatic to be enraged by such misdemeanors, and his quick and violent reflex may have been instinctive and unplanned. The theory that he must have had powerful support, and that he could not have "succeeded unaided in driving from their place of legitimate business a company of traders when engaged with their customers who needed their services to fulfill their religious duties,"[32] appears to be irrelevant, if our premise is correct that the traders in question were caught by Jesus in illicit transactions. They might well protest at his interference, but the customers—and there may have been very many of them—would at once rally to his side; the traders would never summon the temple police, because Jesus and the customers would then have lodged complaints against them, rather than contrariwise.

It is human nature that for people who day in, day out, carry on a routine business in the very shadow of a holy place the sanctity of it will gradually be dimmed: what fills the worshiper with awe and reverence finds shopkeepers of long standing cold and unmoved. It would not be surprising, therefore, if, on that occasion, Jesus had seen traders quitting their stands and carrying merchandise or tools into one of the temple porches (Mark 11:16), whether to help a customer handle his purchase or even to traffic there. This was a grave offense, for no one might enter the temple in a state of impurity (Lev. 15:31). Entry into the precincts was forbidden even "with one's walking-stick, shoes, briefcase, or with dusty feet." They must not be used as a short cut on one's way; one must not spit in them.[33] All that being so, any assistance lent by the people to get rid of transgressors who, in bearing or outfit, profaned the sanctity and purity of the place would assuredly earn the approbation and thanks of the temple police.

Assuming that Jesus did upset the tables of moneychangers and cast out traders and would not suffer dealers to sully the holiness of the temple,[34] and assuming further, as we must, that in so doing he acted from the best and purest of motives, there is nothing, even on the face of the Gospel accounts themselves, to warrant any counsel or design on the part of anybody, except, maybe, those selfsame traders and moneychangers, to seek revenge. The only grievance that the authorities could possibly have entertained—in the sound perception of the author of the Gospel According to John—was that Jesus had acted without formal authority or competence: he should have lodged a complaint with the powers-that-be and asked that proper steps be taken by them. And even that vagary would scarcely have irked the authorities in the case of a man who, as Jesus did, acted on the spur of the moment, coming upon delinquents *in flagrante delicto:* it was not the law then, any more than it is generally the law nowadays, that instead of preventing, as best you can, the continuation of an offense which is being committed in your presence, you have to let the offenders go on with their criminal pursuits and content yourself with informing the police. In the situation in which Jesus found himself, it was natural and lawful for him to act as he did, and no one would have welcomed that more than the temple administrators.

In the Gospels of Matthew (21:23), Mark (11:28), and Luke (20:2), "chief priests and elders," with or without "scribes," asked Jesus, "By what authority doest thou these things, or who is he that gave thee this authority?"; the question was put, not necessarily in connection with the cleansing of the temple, but generally, in respect of his doings and teachings. At a very early stage in Jesus' ministry, when he taught in the synagogue in Capernaum, people "were astonished at his doctrine: for he taught them as one who had authority, and not as the scribes" (Mark 1:21–22). Matthew (7:28–29) makes this same astonishment follow upon the Sermon on the Mount. Teaching as one who has "authority" cannot merely mean that his speeches were powerful and his doctrines impressive (cf. Luke 4:32); it is that his authoritative teaching is, ostensibly, differentiated in a particular way from the teachings of scribes, which might be impressive and powerful as well. For everybody knew that Jesus had no "authority"—hence the astonishment that he taught as if he had; not as the scribes, who would, like all ordinary preachers, describe and explain to you in intelligible form what the laws required of you and how best to observe them if you wished reward and not punishment, but rather as one who had the "authority" to lay down the law and determine it for you and prescribe new rules of conduct. Such "authority" no man might take himself: it had to be conferred by a person already in "authority," in a formal act of ordination, a scholar already ordained "authorizing" a second.[35] In the time of Jesus such ordinations were very rare,[36] so that everybody knew who was and who was not ordained. The astonishment that Jesus spoke as if he were is suggestive of admiration rather than spleen: here is a man, the people might have said, who has the courage of his own opinions and looks at the world with eyes of his own. But what, for the impressed listener, was something to admire was, for the authorities, a matter for concern: if Jesus desired to teach with "authority," he should observe the procedures and first seek ordination. The question which the chief priests and elders are said to have addressed to him may reflect that concern: having no lawful "authority," how is it that you purport to teach as if you had? Jesus' answer could have simply been: I do not purport to teach with "authority," I never professed ordination, and it is none of my fault if people misunderstand. But there is, of course, an "authority" other and better than formal ordination: if John the Baptist, who had not been ordained either, nevertheless spoke with "authority," he must have had that authority from Heaven; and so may I. But, as you cannot tell whether he had divine authority, "Neither do I tell you by what authority I do these things" (Mark 11:33; Matt. 21:27) .[37]

The theory has been put forward that the chief priests and elders posed their question as a means of procuring evidence against Jesus as a "rebellious elder" (Deut. 17:12) ,[38] but it is untenable, if only for the reason that the rebellious elder was, by definition, an ordained scholar,[39] and the questioners well knew that Jesus had not been, and would not be, ordained. Apart from that, none of Jesus' teachings would appear to fall within the category of a rebellious elder's offense:[40] at that time, already, the law as to rebellious elders was held to apply to Sadducees only,[41] and Jesus was certainly not one.

His implicit claim that, like John the Baptist, he had his "authority" from Heaven cannot have been sensational tidings to his questioners. First, that he had succeeded in gathering around him throngs of enthusiastic listeners would to anyone conscious of ever-present divine guidance and determination afford at least prima-facie proof of divine approbation. Second, it certainly was always legitimate for any deeply religious man to believe in his own divine mission: God had bestowed on him the power to persuade and inspire and guide other men for some purpose, and what finer purpose could there be than to bring God nearer to their hearts and minds? But, third, Jesus seems to have claimed divine "authority" before: when he had wrought certain miraculous feats, the "Pharisees," with or without "scribes," "came forth and began to question with him, seeking from him a sign from heaven" (Mark 8:11; Matt. 12:38), which surely means perceptible proof of a kind that he was, indeed, doing God's will. The evangelist's gloss that, by this question, they wished to tempt him (Mark 8:11) is altogether unwarranted: it was very common usage in those days for contentious scholars, each insisting that his was the true interpretation of God's laws and his the true precept to do God's will, to appeal to Heaven for a "sign" as to who was right and who wrong; and several instances are recorded in which a "heavenly voice" was heard to pronounce the divine verdict.[42] It is characteritic of the Pharisaic frame of mind that in one of these talmudic instances the vanquished disputant flatly rejected that verdict and would not abide by "heavenly voices," affirming that the true law is no longer "in heaven, that thou shouldest say, Who shall go up for us to heaven and bring it unto us?" But it has been handed down to humans on earth, and "is very nigh unto thee, in thy mouth and in thy heart" (Deut. 30:12–14). In the same spirit, they might well have regarded any divine authority claimed by Jesus as less than enough to make up for the ordination required by human laws; but their challenge to him to show them a "sign" from Heaven only goes to show that they were very far from dismissing his claim out of hand.

No Pharisee would ever count as blasphemous or otherwise improper an assertion of divine authority. Whoever aired an opinion, suggested a course of action, or propounded a norm of law or ethics would aver that he was divinely inspired or his the only true, "authorized," or authentic interpretation of God's will and word: there would be no listeners if all that he had to convey were his personal views, unless, of course, it was a case of royal bidding backed by physical enforcement. Express or implied ascriptions of divine "authority" were inherent in any teacher's qualification: if he himself did not, or could not, assert it, what could there be at all in what he taught? Naturally, therefore, the divine "afflatus" would be preferred not only by the many saviors and messiahs who appeared at that phase,[43] seeking to comfort the oppressed and the depressed with vistas of early salvation at God's hands through their own good offices, but also by the "scribes," who, according to the Gospel texts, were, with sanction, teaching and preaching everywhere. In contemporary Jewish society the nexus between man and God was direct and immediate: a Jew's approach to God was unhampered by priestly or rabbinical barrier, so that a claim to be divinely inspired was nothing extraordinary and in no wise a trespass on priestly or rabbinical privilege or monopoly. In this respect, Jesus was no different from scores of his fellow Jews, and his arrogation of divine "authority" could not have given either the "Pharisees" or anybody else the slightest ground for pique or ill will.

It was the author of the Gospel According to John, again, who felt that the claim to divine authority or inspiration could in itself neither explain nor warrant a hostile attitude to Jesus; so he added to his breach of the Sabbath a stronger provocation, namely, that he had "said also that God was his Father, making himself equal with God" (5:18). Let it be set down at once that there is nothing in any of the Synoptic Gospels to hint that Jesus ever said anything of the kind; if there was a tradition that he had, the evangelists would indubitably not have suppressed it: they would have underlined and emphasized it. That even the author of the Gospel of John was not too sure on the point appears from the fact—otherwise inexplicable—that when he was interrogated and charged afterward, no complaint was lodged against Jesus, even according to John, in respect of any claim that he was the son of God and equal with Him, and one would have expected this to be the first and foremost indictment. Moreover, while the Sabbath breaches and the claim to be a son of God and equal to Him are represented as grounds why the Jews persecuted Jesus and "sought to slay him" (5:16), yet, when he challenged them, "Why go ye about to kill me?" they are said to have answered: "Thou hast a devil: who goeth about to kill thee?" (7:19–20), the innuendo being that they untruthfully denied a true charge but did not trouble to renew the previous charge of divine pretensions.

It will have been observed that in tracing the mutual relations of Jesus and the Jews we have relied almost exclusively on the Synoptic Gospels, and only once or twice referred to the Gospel According to John. Our submission is that clashes and disputes between Jesus and the Jews, for which the earlier evangelists appear to have possessed no traditions and which are reported in John alone, cannot prima facie be regarded as authentic, but must be taken as tendentious accretions by the author of John, whose Gospel, it will be remembered, was written for Romans and non-Jews when Christianity and Judaism had finally parted ways. He begins with the rejection of Jesus by the Jews, his own people (1:11), and places the episode of the cleansing of the temple almost at the start of his story (2:13–17): his intent was to keep the picture of Jesus as an active rebel against the authorities, and the reasons for Jewish rancor and persecution, in the mind of the reader as an ever-recurring theme. The report of the Jews' resolve to kill him for his Sabbath sins is followed at once, in the words of the Reverend James Parkes, by

one of the long and unsympathetic denunciations of the Jews which mark the Gospel, and which contain words which accurately reflect the situation at the time when they were written, but which would seem strange in one of the earlier Gospels. . . . From this moment onwards every time that Jesus is made to speak to the Jews, He appears deliberately to mystify and antagonize them. He does not attempt to win them, for He knows His own, and treats the rest with hostility and unconcealed dislike. The Jews themselves are represented as perpetually plotting to kill Him, and afraid to do so, because of His moral power. Even when Jesus addresses those Jews "which had believed on Him," He says of them that they are of their "father the devil" (8,44). In the middle of His ministry the Jews decide to expel from the Synagogue any who believe in Him (9,22), so that people are afraid to speak openly of Him (7,13). All this is redolent of the atmosphere which must have existed at the end of the century, when, indeed, confession of Christianity meant expulsion from the Synagogue, and exposure to the unknown dangers of Roman persecution.[44]

But it has no real bearing on the relations as they may have existed, or actually did exist, between Jesus and the Jews or the Jewish authorities of his day.

Still there is, even in the Gospel According to John, at least one Pharisee in splendid isolation, "named Nicodemus, a ruler of the Jews," who would come to Jesus, albeit only "by night," address him as Rabbi, and confess that "we know that thou art a teacher come from God" (3:1-2).

Two incidents, reported only in John, are often cited to prove Jewish enmity against Jesus: they are incidents of stoning, when that animus took violent form. When they heard him say in the temple—of all places—that he had been before Abraham, the Jews "took up stones to cast at him" (8:59); and again, when he proclaimed that he and God, his father, were one, "the Jews took up stones again to stone him" (10:31). Jesus is said to have asked for which of his good deeds he was being so ill used, and they replied: "For a good work we stone thee not, but for blasphemy, and because that thou, being a man, makest thyself God" (10:33). Had either of these stonings really happened, some tradition concerning them must have been accessible to the earlier evangelists, who are most unlikely to have shelved it. But aside from their inconsistency with the popular affection for Jesus, to which not only the Synoptic Gospels testify but even the Gospel of John itself (12:12), the reports also contradict the Johannine version that when Jesus had spoken and taught in the temple, "no man laid hands on him, for his hour was not yet come" (7:30; 8:20). How then can it be that, though his hour was not yet come and no man would lay hands on him, the Jews stoned him? If his hour was not yet come, why did they seek to take him, and he had to escape out of their hands (10:39)? The words "for his hour was not yet come" carry a double meaning. On the one hand, they prepare the ground for what will happen when the hour comes: then, it appears, the Jews will be free from all inhibitions and give full play to their murderous aggressions. On the other, there is a hint of the predestination of Jesus' fate, as if it were not the hostility and contumaciousness of the Jews which determined the event, but solely the will of God, Who appointed His own time and chose His own instruments.

This consciousness of "fulfillment" of a fate predestined is present in the Synoptic Gospels as well. Jesus taught his disciples, and said unto them, "The Son of Man is delivered into the hands of men, and they shall kill him; but after that he is killed, he shall rise the third day" (Mark 9:31). The "men" who will kill him are soon more specifically pilloried as the "chief priests and scribes," into whose hands he will be delivered and who will "condemn him to death and deliver him to the Gentiles" (Mark 10:33). Luke has it that Jesus said, "The Son of Man must suffer many things, and be rejected of the elders and chief priests and scribes, and be slain, and be raised the third day" (9:22). The version in Matthew is that "he must go unto Jerusalem, and suffer many things of the elders and chief priests and scribes, and be killed, and be raised again the third day" (16:21); and, later on: "Behold, we go up to Jerusalem; and the Son of man shall be betrayed unto the chief priests and unto the scribes, and they shall condemn him to death. And shall deliver him to the Gentiles to mock, and to scourge, and to crucify him; and the third day he shall rise again" (20:18–19). The twofold purport of this prophecy, in its different versions, is again clearly discernible: first, the predestination of the future happenings, and their predetermined culmination, or ultimate purpose, in the resurrection; and, second, the prophetic designation of chief priests, elders, and scribes as the instruments chosen for the killing which must precede the resurrection. Even if Jesus did make these prophecies, which in the circumstances as we have retraced them is highly improbable,[45] at any rate they cannot serve as proof of what actually took place afterward, all the less so as their variants allow of several possibilities among which the chronicler of the eventual happenings could make his choice. But the very recording and repetition of the prophecies are likely, and are calculated, to mislead the reader, if only as a matter of faith and theology, into believing that what eventually happened was but a fulfillment of them; this being so, there was no further need, or, indeed, any justification, to inquire and find out whether what did happen was or was not consistent with them. In other words, as it had to be the Jews and not the Romans who, from the evangelists' point of view, must be blamed for the death of Jesus, his own prophecy that the Jewish chief priests, scribes, and elders would be the main and decisive actors in the tragedy would be well-nigh determinant evidence that, in fact, they were, and would anyhow be a most apt overture to a description of the events in which they would obligatorily be portrayed as such.

It is not without interest that in these prophecies Jesus is said to have refrained from mentioning the Pharisees, as if his arch-enemies, the veritable incarnation of evil, would have no hand in his death. It has, indeed, been contended that, the Pharisees not being expressly named, it was only Sadducean chief priests and elders who condemned Jesus.[46] But we have seen that "chief priests, scribes, and elders" is a description wide enough to comprise, at the lowest, a very strong Pharisaic minority, and the sounder opinion seems to be that in the prophecies, as elsewhere in the Gospel texts, the terms "Pharisees" and "scribes" are used somewhat indifferently.[47]

The Pharisees, however, appear to form part not only of the "chief priests, scribes, and elders" who are depicted as the persecutors of Jesus, but also of the masses described as his lovers and admirers. Jesus, as we have seen, gathered multitudes around him, many more than had followed John the Baptist. King Herod, who had ordered that John the Baptist be killed (Matt. 14:10), feared that Jesus, with his vast congregation, was "John the Baptist risen from the dead" (14:2), and therefore sought to lay hands on him, too. According to Matthew, Jesus departed "by ship into a desert place" (14:13) on hearing of Herod's design; and according to Luke, it was, amazingly enough, "certain of the Pharisees" who came and said to him, "Get thee out and depart hence: for Herod will kill thee" (13:31). This seems to show that some Pharisees, so far from seeking to destroy Jesus (Matt. 12:14; Mark 3:6), sought to save him. That we have here a glimpse, solitary though it be, into the true Pharisaic feeling about Jesus seems to be borne out by what Josephus tells us of Jewish reaction to the killing of John the Baptist:

Herod had ordered John to be killed, although John was a noble-minded man who entreated the Jews to strive for perfection and admonished them to do justice to each other and piety to God and come to him to be baptized. . . . These beautiful speeches attracted great multitudes, and Herod was afraid that this man whose reputation seemed to be well established and whose advice everybody seemed to follow, might lead the people to rebellion; and he therefore thought it better to eliminate him before John would have the time to create a situation of real danger, lest he shall regret afterwards, when it would be too late, his failure to act in time. This suspicion prompted Herod to have John arrested and brought in chains to the fort of Machaerus and have him killed there. The Jews were firmly convinced that John's death was the cause of the defeat of Herod's army—this having been the punishment with which God in His wrath had visited the King.[48]

There is no valid reason to assume that the general Jewish feeling about Jesus was any different: his speeches were no less, indeed, inferentially much more, beautiful than John's; his admonitions to justice and piety must have aroused the same echo in Jewish hearts; and the "multitudes" flocked to him and made no secret of their delight and reverence. As did the death of John the Baptist, so would a violent death of Jesus evoke God's wrath and punishment, entail the severest shock and bitterest grief. The truth is that the only quarter from which any present danger to Jesus threatened was Herod the Great King, and none but "Pharisees" warned him of it and sought to see him in safety.

There would soon be another dire peril darkening Jesus' life. His great popularity, his hold on the "multitudes," would be brought to the attention of the Romans. Was it, indeed, "chief priests, elders, and scribes," or the "Pharisees," or, in short, the Jewish leadership that would deliver him into the hands of the Gentiles? We saw that there was no plausible reason why they should; and if they did, they would be quite untrue to the character which they had exemplified on the previous occasion when Jesus was in jeopardy, and by their general relations with the Romans. But let us see what did take place.

PART TWO

What Could Really
Have Taken Place

4 THE ARREST

The story of the trial and death of Jesus starts with his arrest. If a trial is wrapped in mystery, whether for lack of information or by reason of contradictory reports, particulars of the arrest might afford a clue to the solving of the enigma. If you know of what a man is suspected, for what he is arrested, and by whom and on whose orders, you can draw some conclusions as to the charges on which he was eventually tried and the tribunal which tried him. Not that we have clear and unequivocal accounts of the particulars of the arrest of Jesus, but such as we have must be carefully examined lest any clue be overlooked.

When Jesus and the disciples had finished their meal (the "Lord's Supper"), they went out of the city of Jerusalem unto the Mount of Olives (Mark 14:26; Matt. 26:30; Luke 22:39) and there came to a place called Gethsemane (Mark 14:32; Matt. 26:36), which might be identical with what is described in John as a garden over the brook of Cedron (John 18:1). It is significant that, according to Luke (22:39) and John (18:2) alike, Jesus often resorted to this place with his disciples; it may well be that the gardens and hills surrounding the city were then, as they are today, favorite and popular walks.

As Jesus speaks to the disciples (Mark 14:41–42; Matt. 26:45–46; Luke 22:46), there suddenly appear people led by Judas, and it is at once apparent that they come with hostile intent. According to Mark, they were "a great multitude with swords and staves, from the chief priests and the scribes and the elders" (14:43); according to Matthew, there were also "elders of the people" (26:47); according to Luke, Jesus first beheld "a multitude" (22:47), but straightway addressed himself to "the chief priests and the captains of the temple and the elders which were come to him" (22:52); and according to John, they were "a band of men and officers from the chief priests and Pharisees . . . with lanterns and torches and weapons" (18:3), but the arrest was carried out by "a band and the captain and officers of the Jews" (18:12). There is no longer any controversy among the scholars that the band and the captain were a cohort and its tribune, that is, a Roman military unit commanded by a Roman officer,[1] so that while the Synoptic Gospels tell of the presence of Jews only at the arrest, the Johannine tradition is that both Roman soldiers and Jews took part in it.

Before we examine that tradition meticulously, let us try to identify the "Jews" who, according to all the evangelists, took part. A modern writer suggests that while they were the emissaries of the Jewish priests, these participants were not themselves Jews but Gentiles, his argument being that the "sinners" into whose hands Jesus said that he would be betrayed (Matt. 26:45; Mark 14:41) are never Jews but always Gentiles (cf. Gal. 2:15; Matt. 9:10–11); and "the chief priests had at their disposal a small force recruited from many nationalities, and also non-Jewish servants and slaves."[2] However that may be, and whatever the right construction of the term "sinners" used by Jesus on that occasion, words which he used before the event can hardly be adduced as proof of the identity of the men who afterward came to arrest him. Moreover, even if "sinners" can denote only Gentiles, his prophecy, at least according to John, would have been realized by the presence of Roman troops, notwithstanding the presence of "nonsinners."

The presence and active part of Jews seem to be established by the fact that, on his arrest, Jesus was at once led not into Roman custody, but into the home of the high priest, or, according to John, that of the high priest's father-in-law. It stands to reason that it was Jewish temple police who would lead him there, that constabulary being under the high priest's supreme command; and, as will be shown, Jesus could not have been brought into the high priest's home without express instructions to that effect from that dignitary himself.

Some of the Gospels, however, speak of the presence, at the arrest, not of orderly contingents of temple police, but of "multitudes," giving the impression of an indeterminate number of people sent by the "chief priests" or "elders" or "Pharisees," whether as hirelings or just as an incited mob. Luke even suggests the presence of "elders," a suggestion unreasonable on the face of it: an arrest is not normally made—nor was it then—by an "elder" or judge, and certainly not by many elders or judges assembled together; the authority desiring an arrest will dispatch for the purpose one or more armed officers trained in police work such as this. Nor would any "elder" or notable let himself be troubled, at such an hour of the night, to go out of house and city and walk uphill for no little distance simply to attend in person the arrest of a suspected criminal, whoever it might be. If that is true any ordinary night, it must be all the truer on this particular night: whether it was, as the Synoptic Gospels have it, the very night of the great feast of Passover or, as John reports, only the night of Passover eve, every Jewish householder was busy at home either celebrating the Seder or preparing for the feast and its sacrifices. It is inconceivable that on such a night he could be lured out into the hills to share in a police expedition. Finally, if the "elders" were, indeed, the instigators of the arrest, it does not make sense that they should attend and take part in it in person: on the contrary, they would send their agents, but be extremely careful not to be seen and identified themselves.

The real identity of the Jewish participants in the arrest is deducible from the reference in Luke to "the captains of the temple" (22:52). The term here translated into English as "captains" is the Greek *strategoi*, military commanders. It has been suggested that these "temple commanders" are the vice-priests (*seganei kohanim*),[3] of whose functions we have some knowledge in the Jewish sources: wherever *seganim* occurs in the Bible (e.g., Jer. 51:23, 28, 57; Ezek. 23:6, 12, 23), it is rendered in the Septuagint as *strategoi*. These vice-priests were charged, *inter alia*, with the public relations of the temple administration: they had to proceed to the gates of the city and there welcome the people arriving from other parts of the country with the first fruits of their fields and vineyards as a gift to the temple.[4] There is a list of precedence of temple officers, in which *seganim* rank after officiating priests and before the commanders of the temple police,[5] from which it would appear that police commanders were their immediate subordinates. Since, in the verse quoted from Luke, the "captains of the temple" are mentioned as present together with the "chief priests," it has been argued that the *seganim* represent the "chief priests," whereas the commanders of the temple police are the "captains of the temple,"[6] suggesting that the police commanders and their immediate superiors might both have been present. But it seems clear, on any view, that the term *strategoi* can refer only to a commanding officer of military or quasi-military character and, in the context of the temple, to none but officers of the temple police.

While we have discarded as unreasonable the report that "elders" or "chief priests" may have attended Jesus' arrest in person, the version that temple police, and their commanding officers, did so appears eminently sound. The arrest of a suspect, as we have remarked, is normally carried out by a police unit and not by "multitudes" of people or by elders and notables. In the Gospel of John we find striking corroboration of our preference: the Jewish participants are there described as being "officers" from the chief priests (18:3) or "officers" of the Jews (18:12), and the only "officers" competent to carry out arrests for the "chief priests" in particular and for the "Jews" in general were the officers of the temple police.[7]

Our starting point will, therefore, be the premise that the temple police was detached by the "chief priests," that is, as we shall see, by the high priest and his entourage, to apprehend Jesus; and it is immaterial whether the unit or units that carried out the task were under the command of lower-ranking or higher-ranking officers. But the fact that it was temple police who arrested Jesus does not exclude the possibility that other persons were on the scene, and the question arises whether the "multitudes" of Mark and Matthew cannot be accounted for in some way or other. It appears intrinsically improbable that townspeople, of their own accord, should join the temple police in a march out of the city at night to arrest no matter whom. It has been suggested that, as is, indeed, implicit in the language of the Gospels, they did not join in spontaneously but were hired by the "chief priests" and elders, either to aid the temple police in overcoming any possible resistance or by their very presence to overawe Jesus and his disciples into submissiveness.[8] But "multitudes" milling about at the place of arrest would be an obstacle to the police rather than a help: nothing would have been easier for Jesus and his handful of disciples than to mingle among the crowd and to all intents and purposes disappear, or anyhow stir up such confusion as to thwart any orderly police action. Furthermore, the Gospels which report the presence of "multitudes" tell that they were led there by Judas, who had treacherously conspired with the "chief priests and captains" (Luke 22:4) to that end, and surely none of the conspirators, least of all the ringleader, would want a "multitude" of witnesses to the plot and its success. It is in the nature of a conspiracy that it is concluded in secret and carried into effect in secret, with a minimum of partners and potential informers. If the "multitudes" have any meaning at all, they must mean something different from multitudes of Jews.

There is one other discrepancy which goes to the heart of the matter, and we shall meet it again: it concerns the attitude of the Jews at large to Jesus in particular and, in general, to any suspect threatened with arrest. Any Jewish "multitude" would have to be recruited from the lower strata of the people: others would not let themselves either be hired or be facilely inflamed. Of these same "multitudes"—even the term used is the same—we know that they greeted Jesus rapturously on his arrival in Jerusalem only a few days earlier: "a very great multitude spread their garments in the way; others cut down branches from the trees, and strawed them in the way," and "all the city was moved" (Matt. 21:8–10). So far from enlisting the help of such "multitudes" against Jesus, the chief priests and the scribes were in no doubt that "the world is gone after him" (John 12:19), and they dreaded, rightly, "lest there be an uproar of the people" (Mark 14:2) if they did him harm. If they wanted Jesus taken into custody, the last thing that they would do would be to let the Jewish "multitudes" be present, for the inevitable outcome of that indulgence would be Jesus' rescue from the hands of the temple police into safety. The more so if, as is reported, the "multitudes" were armed "with swords and staves" (Mark 14:43; Matt. 26:47): as likely as not, the outraged sympathizers would have given the police short shrift and led Jesus home in triumph.

There was good reason, verily, why the people should love Jesus: not only was he one of their own who had risen, by the manifest grace of God, to that intellectual and moral stature to which, consciously or not, each of them aspired, but his fame as a worker of miracles, healer of the sick, consoler and redeemer of the poor and persecuted, castigator of corruption, and, like themselves, sworn enemy of the rich and mighty was more, far more, than enough to win him popular affection and devotion. That "multitudes" of such ardent well-wishers should be forthcoming at anybody's invitation to help in arresting Jesus cannot seriously be credited.

But let us, for the sake of argument, assume that the "multitudes" enlisted that night did not know, and were not told, that it was Jesus who was to be arrested. It is, perhaps, conceivable that the temple police turned to the general public for help in catching a dangerous fugitive from justice who might be expected to resist arrest violently and so must be overcome by greater numerical strength. It is, however, doubtful, to say the least, that any number of citizens would have answered such a call unless first told who the offender was and what his offense. Once the identity of the "fugitive" was revealed, it would, for the reasons given, have put a speedy end to any cooperativeness of the people; if misleading information was offered by the temple police, the deception would be visible as soon as the people beheld the "quarry": in the best case, they would lay down their arms and go home; in the worst, they would rescue Jesus and thus frustrate the whole purpose of the temple police. And, insofar as concerns divulging the grounds of arrest, it is open to doubt whether the temple police knew what they were at all: at any rate, they did not disclose them to Jesus on his arrest; and it will emerge from the subsequent proceedings that, from the point of view of the Jewish authorities, there was no ground which could be reduced to precise legal terms. But even assuming that the "chief priests" had seen fit to accuse Jesus of any of his unorthodox sayings or acts— which in itself, as we saw, was most unlikely—and to order his arrest on any such account, it was just this kind of teaching and ministering that endeared Jesus to the masses. To adduce it as a ground of his arrest would, consequently, agitate them not only to withhold all cooperation from the temple police, but to do everything in their power to rescue him.

Nor should one believe that it would be easy for the temple police, or a commander, to mobilize popular aid in any of its operations outside the temple precincts. Within and around the temple, the temple police exercised their proper competence, and presumably everybody would lend them a hand to prevent disorder or desecration. Outside the holy precincts, it is possible that they might enlist support of the people in a clash with the Roman occupation forces or individual legionnaires, but never in support of action carried out for the Romans or in connivance with them. The people would never degrade themselves to do the "dirty" work of the police against a nonprivileged Jew, their own kith and kin. And it is not only, and not so much, this notorious reaction of the people that would render futile any police appeal for cooperation, but long-standing awareness of it would make the temple authorities refrain, in the first place, from even attempting to secure their help. If the chief priests "feared the people" (Luke 20:19), as they had every reason to, and therefore held themselves back from "laying hands" on Jesus (*ibid.*), and were sure that there would be a popular uproar (Mark 14:2) if any harm came to him, it would be sheer, almost suicidal, stupidity on their part to seek the assistance of the very same elements whose clamor and mutiny they rightly foresaw and feared. No less than the unmistakable antagonism of the people to any proceeding by the temple police against Jesus, it is the fact that the authorities had full cognizance of the people's attitude that renders any recruitment of Jewish "multitudes" for any such proceeding absolutely unthinkable.

It may be that the Gospels use the term "multitudes" not in an objective but in a subjective sense: to Jesus and the disciples, who that night, in that peaceful garden, were surprised by a number of armed men, it might have seemed as if "multitudes" were descending upon them. Indeed, if we take literally the Johannine report of the presence of a "cohort," that must have been the impression: the Roman army was divided into legions, each legion of ten cohorts, and each cohort of six *centuriae;* and, while in each *cen-*

turia, as its name says, there were a hundred soldiers, we find that there were at times cohorts of fewer than six hundred men, and legions of fewer than six thousand, but the common opinion is that a cohort would never count less than three to four hundred.[9] Assuming that the cohort which came to arrest Jesus was a very small one of only three hundred soldiers, nevertheless a contingent that numerous was big enough to be called, and regarded as, a veritable "multitude," much too big, in fact, for the business on hand. And, indeed, it has been suggested that this was not a full cohort, but only part of one, and that the authors of the Gospel exaggerated slightly.[10]

The Johannine version that Jesus was arrested by the whole or a part of a Roman cohort, commanded by its tribune, with the Jewish temple police and its commanding officer in attendance, is now being accepted as the true statement of facts by most contemporary scholars,[11] and it will be accepted by us for its reasonableness and, in the light of subsequent events, its inherent probability. It should be remembered that the author of John was an implacable and uncompromising blackener of Jews and whitewasher of Romans; and unless he had to reckon with a well-established tradition, too well known to be brushed aside, that Roman troops took part in the arrest, he would have suppressed it: certainly he would never have invented it. Nothing would have been simpler for him than to follow the Synoptic Gospels and saddle the Jews, alone and squarely, with total responsibility for the arrest of Jesus, to the exclusion of the Romans; that he did not, but expressly mentioned the cohort and its tribune as carrying out the arrest, is clear indication of a deliberate and well-advised recension of extant reports and one for which there must have been a formidably cogent incentive.

The fact, then, that the arrest was a joint undertaking of Roman soldiers and the Jewish temple police lends added poignancy to the question who it was that ordered the arrest: did the Roman authorities make the first move, or was the Roman part no more than an act of military aid or backing for an arrest which the Jewish authorities had prompted and for which they bore the ultimate responsibility? But there is a preliminary question, surely, concerning the role of Judas in sponsoring and carrying out the arrest: did he serve Jewish or Roman interests? Preliminary be-

cause if it should turn out—as the Gospels have it—that the arrest
was the outcome of conspiracy between Judas and the Jews, that
would afford strong evidence of Jewish and not Roman initiative.

The treachery of Judas is common to all four Gospels. But the
report of a conspiracy between him and the chief priests (Matt.
26:14; Mark 14:10), with or without the elders or captains (Luke
22:4), is found only in the Synoptic Gospels, and only there is the
story told of money (Luke 22:5) or thirty pieces of silver (Matt.
26:15) covenanted as a consideration for the betrayal. The Gospel
of John tells only that "the devil" was "put into the heart of Judas
Iscariot, Simon's son, to betray him" (13:2); that Jesus was "troubled in spirit" and said, "Verily, verily, one of you shall betray
me" (13:21); that when "Satan" had entered into Judas, Jesus
said to him, "That thou doest, do quickly" (13:27); and that
Judas indeed betrayed him (18:2). But there is no mention of any
conspiracy between Judas and the Jews or any other identified
person or group. According to John, therefore, there might have
been the possibility of a conspiracy between Judas and the Romans, which could explain the Roman part in the arrest and even
imply a Roman initiative.

It is not that a conspiracy between Judas and the Romans is
intrinsically less probable or possible than one between them and
the Jews: if he wanted to betray his master, he had only to denounce him to the Romans as a rebel or zealot, and he could be
sure of swift action. It is that the whole tale of Judas' treachery
is so unlikely, so incongruous, regardless of who his fellow conspirators might have been, that it merits no credence. It may, of
course, be that a story of the disciple who betrayed his master and
even brought about his death, sinking thus to the lowest depths of
shame and immorality, and all because the devil had entered
into him (John 13:27), is meant to convey a profound and significant religious message. Nobody, not even the greatest disciple
of the greatest master—so the moral would be pointed—is proof
against the temptations of Satan or his own criminal inclinations;
or there is no escape from doing evil if God has chosen you as His
instrument thus to attain His purpose. Perhaps, then, the story
was included in the Gospels for purely theological reasons, although some of the early theologians considered it "a terrible
scandal"[12] and insisted that its inclusion had been imperative

solely because the thing had actually happened: "it would lift a very heavy burden from the heart of Christianity if it could be proved that the betrayal of Judas did not take place, and that it is the product of Christian imagination; unfortunately this cannot be proved."[13]

I do not think that one should give up so quickly. Let us take a more realistic look at the details. When Jesus "walked no more openly among the Jews, but went thence unto a country near to the wilderness" (John 11:54), the authorities interested in tracking him down and apprehending him might have needed the help of an outside informer: he had gone away to hide, and must have been at pains to keep his whereabouts a well-guarded secret. But when he returned to Jerusalem, it was openly and triumphantly: "much people that were come to the feast" had heard in advance that he would be coming (John 12:12), and there can be no reasonable doubt that the authorities—if they were interested in him —knew of his impending advent. And when he arrived, he did not mingle with the huge crowds that filled the streets of Jerusalem at this festive season, but rode on an ass (John 12:14) to the welcome of loud and prolonged ovations (John 12:13; Matt. 21:8-10). Now the conspiracy between Judas and the priests is reported as having been arranged two days before the feast of Passover (Mark 14:1; Matt. 26:2), that is, either on the very day of Jesus' triumphant entry or on the next, when everybody was already fully apprised of his whereabouts. There would have been no difficulty whatever in tracing him, neither for the Roman authorities nor, least of all, for the temple police of the chief priests. According to Luke, Jesus himself, when arrested, said: "Be ye come out, as against a thief, with swords and staves? When I was daily with you in the temple, ye stretched forth no hands against me" (22:52–53); and Luke records as well that Jesus was in the daytime teaching in the temple, "and all the people came early in the morning to him in the temple for to hear him" (21:38). He could have been arrested there, in the very bailiwick of the temple police or on his way from or to the temple, or easily followed wherever he went, as he presumably was. There was no need for any "betrayal" or conspiracy, and any money spent for such services as Judas volunteered to render was a sheer waste.

The explanation commonly offered to make the story plausible is that the chief priests, as has been said, were very much afraid of public uproar if Jesus were to be arrested in the open (Mark 14:2), and determined, therefore, to take him at night, under cover of darkness and outside the city, where no citizen protest could be stirred. It was the nocturnal haunt of Jesus, with which his disciples, Judas among them, were familiar, but which could not be discovered by uninitiated strangers, that was the subject matter of Judas' deal. Now, however, we are told that while in the daytime he was teaching in the temple, Jesus every night "went out and abode in the mount that is called the mount of Olives" (Luke 21:37) ; and the spot whither Judas traced him was no secret hiding place, but "Jesus ofttimes resorted thither with his disciples" (John 18:2). He could be followed there with no difficulty, without the aid of any informer. Nor need we imagine that the hillside around Jerusalem was less easily accessible in those days than it is in ours: the Mount of Olives rises not far from the city wall to the northeast, with all of its possible avenues easily overlooked from the battlements; and however flourishing and fertile the "gardens" on the mount may then have been, the distances are not such that a person entering them could not at once be detected. Not even the alien legionaries would have required a guide to find their way around the mount; and the indigenous temple police would be bound to regard the offer of any such guidance as an insult to their intelligence.

The same considerations apply to the device adopted by Judas to identify Jesus: "Whomsoever I shall kiss, that same is he: hold him fast" (Matt. 26:48; similarly Mark 14:44). Jesus was well known to the temple police: he preached in the temple daily and attracted huge crowds. There could have been no need for extra identification, not even at that time of night. It was the fourteenth or fifteenth of the month, the moon was full, and visibility in Jerusalem excellent; and while only the Gospel According to John expressly mentions that the troops and police were equipped with torches and lanterns (18:3), they would hardly have embarked on this expedition of search and seizure after nightfall without lighting of sorts. It is not without significance that the authors of the Gospel of John reject the tradition that Judas betrayed his master by kissing him, a mode of betrayal which Jesus himself censured (Luke 22:48) : according to John, Jesus was not identified by Judas but himself stepped forward and asked, "Whom seek ye?" and when he heard it was he whom they sought, he said, "I am he," while "Judas also, which betrayed him, stood with them" (18:4–5). As the Gospel of John is mute as to the details of Judas' conspiracy, so does it not divulge how he betrayed Jesus. The truth is that neither the conspiracy nor the betrayal was at all required for the arrest: whoever desired to seize Jesus could do so, in daytime or at night, with no outside help.

If it were true that the chief priests had mobilized "a mob of ruffians armed with clubs and swords," "brigands . . . diverted from robbing lesser priests of their dues at the threshing-floor to another task," the kidnaping of a man on whom murder was about to be committed, then it might be that these ruffians and brigands "required a sign to identify their man."[14] We have shown that the men who came to arrest Jesus were Roman soldiers and Jewish constables. There is nothing whatsoever in the Gospels to warrant the assumption that the priests hired gangsters to seize Jesus, except the story of his identification by a recreant Judas; for "one cannot conceive that any regular officer of the law would have had to resort to bribery to identify Jesus. He had been a central figure in the courts of the temple for nearly a week."[15] Therefore, if Judas kissed Jesus to identify him, it must have been ruffians and brigands who had come to take him. But such an inference, however ingenious it seems, cannot be squared with the Gospel texts. Jesus addressed the men who had come to arrest him as the same who sat daily with him when he taught in the temple (Matt. 26:55; Mark 14:49; Luke 22:53) : if it was not the temple police, at any rate it was frequenters of the temple, who needed no identification of him.

The theory that no formal arrest took place at all, but that Jesus was seized by kidnapers and taken away to be murdered, finds some apparent support in the absence of any declared ground for the arrest: it is said that had Jesus been formally arrested, he would have been informed of the grounds, or at least the grounds would have been mentioned in the Gospel reports. This sort of argument curiously reflects modern concepts of the right of accused persons to be informed without delay of the grounds for their arrest; but apart from the fact that such concepts are far from being put into practice in large parts of the world even today, there is nothing in our sources which entitles us to suppose that any procedure of the kind was in vogue, or prescribed, under either Roman or Jewish law in the time of Jesus. Furthermore, if ruffians and brigands had really been hired for the kidnaping, one would expect that they could at the same time have been hired to murder as well: why had the murder to be staged as it was, why had the kidnaped man to be brought into the home of the high priest, why bother the Roman governor and Roman executioners? Jesus was seized at nighttime, outside the city, in a lonely spot, and his disciples "all forsook him and fled" (Mark 14:50); nothing would have been easier than to kill him, if that was what they wanted, there and then. That those who came did not kill him, but were apparently under orders to take him into the presence of the high priest in person, is indication enough that he was not being kidnaped by criminals but arrested by authority.

One final matter is to be noted regarding the Judas episode, namely, the talmudic tradition that Sadducean high priests were wont to engage in undercover activity, so that a plot with Judas would fit perfectly into the picture. The tradition stems from the "popular squib"[16] preserved in the Talmud in which not only the clubs and fists of the high priests and their servants but also their whispers and pens were deplored:[17] and whispers and pens may, to be sure, have furthered conspiracies with secret informers. As we have seen, the squib was contrived one or two generations after the death of Jesus, and proves nothing about the chief priests of his time; but even assuming that in his time, too, there were men who would not shrink from any vicious malpractice to attain their ends,[18] not excluding machination with paid informers, neither the mental and theological readiness of Judas to betray his master nor any potential readiness of the priests to hire him as an informer affords proof that anything of the kind had actually been engineered between them. The intrinsic improbability and utter superfluity of such an arrangement far outweigh any conceivability that it might start with.

We shall, therefore, set out from the premise that there was no conspiratorial arrangement with Judas on the part of either the Romans or the Jews, and that the episode reported in the Gospels provides no clue to the question before us, which is: Who prompted the arrest of Jesus?

There is no doubt—though the contrary has been argued—that the Jewish courts were empowered to issue warrants of arrest and in practice regularly did. Arrest procedures are part and parcel of the administration of criminal justice, and a court competent to try criminals has inherent jurisdiction to take all necessary steps to have an accused brought before it for trial. Saul, afterward Paul, is said to have approached the high priest "and desired of him letters to Damascus to the synagogues, that if he found any on his way, whether they were men or women, he might bring them bound unto Jerusalem" (Acts 9:2) ; and defending himself before Agrippa, he declared, "many of the saints did I shut up in prison, having received authority from the chief priests" (26:10). We find explicit references to imprisonment pending trial in talmudic sources also, for instance, for bodily assault in which a fatal outcome is feared and trial is suspended until either death takes place or the danger of it has passed,[19] or for suspected murderers against whom some, but not enough, evidence is as yet available.[20] The mention of specific cases does not exclude the legitimacy and practice of other pretrial arrests, but rather proves that the practice, as such, was followed.

It has been contended that the absence of a formal warrant of arrest indicates that the arrest of Jesus was ordered by the Jews and not the Romans, because the Sanhedrin did not require any formal charge, whereas in Roman criminal procedure one was indispensable.[21] In other words, that the Jews would order the arrest of a suspect even without knowing, or making any effort to know, on suspicion of what offense: during his detention, forsooth, there would be time to find out what could be proved against him. This theory is not borne out by our knowledge of the law, which is that a suspected murderer may not be arrested and imprisoned without trial unless there is at least some evidence to hand against him, however short it may fall of sufficing for his conviction,[22] as the law requires, for instance, two eyewitnesses at least before a man can be convicted of a capital offense (Deut. 17:6; 19:15) ; if only a single eyewitness is momentarily forthcoming, the suspect may be arrested and held in custody, but cannot yet be tried. This means that no arrest or detention may take place unless at least the subject matter of the suspicion, the cause of the arrest, is first established. The fact that no formal written charge was required for the opening of a trial does not, therefore, mean that a person could be arrested and detained whether a charge against him was known to be pending or not.

We have observed that Jesus was given no hint or information of what offense he was suspected and was being arrested for. Had he been told that it was one of a Jewish religious nature, in whose respect the Jewish courts exercised exclusive jurisdiction, the conclusion that his arrest had been ordered by a Jewish court would have been plain. With information lacking, we can only try to use such circumstantial evidence as we have to arrive at a conclusion.

The fact that a Roman cohort and its Roman commander, as well as Jewish temple police, took part in the arrest is index that the Roman and the Jewish commanders acted in unison and by prearrangement. If so, both must have known why the arrest was being made, and in the eyes of both it must have been legitimate and desirable. The Romans would not have lent their hands to an unlawful or an unnecessary arrest; even if it were possible to hire individual legionaries to share in a kidnaping, a cohort and its commanding tribune could assuredly not have been persuaded to, least of all at Jewish solicitation. If, then, the arrest was lawful, what was its lawful purpose?

One possibility is that the Jewish court desired it so that Jesus could be brought to trial before it. If he was to be tried on a charge within the exclusive jurisdiction of the Jewish courts, and the occupation authorities had been approached for assistance in effecting the arrest, that assistance would have been denied: the Romans would rightly have answered: Either you have the power and the means to summon and bring before your courts the Jewish accused over whom you wish to exercise and retain jurisdiction—then, please, use your power and wield your jurisdiction as best you can—or you have neither enough power nor enough means to secure the attendance of your own people before you—then, please, do not profess to claim jurisdiction over them! It is probable that, even in matters within the jurisdiction of both the Jewish courts and the Roman governor, such universal crimes, for example, as murder, in whose prosecution the Romans were presumably no less interested than the Jews, the Romans would have faced the Jewish courts with the alternative: Either you can secure the attendance of the accused before you or you cannot; if you cannot,

he had better be tried before the Roman governor, notwithstanding the concurrent jurisdiction which the law vests in you. The
fact, however, is that the Jewish authorities needed no help from
the Romans to effect any arrest; we have met theories that the
Jewish courts were beholden to Roman aid or consent for the
execution of capital sentences, but no one has ever suggested
that Roman aid or consent was wanted to carry out the arrest of
a suspect pending trial.

It would appear, then, that Roman presence in the arrest of
Jesus is at least prima-facie proof of Roman sponsoring: the
Romans were not used or amenable to sending out their troops on
the initiative of others. What followed renders the proof virtually
conclusive. The arrest of Jesus was the first step in the proceedings
to be held the next day in the court of the Roman governor: attention has been drawn by previous writers to the astounding fact
that Pilate should have been ready to sit early the next morning,[23]
an unusual hour for a procurator to hear criminal cases; but his
very readiness implies previous notice of the cause and of the
man.[24] For that, previous notice must have preceded the arrest:
the governor would hardly be troubled with the intelligence at
night. On the assumption, then, that the trial of Jesus before
Pilate had : en set down the day before at the latest, it is not
material whether the governor himself had issued a warrant for
Jesus to be brought and arraigned before him the next morning
or whether the warrant had been made out by one of his subordinates: the tribune would not go to the place, or take his troops
there, save by order of his superiors, and the order would not be
given except for Roman purposes. Indeed, considering the high
rank of the tribune, it has been asserted that the warrant must
have come from the governor in person.[25]

If Jesus was arrested on Roman initiative and by order of the
governor in person or one given on his behalf, what were the
Jewish temple police doing there? As there was no need for a guide
or informer, like Judas, to have him tracked down, so was there
none for help from them, either to detect or to seize him. Two
main theories were propounded in explanation. One is that the
Sanhedrin had previously issued a warrant of arrest (John 11:57),
and that it was for its better or speedier execution that the Jewish
authorities asked the governor to issue a second of his own.[26] But

the previous issue of a warrant by a Jewish court would not, in Roman eyes, have afforded the least reason for issuing a second, and Roman, one; on the contrary, the Roman authorities would rightly have held another warrant wholly superfluous. Furthermore, a wish of the Jewish authorities to see a Jew arrested would not in the slightest move the Romans to arrest him: first, they would have to be satisfied that the arrest was in the best Roman interests, and if it was, it would not normally be in the interests of the Jews. But let us suppose, for the sake of argument, that the "commandment" given, according to John, by "chief priests and Pharisees," to whoever knew of Jesus' whereabouts to disclose them to the authorities so that "they might take him" (11:57) was in the nature of a warrant of arrest, and had in fact been issued by a competent Jewish authority. A "council meeting" reported by Mark and Matthew to have taken place two days before the feast of Passover, at which "the chief priests and the scribes sought how they might take him by craft, and put him to death; but they said, not on the feast day, lest there be an uproar of the people" (Mark 14:1–2; and similarly Matt. 26:3–5), would appear to be the very same meeting as reported in John (11:47–57), whereafter the said warrant was allegedly issued;[27] though its timing varies in the Gospels, being predated in John to when Passover was "nigh at hand" (11:55). But while the account of the council proceedings in Mark is short and fragmentary, in John there is greater elaboration, thus phrased: "What do we? for this man doeth many miracles. If we let him thus alone, all men will believe on him; and the Romans shall come and take away both our place and nation" (11:47–48). The high priest suggested thereupon that it was "expedient" that one man should die rather than the whole nation perish (11:50; 18:14). Whatever may have been the council's apprehensions in respect of Jesus—and it appears that it feared his ever-rising popular support—it is entirely out of context that it would turn to the Romans: if its concern was lest he be the cause for the Romans to "come and take away" its office, as no longer enjoying the people's trust, it is hardly to the Romans that it would hasten to be rid of him. The first question which the councilors would be asked would be what was the ground for issuing the warrant to arrest Jesus; and if they had no better answer than the truth, they would certainly be thrown out

instanter. On the other hand, to invent a better—that is, a Roman
—ground for arrest, they need not, and could not, rely on their
own warrant, which, in the nature of things and in view of the
limits of Jewish jurisdiction, must have been issued on other
grounds. Furthermore, it appears from Mark (14:1–2) that the
council's deliberations and resolutions were of a conspiratorial nature; how, then, would the councilors go to the Romans and so
give their plot a publicity which they could no longer control?
And, finally, it is said in Mark (14:2) that they had better wait
until after the feast, to avoid public protestations; how, then,
would they go to the Romans on the very eve and insist that Jesus
be arrested at once?

The second theory was "that the arrest ordered by Pilate was
provoked by the Jews, but that Pilate, who was on bad terms with
the Jewish authorities, was able to insist, although he followed
their suggestions, that they should not lead him into a trap."[28] His
insistence was not only that Jewish police should take part in the
arrest, but also that the Jewish court should hold a pretrial—all
this to make sure that the Roman governor would not be "led into
a trap," and it was to demonstrate sincerity and good faith that
the Jewish authorities made compliance.

But any such theory presupposes that the Jewish authorities,
anxious as they were to see Jesus arrested, could not have it done
without the concurrence or fiat of the Roman governor, a presup-
position which, as we saw, is factually misconceived. It is true
that if Pilate issued his warrant at that instance, he could well
attach all sorts of conditions to it, even that of active Jewish part
in the arrest; but there is nothing, not even the council resolutions mentioned, to justify the assumption that Pilate acted upon
a Jewish petition in ordering the arrest. That he was "on bad
terms" with the Jewish authorities is a slight understatement: we
have observed that he would never respond to Jewish prompting
unless he was satisfied in his own mind that to do so was in the
best Roman interest; if he were satisfied, prior Jewish prompting
was irrelevant; if he were not, it became a nuisance. In any
event, he would not rely on any "sincerity" or "good faith" on the
part of the Jews, or be interested in such virtues; and the possibility that the Jews would or could "lead him into a trap" would
not enter his mind; it was not they whom he served but only and

exclusively himself. The least suspicion of insincerity, in the sense of a possible disservice to the Romans or the possible value-lessness, from the Roman point of view, of the action sought, would have induced Pilate to dismiss the matter out of hand, and there would be no opportunity for him to make conditions.

ọ We are thus left with the fact that the order for the arrest of Jesus was made by the Romans, and that a tribune with his cohort was sent to carry it out. No Jewish instigation behind that Roman order has been proved or can be reasonably assumed. The presence of Jewish temple police at the time and place of arrest cannot be explained by any Roman instruction or requirement. Only one possible explanation remains, and that is that they were permitted to be present at their own asking.

There must have been a cogent reason for their being instructed to ask the Roman authorities, presumably the tribune in charge, for that permission: they would not be eager to be present just for the doubtful edification of it. Nor may we underrate the import of a decision to detach a contingent of temple police for duty outside the temple precincts on a night such as this, when city and sanctuary overflowed with visitors from all parts of the country and all manpower was required to maintain peace and order. There was surely a momentous interest at stake if the Jewish authorities deemed it imperative to send a temple police unit on this kind of mission at this particular hour. What their purpose was will become plain as we study subsequent events.

It was but natural that, on his arrest by Roman troops, Jesus would be taken into Roman custody. We know that the Romans had places of detention in Jerusalem (Acts 23:10), and there was no reason why he should not have been conducted there. (This, indeed, is so self-evident that one scholar, for this reason only, dismisses the entire story of Jesus being brought into the home of the high priest, and suggests that he spent the night in Roman custody and was arraigned before Pilate the next morning.)[29] If Jesus was not held in Roman custody, it was because he had been handed over to the Jewish temple police, and it must have been at the instance of their commander that the tribune agreed to leave Jesus in Jewish custody. To ask for this was nothing out of the ordinary: local prisons may well have served the Romans, too, and it would not matter much to the tribune where his prisoner was locked up.

The undertaking of the temple police commander to deliver Jesus the next morning at the Roman governor's courthouse would suffice: breach of it would be bound to cost the temple police not only their precious competences but their very existence, and for their commander would be virtual suicide. It is probable, also, that the Romans knew from previous experience that they could rely on such an undertaking, and it might be that they preferred the use of local prisons for Jewish prisoners so as to avoid the many dietary and other complications of looking after them.

So permission for the temple police to be present at the arrest was sought with a view to getting the Roman officer in command to agree to their taking Jesus into Jewish custody pending his trial before the Roman governor. When this was conceded, they thereupon took Jesus not into prison,[30] but into the mansion of the high priest: a wholly unprecedented move, and one, it may be presumed, altogether unexpected by the Romans, which can be explained only on the assumption that the temple police were under orders from the high priest himself to bring him there. It would, then, also be the high priest by whose bidding a unit of the temple police was detached that night for the special duty: he must have known of the warrant of arrest issued against Jesus, and that the arrest would be carried out not later than that night so that arraignment before Pilate might proceed early the next morning; and he must have been concerned to have Jesus brought to him and not taken into Roman custody. This concern was, it would seem, so grave and so pressing as to justify and require the diversion of the temple police from their many and urgent responsibilities within the temple precincts that night. It could hardly have been an easy decision to make, psychologically: it implied a directive from the high priest to the temple police commander to address himself with some humble plea to a Roman tribune, a procedure certain to be intensely distasteful to the commander no less than to the high priest—whether or not they could be reasonably sure that such a plea would be granted. But if any of these considerations counted with them, they were far outweighed by the seemingly paramount importance of the purpose in hand.

It appears that the high priest's orders had to do with Jesus only: it was Jesus who was to be taken to the priestly residence, not any of his disciples or attendants. It would, however, be very surprising, if the desire really was to arrest Jesus and have him punished for dangerous dissemination of unorthodox and non-conformist doctrine, that his disciples, confessed instruments and organs in spreading that doctrine, should be let go free to teach what and where and whom they pleased. Had the intention been to put Jesus on trial for heresy or nonconformity or messianic aspirations, nothing would have been accomplished by laying hands on him alone: his teachings had already found a wide and enthusiastic audience, and disciples had been schooled to continue where, and if, he had to stop. To be reasonably effective, any action against him had also to be taken simultaneously against his disciples, as, indeed, happened some years later, when Peter was brought to trial and "the other apostles" were charged and tried together with him (Acts 5:18, 29). But the high priest, and hence the temple police, were not interested in the disciples or attendants: they were looking only for Jesus.

Still more surprising, and, indeed, at first sight inexplicable, would it be that the disciple who "stretched out his hand, and drew his sword, and struck a servant of the high priest's, and smote off his ear" (Matt. 26:51; similarly Mark 14:47; Luke 22:50; John 18:10) should not have been seized there and then by the temple police, even though, by miraculous doing of Jesus, no further harm might have befallen him (Luke 22:51).[31] It is reported in John that one of the high priest's servants identified Peter as the one who had cut off the man's ear (18:26), yet he was allowed to go free as a matter of course, and nobody bothered to detain him (Matt. 26:75; Mark 14:72; Luke 22:62). (That all the disciples had declared solemnly that they would go with Jesus unto death [Mark 14:31] did not prevent them from forsaking him; but there is no indication in any Gospel report that any ill would have come to them even if they had not "denied" him.) The simple reason for all this is that the high priest had given strict instructions to have Jesus, and nobody else, brought into his presence, and those the temple police faithfully obeyed. The Roman officer, on his part, equally had no warrant of arrest against anybody except Jesus: it was Jesus alone who was to stand trial before the governor on the morrow. But it is significant, and throws some light on the general attitude of the Romans toward indigenous concerns, that violence committed against a Jewish policeman, even in the presence of Roman troops and their officer, would not move them to action. Whether they thought that it was a matter for the Jewish police to take care of, or even rather enjoyed this sort of domestic fracas, they did not feel beholden to intervene. Nor are the temple police reported to have done anything: they may have been impressed, and satisfied, with Jesus' reprimand that "all they that take the sword, shall perish with the sword" (Matt. 26:52), or with his piety and mercy when he said, "Put up thy sword into the sheath: the cup which my Father hath given me, shall I not drink it?" (John 18:11); or so preoccupied with the urgency of their purpose, which was to have Jesus given into their custody and brought into the high priest's home, that nothing else mattered to them at that moment. Their mildness toward the assailant may also reflect that while they may have known that Jesus was to be brought into the home of the high priest himself, and with no hostile intent, his disciples, perhaps fearing lest he be thrown into jail and mishandled, may have given vent to their helpless anger. If Peter indeed was the assailant, he must have felt confident that he would suffer no hurt; he would not otherwise venture to follow Jesus into the high priest's home (John 18:15), after first declining to enter (18:16). Because of these incongruities, the historicity of the whole incident has been doubted,[32] but the tradition, common to all the Gospels, lends itself to acceptable interpretation if it is assumed that the temple police had no business at the arrest of Jesus except to get him out of Roman custody as quickly and unobtrusively as possible and into the presence of the high priest, and that nothing else was of consequence.[33]

Jesus was "led away" to the high priest's house (Matt. 26:57; Mark 14:53; Luke 22:54). There is no mention in the Synoptic Gospels of the chains or shackles that usually figured in the arrest of a suspected criminal. Only according to John was Jesus "bound" before being "led away" to Annas (18:12) and again sent "bound" from the house of Annas to the high priest's (18:24). It seems that the fourth evangelist could not conceive an arrested suspect led away unbound, and accordingly added this —for him self-evident—complementary detail. Had there been any tradition of a bound or shackled Jesus, would any evangelist be likely to omit from his report that further act of Jewish humiliation, that further suffering of Jesus? All would rather have made the most of it, another and not unimportant item to substantiate their charges of Jewish cruelty. Arguing, then, *ex silentio,* we have it on the authority of the evangelists that Jesus was led away unfettered, that he went with the temple police as if he were one of them. And when he arrived at the palace of the high priest, he was not taken into a lockup or a cellar, or placed in solitary confinement, and there is nothing in the Gospel reports pointing to any measures to prevent his escape or mark his status as a prisoner. He was led into the splendor of the palace, doubtless into the largest and stateliest of its halls, where all the councilors could assemble. And not Jesus alone would be led and seated there, but his disciples and attendants with him if they had but chosen to follow him in, not chosen to forsake him and flee (Matt. 26:56; Mark 14:50) or to "deny" him (Matt. 26:74; Mark 14:70–71).

The Roman tribune granted the petition of the temple police commander and gave Jesus into the custody of the Jewish authorities, pending his trial before the governor the next morning. The temple police led him into the palace of the high priest, and there Jesus would find him and all the chief priests and elders of Israel foregathered. It was in the middle of the night, and the great feast of Passover was in the air and in everybody's mind. What had transpired to make the high priest insist on having Jesus brought into his palace? What had actuated him to detach a unit of the temple police from exacting duties in the temple, just to have Jesus escorted into his presence? For what purpose had all the chief priests and elders and scribes and all the council come together in his house? Why was Jesus brought before that august synod at that time of night?

5   IN THE HOUSE OF
THE HIGH PRIEST

The Gospels are divided about what happened in the high priest's house when Jesus had been brought there. According to Luke, he had to spend the whole night in the company of the men who had arrested and "held" him (22:63), and they blindfolded and beat and mocked him (22:64–65). Only when "it was day, the elders of the people and the chief priests and the scribes came together and led him into their council" (22:66). According to John, Jesus was led into the house of Annas first, "for he was father-in-law to Kaiaphas, which was the high priest that same year" (18:13); it seems that he there was interrogated by "the high priest," which may be either Annas or Kaiaphas, and thereafter Annas had him sent "bound unto Kaiaphas the high priest" (18:19–24). There, nothing is reported to have taken place until they "led Jesus from Kaiaphas unto the hall of judgment" of the Roman governor (18:28). Only the Gospels According to Mark and Matthew tell that he stood that night in the high priest's house before all the council.

A good many scholars hold that what in truth transpired was the interrogation reported in the Johannine Gospel: it was the high priest, or his father-in-law, who questioned Jesus; there was no council present; and the purpose of the interrogation would then appear to have been preliminary to, and preparatory for, the trial before Pilate on the following morning. The contention is that the author of the Gospel of John rightly dismissed as unhistorical and untrue the report in the Synoptic Gospels of a night or early morning meeting of the Sanhedrin: had there been a valid tradition behind it, he neither would, nor could, suppress it; on the contrary, he would be the first to grasp a further and excellent opportunity to incriminate the Sanhedrin unequivocally for Jesus' death. His subsequent effort to whitewash Pilate would have been rendered much easier and have sounded much more natural had he followed Mark and Matthew and prefaced the proceedings before him with the formal and solemn pronouncement of a death sentence by the Great Sanhedrin of the Jews. That, although aware of the reports in Mark and Matthew, he did not is said to indicate that the Sanhedrin conducted no trial and pronounced no sentence.[1]

We shall not seek to resolve the question of the historicity of the nocturnal proceedings reported in Mark and Matthew, but take our start from the premise that the Great Sanhedrin did that night assemble in the high priest's palace. And this in spite of formidable exegetical arguments propounded to disprove the authenticity of the passage in Mark,[2] which served Matthew as model, and not because we would necessarily maintain the authenticity or reliability of the report, but because—looking at the events from the Jewish point of view—this is an assumption against us: the Jewish case must be much stronger if the Sanhedrin did not meet at all that night and if anything that did happen could be blamed on the high priest alone. The high priest may have been, in person, a Roman puppet, without moral or political stature, from whose acts and conduct the Jewish community as such would have vehemently dissociated itself; and it could be— and has been—held that what he said or did could in no way be blamed on the Jews or on the Jewish authorities as a whole. It is entirely different with the Sanhedrin: if the high priest acted in accord with, and presiding over, that august and most representative body, it was no longer he personally who would bear responsibility, or his personal character or prestige that would be of relevance: the Sanhedrin spoke for all sections and factions of the

Jewish people, and its acts and decisions commanded general and undisputed authority. Postulating, therefore, as we do, that it was the Great Sanhedrin that assembled that night, we assume the burden of an "admission against interest," because we follow the evangelists in involving the Jews and Jewish authorities as a whole in the night's events.

It was at the instance of the high priest that Jesus had been brought into his palace: he had detached temple police to prevent Jesus' being taken into Roman custody and to procure his delivery, for the night, into Jewish custody. He knew, of course, of Jesus' arrest by Roman troops, and had sent his police officers to negotiate with the Roman tribune; hence he also knew that Jesus was to stand trial the next morning before the Roman governor—that being the reason for his arrest. He would know all that, even if he had himself no hand in provoking Roman suspicion and prosecution of Jesus; and a fortiori if he was so involved. He must have had some reason for asking the Roman authorities to deliver Jesus into his custody that night, and no less for convening the Sanhedrin and bringing Jesus before it. To clear the way for our inquiry into those reasons, we must first dispose of the theories that the Sanhedrin was convened either to try Jesus and sentence him to death, as the Gospel reports convey, or to hold a preliminary investigation into the charges to be leveled the next morning in the Roman governor's court.

Of the scholars who hold that Jesus was tried and sentenced by the Sanhedrin, some think that he was tried twice, that is, first in a religious trial before that tribunal and afterward in a political trial before the Roman governor;[3] others that the trial before the Sanhedrin was the only real one, and that the governor was then desired by the Jews to carry out the capital sentence, because that was beyond the Sanhedrin's powers.[4] We have already dismissed the theory of incompetence as inconsistent with the fact that, at that and later times, the Sanhedrin did carry out capital sentences itself;[5] but it is untenable for two further reasons, one of a legal and one of a political nature. As a matter of law, the mode of punishment prescribed in Scripture—stoning, burning, or slaying[6] —could not be replaced by any unauthorized and alien mode of execution; any mode other than that prescribed in Jewish law would not amount to lawful carrying out of a sanhedrial sentence but, on the one hand, would leave it unexecuted and, on the other, constitute unlawful killing. And as a matter of politics, neither would the Sanhedrin have asked the Roman authorities to carry out its capital sentences for it, nor would the Romans have condescended to: as we have seen, the Sanhedrin exercised capital jurisdiction only over Jews, and it is inconceivable that a Jew would be delivered by a Jewish court to the Roman enemy for execution, whatever his crime; the Sanhedrin would rather have abstained from passing capital sentences than have them carried out by a hateful adversary in a manner incompatible with Jewish law and repellent to Jewish sentiment. As for the Romans, they would not have left any jurisdictional powers in the hands of the Sanhedrin if it had declared its inability to see to it that its judgments and orders were duly executed: if and so long as it was able to do so, well and good—the Romans would not interfere with its internal jurisdiction; but were it not, they would certainly have declined to relieve it of its duty, however abhorrent to it, of executing its own criminals.

There remains, then, the theory that Jesus had to stand two different trials, one Jewish—religious—and one Roman—political. We are for the time being concerned with the Jewish trial only, said to have taken place at night before the Sanhedrin in the high priest's house. Before we examine the Jewish Trial Theory, it is only fair to say that the overwhelming majority of modern scholars has by now abandoned it, although, since the early days of Christianity, all generations and sects of Christians were brought up in the unshakable belief that Jesus had that night been tried and sentenced to death by the Jews. The rejection of the Jewish Trial Theory by theological and historical modern scholarship alike has moved a recent writer to the bitter complaint that the faithful traditionalists seem to be encountering a wall of consensus that no Jewish trial in fact took place.[7] We shall not content ourselves with this consensus, but inquire into the theory on its merits, if only for the reason that most legal writers on the subject[8] still adhere to it.

It is that the high priest convened the Sanhedrin that night in his private home; that there and then Jesus was tried under Jewish law on a charge of blasphemy; that he was convicted of that offense upon his own confession; and that he was sentenced to death. On the face of it, the theory appears incompatible with the following well-established provisions of Jewish law:

1. No Sanhedrin was allowed to sit as a criminal court and try criminal cases outside the temple precincts, in any private house.[9]

2. The Sanhedrin was not allowed to try criminal cases at night: criminal trials had to be commenced and completed during daytime.[10]

3. No person could be tried on a criminal charge on festival days or the eve of a festival.[11]

4. No person may be convicted on his own testimony or on the strength of his own confession.[12]

5. A person may be convicted of a capital offense only upon the testimony of two lawfully qualified eyewitnesses.[13]

6. No person may be convicted of a capital offense unless two lawfully qualified witnesses testify that they had first warned him of the criminality of the act and the penalty prescribed for it.[14]

7. The capital offense of blasphemy consists in pronouncing the name of God, Yahweh, which may be uttered only once a year by the high priest in the innermost sanctuary of the temple; and it is irrelevant what "blasphemies" are spoken so long as the divine name is not enunciated.[15]

The obvious inconsistencies with, and the deviations from, these rules of law and procedure[16] were taken into due account for the most part by the propounders of the Jewish Trial Theory, and furnish them with the all but conclusive argument that the whole trial, and the resulting sentence, were tainted with illegality.[17] In the words of Chief Justice MacRuer: "The Hebrew Trial . . . steeped as it was in illegality, . . . had been a mockery of judicial procedure throughout. Jesus was unlawfully arrested and unlawfully interrogated. . . . The court was unlawfully convened by night. No lawful charge supported by the evidence of two witnesses was ever formulated. . . . As he stood at the bar of justice, he was unlawfully sworn as a witness against himself. He was unlawfully condemned to death on words from his own mouth. . . ."[18] The very violation of all rules of law and procedure goes to establish the claim that Jesus was the victim of judicial murder.[19] This claim is further strengthened by the notion "that the result of the trial was formally pre-determined by the judges, without distinction of sect";[20] that is to say, that the whole trial was staged to

give the appearance of judicial proceedings to the resolution previously passed to put Jesus to death (John 11:53; Mark 14:1;
Matt. 24:6) . And if the whole trial was, anyhow, only a travesty,
why should the judges have troubled about the niceties and technicalities of law and procedure?[21]

Other writers have not been quite so nonchalant. To eliminate
at least certain of the incongruities, namely, that the trial was held
at night and on the eve of a festival or on the festival itself—which
present, in fact, not only legal but also psychological difficulties—
attempts have been made to predate the trial: it is said that the
occurrences set by the Gospels in the one night and the one following day actually took place in the course of three consecutive days
("Three Days Chronology") , so that the trial need not have been
conducted either during the night or on the eve of a feast day.[22]
The liberty here taken with the Gospel calendar calls to mind the
Pharisaic rule of scriptural interpretation that what is reported in
Scripture to have happened first may have happened last, and that
what is reported to have happened later may have happened
earlier.[23] Whatever may be the merits of this revision of datings,
it can solve only one or two of the procedural difficulties, and
leaves the substantial irreconcilabilities unanswered.

The weightiest argument which seems to have been advanced to
save the Jewish Trial Theory is that the law under which the trial
was held was not the Pharisaic, which we know from the talmudic
sources, but the Sadducean, which has since become obsolete and
fallen into oblivion;[24] and it is said that the trial that night in the
high priest's house was in full conformity with Sadducean law and
procedure. Now while it is true that, if any such Sadducean law
and procedure ever existed, they have been consigned to limbo,
nevertheless some fundamentals of Sadducean legal doctrine are
well known and well vouched for,[25] and we can test the argument
by applying them to the trial reports. We have noted that Sadducees differed from Pharisees in their acceptance, as binding, of
only the written precepts of Scripture, whereas the Pharisees pos-
tulated, as well, the divine authority of the oral law expounded by
them.[26] Insofar, then, as the violations of law observed in the trial
affect oral law not enshrined in Scripture, it might be that a Sadducean court would not have regarded them as violations at all,
not having recognized that law; on the other hand, even a Sad-

ducean court would presumably not break rules laid down in Scripture itself, or deducible from it. Now there is no scriptural prohibition of holding criminal trials on feast days or the eves of festivals:[27] in this respect, the trial of Jesus might, under Sadducean law, have been in order. But the ban on night trials already gives rise to doubts: it is based on the scriptural injunction to impale offenders "against the sun" (Num. 25:4), interpreted as requiring the trial and punishment of criminals only while the sun shines, that is, during daytime.[28] As this kind of scriptural authority was often superimposed ex post facto on an existing rule established independently of Scripture, we might give the Sadducees the benefit of the doubt and assume that they had seen no objection to night trials either.

It is then said that while, as we know, criminal jurisdiction under the Pharisaic law was exercised only by the Small Sanhedrin of Twenty-three, under Sadducean it was the Great Sanhedrin of Seventy-one, that which in fact met that night in the high priest's house, that would itself exercise the jurisdiction because of the seventy elders who, according to Scripture, joined Moses to lead the people (Num. 11:16). But first, there is no indication in Scripture that the seventy elders with Moses ever exercised criminal jurisdiction; nor, second, have we any record of the Great Sanhedrin of Seventy-one ever having done so. It is true that the scriptural choice of seventy, besides Moses, served as precedent for the membership of the Great Sanhedrin, but the number appears to have no bearing on the nature of its functions and competences.

With all that, the main difficulty in the way of a Sadducean trial is that it is explicit scriptural law that a capital charge must be proved by two or three witnesses (Deut. 19:15; 17:6). Even assuming that the rule against self-incrimination and the inadmissibility of confessions was expounded only by Pharisaic teachers as a matter of oral law,[29] the availability of a confession could not be held to dispense with the necessity of witnesses: a criminal charge could be established only "at the mouth of witnesses" (Deut. 19:15). Since, in the trial of Jesus, all witnesses were dismissed as untrustworthy or disqualified (Mark 14:59; Matt. 26:59–60), and the conviction was based on Jesus' confession alone (Mark 14:63–64; Matt. 26:65–66), the scriptural—that is, Sadducean—law cannot have been complied with.[30] Biblical instances have sometimes been adduced as proof that, under strict scriptural law, men could be punished on the strength of their confessions, notwithstanding the requirement of witnesses: thus, it is said, was the killer of Saul punished by David, after "David said unto him, Thy blood be upon thy head; for thy mouth hath testified against thee, saying, I have slain the Lord's anointed" (II Sam. 1:16); or, Achan was stoned by the people after he had made a full confession to Joshua (Josh. 7:19–25). From the scriptural texts, however, we cannot know whether the punishments were judicial or extrajudicial, or whether witnesses were available besides; the ancient Jewish tradition is that Achan made his confession only after conviction;[31] and as for the Amalekite who "confessed" to David, his tale was that Saul had asked to be killed (II Sam. 1:9–10), and he thought that he had done a good deed which he could vaunt, not committed a crime to be confessed: David reacted to a violation of "the Lord's anointed" rather than to any known offense punishable by ordinary process of law.[32]

There is, as well as this problem of evidence, the question of substantive law. It is not oral but scriptural law that "Whosoever curses his God shall bear his sin" (Lev. 24:15), but he that pronounces[33] the name Yahweh shall be put to death and all the congregation shall stone him (24:16). A clear distinction is drawn between cursing God, which is an offense not punishable with death, and blaspheming God by pronouncing His ineffable Name, which is a captial offense; the distinction is scriptural, and hence part of the Sadducean law. To get around this, it has been said that Jesus' offense was not blasphemy by pronouncing God's name, but "doing presumptuously" and thus "reproaching the Lord" (Num. 15:30); but it seems to have been overlooked that this alternative offense is not a capital one either, but earns only divine punishment (*ibid.*) or flogging.[34] It is, further, argued that there is evidence to show that the Sadducean notion of blasphemy was much wider and not restricted to pronunciation of the divine Name: the witnesses who testified against Stephen said of him, "We have heard him speak blasphemous words against Moses and against God" (Acts 6:11), and again, "This man ceaseth not to speak blasphemous words against this holy place and the law" (6:13), implying that there can be blasphemy without utterance of the Tetragrammaton, for which a man can be tried (6:12) and stoned (7:58). From the description of the stoning, it could be maintained that Stephen was lynched by a maddened mob rather than formally put to death;[35] but, be that as it may, the blasphemies alleged against Stephen are so similar to those for which Jesus was allegedly sentenced that they afford no least independent proof. Stephen—just before the stoning—is said to have proclaimed that he saw "the glory of God, and Jesus standing on the right hand of God, and . . . the heavens opened, and the Son of man standing on the right hand of God" (7:56–57), while Jesus had already promised, "Hereafter shall the Son of man sit on the right hand of the power of God" (Luke 22:69), a promise that provoked the finding of blasphemy against him. It is the precedent of Jesus which explains the blasphemy of Stephen, not conversely. Even more spurious is the argument from the stoning incidents reported in the Gospel According to John: we have shown[36] why they cannot, in fact, have taken place; but even if they did, they afford no proof, for although the Jews are said to have taken up stones to stone Jesus (John 10:31) for blasphemy (10:33), they did not purport to do so in execution of a judicial sentence, and are not to be taken as using the term "blasphemy" in any technical sense.

It appears, therefore, that even had the Sanhedrin that tried and sentenced Jesus been a Sadducean court applying Sadducean law, it could not have convicted him of blasphemy, and it does not appear from any of the Gospels that he had been charged with any other offense or convicted of it. But the theory that the Sanhedrin could have been a Sadducean court is a priori untenable from start to finish. It is true that the Sadducees may have had courts of their own: one such is mentioned in the Talmud[37] as carrying out the punishment of burning in divergence of the manner of Pharisaic law. But while a Sadducean court may well have used modes of execution differing from the usage of Pharisaic courts, that would not, either in the devising of such modes or at all, transgress the rules of scriptural law which the Sadducees regarded as sacrosanct and inviolable. The story reported in the Johannine Gospel of Jesus and the adulteress has been cited to establish the prevalence of Sadducean courts which rejected the Pharisaic modes: Jesus is told that "Moses in the law commanded us" that an adulteress ought to be stoned (8:5), whereas the Pharisaic law is that an adulteress is liable to death by strangulation.[38] But the disputants of Jesus here are expressly identified as Pharisees (8:3), not Sadducees; the woman was neither tried nor condemned, and we do not know what would have been the outcome of a trial in a Sadducean or a Pharisaic court; and, finally, the episode seems to have been inserted in the Gospel for the sake of the moral: the allegory of stoning was required so that Jesus' exhortation might apply, "He that is without sin among you, let him first cast a stone at her" (8:7).[39]

It is a fact that there were departures time and again from prescribed modes of execution and from rules of procedure and practice, but they need not be taken as evidencing a Sadducean bench or a court proceeding under Sadducean law. We find instances of judicial error, "because the court was not learned enough";[40] of illegitimate usurpation of judicial powers, where kings, for example Herod, arrogated to themselves the power to try and punish criminals;[41] or of legitimate excesses of jurisdiction by reason of emergency.[42] It is this permissible exception from the strict applicability of rules of law and procedure that has provided some scholars with a clue to their theory: in the case of Jesus, the Sanhedrin had proclaimed an "emergency," and hence freed itself from all the rules, so that there could no longer be any difficulty about their nonobservance.

The principal modern proponent of this theory goes so far as to maintain that the "emergency" is the *ultima ratio* of Jewish law:[43] according to him, substantive and procedural law alike could in every case, and in cases of apostasy normally would, be suspended by the president of the Sanhedrin, so as not to be hampered in the campaign against apostates and other dangerous elements by burdensome provisions.[44] The main, if not the only, authority for this view is the report of a hanging of eighty witches on one day in Askalon, ascribed to Simon ben Shetah,[45] who presided over the Sanhedrin more than a century before Jesus' time. We shall return to this report in another context;[46] here it suffices to say that, according to tradition, Simon ben Shetah did, indeed, act in an emergency, and consequently his action would not be accepted as a precedent.[47] But this is the only case that we know of a president of the Sanhedrin invoking emergency powers; and it is entirely improper to deduce any general rule from it. Moreover, nothing in the Gospel reports justifies the conclusion that the high priest, or any other president or officer of the Sanhedrin, or the Sanhedrin in plenary, did in fact proclaim an emergency and suspend all or some rules of law or procedure; on the contrary, the quest for witnesses against Jesus (Mark 14:55) and the plenary meeting without delegation of powers indicate prima facie that no emergency was proclaimed.

Another author regards this emergency power as a kind of fiction or subterfuge, which the court would plead after the event to excuse irregular deflections from rules of law and procedure: to forestall or avoid any subsequent attack on the validity of its proceedings, it would pretend to have sat under conditions of emergency, even without any prior or formal proclamation of one, and any infraction of the law would automatically be cured.[48] Again, it is not impossible that the wholesale hanging of witches in Askalon was, after the event, sought to be legitimized, if only for the sake of the reputation of Simon ben Shetah, by providing a plea of emergency; but if that was so, it would follow that emergency powers did not exist at all as an institution of Jewish law, the single incident at Askalon not being such as would set a general precedent. I am inclined to think that, so far from providing high priests and Sanhedrin with ex post facto pretexts, the emergency powers offer our authors a welcome cloak for the insolubility of their dilemma.

We have seen that the Pharisees were rightly reputed—or notorious—for a rigorous legalism and punctilious formalistic exactitude in the observance of every particle of the law. This is how the "Pharisees" are depicted in the Gospels: and for the orthodox interpreter, the glaring contradiction between the typical strictness in complying with the law and this particular failure to do so must be somewhat embarrassing. The Sadducean theory seemed to provide the answer: there were no Pharisees that night in the high priest's house, or if there were, they were in a minority that could not make itself heard. But—apart from the difficulties already mentioned—this answer raises a new riddle. We know that it was the "Pharisees" who were the archenemies of Jesus, according to the Gospels; it was they who "sought to destroy him" and consulted together how best to. How, then, could it be that they, of all people, had no hand at all in the final piece of destruction?

We also know that the Pharisees and the Sadducees were at logger-heads: how, then, could it be that the Pharisees would trustingly delegate to the Sadducees the conduct of the trial and the pronouncing of the sentence upon Jesus? After all the eagerness that the "Pharisees" have displayed in trying to persuade Jesus to wash hands and keep fasts and pay more regard to technicalities of sabbatical laws, we are to believe that they would suddenly deliver him into the hands of heretical Sadducees for trial in disregard of all the binding rules of substantive and procedural law! Even if a Sadducean court had claimed jurisdiction to try Jesus, there can be no doubt that the Pharisees would have objected, or that Jesus would have demurred: if he had to be tried at all, the least that they and he would have asked for was his trial according to law.

The main point that the Sadducean theory overlooks, however, is that the Great Sanhedrin of Seventy-one, while including Sadducees and Pharisees, went by Pharisaic law—not only because Pharisees would not otherwise have taken part, but also because the people would not have it otherwise.[49] If we take it that it was the priests and elders and scribes and all the council, that is, the Great Sanhedrin, that assembled that night, then *ipso facto* we exclude the possibility that Jesus was tried by a Sadducean court: even if such courts did exist, they were not, and could never be, identical with the Great Sanhedrin.

The Jewish Trial Theory thus falls to the ground, in the light of legal and logical considerations no less than for exegetical reasons. Jesus could not have been tried by the Sanhedrin in the manner, and at the time and place, described in the Gospel reports, or convicted of the offense of which, according to those reports, it is said to have convicted him. It has, therefore, been suggested that what the Sanhedrin did that night was to hold a preliminary inquiry into the charges on which Jesus would, or could, be tried the next morning before the Roman governor.

The fact that Jesus was tried, and was sentenced, the next morning by Pontius Pilate is commonly agreed: why, then, should that trial have been preceded by another? If a criminal trial on a capital offense is preceded by trial-like proceedings, it stands to reason that those proceedings are in the nature of a preliminary investigation for the purposes of the trial. This conclusion is apparently fortified by the fact that, according to Gospel reports, the proceedings in the high priest's house began not with a recital to Jesus of any formal charge or accusation but with the search for witnesses—not to prove a given and defined offense, but to find out whether testimony would be forthcoming to prove any offense against him at all. The most formidable argument in favor of the investigatory theory is that the high priest interrogated Jesus himself: interrogation of the accused is unheard of in a criminal trial under Jewish law. A sentence ("condemnation") of the Sanhedrin is recorded only in Mark (14:64); according to Matthew, they all "said" that he was guilty of death (26:66), and may have said so informally; and, according to Luke, they just "said, What need we any further witness?" (22:71); and the lack of any formal sentence in the two later Gospels—coupled with the entire absence of any trial proceedings in the Gospel of John—might point to the fact that the proceedings ended not with a judgment against Jesus but only with a decision to indict him before Pilate. It is said, indeed, that the Sanhedrin acted that night not in its judicial capacity, but as an administrative body, and there can be no doubt that it had administrative as well as judicial functions. The investigatory theory, according to some of its protagonists, finds significant support in the terminology of the Gospels: the term used in Mark (15:1), translated as "consultation," is the Greek *sumboulion,* meaning council session; if the Sanhedrin had sat as a court, it would have been *krisis* or *krima.*[50]

It appears prima facie difficult to understand that, while it was unlawful for the Sanhedrin to meet at night or on the eve of a feast day to hold a trial, it was lawful for it so to meet for a preliminary inquiry. One would have thought that if even a trial was unlawful at such a time, a fortiori a preliminary inquiry must be. But the opinion has been offered that the prohibition to sit on the Sabbath and festival days applied only to judicial trials, where an accused had to be sentenced and put to death, not when the Sanhedrin met in an administrative capacity, or for political or other debate.[51] It is true that the reason for the ban was probably not the requirement of sabbatical or festival repose for the members, but rather the humane consideration that an accused should not be placed in jeopardy on such a day; from his point of view, however, it was almost as bad to be subjected to a preliminary investigation as to be required to stand trial, and neither of the one nor of the other should he be victim on his day of rest. And as for the embargo on nocturnal proceedings, reliance has been placed on a rule that where a trial was adjourned from one day to the next, the members of the court would consult with each other during the night,[52] to show that consultations at night, as distinguished from trials at night, were perfectly lawful.[53] But, for these consultations, the judges met in their homes, and not necessarily all of them together; and there is no record of any plenary night meeting of the Sanhedrin for any purpose. Furthermore, while consultations among the judges could be held at night without in any way inconveniencing the accused, any nocturnal inquiry, including his interrogation, would infringe his right of rest no less than a nocturnal trial would; and as with sabbatical and festival rest, so must the night's rest be taken as a right conceded to the accused rather than to his judges.

If, indeed, the Sanhedrin did hold a preliminary investigation, it must have been held for the Roman authorities. It has been said that a "preliminary examination was required before the trial before Pilate could take place. There was the necessity to question Jesus, interrogate witnesses, translate their depositions, and prepare the charge sheet. . . . Differences of language, custom and conventional habits between the Roman officers and the indigenous population would necessitate that the preparation of the case should be entrusted to Jewish officials on the High Priest's staff."[54] We shall shortly see that the Romans stood in need of no Jewish help in that regard; but, assuming for a moment that they did, how could it be that, of all the Jewish "authorities" or "officers," it had to be the Great Sanhedrin of Israel that must render them technical assistance such as this? The answer, of course, can only be that it was not the whole Sanhedrin that met that night, but the high priest and some of his clerks and officers;[55] the "chief priests and elders and scribes and all the council" would then be a later interpolation into the text, as is said to be shown by the fact that the "whole council" is mentioned in Mark (15:1) in connection with the delivery of Jesus the next morning into the hands of Pilate, but not (14:53) in connection with the night's proceedings. (The same textual variations led other scholars to the assertion that while a preliminary investigation was held by the high priest and some of his officers during the night, the Sanhedrin assembled early the next morning and held a trial.) [56] The theory that the preliminary investigation was carried out that night by the high priest and some of his officers finds support in the Johannine Gospel, which tells that Jesus was interrogated that night by the high priest alone (18:19–24), and that no council assembled in the high priest's house. But what of the "chief priests and elders and scribes" (Mark 14:53), or "the chief priests and elders and all the council" (Matt. 26:59), or "the chief priests and all the council" (Mark 14:55), who are plainly mentioned as attending and active in the night's proceedings? To dismiss all of this as a later interpolation is too easy and too little justified. I think that we have to abide by our premise that it was the Great Sanhedrin that convened that night, with the question still unanswered how that body should come to conduct an inquiry such as this for the Romans.

Authority for the thesis that it did, in fact, perform such tasks for them is claimed in the report on the arrest of Paul: the Roman captain, having arrested him (Acts 21:33), sought to examine him by scourging (22:24); Paul protested, claiming immunity from scourging as a Roman citizen (22:25–27); and the captain then "commanded the chief priests and all their council to appear, and brought Paul down, and set him before them" (22:30). It is said that Paul was "set before" the Sanhedrin by that command for the purpose of an inquiry in preparation of a Roman trial; but since Paul protested only his right as a Roman citizen not to be scourged, the captain could very well have questioned him without scourging, for no Roman citizen was entitled to immunity from interrogation, and no such immunity had been claimed by Paul. Moreover, if he could, as a Roman citizen, lawfully object to questioning by a Roman officer, he could a fortiori, as a Roman citizen, object to questioning by a local Jewish court. That the captain convened the Sanhedrin for no Roman purpose is evident from his letter to Felix, the governor, writing that he brought Paul before the council because he "would have known the cause wherefore they accused him" (23:28), and he then "perceived" that Paul was accused by them, that is, by the Jews, "of questions of their law, but to have nothing laid to his charge worthy of death or of bonds" (23:29). In other words, it turned out that Paul was charged with offenses under Jewish religious law that, under Roman law, were punishable neither with death nor with imprisonment; and the Sanhedrin was concerned with questions of Jewish law within its own and exclusive competence, not with any offense which might have been committed under Roman law and be triable in a Roman court. In his speech for the prosecution before Felix, Tertullus said that the Sanhedrin would have judged Paul according to Jewish law (24:6) had not the Roman officer taken Paul away "with great violence" (24:7). What took place before the Sanhedrin was, therefore, the first stage of a trial under Jewish law, and not a preliminary inquiry to assist a Roman court, and would presumably have been concluded in due course if the Roman officer had not been informed of the plot to lynch Paul (23:21).

There is not a single instance recorded anywhere of the Great or Small Sanhedrin ever acting as an investigatory agent of the Romans. If such a custom or practice had existed, and surely if there had been any rule of law whereunder the Sanhedrin would be competent, or could be compelled, to render such legal services to the Roman governor, we would have some information about it in a Roman, Jewish, or Christian source. From what we know of the relations between the Romans and the Jewish authorities in Judaea, it is conceivable that the governor might ask for and obtain legal and administrative aid from the king, who was Roman-appointed and a Roman vassal; but it is almost unimaginable that he would have asked the Sanhedrin, knowing, as he did, what its attitude was toward all things Roman. From the story of Paul, it would seem that it readily met at the Roman officer's bidding, when it was called upon to assume jurisdiction over a Jew held by the Romans; but no Sanhedrin would have lent its help when called upon to deliver a Jew into Roman jurisdiction.

The same story affords proof, by the way, that Roman officers were perfectly capable of conducting investigations themselves, and the "scourgings" inflicted on all non-Romans certainly contributed to render the investigations very effective, much more so than any sanhedrial inquiry could hope to be. There were no language difficulties either: both Jews and Romans—at least the educated ones—would normally speak Greek (Acts 21:37), and

Roman officers always had Aramaic interpreters—tax collectors and that tribe—in their service.

Under Roman law, it does not appear that any preliminary inquiry, in the technical meaning of the term, had to precede a criminal trial, even of a capital offense. The prosecutor would normally bring his charge before the magistrate by word of mouth, whether at the beginning of the trial or with an application to arrest the accused and have him brought to trial.[57] There were preliminary investigations in the sense that the prosecutor would have to search for witnesses to prove his case: these were his responsibility, not the court's. Considering that a prosecutor was liable to a fine for failure to prove his case,[58] it may be assumed that such investigations were common and thorough; but that does not alter their essentially private character.[59] The governor, as a court, could not ask either the Sanhedrin or any other organ or authority to embark on a preliminary investigation of that kind: for the purpose of his court and the trial to be held by him, he simply did not need it. If the prosecutor—whoever he was—could not prove his case, the accused would be acquitted, and the prosecutor possibly fined; but it was no concern of the court to provide him with evidence.

This would open up the possibility that the Sanhedrin carried out a preliminary investigation not at the behest of the Roman authorities but on its own initiative, and not as a court but as a prosecutor.[60] Such a hypothesis must start from the premise that it was competent, and in fact purported, to act as prosecutor before the Roman governor in the trial of Jesus. But neither the one nor the other is the case. As for competence, the rule in Roman law was that the prosecution was conducted by a private accuser: a body of accusers or a number of accusers was not admitted.[61] The reason is that the law laid upon the prosecutor personal liabilities which could not be laid upon or shared by collective prosecutors: for example, an accuser might have to pay damages, as well as forfeit his civil rights, for frivolous prosecution (*calumnia*);[62] a false accuser might be liable to the punishment which the person falsely accused had faced, including death;[63] if a prosecutor gave up his case too soon (*tergiversatio*), or was negligent in pleading and proving it, he might have half his property sequestered, besides being punished with infamy;[64] and for any collusion with the accused, by which that person might go free or be punished only mildly (*praevaricatio*), he would be similarly liable.[65] These penalties could be effectively enforced only against individuals: neither in Rome nor in the colonies, to our knowledge, had an accusation ever been presented save by an individual accuser.

But neither do the Gospel reports suggest that the Sanhedrin acted as the prosecutor of Jesus before the Roman governor. What it did, according to the Gospels, was to resolve to have him delivered for trial to Pilate (Matt. 27:2; Mark 15:1; Luke 23:1). The accusations—insofar as they are reported—were brought before Pilate by multitudes (Luke 23:2) or chief priests (Mark 15:3) or the Jews (John 18:30–31), all unidentified groups which might or might not represent the Sanhedrin. The fact that it cannot well be the Sanhedrin as such that acted as prosecutor is, however, borne out by the nature of the charges: had it held a preliminary investigation to frame the charges on which Jesus was to be prosecuted before Pilate, the said charges would have been identical with those found against him in the preliminary proceedings of the Sanhedrin. But, instead, we find Jesus accused before Pilate of stirring up the people (Luke 23:5) and perverting them (23:14), of being a "malefactor" (John 18:30) and of making himself a king (19:12), but not of any blasphemy, or of any of the "doctrines" extracted from him in his interrogation by the high priest (John 18:19). Nor does the high priest, who, according to John, would have held the preliminary investigation, appear as accuser: in John, it is always "the Jews" who negotiate with Pilate (18:13, 38; 19:7, 12, 14). To answer the purposes of the Roman trial, the Sanhedrin would have had to conduct the preliminary inquiry into an offense under Roman law; what it did was to inquire into an offense purely under Jewish law. If the search for witnesses was intended, also, to unearth evidence of a Roman law offense, it proved abortive, and no such witnesses were forthcoming. Even when Jesus himself was questioned, he was not once asked about matters which could be relevant in a Roman trial: nobody bothered to put the crucial question which would be thrust at him by Pilate the next morning (Matt. 27:11; Mark 15:2; Luke 23:3; John 18:33). All the Gospels are agreed that the Sanhedrin did not concern itself at all with any possible offense under Roman law: it concerned itself with what Jesus had said and done about the temple, and with his messianic and doctrinal aspirations, subjects of no interest to the Roman governor. It follows that, whatever it did, it did not upon the instance or order of the Roman governor and for his needs, but solely on its own initiative and for purposes of its own.

As distinguished from the case of Jesus, in the case of Paul the Sanhedrin does, indeed, seem to have instigated the prosecution before Felix, the Roman governor, but to secure a *locus standi* under Roman law it had first to appoint an individual accuser in the person of Tertullus, "a certain orator who informed the governor against Paul" (Acts 24:1). Rather than the trial and sentencing of Paul for any offense under Roman law, which Tertullus did not specify, the purpose of hiring an accuser against him seems to have been to have him return to Jerusalem to be tried by the Sanhedrin (24:7–8). It is significant that, even for that limited purpose, the "Jews" or the "high priest with the elders" (24:1) would not themselves appear before the governor: they would appoint an "orator" versed in Roman law, as a matter of course and prudence, leaving aside any question of competence.

The Sanhedrin which assembled that night in the high priest's house did not try Jesus, or conduct any preliminary investigation. What, then, did it do, and for what purpose was it convened?

Let us, once more, remember that this was the night preceding the Passover festival (John 13:1), or even the festival night itself (Mark 14:12; Matt. 26:17; Luke 22:7). As anyone familiar with Jewish rites and customs knows, each single member of the Sanhedrin, not least the high priest in person, must have been busy and preoccupied with the somewhat cumbersome and complicated preparations for the feast or with its celebration, whether in his home or in the temple or both. That the Sanhedrin should have been called that particular night to a meeting in the high priest's residence, and should eventually have spent long hours there until well into the next morning, requires very cogent and convincing explanation to be credible. There must have been a matter of utmost urgency on the agenda, important enough to necessitate the instant consultation of the entire council, so important that no member, being summoned to attend, would raise a question of importunity. To hold a preliminary or other investigation, or to try a man on any criminal charge, was a matter neither of urgency nor of particular moment: and any member apprised of the purpose for which he had been summoned, if it was that, would at once have excused himself and gone back home. There was no judge then, nor would there be any judge today, who did not know that criminal proceedings are not held at night or on festivals; even if there had been no explicit legal rule to that effect, no judge in his senses, and certainly not seventy-one judges collectively, would have agreed to spend the festival night trying a criminal case, whatever it might be about. It could, perhaps, be imagined that a clandestine and illegal court might hold its sessions at night and in private premises; but the Great Sanhedrin of Israel, a court of seventy-one members and of unlimited jurisdiction, holding its sessions daily and openly in the temple, would never degrade itself to meet surreptitiously, any more than would any court of competent jurisdiction today. It was said that the nocturnal meeting had been arranged "lest there be an uproar of the people" (Mark 14:2), if they got wind of Jesus under trial; but not only was the "uproar of the people" feared if Jesus were taken on the feast day (*ibid.*), and not if he were taken and tried on an ordinary weekday, but meanwhile—or so Mark tells us—"great multitudes" of people (14:43) had already taken part in the arrest of Jesus, and the uproar could anyhow no longer be averted. If the "chief priests" were concerned to prevent Jesus' appearance at the temple during the Passover festival, when large crowds gathered there, nothing would have been easier for the high priest, once having secured the custody of Jesus that night, than to detain him until after the feast and then have him put on trial before the Small Sanhedrin in due course according to law. Nor would there have been any difficulty, if it was desired to avoid public disorder, in holding the trial *in camera*, during daytime and regular working hours, and in the proper court hall of the Sanhedrin.

There is no escaping the conclusion that it had not been in the hands of the Sanhedrin, or in the high priest, to fix the timetable: the timing had been forced upon them. We have seen that the high priest knew that Jesus was to be tried before the Roman governor early the next morning: the trial had been fixed beforehand to suit the governor's convenience—one could not know whether he would stay for yet another day in Jerusalem, or perhaps was due to return to Caesarea the very same day. At any rate, no Jewish body or individual could have had any influence on particulars of the governor's schedule. If anything was to be done by the Jewish leadership about the trial of Jesus, it had to be done forthwith, during the night. But what was so important about the trial of Jesus as to warrant an emergency meeting of the Great Sanhedrin by night? The Sanhedrin had no power, or any illusion of power, to prevent the Roman governor from holding the trial, certainly not by forestalling him clandestinely and holding a trial itself. Nor was it called upon to undertake, or interested in undertaking, any services preparatory to the trial before him. There can, I submit, be only one thing in which the whole Jewish leadership of the day can have been, and indeed was, vitally interested: and that was to prevent the crucifixion of a Jew by the Romans, and, more particularly, of a Jew who enjoyed the love and affection of the people.[66]

If there was still any chance of saving Jesus, this was the last opportunity: the Roman governor could not be expected to consent to an adjournment or delay of the trial. Anything that could be done must be done that very night. Yet the question persists: Why had anything to be done? What if a Jew, one of the many teachers of the young who had messianic dreams and indulged in prophecies, was tried by the Roman governor? What even if he was sentenced and crucified? Just one more lamentable casualty in the bitter war with Rome. I do not allow myself to speculate that the Jewish leaders might have been prompted by ethico-religious considerations, such as the prohibition of standing by quietly when the blood of a neighbor is shed (Lev. 19:16), or the prescript to save the persecuted from the hands of his persecutor.[67] The great importance of the matter inhered not in its moral and religious aspects, but in wholly realistic, political factors. We saw that the high priest found himself in a very precarious situation vis-à-vis the people: unless he did something about it, his standing and prestige in their eyes would steadily decline.[68] He must have been desperately anxious to raise the esteem in which the public held him, and especially to demonstrate that he was a good and loyal Jew, admirably qualified for Jewish leadership, and not merely an instrument in Roman hands. The Sadducees, on their part, were generally despised, if not detested, by the people for their wealth as much as for their religious schismatics, and, with the growing popularity of the Pharisees, had every reason to fear for their places of power and influence and for their seats in the Sanhedrin if they did not regain some popular support. And as for the Pharisees and the Sanhedrin in general, there was a growing tendency—or so it was apprehended—on the part of the Roman authorities to restrict sanhedrial jurisdiction and autonomy and undermine its influence upon the people and its prestige among them. While the Sanhedrin had to be circumspect not to alienate such Roman goodwill as it could still enjoy, the first and foremost condition for its survival and effectiveness was to retain the people's confidence and fealty. Nothing could have been further from the intentions of its leaders, or more harmful to their purpose, than to provoke the discontent and disaffection of the people by conniving at the trial and crucifixion by the Romans of one who was in their very midst, whereas any action on their part to avert crucifixion would, if it succeeded, be likely to awaken popular applause and enthusiasm and to reinstate the high priest and the Sanhedrin in the regard of the people as their natural and accepted leaders.

Jesus was one of the people. Otherwise he would perhaps not have been loved by the people as he was: when he came into Jerusalem a few days before, "a very great multitude spread their garments in the way; others cut down branches from the trees, and strawed them in the way. And the multitudes that went before, and that followed, cried, saying, Hosanna to the Son of David: Blessed is he that cometh in the name of the Lord" (Matt. 21:8–9) ; and many people "took branches of palm trees, and went forth to meet him, and cried, Hosanna: Blessed is the king of Israel that cometh in the name of the Lord" (John 12:13) . Such, indeed, was the ecstasy of the crowds that certain of the Pharisees among them are reported to have suggested to Jesus that he restrain them a little: "some of the Pharisees from among the multitude said unto him, Master [that is, Rabbi], rebuke thy disciples" (Luke 19:39) . It is clear that all the "chief priests and elders and scribes" knew very well what was going on and saw that "the world is gone after him" (John 12:19) ; nor could any such "triumphant entry" into the city, any such acclaim by the masses, pass

unnoticed. Anybody who wished—and some of the Jewish leaders
might have wished—to divert a measure of the popularity away
from Jesus and unto themselves was in fact estopped "for fear of
the people" (Luke 20:19). The considerations which may have
prompted the leaders to try to get rid of a man of progressive
and reformist aspirations and independent thinking, and a worker
of miracles, such as Jesus was, were far transcended by their
conviction—which found expression in the Gospels—that any
attempt at interference with Jesus would at once cause a "public
uproar" (Mark 14:2). But the stage of such a conflict of motives
would never actually be reached, as no individual success, no particular doctrine, and no religious or political aspirations could
have any relevance as against the paramount necessity for the
Jewish leadership to win and keep popular support. That a particular individual, for whatever reason, was a favorite of great
masses of the people must have been ground enough for the Jewish leaders to foster and endorse and protect him: by denying him
their backing and protection, they would automatically forfeit
popular sympathy; by according him their backing and protection, they would gain the people's goodwill and esteem for themselves. To become accomplices of the Roman governor in the persecution and prosecution of Jesus was the surest way to earn the
abhorrence of the people: it was bad enough, in all conscience,
to collaborate with the Romans, but to join forces with them to
harm or destroy the best-beloved and most popular of Jews was
close to unforgivable. On the other hand, to dissociate themselves
from the Roman authorities and do everything in their power
to render the persecution of Jesus abortive and save his life would
not only earn them the popularity that they coveted, but also
demonstrate to the people that the voice of the Sanhedrin was
still heard even in the court of the Roman governor.

It is from the standpoint not only of internal Jewish relations,
but also of those between the Sanhedrin and the Romans, that any
intervention by the Sanhedrin had inevitably to be in favor of
Jesus. By delivering him to the Roman governor for trial or crucifixion, it would have confessed its inability or incompetence to
maintain law and order among the Jews. Such an admission was
exactly what the Romans would have hailed as a welcome pretext for depriving the Sanhedrin of the last vestige of its au-

tonomy and establishing Roman jurisdiction throughout. If, from the domestic Jewish aspect, it was really necessary to bring the ministry of Jesus to an end and prevent him from spreading his teachings further, it was the Sanhedrin which ought to have been equipped to take the requisite steps, judicial or administrative or both. If it was not so equipped, more the pity! But what would the Roman governor have to do with any such purely Jewish predicament? His reaction was bound to be either refusal to handle matters of no concern to him or acceptance of the Sanhedrin's abdication of its own competences and privileges, and it could have intended neither. There was no earthly reason why it should deliberately run the risk of either rebuff or forfeiture of jealously guarded privileges. Moreover, as a point of Jewish law, it would have breached its judicial duties by delivering into the hands of an alien court an offender due for trial under that law. For it to deliver Jesus into the hands of the Roman governor would, then, in the governor's eyes, have been tantamount to admission of sanhedrial failure and incapacity to preserve law and order; and, in the eyes of the people, to a contemptible infringement of national solidarity and treasonable collaboration with the enemy. Even if there were sinful and wicked members of the Sanhedrin—and there is nothing to substantiate the view—who would qualify as potential traitors and quislings, its membership cannot, in any circumstances, be presumed to have been blind and stupid: we must take it that all the judges knew the natural and probable consequences of their acts and would do nothing likely or liable to work out to their own hurt.

There is no difference, in this respect, between the Pharisaic and the Saducean membership. We know that Saducees may have been antagonistic to Jesus, not only for being a Pharisee himself, but mainly for despising the rich (Matt. 19:24; Mark 10:21; Luke 18:22–25); but he may, of course, have found Pharisees inimical, too, if only out of their envy[69] or because he taught "without authority." It was not the personality of Jesus that would inspire his advocates as well as his adversaries to take their stand: if it was his personality, or the merit of his doctrines, that was an issue, the Sanhedrin might have been divided. But it was unanimous, because not the personal fate of Jesus, or the merit of his doctrines, was at stake, but the standing and popularity of the Sanhedrin. The merit of his doctrine was actually the less relevant factor, seeing that it was his teachings and miracles that had won him his far-reaching popularity, and it was in the interest of the Sanhedrin—an interest of sheer self-preservation —to have that popularity serve its own purposes to the fullest possible extent.

With the high priest and the Sanhedrin so circumstanced, with Jesus awaiting trial early the next morning before the Roman governor and the people unaware of it, what more natural than that they should assume that, if they were looked to for leadership, the people would expect them to take some action to prevent the trial and the possibly or probably resulting crucifixion? If the trial and crucifixion of a Jew by the Romans were an affront to the Jewish people, the trial and crucifixion of an outstanding Jew, one of the people's favorites, were an outrage which the people would surely not suffer quietly; and it was essential that the leaders should be able to come forward and satisfy the people that they not only had no hand or part in the proceedings but, on the contrary, had done everything in their power to avert the tragedy. Now the only way in which the Sanhedrin could possibly prevent the putting to death of Jesus was to bring about either his acquittal or a suspension of sentence subject to good behavior. For an acquittal, Jesus had first to be persuaded not to plead guilty to the charges, and then witnesses must be found to prove his innocence. For a suspension of sentence, if he were found guilty, he had to be persuaded to promise that he would not again engage in treasonable activity. No other way was open to the Sanhedrin, because Jesus—as we saw—had been given into the high priest's custody on an undertaking that he would be delivered for Roman trial the next morning, and a breach of that undertaking would have resulted in the temple police, and maybe the Sanhedrin, being stripped of their powers and competences. Once duly delivered to stand his trial, Jesus must conduct himself in such a manner, and evidence be provided for him to such effect, that either an acquittal or, at least, a suspended sentence would in all probability follow.

It is true that the high priest might conceivably have done all this alone: have talked to Jesus himself and have himself sent out his emissaries to look for witnesses. Indeed, the Johannine tradition is that it was the high priest (or his father-in-law) alone who questioned Jesus that night. But the high priest, head, as he was, of a very rich Sadducean family, could rightly have been apprehensive lest his personal influence on Jesus might not be strong enough to assure a reasonable prospect of success if he worked alone. Moreover, he took the hazard of not only failing to impress Jesus, but of being denounced by him to the Roman governor as seeking to interfere with the due process of justice, a denunciation which Jesus would never have made of the Sanhedrin, but which, it is possible, he would have had little compunction about making of the Roman-appointed high priest. The high priest may also have reflected that this was a matter for which the whole Sanhedrin should bear responsibility, more particularly if the law-abidingness of Jesus thereafter had in any way to be vouched for. And it was no small or inconsequential matter for the Jewish authorities to talk to a prisoner in technically Roman custody and awaiting trial under Roman law before the Roman governor, to the end of procuring acquittal or suspension of sentence: it was a clear meddling with Roman justice, unjustifiable perhaps from the Roman point of view, but, as it would seem, indicated, nay, even required, from the Jewish, only because of the prevailing political situation, that is, the popular resentment of Roman occupation and oppression and the concomitant resistance. In other words, this was in the nature of a political decision and answerability for it had better rest on the Sanhedrin as a whole. The fact that opinions within and without the Sanhedrin may have been divided as regards the personality and teachings of Jesus may have been another reason why the high priest chose not to act alone in taking a stand in his favor. He might even have felt himself incompetent to determine, in his own discretion, to what lengths he had to go to save Jesus, the merit or demerit of Jesus' teaching being, at least formally, outside his personal judgment.

Thus it came about that in that festival night all the members of the Great Sanhedrin were suddenly bade to proceed forthwith to the high priest's palace: there would be a trial, early the next morning, before Pontius Pilate, the governor; Jesus—the popular preacher who taught in the temple and attracted such huge audiences, the same man who showed such courage and presence of mind the other day in the temple bazaar—has been arrested on a charge, it seems, of treason or sedition; temple police have succeeded in abstracting him into their custody for the night; if anything is to be done to save him, it must be done at once; and there can be no doubt that we must do everything to save him— it is a matter of life and death, which we must attend to even at night and even on a festive day;[70] please come at once! And they all came, every one, unfailingly.

The Gospels tells us that when they had assembled, the first thing was that they "sought false witness against Jesus to put him to death" (Matt. 26:59) : that is to say, they had assembled to find him guilty of some crime and sentence him to death. But how could they do that by seeking "false" witnesses? To find him guilty, they would, one should think, have to seek true witnesses to testify against him! Not enough that the trial was prearranged and the death sentence predetermined; even the witnesses had to be "false," presumably to fill the cup of judicial perversion to the brim. In this as in many other respects, the author of the Gospel of Matthew outdid the author of the Gospel of Mark: in Mark we read that they "sought for witness against Jesus to put him to death; and found none. For many bare false witness against him, but their witness agreed not together" (14:55–56) . Meaning that they sought witnesses, not necessarily false, but preferably true, but all that came forward and testified proved to be false, in that their testimonies did not "agree together." It seems that all the witnesses against Jesus had to be "false," so as to lay the foundations for subsequent allegations of judicial murder,[71] but then the Gospels themselves proceed to found his conviction entirely on a confession of so-called blasphemy; the false witnesses—presumably because of their falsity—are discarded as instrumental in the verdict. On the face of the Gospel stories, the episode of the witnesses is completely unintelligible: Jesus himself had pointed out that he had always spoken "openly to the world" (John 18:20) and taught in the temple and in the synagogues "where the Jews always resort" (*ibid.*) ; "all the people came early in the morning to him in the temple for to hear him" (Luke 21:38) ; thousands must have listened to him teach and preach, and many of them could, without any great effort, be made available to testify exactly what his teachings and his preachings were.

Such could not be labeled "false" witnesses, nor would they have contradicted one another, because the sayings of Jesus had left an imprint on people's minds and would have been rehearsed countless times by and among them. Indeed, the specific "false" testimony recorded in the Gospels, namely, as to Jesus' words that he would rebuild the destroyed temple within three days (Mark 14:58; Matt. 26:61), actually appears to refer to an utterance by him in public in the temple (John 2:19),[72] and there is no reason why it should not have been accepted as true, for what it might be worth as incriminating evidence. It comes to this, then, that the Sanhedrin sought "false" witnesses to testify against Jesus, but could not find any; the witnesses appearing and testifying before it were true witnesses, but were proved false, because they would not "agree together"; and whether they were false or true, and whether they agreed together or not, no attempt was made to rely on their testimonies in any way; nor are we given any hint or intimation of the points on which they failed to "agree together," or the manner of their disagreement, or why it was that they were first "sought" and inexplicably abandoned in the end.

We shall accept it as a fact, and start from the premise, that the Sanhedrin which assembled that night in the high priest's house did "seek for witnesses." As we said, it could not, even at that time of night, have encountered any difficulty in finding a good number of people able and willing to testify about Jesus' public teachings and preachings. But it did not need any such testimony for its own information, or to have any specific allegation against Jesus proved or disproved: not only was there nothing of the kind against him before it, but its members can reasonably be presumed to have been familiar with his teachings, if only from hearsay. What the Sanhedrin needed was a finding that the witnesses who had come forward to testify against Jesus were false ones, men who could not be relied upon and who had not "agreed together": it was not that they were unreliable and untruthful—on the contrary, they presumably were truthful and reliable; it was that they had to be pronounced, formally and solemnly, as false witnesses. It was altogether irrelevant to what particular teaching or deed or saying of Jesus they would testify: it happened to be the destruction and rebuilding of the temple; it could as well have been any other of his prophecies or parables. What mattered was that, to

whatever item they would testify, they ought not to "agree together," so as to warrant a finding that they were "false" and
unreliable.

The question whether, and to what extent, a witness is truthful
and his evidence credible is, in every case, to a very large degree
determined as a matter of impression and discretion of the trial
judge or jury. If, that night, the Sanhedrin had indeed been resolved in advance "to put Jesus to death," nothing would have
been easier than to find the witnesses testifying against him truthful and reliable and "agreeing together," and extract from their
evidence a capital offense that would serve its purpose. But it
simply does not make sense that, though resolved in advance "to
put Jesus to death," it dismissed the witnesses testifying against
him as "false," without even troubling to inquire whether their
testimonies did or did not disclose a criminal offense. The inevitable conclusion is either that the Sanhedrin was not resolved in
advance to put Jesus to death at all or that it did not dismiss the
witnesses as "false," or that both these things were so: if it dismissed the witnesses as "false," it did so because it wanted to, and
because, for its own true purpose, it did not need the evidence of
any witness. The purpose was to provide Jesus with a judicial
finding that all witnesses who had come forward to testify against
him had been proved false and unreliable. Such a finding of the
Sanhedrin was not, of course, in any way binding on the Roman
governor; but there was always the chance that the evidence available against Jesus before the governor would not be strong and
conclusive, in which case a sanhedrial finding that witnesses against
him had been forthcoming before the Jewish courts also and
dismissed as untrustworthy might well turn the scales in his favor.
The Sanhedrin could, in the circumstances, and in view of Jesus'
popularity, be reasonably confident that Jewish witnesses would
not volunteer to give evidence against him before the governor;
there remained the possibility that Roman agents had overheard
Jesus' speeches in the temple or in the synagogues, and, as against
their evidence, there might be some force in the sanhedrial finding
that witnesses who had testified to some seditious content in those
speeches had been proved false. The very fact that witnesses had
come forward before the Jewish courts, too, to testify against
him might raise the suspicion that Jesus was the object of persecu-

tion for private and ulterior motives, and the finding of perjury would strengthen that suspicion considerably.

A criminal court, under Jewish law, had to satisfy itself of the reliability of witnesses and of their "agreeing together" by directing to them certain questions which the law laid down, as, for instance, on what day, at what hour, and in what place the event to which they testified had happened.[73] From the Gospel reports, it does not appear that any such obligatory examinations were conducted before the witnesses were found "false." If, being examined as to the date of a speech of Jesus to which they had testified, one gave one date and a second another, that would, in law, suffice for the rejection of the evidence of both, however irrelevant the date might appear to the issue whether the speech contained any illegal matter. All the same, the Gospel reports do not exclude the possibility that such examinations were duly conducted: "their witness agreed not together" (Mark 14:56) and "But neither so did their witness agree together" (14:59) presuppose some examination to find out whether or not the testimonies were interconsistent. Anyhow, statutory examination of witnesses was not confined to the obligatory questions, and the more a judge pressed it, the better would it be. This power of further questioning is especially required in the case of witnesses who "agreed together" on the obligatory questions, for it would be easy for perjurers to have concerted answers to those questions ready in advance; it is really only by surprise questions that discrepancies are likely to be detected. In contrast to the obligatory questions, those put in supplementary examination are in the judge's discretion: he must choose the line that fits the demeanor and reactions of the individual witness under questioning, and he may draw from the way in which the witness behaves and reacts his own conclusions as to the truthfulness of the answers.[74]

That the Sanhedrin found that the testimonies of witnesses did not "agree together" is nothing extraordinary: many accused persons must have been acquitted for the same reason. But, contrary to the traditional thinking, there is no reflection, in a finding of this sort, on the witnesses: they may be perfectly honest people, testifying in the best of faith, and the inconsistencies which marred their evidence may have been due to natural and unavoidable shortcomings of the human memory. To have all been found "false" proves nothing against the witnesses who testified against Jesus before the Sanhedrin, but it proves something in regard to the court. Whereas one court would use its power to pursue examinations to try to smooth out minor inconsistencies, as in modern "re-examination," so as in the end to find the witness reliable and convict the accused, another would do everything it could, in that use, to multiply inconsistencies, so as in the end to find the witness unreliable and acquit him. This, apparently, is what happened here: the witnesses all said of Jesus, "We heard him say, I will destroy this temple that is made with hands, and within three days I will build another made without hands" (Mark 14:58), without any discrepancy between their stories being reported, yet the court found that "neither so did their witness agree together" (14:59), though, on the face of it, that witness agreed perfectly. The court exercised a discretion: to attain its ultimate purpose, it found some natural and minor inconsistencies—which did not have to be reported—enough to reject the evidence as false. It does not matter whether, in exercising that discretion and making that deliberate and intentional choice, some of the members of the Sanhedrin were, perhaps, also anxious to reassure their own consciences that in fact no valid evidence was available to incriminate Jesus, or whether they only wanted to be able to certify and attest that the witnesses who had testified against him had perjured themselves.

While, under Jewish law, the admissible and reliable evidence of at least two eyewitnesses, and of two witnesses who had warned the accused of the punishability of his offense, was a *sine qua non* for any criminal conviction,[75] under Roman law the nonavailability of witnesses did not suffice to warrant an acquittal: the accused could always be convicted of his plea of guilty,[76] even where no witnesses were called or were forthcoming. Since the trial before Pilate would go forward under Roman law, it would not suffice to put potential witnesses out of action or impugn their credibility: it was much more important to dissuade Jesus from pleading guilty and so prevent his conviction upon his own confession. Wherefore Jesus had not only to be instructed what and how to reply to questions which would be put to him in the governor's court, but also, and first of all, persuaded to cooperate with the Sanhedrin. We must assume that Jesus knew of his impending trial before Pontius Pilate: if he had not known it before, his arrest by Roman troops could not have left him in any doubt. We shall also assume that he knew, or took it for granted, that the Sanhedrin had nothing against him, to put it at its lowest: if he had not been aware of that all along, the examination of witnesses in his hearing and the branding of them as "false" and unreliable must have removed the last doubt. But he was no less conscious of his own immense popularity and of the shaky posture of the high priest and the Sanhedrin internally as well as externally, and well informed enough to make his own appraisals. He would not, therefore, have harbored any fancies that the Sanhedrin's attitude toward him was born of pure neighborly love: he would have guessed the egoistically political motivation behind it and naturally have weighed in his mind his own religious and messianic concerns as against general Jewish and sanhedrial politics. His own "religious and messianic concerns" may have included a resolute and preconceived expectancy toward his peril and ultimate fate in a trial before the Roman governor. And, on the part of the Sanhedrin, "persuading Jesus to cooperate" meant not only inducing him to plead not guilty and to promise Pilate to be of good behavior, but also—and perhaps mainly—making him forsake his own "religious and messianic concerns," insofar as they were incompatible with sanhedrial sanctions: the Jewish leadership could not be expected to vouch for Jesus before the Roman governor unless he were ready and willing at least to bow to its authority and assure it of his loyalty.

Jesus' loyalty and goodwill could not be established negatively by the absence of trustworthy incriminating evidence. It had to be established positively, out of his own mouth. Hence his interrogation by the high priest himself: its purpose was to persuade him to accept the Sanhedrin's authority and desist from dangerous pretensions.[77]

So long as the "false" witnesses testified against him, Jesus answered nothing, but "held his peace" (Mark 14:61; Matt. 26:63), though he was seemingly expected, and entitled, to cross-examine and rebut them. But since they were speaking the truth, his intervention would have been pointless. It was when the high priest started questioning him that he first reacted. Asked whether he was "Christ, the Son of the Blessed" (Mark 14:61), Jesus admitted that he was (14:62) and added: "and ye shall see the Son of man sitting on the right hand of power, and coming in the clouds of heaven" (*ibid.* and Matt. 26:64). According to Matthew, the question of the high priest was in the following terms: "I adjure thee by the living God, that thou tell us whether thou be the Christ, the Son of God" (26:63); according to Luke, Jesus was simply asked, not necessarily by the high priest: "Art thou the Christ? tell us" (22:67). It has been shown that the references in Matthew to the "Son of God" and in Mark to the "Son of the Blessed" must be interpolations[78] from a time when the dogma of the divine descent of Jesus had already been introduced into Christian belief.[79] We shall, therefore, take as the true tradition that recorded in Luke, "Art thou the Christ? tell us," to which Jesus is said there to have answered: "If I tell you, ye will not believe: And if I also ask you, ye will not answer me, nor let me go. Hereafter shall the Son of man sit on the right hand of the power of God" (22:67–69).

We do not know whether this was the sole question asked of Jesus by the high priest, or whether the high priest had questioned him before as to his teachings, opinions, and intentions in general, as would appear from John 18:19. If he had, the question recorded in the Gospels may have been the last of a series in a more prolonged examination; Jesus may have answered them specifically, in which case his answers seem not to have aroused any disdain; or he may have reacted in a manner similar to that reported in John: "I spake openly to the world; I ever taught in the synagogue, and in the temple, whither the Jews always resort; and in secret have I said nothing. Why askest thou me? ask them which heard me, what I have said unto them: behold, they know what I said" (18:20–21). Be that as it may, his reply to the last question, "Art thou the Christ?," apparently led the high priest and the Sanhedrin to give up in despair. Before we inquire into the reasons why they did, let us consider the question and the reply themselves.

It has been said that the claim to be Christ, sitting at God's right hand in heaven, was an admission of blasphemy in Jewish law, amounting to a denial of the fundamental principle of monotheism which would not, *ex definitione,* brook a divine being besides God.[80] But by asserting that, as Christ or Messiah, he would be privileged in heaven to sit at God's right hand, Jesus did not in any way infringe the oneness of God. It might be different if he had actually claimed to be the Son of God; but, as we have noted, any such claim put into his mouth by the evangelist must be rejected as a later interpolation.[81] According to what may be regarded as Jesus' own words, peacemakers "shall be called the children of God" (Matt. 5:9), and so "that ye may be the children of your Father which is in heaven," you must "love your enemies, bless them that curse you, do good to them that hate you, and pray for them which despitefully use you, and persecute you" (5:44–45). It is the great reward of doing good that "ye shall be the children of the Highest" (Luke 6:35). In the sense in which Jesus employed the metaphor "children of God," the terms "Son of God" or "Son of the Blessed" may also bear a purely allegorical as distinct from a biological meaning, and indicate the chosen rather than the natural son. In this respect, there would not be much difference between the Christ—or Messiah—and the Son of God: the Christ was chosen by God as His messenger or prophet. The Greek *Khristos* is a translation of the Hebrew *Mashiah* (Messiah), signifying the anointed. Not only the Messiah but all God's favorites are anointed, such as priests,[82] kings,[83] prophets,[84] and even holy places and chattels.[85] The anointing may be a mark of divine distinction, but it is a distinction conferred on human beings, and by its very nature not at all apt for divinity. It is a human being who is chosen by God to serve Him, or inspired by God to prophesy, or to whom God has revealed Himself, and it is a human being whom God would love as His son. That, in the original tradition, Jesus was a son of God only in this figurative sense seems to be borne out by his genealogy as recorded in the Gospels (Matt. 1:2–16; Luke 3:23–38).

As for the "Son of Man," that may simply be a translation of the Hebrew *Ben Adam,* meaning man (literally, "son of Adam," the first man), or the title by which God addressed some of His prophets, Ezekiel, for example, or an allusion to the Son of Man whom Daniel announced as arriving on the clouds of heaven and entering upon "a dominion which shall not pass away and a kingdom which shall not be destroyed" (Dan. 7:13–14).[86] It has been pointed out that "Son of man" is a self-appellation used exclusively by Jesus and of himself.[87]

The Synoptists are themselves witnesses confirming this usage as a historical fact, as they never by any chance allow the term to glide into their own language. Even to the evangelists themselves it did not seem to be a regular messianic title. . . . Ignatius, Justin, Irenaeus, Origen, Eusebius, Athanasius, Gregory of Nissa, Gregory Nazianzus, Cyril of Alexandria, Chrysostom, as well as Tertullian, Ambrose, Cyprian, Augustine, with one consent, though in variously conceived modes, have seen in this title a reference to the human side of the descent of Jesus.[88]

Speaking of himself as son of man, he desired to be known as son of a man: there could have been no clearer or better repudiation of any claim to divinity. When Jesus said to his disciples, speaking of himself, "that ye may know that the Son of man hath power on earth to forgive sins," "they marveled, and glorified God, which had given such power unto men" (Matt. 9:6–8), the specific reason for marveling, and for glorifying God, being that not only God, but a human being, could forgive sins. It is true that the style "Son of man" in itself, and when Jesus uses it in speaking of himself in the third person, suggests that he regarded himself not just as a member of the human race like any other, but as the chosen one whom God "will make Lord of the world."[89] He may have taken his cue, drawn his analogy, from the words of the Psalmist, "What is man, that thou art mindful of him? and the son of man, that thou visitest him? For thou hast made him a little lower than the angels, and hast crowned him with glory and honour. Thou madest him to have dominion over the works of thy hands; thou hast put all things under his feet" (Ps. 8:4–6).

The import of the term Son of Man, and the significance of Jesus using it of himself, may have interesting theological implications—and it is perhaps not surprising that it has provided generations of scholars with an inexhaustible subject of thought and research. For the purposes of our inquiry it is sufficient to state that the expression is simple and straightforward Hebrew (or Aramaic) of biblical provenance, and that the use of it, even in relation to oneself, was neither prohibited nor offensive—as, indeed, it is not in the spoken Hebrew of today.

The association of the Messiah with "clouds of heaven" or with a seat at the right hand of God was nothing new either, and no one using such a metaphor was ever suspected or accused of blasphemy. Moses went into the clouds (Exod. 24:18); even the enemy shall come up as clouds (Jer. 4:13); and Daniel's "Son of man" came on the clouds of heaven (7:13). And the "Lord said unto my Lord, Sit thou at my right hand, until I make thine enemies thy footstool" (Ps. 110:1). A minor altercation is reported in the Talmud between two illustrious scholars which throws some light on the manner in which "blasphemies" of this sort would be dealt with. Daniel had a vision of two thrones, on one of which sat "the Ancient of days," whose garment was white as snow, and his throne was like the fiery flame (7:9). Said one scholar: This was the throne of God, and the other, next to it, was the throne of David. He was rebuked by the second: How can you so profane God's holiness?[90]—suggesting that a mere mortal such as David would not be suffered or imaginable on a throne next to God's. The rebuke may or may not have been called for, but it did not diminish in any way the great prestige of the "profaner," nor would anybody have for a moment envisaged the possibility that any such "profaning" could be a criminal offense.

Even, therefore, on the assumption that Jesus uttered in front of the Sanhedrin the messianic declaration of the Son of Man, meaning himself, sitting at the right hand of God and coming in clouds of heaven (he had said much the same on earlier occasions: Mark 13:26; Luke 21:27),[91] there was nothing either in the words themselves or in messianic claims or arrogations in general that would constitute an offense under Jewish law. Not only was there nothing criminal in his words, but there was nothing in his pretensions or pretentiousness that could, in reason, shock or scandalize his hearers.[92]

We are told, however, that, upon hearing the words, the high priest "rent his clothes, and saith, What need we any further witnesses? Ye have heard the blasphemy: what think ye?" (Mark 14:63–64; Matt. 26:65). (The version in Luke 22:71 is: "And they said, What need we any further witness? for we ourselves have heard of his own mouth"; there is no mention of rending garments.) It is, indeed, a rule of Jewish law that, on hearing the divine Name desecrated, the court and the witnesses must rend their garments,[93] and most scholars, not surprisingly, regard this gesture on the part of the high priest as the proper and prescribed reaction to blasphemy uttered in his presence. They do not pause to ask why it was only the high priest who rent his garments, and not also all the other members of the Sanhedrin present, for the rule of law applied equally to all and each of them.[94] We may perhaps see in the lone act of the high priest a first indication of the fact, yet to be demonstrated, that it was not this rule of law which had here found its application.

We have seen that, under Jewish law, the capital offense of blasphemy is not, and at no time was, committed unless the holy and ineffable Name of God, composed of the letters YHWH (Yahweh), had been expressly pronounced by the blasphemer.[95] The rending of garments—like capital punishment—follows the enunciation and desecration of this one and only divine Name alone; it does not follow any other reviling of God in which the Name was not spoken (Lev. 24:15–16), however bad the reviling be. The theory that the rending of garments, and capital punishment, had been justified by Jesus' use of the divine Name of "Power" (at whose right hand the Son of Man will sit) has been disproved by prominent commentators of the New Testament.[96] In fact, the designation "Power" has been used of God only in postbiblical times: it was a Pharisaic device—apparently adopted by Jesus as a matter of course and of piety—to provide a nonsacred name by which God could be referred to in general conversation.[97] Some Christian theologians have held that Jesus' blasphemy consisted in his reply to the high priest, "I am" (Mark 14:62), reasoning that the words "I am" (*Ani Hu*) are a divine name as holy and sacrosanct as Yahweh.[98] It is true that God is said to have used this description speaking of Himself: "I am, and there is no god with me" (Deut. 32:39), and a prophet has also put it into God's mouth (Isa. 48:12). But that does not mean that any sacrosanctity attaches to the words as thus cited, nor is there any reason why they should, in this respect, be distinguished from the many other words that God is said to have used in speaking of Himself. Anyone conversant with the rudiments of Hebrew knows that the words *Ani Hu*, whether jointly or severally, are articulated hundreds of times in everyday speech—in fact, one cannot do without them; and to make their enunciation or profanation a capital offense is tantamount to rendering each single citizen, each day of the year, liable to the death penalty. That absurdities like this should have been propounded by scholars of repute goes to show how desperate were the efforts that they had to make to bring Jesus' words within the category of blasphemies under Jewish law. In the result, they all failed utterly.

Nor did Jesus commit the minor offense of reviling God without desecrating the Name. On the contrary, his boast of the heavenly distinctions that God would shower upon him, of his choice by God as the Messiah (the "Christ"), bespeaks his recognition and worship of God: so far from reviling God, he was invoking God's "power" and wisdom, and the heavenly distinctions to which he laid claim would be exiguous unless God were indeed the *ultima ratio* in perfection and insight. And the fact that he relied on God for his choice and election was—as we have pointed out—the most natural and common thing to do:[99] he might have been regarded as an apostate or an atheist if, for his teachings and aspirations, he had relied on his own strength and not on God's choice and call; but his persistent and unfailing dependence on God, his invocation of God, attest piety and devotion, however mistaken and misguided his teachings or aspirations may appear to this or the other listener.

Some corroboration for the hypothesis that Jesus could not have been convicted of any offense because of his teachings and aspirations, or, in particular, of his claim to be the chosen Messiah, is to be found in the report of the trial of Peter, which, as we know, took place before the Sanhedrin about a decade later (Acts 5:26–39). Like Jesus, Peter and his disciples were pious and observant Jews and had a following among the people. But while Jesus claimed to be the Messiah, Peter taught and asserted that the Messiah had already appeared in the person of Jesus, which made his doctrine theologically much more prejudicial and dangerous than any personal aspiration voiced by Jesus. But Rabban Gamliel, "a doctor of the law" of high "reputation among all the people" (5:34), who was present at the session of the Sanhedrin, pleaded with his colleagues to "refrain from these men and let them alone: for if this counsel or this work be of men, it will come to nought; but if it be of God, ye cannot overthrow it, lest haply ye be found even to fight against God" (5:38–39). Thus it came about that Peter was acquitted and left to continue his teachings. We shall revert to his trial in another context; for our present purpose we need only observe that Gamliel, a leader of the Pharisees and one of the most eminent scholars of his day, did not purport to fathom God's ways and choices; anybody professing to teach in God's name and to have been graced with divine inspiration must be free to do so, and in due course of time it will emerge whether it had truly been God who had inspired him. Had the Sanhedrin seen, in the messianic teachings or aspirations of Jesus, any blasphemy or idolatry or false prophecy or any danger to the public peace or the established faith, it would certainly not have failed in its duty to administer justice and uphold the law—against Jesus and Peter alike. But in the case of Peter it was content to leave the matter in the hands of God, because it could not, and would not, exclude the possibility that Jesus had, indeed, been divinely inspired. It has been sagely remarked that this sanhedrial decision, on Gamliel's plea, may have been among the first precedents for the relatively modern, but still widely unheeded, rule that no one is to be punished merely for expressing unpolitic or unorthodox opinions.[100] The rule may not, at that time, have been required to protect individual views for which the proponents did not claim divine authority; if it was required, it was for people who dared to challenge orthodox tenets and established religion on the purported authority of divine call and afflatus, for it was only God's backing that would render their sermons worth listening to.

There is no valid reason to doubt that the same Gamliel who persuaded the Sanhedrin in Peter's case was present and prominent also during the meeting at night in the high priest's house, when Jesus stood before it. To regard the outcome of the "trial" of Jesus that night as proof of Gamliel's absence appears to be in the nature of a *petitio principii;* but there are scholars who, on the one hand, agree that he could not have found Jesus guilty and would very much like to know what he would have said or done had he been present,[101] but, on the other, take Jesus' conviction by the Sanhedrin for granted, notwithstanding the undoubted presence and concurrence of judges of Gamliel's school of thought. Had Gamliel, in the trial of Peter, vented only an individual opinion, a discussion would presumably have ensued, with some members relying on the stand of Gamliel or other Pharisaic scholars in the matter of Jesus a few years earlier, if indeed any Pharisaic scholar had then taken such a stand. Gamliel, however, certainly did not: he gave authoritative expression to what must have been a matter of general consensus that God's way and choices are unfathomable to men, and that, however much this way of choice may contradict that way or choice, both may be the "words of the one living God."[102] Thus, whether or not Gamliel himself was there to speak in the case of Jesus also, his opinion and manner of thinking were most certainly well represented, so that there is, again, no cause to infer that he may not himself have been present that night, too. Nor is there any ground for the assumption that had Jesus actually stood trial that night, the outcome would have been different from that of Peter's. The fact is that he stood no trial and was not convicted. No blasphemy was charged, no blasphemy occurred: God's holiness was unimpaired, the holy Name was undefiled. Why, then, did the high priest rend his garments?

The easiest way to unravel the riddle, as with most problems arising out of the Gospel reports, is to dismiss the whole incident of the rending of the high priest's garments as unhistorical. The authors of the Gospels of Luke and of John have already shelved it, apparently regarding the traditions of Mark and Matthew as unreliable. But I think that the Marcan version lends itself to a reasonable and satisfactory explanation, and it will be seen that it falls neatly into place, and is not without significance, in the sequence of events that night. It is an ancient and well-known Jewish custom to rend one's garments as a sign of grief,[103] not only on the death of a kinsman or other beloved person, or on suffering calamity or serious misfortune, but also on hearing any bad news, as, for instance, on the outbreak of war.[104] If the high priest rent his garments that night, it was because of his grief not to be able to make Jesus see his point, his anguish that Jesus ostensibly refused to cooperate and was moving stubbornly toward his disastrous fate, and, not least, that Roman oppression would claim another Jewish victim, with all the consequences that might flow from Roman killing of a man of Jesus' standing and popularity. His declaration before the Sanhedrin that he was the Messiah (the "Christ"), while it was not a criminal offense, amounted to a rejection by Jesus of the offer made to him by the high priest and the Jewish leadership: cooperation between them would be possible only if they would accept his assertion and recognize his claim. This, of course, they could not and would not do, not only because they did not believe in him, and would have regarded their submission to his authority as a dereliction of duty and a transgression of law, but also because sanhedrial recognition of the messianic pretensions of Jesus would surely have meant, in the eyes of the people as well as of Pilate, a confirmation of the very charges of which Jesus stood accused before the Roman authorities. So far from agreeing to abstain thenceforth from activity that might bring him into conflict with the powers-that-be, he reasserted his messianic mission and insisted on its fulfillment; he would not bow to the authority or accept the guidance of the Sanhedrin. It was no blasphemy which made the high priest rend his garments, but the failure of his efforts to bring Jesus to reason and save him from his doom—and a foreboding of the catastrophic aftermath.

But it was only the high priest who rent his garments: there was no conviction for blasphemy, no desecration of the holy Name, and so no legal duty of rending, nor were the others present under any obligation to follow the high priest's example.[105] That the rending of his garments is almost conclusive evidence of the high priest's grief—if it was not just formal compliance with a ritualistic prescript—cannot be seriously contested; but if—as the protagonists of the Jewish Trial Theory maintain—it was his purpose, in interrogating Jesus, to extract a confession, then, according to the Gospel reports, he had accomplished that purpose easily. What cause had he, therefore, for any grief?[106] The cause can be understood at once if we assume that the last thing that he desired was to extract a confession; on the contrary, he wanted Jesus to give up his messianic aspirations or at least keep silent about them: he got exactly the contrary of what he wished, and hence had reason to mourn. If we take into consideration the trouble to which he had gone, ordering temple police to seek the custody of Jesus, calling the full membership of the Great Sanhedrin into his own palace, and devoting the whole festive night to frantic efforts in behalf of Jesus, we cannot be surprised at his total disappointment and despair when he saw that everything had been in vain.

While others present did not rend their garments, there is, in the Gospel reports, some backing for the surmise that they may have given vent to their indignation and disillusionment in different, less civilized, ways. According to one version, they "did spit in his face, and buffeted him; and others smote him with the palms of their hands" (Matt. 26:67); according to another, "some began to spit on him, and to cover his face, and to buffet him; and the servants did strike him with the palms of their hands" (Mark 14:65). A third has it that it was "the men that held Jesus," that is, presumably, the temple police, who "mocked him and smote him, and when they had blindfolded him, they struck him on the face" (Luke 22:63–64). The most probable story of all, however, if we must assume that Jesus was, in fact, bodily assaulted, is that of the Fourth Gospel, that one of the Jewish officers "struck Jesus with the palm of his hand, saying, Answerest thou the high priest so?" And Jesus' reply, "If I have spoken evil, bear witness of the evil: but if well, why smitest thou me?" (John 18:22–23), lends both the question, with the accompanying violence, and the response a very authentic flavor. But let us say that, following Jesus' "confession" and the final conclusions to which the members of the Sanhedrin were driven by it, some of them actually exploded in fisticuffs, or servants or other bystanders reacted violently. In a more sophisticated and less turbulent society, people might have turned away in silence and disgust or, at most, used strong words. But in those tumultuous days in an enemy-occupied Jerusalem, people may not always have been as self-controlled and disciplined as that. And after a nerve-racking night, which each and all of them would rather have spent in celebrating, or in preparing for, the feast at home and in the temple, or in slumber, than in trying to persuade Jesus to accept their authority and be saved from his fate, the anger and frustration which took hold of them could not easily, in every individual case, be confined within civilized limits. Had a sentence of death been pronounced against Jesus by the Sanhedrin that night, as reported in Mark 14:64, any impatience with his obduracy that might have incensed any member of the court would have found its quick release in the carrying out of the sentence: it is virtually inconceivable, and, of course, highly improper, for a judge to raise his hand against a prisoner in the dock. The biblical prescript "Love thy neighbour as thyself" (Lev. 19:18) was interpreted as an exhortation to judges to make as light and fair as humanly possible the last hours of a prisoner sentenced to death;[107] and not only judges were forbidden even to lift a finger to strike another man.[108] But, if it be true that the Sanhedrin did not, that night, pass any death sentence, the ineffectuality, after a long and tiring vigil, of the desperate efforts to bring Jesus to reason, and agonizing thoughts of impending and now probably unavoidable tragedy, might well have robbed the more passionate judges and bystanders of their last traces of self-restraint.

It is only in Mark (14:64) that we find a formal condemnation to death; according to Matthew, they—the judges—answered the high priest "and said, He is guilty of death" (26:66) ; according to Luke (22:71), they did not even say that. Thus each Gospel has a version of its own: John has no death sentence, because according to him there was no trial before the Sanhedrin; Luke has none either, although according to him there was some sort of trial before the Sanhedrin, albeit only in the early morning hours; according to Matthew, they all exclaimed, "He is guilty of death," but no "condemnation," as such, is recorded; only in Mark is one recorded.[109] Had there actually been a formal condemnation, it would necessarily have to be assumed that some sort of trial did precede it, and also to be expected that the formal sentence would duly be carried out, whether by order of the Sanhedrin itself or, on the view that it lacked the necessary power, of the Roman authorities. The ultimate event, as all the Gospels report it, seems to attest cogently enough what had—and had not—taken place before: in the issue, the Sanhedrin did not purport to carry out any death sentence of its own, nor did the Roman authorities—or anybody else—carry out any death sentence of the Sanhedrin; nobody informed Pontius Pilate that a trial had been held before the Sanhedrin, and that Jesus had already been sentenced to death! Yet one would have thought that this was the first thing to tell the Roman governor if "the Jews" were indeed so eager to see Jesus condemned: the Great Sanhedrin of Israel had already assembled and had unanimously found Jesus guilty of a capital offense! Not even the author of the Gospel of John, according to whom the Jews said to Pilate, "It is not lawful for us to put any man to death" (18:31), puts a plea into their mouths that he order a death sentence, which had already been passed, to be carried out by the Romans; on the contrary, he lets the Jews refuse

to "judge him" (*ibid.*) . Even if, then, there was no formal condemnation by the Sanhedrin, that does not necessarily mean that
members of the Sanhedrin may not have exclaimed some such
words as are reported in Matthew, that Jesus was now doomed.

We started from the premise that the high priest, and hence
the members of the Sanhedrin, knew that Jesus was to be tried
early the next morning before the Roman governor, and that they
regarded it as absolutely indispensable to do everything possible
to prevent the unfavorable outcome of that trial. It follows that
they anticipated that the probable outcome would be fatal, and
did not believe that Jesus stood a chance of acquittal or of a
punishment less than death. We have pointed out that saving
another's life warranted violation of the feast, but nothing short
of saving the life of a man in direst jeopardy would warrant it.
The men of the Sanhedrin were acquainted with their governor,
and had no illusions about him: if Jesus were tried and did not
formally and solemnly recant his pretensions, he had no hope of
escaping death. When their efforts to get him to agree to give up
those claims and promise to desist from messianic activity had
availed nothing, they all knew that he would be found guilty and
sentenced to die—by virtue not of any sentence or judgment of
theirs, but of what that governor would pronounce against him.
The outcry, "He must die," was the natural and spontaneous
reflex to the words which Jesus had spoken, sealing, as they did,
his fate in the coming trial, from whose upshot there seemed no
longer any possibility of rescuing him.

We cannot know whether the evangelists—or some of them—were
aware of what had, in truth, happened that night in the high
priest's house and had framed their reports so as to serve their
particular partisan ends, or reported each according to his traditions, in the honest belief that they were historically true. It has
been said that we must distinguish between "early tradition and
later expansion," and that "only after having eliminated from
the four accounts such elements as are due to secondary traditions
or to editorial accretion, may we use the residue of primary tradition for purposes of making historical deductions."[110] But the
task of differentiation is not easy, and what to one scholar may
appear to be a primary tradition, a second may regard as secondary, and it would be difficult to disprove either opinion. It has

also been said that in reporting the night proceedings in the high priest's house, the evangelists did not purport to convey any traditions which they possessed but described what they knew of trial or interrogation procedures of their own time and place. Thus the high priest is recorded as interrogating Jesus exactly as Roman judges or governors would, in the days of the evangelists, have interrogated suspect Christians.[111] It is, indeed, probable that, to render Jewish responsibility for the death of Jesus plausible, the evangelists would attribute to the Sanhedrin some sort of judicial procedure, and one with which they and their contemporary readers were familiar would be the natural choice. The Jewish law of procedure prevailing in Jerusalem in the epoch of Jesus was almost certainly unknown to them, apart from the fact that, even if it were known, it would not have suited their purpose. We find even such a learned and well-versed Jewish writer as Philo of Alexandria ignorant of Jewish laws: claiming to describe the Jewish canon, he gives in actual fact a description of Greek and Egyptian statutes in force in his own time and place.[112] And what is understandable in a Jewish writer is certainly understandable, and venial, in Christian authors and preachers. But the whole theory falls to the ground for the simple reason that the Gospel reports, whether of the interrogation by the high priest or of the trial by the Sanhedrin, in no way correspond to procedures known to be in use when and where the evangelists lived: in a letter from Pliny,[113] rendering account to the emperor of the manner in which he tried suspect Christians, he speaks of their interrogation, himself questioning and requestioning them until they confessed; but he does not speak of the examination of any witnesses. The normal procedure would be to start, not with the examination of witnesses, but with the interrogation of the accused (*quaestio*), and where the accused confessed, witnesses would no longer be required.[114] But, as will be remembered, the Gospel reports speak of the examination of witnesses first: the accused was not interrogated unless and until that had proved abortive. Just as interrogation of the accused would have been contrary to Jewish law, so would the prior examination of witnesses have been contrary to Roman; and just as there is not in the Gospel reports a true and accurate account of Jewish law, so is there none of Roman.[115]

Scholars who see, in the Gospel accounts of the trial, descriptions of Roman procedures have regarded the beatings and smitings of Jesus that those accounts record as having followed it as an echo of the flagellations which, under Roman law, were implicit in every sentence of death and preceded its carrying out.[116] They hold that no such beatings or smitings actually took place, but as the evangelists knew that every prisoner sentenced to death would automatically be liable to *flagellatio,* they reported the beatings and smitings as if they had to follow the sentence as a matter of course. This theory is equally untenable: according to Luke, the beatings preceded the trial (22:63–64), which in itself would take them out of the category of penitentiary measures; and the other Gospels report some flagellations afterward at the hands of Roman soldiers (Matt. 27:30; Mark 15:19; John 19:1), which would amply account for what was required under Roman law but under Jewish was illegitimate and improper.

"Then they led Jesus from Caiaphas unto the hall of judgment: and it was early" (John 18:28), and in the hall of judgment in the Roman governor's court Pilate was already prepared and waiting for the prisoner to be brought before him for trial. Both John and Luke (23:1) report that Jesus was "led" there, being neither chained nor shackled; according to Mark (15:1) and Matthew (27:2), the Jews bound him first, and so led him to Pilate's court. The second version appears the more probable one: though, as we have seen, Jesus had in all likelihood been led unbound into the high priest's house, the logic would be that he was led bound into the Roman court. He had been delivered into Jewish custody for the night upon the plea of the temple police, on the undertaking that he would be duly handed over the next morning to the Roman court for trial: at least in front of the Roman troops and guards, the Jewish constables would have to act as if Jesus had indeed been their prisoner, in the full sense of the word, through that night, and that they were now surrendering him, as such, for trial. His delivery not as a prisoner, but as a free man, might have aroused suspicion that in asking that Jesus be given into their custody theirs 'had been a purpose other than the one vouched by them, and incompatible with what the Romans planned. The Roman tribune may have agreed to let Jesus stay overnight in Jewish custody on his own responsibility;

but had he—or the governor—seen that Jesus had been freed and accorded special treatment, he might have called the temple police to account for the indulgence. At all events, it can be assumed that, after hearing Jesus' replies to the high priest, the Sanhedrin saw no way out and ordered him to be arrested and brought for trial to the Roman court.

The Synoptic Gospels are unanimous that "when the morning was come, all the chief priests and elders of the people took counsel against Jesus to put him to death" (Matt. 27:1), or that "straightway in the morning the chief priests held a consultation with the elders and scribes and the whole council" (Mark 15:1). According to Luke, this consultation "as soon as it was day" (22:66) took the place of the trial itself, being either identical with it or in lieu of it; but the version in Matthew and Mark raises the question whether it was the conclusion of the trial or a separate and additional proceeding. There is a theory ventilated that the Sanhedrin would always—and had to—pronounce sentence at the dawn of day,[117] another of those unfounded and rather absurd theories invented for the purpose of proving the historicity of some otherwise inexplicable Gospel report: as a matter of law, the Sanhedrin started its sessions in the morning hours and determined them in the afternoon,[118] and even where the trial had been concluded earlier, sentence was never pronounced until shortly before sunset.[119] Seeing that, for Matthew and Mark, a trial had taken place during the night and had resulted in a condemnation or a finding of guilt, the evangelists may have thought an explanation to be due for the subsequent delivery of Jesus into the hands of Pilate instead of his execution by the Jews;[120] they could hardly suppress the trial before Pilate and the resultant crucifixion, because those facts were already too well known. The early morning "consultation" provided them with a solution: though the Jews had tried Jesus and found him guilty, they now consulted together whether it would not be wiser, and more practicable, not to have Jesus put to death but to deliver him into the hands of Pilate. It is significant that no explanation is offered, in either Matthew or Mark, why this would be wiser, or more practicable: anybody who wanted to see Jesus tried and crucified by the Romans could have denounced him to them, and there was no need, with that purpose in mind, for any sanhedrial trial or condemnation, and a night trial at that;[121] on the other hand, if the Sanhedrin had indeed found Jesus guilty of a capital offense under Jewish law, it would have regarded his execution, no less than his trial and condemnation, as its own proper function and duty. The simplest way out of the difficulty is, of course, to say that, as there was no sanhedrial trial, equally there was no early morning consultation, and the consultation report was superadded to the trial report only once more to stress, as the text in Matthew would suggest, the deadly enmity of the Jews toward Jesus and their ever-recurring "counsel to put him to death." But even supposing that this consultation report, as distinct from the trial report, was based upon a valid tradition, it might be said—looking back at the events as we have interpreted them—that neither the failure and lamentation of the high priest nor the frustration of the members of the Sanhedrin was enough in their eyes to justify the delivery of Jesus into Roman hands: they still had compunctions, still felt the need to consult with each other, before making a decision which would be irrevocable. Maybe, by this further consulting together, they could find some other, as yet untried, stratagem to persuade Jesus to desist or a pretext to withhold or postpone his surrender for trial; and it was only after such renewed deliberations, unable to discover stratagem or pretext, that they made up their minds. They saw, and satisfied themselves and each other, that they could do nothing more. They had done everything humanly possible, and now concluded that, in the circumstances, they would have to honor their undertaking and deliver Jesus up for trial. Whatever forebodings they may have entertained of what that trial might hold in store for Jesus, they had no power to prevent it, or any practical possibility of withholding and concealing Jesus. Not that Jesus had desired to be withheld or concealed, or his trial prevented. And so—as we shall presently see—the members of the Great Sanhedrin left the high priest's palace and dispersed, each going to his home and after his business; and the impending fate of Jesus—and their own inadequacy—must have hung over them like a dark and sinister shadow.

6 THE TRIAL

All four Gospels are agreed that Jesus was tried before Pontius Pilate, the Roman governor, and that he was brought into his presence by the Jews. But they differ on the very first question which antecedes the many problems arising in connection with the trial proper: Who were "the Jews" that did so? Mark (15:1) reports the consultation between the "chief priests . . . elders and scribes and the whole council," and continues to speak of the binding of Jesus and his being carried away and delivered to Pilate, as if all of these had actually taken part in the consultations and, as well, in binding Jesus, carrying him away, and delivering him for trial. Luke (23:1) says that "the whole multitude of them arose, and led him unto Pilate," seemingly referring to the multitude of "the elders of the people, and the chief priests, and the scribes" mentioned earlier (22:66). Matthew (27:1-2) speaks of "the chief priests and elders of the people" who took counsel against Jesus, and then goes on to say that "when they had bound him, they led him away, and delivered him to Pontius Pilate the governor," a context in which "they" presumably means the chief priests and elders. Only in John is the question open: Annas had sent Jesus "bound unto Caiaphas the high priest" (18:24), and "then they led Jesus from Caiaphas unto the hall of judgment" (18:28), so that we are left in the dark as to who "they" may have been: were they the same as "them" that presently converse with Pilate and are afterward identified as "the Jews" (18:31), or other Jews than those reported to have played an active role in the subsequent proceedings?

It is significant that, according to Mark, it was emissaries of "the chief priests and the scribes and the elders" that arrested Jesus the night before (14:43), the same "chief priests and elders and scribes" that consulted together and delivered him to Pilate the next morning. Similarly, it was a "great multitude" from "the chief priests and elders of the people" which, in Matthew's version (26:47), arrested him, those very "chief priests and elders of the people" that took counsel together and delivered him the next morning to Pilate. We have shown that any part of the chief priests or elders or scribes, or other council members, in the arrest of Jesus, or, indeed, in any arrest, must be rejected out of hand as just not thinkable, for all the report of it in Luke (22:52), and we have identified the emissaries "from the chief priests and elders" with or without "scribes" as a contingent of the temple police detached to attend the arrest. Logic suggests, and we may, I think, safely assume, that the same contingent which had taken Jesus into its custody and brought him into the high priest's palace was now ordered by the "chief priests, elders, scribes, and all the council" to deliver him to Pilate for trial. The view has been taken that "the soldiers belonging to the [Roman] cohort which had arrested Jesus, and who had led him before the high priest, now brought him before Pilate,"[1] which would mean that, as a result of its consultation, the Sanhedrin notified the Roman authorities that Jesus was at their disposal, whereupon the cohort came to the high priest's palace and took him away. This construction appears unnecessary: not only is it irreconcilable with the Gospel reports that Jesus was brought before Pilate by Jews and not by Roman soldiers, but it is based on the premise, which we have found untenable, that Jesus had been brought into the palace by the Roman soldiers who arrested him. Indeed, the same posse which had brought him into the palace the night before may be assumed to have brought him into the Roman governor's court the next morning, but it was one of Jewish temple police, not of legionaries.

Having brought Jesus to the governor's court and delivered him into Roman custody, what did the detachment of Jewish temple police do? Stay or depart? If it stayed, did it attend the court session or was it posted outside the courtroom to await further orders? Whether it was the eve or the day of Passover, the temple police would in either case have a host of things to attend to within the temple precincts and the avenues leading to them, and it might reasonably be expected that, having performed its immediate task, it would be ordered back to temple duties at once. On the other hand, the high priest and the members of the Sanhedrin must have been critically interested in obtaining prompt and firsthand reports of all particulars of the trial; and it may be that the temple police contingent, or some of its officers, were ordered to attend and report, that is, of course, if the "chief priests" (Mark 15:3), with or without "elders" (Matt. 27:12) or "scribes" (Luke 22:10), were not present themselves. Here again, the Gospels are all agreed that chief priests and elders and scribes, or some of them, were not only present but prominent: "the whole multitude of them" is said to have accused Jesus (Luke 23:1–2); "the chief priests accused him of many things" (Mark 15:3); and "when he was accused of the chief priests and elders, he answered nothing" (Matt. 27:12). Not only that, but it would appear from the Gospel reports that the "chief priests" were there not with elders and scribes alone, but with multitudes of people besides (Matt. 27:24–25; Mark 15:8; Luke 23:13; John 18 and 19, *passim:* "the Jews"). If that was so, there would have been no point in having temple police attend to report the Roman hearing.

Who, then, was it, and, in particular, what kind of "Jews," that attended the trial of Jesus before Pilate? It is because the Gospels ascribe to "the Jews" so much activity in the trial, even ultimate responsibility for its outcome, that this preliminary question is decisively important. If we can identify the Jewish attendance, that responsibility may have to be reduced and confined accordingly. Our task is not simplified by the vagueness of the Gospel descriptions ("the Jews," "multitudes," "the people") and their inconsistency ("chief priests" with and without "elders," "scribes," "officers"). We shall have to look outside the Gospels for a solution of our problem.

It is submitted that no Jew, and no other outsider, could have been present at the trial, for the Roman governor held it *in camera,* and the public was not allowed in at all.

The *praetorium* where the Roman governor held his court is mentioned expressly as the place of Jesus' trial only in the Gospel According to John (18:28). But Matthew and Mark mention it, too, if only as the place where Roman soldiers led Jesus after sentence (Matt. 27:27; Mark 15:16); and Matthew also alludes to the *sella,* that is, the bench or judgment seat on which the governor sat (27:19) and from which he pronounced the sentence (John 19:13). *Praetorium* was the name of the governor's residence;[2] like the emperor in Rome, so did the governors in the provinces hold their courts in the palaces where they lived.[3] By contrast, trials before professional or lay judges were held in a *forum* or public square, and while we find the emperor or a governor exceptionally holding a court in a *forum,* the conduct of a trial within the *praetorium* was the exclusive privilege of the governor who tenanted it. Needless to say, trials held in a public square were open to the public, but those held in the imperial palace or a governor's *praetorium* took place in private, and only *apparitores,* clerks of specific appointment, were admitted into the courtroom.[4] That the actual chamber or hall in the palace or *praetorium,* where trials were held, was called *secretarium* confirms the secrecy of the proceedings:[5] it seems that it was cut off from the other parts of the building by a wall or curtain, called *velum,* which could be opened if it were desired, or ordered, that anybody enter the courtroom, but had otherwise to be closed throughout the proceedings.[6]

The principle of publicity of judicial proceedings, in which Roman law excelled from its early beginnings, is not necessarily inconsistent with the secrecy of proceedings conducted by a governor or by the emperor. It must be borne in mind that the governors, like the emperor, were in essence executive authorities, not judicial organs: their judicial powers flowed from their *imperium* and were restricted to criminal jurisdiction (*imperium merum*),[7] in other words, confined to matters whose adjudication was required to maintain public order and security and to safe-guard the political regime and the personal safety and authority of the rulers; as such, they were part and parcel of the general governing power or *imperium*. The governor's authority to pass capital sentences was said to flow from the *ius gladii*, the right of the sword, vested in him, the sword by which, symbolically, he governed the occupied territory and held it in subjugation. Even though he might at times hold a court and exercise judicial func-tions, he always abided the executive ruler, and thus it was that, even in judicial proceedings, the procedure which he observed was that not of a judge but of an executive.[8]

We do find emperors in subsequent periods directing their minds to complaints that the secrecy of judicial proceedings held by provincial governors resulted in miscarriages of justice: im-perial letters to offending governors are preserved which warn against sitting in private, and laws prescribed that "the governors shall conduct criminal trials with their tribunals open to crowds of people . . . and shall not hide themselves in their private council chambers so that parties can have no chance to appear before them unless they bribe the court officials."[9] And again: "The governor shall not doubt that there is imposed upon him a special duty in conducting judicial proceedings, namely, that he shall not pronounce in the seclusion of his palace a decision con-cerning the status of men or property, but he shall hear both civil and criminal suits with the doors of his private council chamber open and with everyone invited inside." The codifiers added the comment that "whatever decision he renders in accordance with the regular procedures of law and with the requirements of truth shall be concealed from no man."[10] In those times, governors—especially in the North African provinces—were ex officio also judges ordinary, *rectores,* with general civil and criminal juris-diction. It is quite mistaken to assume, as Mommsen did,[11] that these later laws and imperial admonitions only recapitulated the principle of publicity as it had been applied down the centuries in Rome and in the provinces, by ordinary tribunals and by governors: from the tenor of them it is abundantly clear that their purpose was to abolish a well-established custom, that is, the governors' privilege to hold their courts in the privacy of their own residences to which no stranger could have access, except, it seems, by bribing the *apparitores*.

We know that the *praetorium* of the governors of Judaea was in Caesarea, not Jerusalem.[12] There is some indication in the New Testament that even in Caesarea it was the Jewish king's palace that served the purpose (Acts 23:35), but it may be that the palace is referred to as Herod's because he had built it, and that it was, in fact, used solely as governors' residence and not as royal home.[13] It is, however, reasonably certain that when the governor was in Jerusalem, he resided in the king's palace, and that is the *praetorium* where he held his court.[14]

Corroboration for our view that the people, the public, did not enter Pilate's courtroom at all comes from an unexpected source, the Gospel According to John. It is there reported that "they themselves," that is, the people who had led Jesus "unto the hall of judgment," "went not into the judgment hall"; and the reason given is their apprehension "lest they should be defiled; but that they might eat the passover" (18:28). This would presuppose that by entering the palace in general, or the courtroom in particular, Jews would so "defile" themselves as to be disqualified from partaking of the paschal sacrifice. Nothing in Jewish law or ritual, however, would support the contention that by entering the king's—or anybody's—palace or a courtroom a Jew could become impure: that would happen only if a corpse lay beneath the palace roof,[15] or the palace were a place of idolatrous worship,[16] and there is no reason here to assume either the one or the other. But let us, for the sake of argument, assume that within the palace was a potential cause of impurity: even then, no Jew entering would be barred from partaking of the paschal sacrifice. The law was that even the impure might eat of it, their impurity notwithstanding,[17] and, more than that, even if priests had caught some impurity, they might still officiate in Passover sacrifices, so long as the majority of the people were pure.[18] It is not credible, therefore, that anyone feared that he would be "defiled" by entry into the palace or the judgment hall and thereby excluded from the Passover. If—as is reported in John—people did not enter the palace and the courtroom, it was for an entirely different reason, namely, that they were simply not allowed to, willy-nilly. That the author of the Gospel of John did not offer that true explanation, which was presumably known to him from the general practice of provincial governors, may have been because, to continue his story, the frequent intercourse between Pilate and the people was required, and if Pilate wished to consult the people, he could just as well have let them in. The author's switch of a spurious reason—fear of defilement—for the real one— a trial *in camera*—was entirely without risk, because their Roman readers had no knowledge of Jewish sacrificial laws and customs. What they knew was that a Roman governor would normally hold his court in his *praetorium;* and the author of the Fourth Gospel rightly perceived that there was no valid ground to suppose that Pilate departed from the normal rule in the case of Jesus. But holding a court in the *praetorium* meant holding it *in camera,* with no public present; and so he correctly recounted that the Jews did not enter the palace or attend the trial; his volunteering a wrong reason for that does not necessarily detract from the reliability of his factual report.

It is now said in John that "Pilate went out unto them," that is, to the Jews, several times, first to hear their charges (18:29), then to put them to their choice of a prisoner to be pardoned (18:38–40), then to show them the scourged Jesus (19:4), and finally to hear his sentence pronounced (19:13). This seems to indicate that—whoever they were—the people who did not enter the *praetorium* stayed somewhere outside: it would appear that there was a place reserved for persons awaiting the outcome of a trial or the appearance of the governor for some other purpose than the pronouncing of sentence. What it was is hinted at in the report in John that, when about to pronounce the sentence, Pilate "sat down in the judgment seat in a place that is called the Pavement, but in the Hebrew, Gabbatha" (19:13). Now we know of no Hebrew word or name like Gabbatha, and all manner of theories have been put forward to amend the text by substituting some similar word for it.[19] But this is pointless, because the Greek "stone pavement" may simply have been misleadingly represented to the evangelist, who knew no Hebrew, as being called Gabbatha in Hebrew or Aramaic. Whatever may be the meaning of Gabbatha, it is enough for us that it is surely identical with the Greek "stone pavement"; and this "stone pavement" would appear to be a paved courtyard abutting on the public square or thoroughfare whence the people would have direct access to the palace precincts. We have a report in Josephus that when a governor once decided to hold his court in public, as if in a Roman *forum*, he did so not in a public square in town but in front of the king's palace, where he had his "judgment seat" (the *sella*) brought.[20] Thus in front of the palace there was a paved courtyard which, while belonging to the palace precincts, and presumably separated from the adjoining public square by gates which could be shut and opened as desired, was open to the public generally or on particular occasions, and it was in this courtyard that, according to John, the sentence was pronounced and, until then, people were allowed to wait.

That not the whole proceedings were conducted *in camera*, but only the taking of evidence and the hearing of arguments, whereas the sentence was pronounced in public, is another conclusion which may validly be drawn from the Johannine report. I have not found any explicit statement that, under Roman law, sentence had to be pronounced in public, even where the trial had been conducted *in camera;* but in modern law there is ample authority for a proposition such as that,[21] and it is not impossible that the evangelist had known or heard of governors in his time who used so to act. There is very good reason for pronouncing all sentences in public: an execution without any prior announcement of the sentence and its grounds would, in the eyes of the uninformed, look like judicial or executive and tyrannical murder, while the public announcement of a reasoned sentence, even after a secret trial, would render the execution intelligible and justified as a proper exercise of judicial power. We may, therefore, safely assume that while the trial of Jesus was held in the *praetorium* with no members of the public present or admitted, the sentence was pronounced in public, and until it was, people waited in the courtyard in front of the palace.

But, as we saw, John reports that the governor "went out" of the palace not only to pronounce sentence but also, more than once, to talk to "the Jews" and hear what they had to say, while the trial proper was still in progress; and at least once he took Jesus out with him for a confrontation with them. In law or procedure there was, of course, no precedent or formal justification for this behavior, though one scholar erroneously maintains that Roman judges, including governors, invariably inquired for the *vox populi* and adjudicated according to the will of the people assembled.[22] The truth of the matter is that the author of John had before him the tradition already conveyed and perpetuated in the three Synoptic Gospels, that it was the chief priests and elders and scribes of the Jews, and Jewish "multitudes," that persuaded Pilate to condemn Jesus and insisted on his crucifixion: when the Gospel of John was written, that tradition was too well established to be set aside, and it was, moreover, especially for the author of that Gospel, much too welcome and indispensable a ground for accusing the Jews rather than the Roman governor, and saddling them with responsibility, to be possibly suppressed. So John contrived to insert the story of the presence of "the Jews," whether as denouncers or onlookers or noisy inciters, or as performing any other function that the Synoptic Gospels ascribed to them, into his own report of a trial held *in camera*, by making the governor interrupt the proceedings time and again and go out of the *praetorium* to see the people.

The result of these efforts at adjustment is so ludicrous as to border on the absurd: what proud Roman governor would keep jumping from his lordly seat of judgment at odd intervals and running out into the courtyard to talk with a mob of natives? The question has only to be put to be dismissed as nonsensical. The governor was surrounded by his *apparitores* or court clerks and by guards and officers: if he wanted information from everybody or anybody waiting outside, he would have sent an *apparitor* or officer there, as a matter of course, to make the inquiry and bring him the answer; he would never have gone himself. Or he might have sent out an *apparitor* or officer to bring anybody whom he wished to consult into the *praetorium* and into his presence, but never have troubled himself to get up and go out in person, and most certainly not for the rather impertinent reason that, by coming into his presence, some wretched Jew would "defile" himself! As we shall presently show, he did not, in fact, desire or need information from any of the Jews waiting outside; and if he just wanted to inform them that he had found in Jesus "no fault at all" (18:38), he could—and would—have proceeded to the judgment seat in the paved courtyard and pronounced sentence of acquittal. The theory has, indeed, been expounded that each time that Pilate went out to the Jews in the courtyard, it was to pronounce a formal acquittal of Jesus,[23] but it is unexplained how it was that the proceedings were still allowed to go on.

The squaring of the correct report of a trial *in camera* with the role attributed to the Jews at the hearing set the author of the Gospel of John a truly formidable task: if it were the Jews who sought to have Jesus tried and crucified, why did they not themselves do both? Why deliver him to the Roman governor for trial *in camera,* where they would have no opportunity to attend and make their demands and charges? Why engineer proceedings in which they would have to make themselves heard in the most unorthodox and intrinsically improbable manner? No such difficulty was encountered by the authors of the Synoptic Gospels, first, because the Sanhedrin is made to try Jesus itself first, and, second, because, in their rendering, Pilate tried Jesus in public, or so it would seem. But John, who had rightly abandoned the tradition of a trial by the Sanhedrin and, again rightly, has the trial before Pilate take place *in camera,* is in this dilemma that the Jews, though not present, had to take part, and, though wishful to see Jesus put to death, had not tried and put him to death themselves. Let us see how the evangelist solved his dilemma.

Pilate "went out unto them, and said, What accusation bring ye against this man?" (John 18:29) , indicating that, so far, none had been brought. This is—to say the least—most surprising: how could Jesus have been admitted into the *praetorium* unless a charge was pending against him? If he was, as yet, under no indictment, he would not be let in any more than any other member of the public. Or, if indeed there was apprehension of impurity attaching to entry, that would have applied as forcefully to Jesus as to any Jew. It is entirely out of the question that the temple police, or any Jewish authority, could deliver a man for trial before the Roman governor, and have him so accepted by the troops guarding the palace, without the charge against him being known and without the governor's prior consent to try him. Furthermore, as we have submitted, a Roman cohort under the command of a tribune would never have been detached for the arrest of Jesus unless a charge had already been preferred against him. Nor would the governor be found ready to sit in his court early in the morning to try Jesus, unless—and it bears repeating—he had advance notice of the trial and what it was about. To give the Johannine report the best possible interpretation, we must assume that there had been some accusation against Jesus before the governor when Jesus was first brought to his court; that the governor went into the charge by interrogating Jesus about it and was not satisfied that it could be sustained, whether by reason of formal or other defects or by reason of jurisdictional doubts; and that, being informed that "the Jews" had delivered Jesus for trial, he went out to "the Jews" to ask them whether they had no better charge against him.

Instead of giving the governor a reply and formulating a specific charge, the Jews are reported to have "answered and said unto him, If he were not a malefactor, we would not have delivered him up unto thee" (18:30). This is no less surprising: if the Jews were as interested as all that in having Jesus tried on a capital offense, why did they not take the opportunity offered and formulate a charge accordingly? By their failure to give a direct and straightforward reply to the governor's question and to accuse Jesus of a capital crime there and then, they endangered the very purpose for which they were allegedly there. The natural reaction of the governor to their evasive and somewhat disrespectful reply would have been to discharge Jesus at once: if you do not want to disclose the particular charges that you may be able to refer against Jesus, I shall have nothing to do with him and shall not waste my time. On the assumption, however, that he already had in his hands a charge which he found inadequate, the reply of the Jews lends itself to a better construction, too: before putting his question, Pilate must have told them that he had gone into the charge laid before him and had found it defective; whereupon the Jews replied: We would never deliver an accused person for trial before you unless we held strong evidence to prove our case; and the charges laid against Jesus are well supported by evidence which will duly satisfy you that he is indeed "a malefactor."

Then Pilate is said to have told them, "Take ye him, and judge him according to your law" (18:31): if you have investigated

the charge and found it upheld by sufficient evidence, why did
you not try Jesus yourselves? Why deliver him to me for trial and
not to your own courts? If you have satisfied yourselves that the
charges brought against Jesus disclose a capital offense, and that
there is strong evidence to prove his guilt, you could have convicted and put him to death yourselves! But the Jews are said to
have replied, "It is not lawful for us to put any man to death"
(*ibid.*) : we would gladly have tried Jesus and put him to death
ourselves if we but could—but we have no power under the laws
to do so, and therefore had no option but to deliver him up to
you for trial. As we have seen, this reply, put into the mouths
of the Jews, was generally taken as an authoritative admission
that the Jewish courts had no jurisdiction to try capital offenses
or carry out capital sentences;[24] but it could also be taken as an
entirely nontechnical assertion of the unlawfulness, under Jewish
law, "to put any man to death." We Jews, they might have said,
do not kill people; we must honor the divine commandment
"Thou shalt not kill" (Exod. 20:13), which is one of our most
fundamental and sacred laws; and that is why, this man being
charged of a capital offense, we deliver him up to you rather than
kill him ourselves. This kind of argument is reminiscent of the
position which the Church took in the days of the Inquisition: as
the Church abhors the shedding of blood (*ecclesia abhorret e san-
guine*), convicted heretics would be delivered to the secular arm
for execution;[25] under canon law, any priest taking part in a capital conviction and sentence is guilty of an "irregularity": the
hands of priests must be clean, and the blood—even of the guilty
—would sully them.[26] I do not know that the Church adopted this
line of thought from what the evangelist put into the mouths of
the Jews; but, in a way similar to how the Church was to argue in
later centuries, the Jews may well have said to Pilate, or so perhaps
the author of the Gospel thought: We have indeed satisfied ourselves that this man is guilty of a capital offense, and that under
the law he ought to be executed; but we do not shed blood, not
even of the guilty, being under our law—as distinguished from
your Roman law—forbidden to kill and render ourselves impure,
wherefore it is our humble petition that you try him and put him
to death. The practical experience which the Inquisition was to
gain goes to show that "the secular arm" is not normally disin-

clined to accede to such a petition. It is true that certain material benefits, such as a share in the property confiscated from the convict, accrued to the secular arm in consideration of its services; but then it was the rule in ancient Jewish law, too, that the property of convicts executed by the king or governor passed to the king's or the governor's treasury, whereas the property of a convict executed by order of a court passed to his legal heirs.[27] The governor would, then, under Jewish law, be entitled to the estate of any convict executed by Roman authorities.

But let us assume, as is generally done, that what the Jews said to Pilate was, in effect, that they had no jurisdiction to try Jesus and put him to death, and therefore there was no option but to have him tried by Pilate. It is true—as we saw—that if Jesus was charged with an offense under Roman law only, the Jewish courts would have no jurisdiction to try him: their jurisdiction was strictly limited, under both Roman and Jewish law, to offenses known and punishable by Jewish law; and when the offense was known and punishable by both Roman and Jewish law, they could claim jurisdiction only so long as the Roman governor would not. It would appear, however, that the whole jurisdictional issue has no real bearing on the question before us: if the author of the Gospel of John had to adjust his story to that narrated in the Synoptic Gospels, his starting point must have been that Jesus had already been tried and convicted by "the Jews" for an offense under Jewish law, namely, blasphemy, one that was, indeed, within their own exclusive jurisdiction. Why, then, did he not put into the mouths of the Jews the much simpler and more straightforward answer: We have already tried him and found him guilty, but, possibly, we have no power to execute him, or, we would prefer you to order his execution? Moreover, even if, for the purposes of the Gospel of John, we disregard the Jewish trial of the Synoptic Gospels, many offenses under Jewish law could have been charged against Jesus if the Jews really wanted to try him: the interrogation by the high priest at night, as reported in John (18:19), does not appear to have discovered any offense triable and punishable by the Roman governor alone, as distinct from offenses triable only, or also, by the Jewish courts. The things that Jesus "taught in the synagogue, and in the temple, whither the Jews always resort" (18:20) were likely to constitute offenses—if at all—under Jewish no less than under Roman law.

Whatever may be the most plausible reading of the question and the answer to it, I would submit that both are much too improbable and anachronistic to be accepted as true. The Roman governor was personally in charge of the judicial administration of his province, and personally exercised the jurisdiction vested in the Roman emperor by virtue of Roman sovereignty over the province which he governed. It was one of his main tasks and functions to see to it that local courts would not so exceed their limited jurisdiction as to encroach upon that sovereignty. It is, I think, totally inconceivable that this governor should address to the local populace an inquiry as to what his own jurisdiction was and what that of the local courts. It is no less unthinkable that he should have taken their reply as an authoritative and conclusive statement of the law—and a wrong and inexact reply at that.[28] If, by chance, a governor was not, or not yet, well informed about the limits of the jurisdiction of local courts, he had *apparitores* and other advisers learned in the law to consult, and would not seek the information from local sources which, apart from their inherent unreliability, were in the nature of an interested party. And if, by chance, a governor had information of this kind from local sources, surely he would first of all check it with his own legal advisers before acting upon it. The spectacle of the Roman governor coming out of his court to ask the people assembled outside why they would not try his prisoner, and acquiescing in the finality of their reply that, notwithstanding his invitation, they had no power to, is just too grotesque for credence. Any objective jurisdictional theory based upon this piece of information purporting to have been given to Pilate by the Jews rests upon nothing but fallacy and fiction.

As people always believe everything that they want to believe,[29] the author of the Fourth Gospel succeeded in solving his problem: the Jews very much wanted to try Jesus themselves, but could not, because they lacked jurisdiction either to try him or to execute him or both, and therefore had to deliver him to Pilate for trial and execution. And inasmuch as it was really "the Jews" who would have tried Jesus if only they had had the power to, and Pilate was but a sort of *locum tenens* for them, their substi-

tute, so to speak, it was altogether in character for him to interrupt the trial time and again and ask for the advice and assistance
of his sponsors, "the Jews," who, for regrettable ritualistic reasons of their own, did not enter his courtroom but waited outside.
It is in this way that the author of the Gospel of John also succeeded in linking up with the other Gospels and creating the impression that if, as he did, Pilate tried Jesus, it was only ostensibly and at the behest of the Jews: not of his own initiative and
from his own sense of duty or conviction of justice, but rather
against his better judgment, just because of the insistence and
intransigence of the Jews. The question therefore arises—and not
only on the story as related in the Gospel of John—whether, in
the prevailing circumstances, and in view of what we know of
Roman law and procedure, it was actually possible for the Jews,
whoever they were, to have taken any such active part in the trial
before the governor as is ascribed to them.

To probe this question, we shall assume—without believing—
that the Jews were present at the trial, whether it was held in public, as would appear from the Synoptic Gospels, or whether the
governor only conversed with them from time to time during the
trial, as reported in John. Pilate heard the accusers (Luke 23:2;
Mark 15:3; Matt. 27:12) and interrogated Jesus (Luke 23:3;
Mark 15:2; Matt. 27:11) and found no fault in him (John 18:38;
Luke 23:4; Mark 15:14; Matt. 27:23) ; but the Jews, completely
unimpressed by his findings, kept insisting that Jesus be executed,
shouting again and again, "Crucify him, crucify him!" (John
19:6, 15; Luke 23:21–23; Mark 15:13–14; Matt. 27:22–23) . Many
have already drawn attention to the remarkable fact that the
omnipotent Roman governor, surrounded by his officers and
troops, and sitting in judgment in lieu of his imperial majesty,
should ask the local citizens for advice on how to deal with a
criminal arraigned before him, or, in administering justice, should
take heed of hysterical popular demands. The very notion has
been dismissed as unbelievable.[30] Still less credible is it that he
should have crucified Jesus solely because of the bloodthirsty
clamor of the insistent "multitudes" and thereby allowed himself
to be reduced to an instrument in their hands to commit wanton
murder. If he thought Jesus innocent, that is, not dangerous to
Roman interests, nothing would have been easier for the governor

than to acquit and discharge him. And not only that. He would presumably have taken drastic punitive action against all those who had wrongly accused Jesus and, worse still, in spite of the fact that the governor had found no fault in him, had insisted on his crucifixion. Prima facie, this loud clamor for the blood of an innocent man amounted to a wholly improper attempt to pervert and defeat the course of justice: the governor—or so we are led to believe—was pressed to pass sentence contrary to his own judgment and in total disregard of his own conclusions of fact. In his eyes, an attempt such as that would not only be gravely contemptuous and constitute a criminal offense, but was also likely to involve himself in criminal conduct: even the admission of evidence known to be false against an accused was an offense for which the judge was punishable under Roman law,[31] and the execution of an accused known to be innocent would, in Roman law, be murder for which he would be personally answerable.[32] A law enacted in the year 59 B.C., which remained in force and was later codified,[33] laid upon judges and governors the duty to return any bribe or other benefit which they had received as consideration for their deflection from the path of justice, and criminal liability for any adjudication in a criminal cause under the influence or pressure of any interested outsider.[34] It is true enough that not a few Roman governors in many provinces are reported to have ordered unlawful executions: some were duly tried and punished; some got off scot-free;[35] but all such unlawful usurpations of judicial power were prompted by personal motives of the governors concerned, usually motives of personal vengeance, and nowhere and never was any such execution carried out at the bidding and under the pressure of natives and outsiders and in utter disregard of the governor's own personal—and expressly professed—inclinations.

We glanced earlier at the theory that Roman judges and governors used to adjudicate according to the *vox populi*, and hence that Pilate can fairly be assumed to have asked the local populace what to do with the criminal who stood trial before him;[36] that, it is said, was a course of procedure which every Roman judge or governor would consider to be called for in the normal dispatch of judicial business. In fact, however, we have an express provision of Roman law to the exactly opposite effect, and though it dates from a later period, there is no reason to doubt that it restates a well-established legal tradition. The law is: *Vanae voces populi non sunt audiendae*[37]—The vain voices of the people may not be listened to. What the propounders of the wholly mistaken theory may have had in mind was perhaps the *provocatio*, whereby all capital sentences passed against Roman citizens had to, or could, be brought for approval before the people's assembly;[38] but the *provocatio* did not apply either to sentences passed by the emperor or a governor or to sentences against non-citizens; and, at any rate, even if and where it was conducted by acclamation and not by a show of hands, it took place in an orderly manner, and not in hysterical and unsolicited haranguing of the judges. It is true, also, that where criminal trials were held in public, in a *forum,* spectators might at times become agitated and record their approval or disapproval vociferously, as crowds are apt to do; but nowhere do we find a court truckling to the imprecations of the masses where the evidence adduced and the conclusions arrived at by the judges would point to some other course. It is fair to add that even the author who found justification in Roman law for Pilate's conduct in listening to the people admits that, by doing so, he made "a tactical mistake, never again to be mended.[39]

No less unrealistic and unreasonable than the attitude of Pilate in the face of the hectic demands of "the Jews" does the conduct of "the Jews" themselves appear. We have dwelt on the popularity enjoyed by Jesus, which had found such unmistakable public expression in the rapturous welcome accorded to him in the streets of Jerusalem only a few days earlier. What had happened to make all his admirers and followers turn into his murderers overnight, into seemingly implacable enemies? Why should the people—the "multitudes" of them—have suddenly swung from one extreme to the other? What had Jesus done to warrant such a change of heart? Or what had chief priests or any other adversaries of Jesus—if there were any—done to bring about this radical alteration in the popular attitude to him? There is not in any of the Gospels the least attempt or hint at explanation.

It has been said that Jesus' abject stand before the governor convinced the people that he could not, after all, be a true messiah, as the true messiah would surely have overcome all adversi-

ties and easily subdued the governor,⁴⁰ and that disappointment
at seeing their hopes dashed and their faith shattered aroused
feelings of hatred and vengeance in them. But the people could
not have seen Jesus standing before the governor unless they went
to the *praetorium,* and why should they have gone there in the
first instance? In the early morning hours of the feast of Passover
or of its eve they surely all had something better and more
urgent to do than to traipse to the *praetorium* to see whether
a criminal trial was taking place and what it was all about. Moreover, the whole theory is historically and psychologically misconceived: any Jew who had to stand trial before the Roman
governor, irrespective of who he was and what the charge, would
automatically have elicited the sympathy of the people, and nobody would have turned against him in any way; and the poorer
his prospects of acquittal and the graver the peril of his death,
the greater and stronger would that sympathy be. And if the
man standing trial was a popular figure, beloved by the masses,
the fact alone of his being arraigned before the Roman governor
would make him a holy martyr in the eyes of the people, and all
the hatred that they could muster would be centered on the
odious alien. So far from expecting their spiritual leaders to over-
power the might of Rome, they considered that "to perish at the
hands of the hated Romans," the oppressors of Israel, was "to
join that venerated company of heroes who had sacrificed their
lives for their ancestral faith"⁴¹ and paved the way for the ultimate freedom of Israel.

It should not be forgotten, however, that, according to the
Gospel reports, it was not only "the people" or "the Jews" who
were present at the trial, but also "chief priests" who "moved the
people" (Mark 15:11), and it is said that, whatever may have
been the attitude of the people to Jesus before that morning, they
were now persuaded that the "chief priests" had been right all
along in their animosity toward him. They had seen in Jesus
hitherto not only a spiritual leader, however messianic, but the
"invincible king of the Jews, the warlike hero," who would "smite
the earth with the rod of his mouth, and with the breath of his
lips slay the wicked" (Isa. 11:4). All at once, they were faced with
the "most alarming and incredible" spectacle of their great libera-
tor bound, their unconquerable champion paralyzed and speech-

less: "how lucky it seemed that these chief priests and ruling classes, till then held in contempt for their collaboration with the Roman oppressors, should just in time have unmasked that boaster, traitor and coward! Suddenly the chief priests rose in the respect of the people: they turned out to be the only men who had always had the right opinion about this Jesus of Nazareth!"[42] I am afraid that, so far from solving the puzzle, this theory only adds to the bewilderment. It was not enough that the people precipitately changed their minds about Jesus: they did the same, and as precipitately, about the chief priests and "the ruling classes" as well! These abominable collaborators with the enemy and oppressor, to whom the people would not pay the slightest heed, could all of a sudden twist the people around their little fingers and only because they had not shared the popular belief in the fortitude and valor of the people's hero! Let us picture Jesus standing before the governor—and however "speechless" and mute he may have stood, there is not the least reason to doubt that he preserved his dignity of bearing and his loftiness of appearance until the end—and the "multitudes" of his admiring and grieving followers looking up at him. However disappointed they may have been in their hearts that he was not, after all, the invincible hero of their hopes, his plight and suffering could only have brought him nearer to them—no invincible hero, but a Jew and a man like you and me, and he was now prosecuted and stood in jeopardy because it was we who built him up as a king and a revolutionary and wanted him to make our dreams come true of deliverance from the Roman rule. Anybody who, in this kind of setting, arose and said, "I told you so before—I always knew that he was no hero but a mere pretender," would, I think, have run the risk of lynching. The chief priests, who anyway—or so the theory goes—collaborated with the enemy, would surely be identified with the Roman governor prosecuting or trying Jesus if they sought in any way to justify the prosecution or the trial. But they would never succeed in persuading the people that any Roman prosecution of a Jew was justified, and certainly not the particular prosecution of the man whom they knew and loved.

Attempts have been made to arrive at a solution of the question before us by inquiring first into the preliminary issue of who exactly were "the Jews" present at the trial: by first identifying them, we may be able to ascertain whether a change of mind and attitude had really occurred.

As far as concerns the chief priests, whose presence, with or without scribes and elders, is reported by all the Gospels (Mark 15:3; Matt. 27:12; Luke 23:4, 23; John 19:6, 15), we have shown that, under the procedure prevailing in the Roman governor's court, they could not have appeared as formal accusers,[43] by dismissing the wholly unrealistic theory that there could have been a previous agreement or understanding between them and the Roman governor to have Jesus tried and put to death. It would appear, then, that they would not have been present either as accusers or to watch over the due performance of any such pact. Failing these reasons, no sufficient ground for the attendance of the chief priests, and of the elders or scribes, can be, or has been, adduced. On the other hand, all priests were required for temple duties that morning: never were priests so busy and overworked as on feast days, and more particularly on the eve and day of Passover. It is just not to be thought that the "chief priests" would absent themselves from the temple on such a day to witness a trial before the Roman governor except under compulsion. It is only according to Luke (23:13) that Pilate "called together the chief priests and the rulers and the people," which suggests that they may have had no alternative but to appear before him; but the other Gospels indicate that the chief priests were there of their own accord. Maybe the chief priests had to be there from the point of view of the evangelists, for the simple reason that they had been depicted as the archenemies of Jesus, who had already conspired to put him to death (Mark 14:1; Matt. 26:3–4; John 11:47–53) and would be the only agents available to "move the people" to a clamorous demand that he be crucified. That the people had to be moved by somebody, and would not have engaged in any activity against Jesus without forceful instigation, seems to have been obvious even to the evangelists: so they provided the chief priests as the natural and most effective instruments.

If, however, it be assumed, as is reasonable, that "the people" would not let themselves be egged on so easily and so abruptly to turn against the man whom they loved, least of all by "chief priests" whom—if they were enemies of Jesus—they despised, and that no "chief priests" were in fact present, some scholars seek to unravel the mystery by maintaining that the Jews who assembled that morning in the Roman governor's court were people who did not know Jesus at all. These would mainly be idlers who had nothing better to do than to frequent criminal trials and found some justification for their existence in contributing their hysterics to the administration of Roman justice, their hysterics being designed, of course, to achieve the earliest possible presentation of the spectacle of another public execution.[44] There could be no worse disappointment for such onlookers than an acquittal; hence their incessant and impatient interjection, "Crucify him, crucify him!" In a recent scholarly book, a similar "mob" theory has been elaborated as follows:

It is in the realm of historical possibilities that a mob, incited by opponents of Jesus, might have gathered outside the praetorium and shouted slogans of vindictive bitterness and hate. A demonstration by the mob can be construed as having been staged so as to convince Pilate that the masses made no common cause with one who was accused of sedition. Such a demonstration would have been regarded as a declaration of loyalty to the Imperial Government—a tactical move engineered perhaps by the priestly rulers to prove that the population of Judaea was immune against being inveigled into insurrection by political agitation. A report of some such demonstration seems to have been at the disposal of the evangelists—and they seized upon it in their endeavour to exonerate the Roman governor. If the fact of a demonstration by the street-rabble is historically credible, its influence upon a person of Pilate's domineering disposition belongs to the province of apologetics.[45]

It is true that these "mob" theories may provide the answer to the—otherwise, it seems, unanswerable—question as to the swift change of mind of "the people." But they raise a new question at once: How could the Roman governor let himself be influenced by the "street-rabble?" Sitting on his high seat of judgment, he was doubtless able to see and distinguish what kind of people were present and loud-voiced in his court; and if, as a Roman judge, he would not hearken to the real *vox populi*,[46] the less would he heed uninformed crowds of sensation seekers. There is a substantial difference between the orderly expression of popular opinion and the hysterical cries of the masses: the one is normally reasoned and reasonable; the others are always instinctive and spontaneous. While a judge might listen to the one and let himself be influenced by it, he will always guard himself against mass outcry and disregard it. So if it was a mob that was present, it could not have fulfilled the task which the Gospels assign to it: its din and demands would, and could, have made no impression whatever on the governor. To relegate the Gospel reports of the mob's effect on Pilate to the realm of apologetics, as the last-quoted author does, is no better solution than to dismiss the whole "mob" theory from the start: if no mob could have done what the Gospels credit it with, the logical conclusion must be that there was none there at all.

On a point of historical "possibilities," moreover, it is hardly less probable that any "mob" would have been found ready to incite the Roman governor to put a Jew to death than that priests or others would be. It was not only patriotic identification with the Jew and dislike of the Roman that would deter Jewish "mobs" from accepting such an assignment, even for good money, but mainly the very justified fear of retribution by the zealots, who would not let treacherous conduct of that sort go unavenged.

The evangelists must themselves have felt that the story of Jewish crowds or "multitudes" taking vigorous part in the trial before Pilate needed some bolstering to be plausible: they provided it in the episode of Barabbas. We hear that "at that feast the governor was wont to release unto the people a prisoner, whom they would" (Matt. 27:15), and of course "the people" had to present themselves before Pilate to make their demand or choice. According to Mark, the governor released "unto them" at that feast "one prisoner, whomsoever they desired" (15:6). "And the multitude crying aloud began to desire him to do as he had ever done unto them" (15:8); for which purpose, if for no other, the "multitude" naturally had to be present. Luke has it that Pilate had "of necessity," that is, presumably, by virtue of some express law, to "release one unto them at the feast" (23:17), while John describes it as a Jewish custom, the governor telling the Jews, "ye have a custom, that I should release unto you one at the passover; will ye therefore that I release unto you the King of the Jews?" (18:39). It is the right of the "people" as such, established by custom, to pick out the prisoner to be granted the gubernatorial pardon, and that, if nothing else, accounts for the presence of the "multitudes" in the governor's palace, this morning of Passover or its eve.[47]

The Gospels are at one in telling that, faced by the governor with a choice between the pardon of Jesus and the pardon of one Barabbas, the people loudly clamored for the crucifixion of Jesus and the release of Barabbas. But while, according to Luke (23:18–21) and John (18:40), the people did so of their own accord, according to Mark (15:11) and Matthew (27:20) the "chief priests," with or without "elders," had to persuade and move the "multitude" to that fatal preference, the insinuation being that were it not for that instigation by the chief priests and elders, the people would, or might, have voted for the freeing of Jesus. That the chief priests, with or without elders, are depicted as resolved to have Jesus put to death is, to be sure, nothing new; but it has been said that they must have had a particular interest in seeing Barabbas pardoned, because he was an insurgent (Mark 15:7; Luke 23:19), a zealot, and a notable one at that (Matt. 27:16), and that his crucifixion by the Romans would decidedly have led to popular uprisings.[48] Even if that were so, we have it from the mouths of the chief priests themselves, as reported in the Gospels, that any harm which came to Jesus would likewise cause a public uproar (Matt. 26:5; Mark 14:2), and while the Gospels offer ample evidence of the popularity of Jesus, that of Barabbas is conjectural. The theory becomes all the more unlikely if, with certain scholars, we assume that Jesus himself had been associated with the zealots and, like Barabbas, stood before Pilate on a charge of insurrection.[49]

The Barabbas episode is introduced into the reports of the trial at a stage when Pilate had questioned Jesus and had already declared his opinion that he was innocent (Luke 23:14; John 18:38). And having recorded the custom of the paschal pardon, the Gospels create the impression that Pilate desired the people to ask for the release of Jesus rather than of Barabbas (Luke 23:20; John 18:39; Mark 15:9; Matt. 27:22), and at last gave in to the people unwillingly and against his better judgment (Mark 15:15).

The incongruities of this story are so many that no historicity can be attributed to it. They have all been pointed out before, but I may be allowed to stress these:

1. Pilate wanted to pardon Jesus, or so we are led to believe; why, then, did he not pardon him?

2. Assuming that there existed this *privilegium paschale* of the people to have a prisoner pardoned: why was the choice confined to either Jesus or Barabbas? What, for instance, of the two convicts who were crucified together with Jesus?

3. And supposing that such a privilege was, indeed, vested in the people: were the "multitudes" that happened to be present there its incumbents? Why they and not others? Whom did they represent? What were their qualifications and credentials?

4. Pilate had found no fault in Jesus: why did he not acquit him? Why should he have to pardon him? The natural course for him to take would have been to acquit and discharge Jesus, and then pardon Barabbas if he so desired, and set him free as well.

5. Barabbas was not only an insurgent and a zealot, but responsible also for a murder that had been committed in the course of the insurrection which he had led (Mark 15:7; Luke 23:19). We are to believe that this is the kind of man whom Pilate would have pardoned, even at the entreaty of the people. He was a "notable" resistance fighter "who had just proved how dangerous he could be. We may well ask how Pilate would have justified his conduct both to his Roman officers and officials, and, even more important, in his report to the emperor Tiberius."[50]

6. When the governor saw that the people were uncertain whose pardon to elect, and that the intervention and persuasion of chief priests and elders were required to help them make up their minds, he could very well have taken their hesitancy as a sufficient sign of their true and instinctive inclination, and pardoned Jesus on the strength of it.

7. It is not reasonable that the people would let themselves be "persuaded" by chief priests at all. We know beyond a peradventure that there was not much sympathy in the hearts of the people for the "chief priests" in power, and their political consciousness at that time was so highly developed that any advice tendered, let alone any suasion essayed, by the chief priests would in itself have been looked upon by them as most suspicious, especially if directed against one of themselves, and one so beloved as was Jesus. Neither persuaders nor persuaded were suited for the role in which they were cast.

8. No less improbable is it that such persuasion could have been exerted on the spot, in the presence of the governor. He would surely have interfered to stop such flagrant meddling. If it was the choice of the people that he wanted, he presumably did not want the choice of chief priests or elders, or a proclaiming by the people not of their own but of the chief priests' selection.

9. Except only from Gospel reports, we have no record or knowledge of the existence of any such *privilegium paschale*. Had such a custom existed, and, a fortiori, had there been any Roman or Jewish law establishing or recognizing it, we would somewhere have found a record of it or of its application in some preceding or subsequent year, and by some governor more susceptible to mercy than Pilate. It has been said that this was a personal gesture of Pilate alone, not precedented or emulated by any other governor, which he had introduced to ingratiate himself with the people.[51] But such a gesture would be entirely out of tune with all that we know about Pilate's character: nothing, indeed, would have been further from his leanings than a wish to find favor with anybody, least of all with the Jews; and furthermore, if such a gesture of propitiation had been practiced by Pilate of all governors, it could not have passed unnoticed and unchronicled. Josephus, who "was specially intent on recording all the privileges which the Roman government at various times had accorded to the Jews," nowhere mentions so remarkable a privilege and, while tallying all the misdeeds of Pilate, is silent over his extraordinary act of compassion: if Josephus had "by chance forgotten" to mention the privilege as such, it is inexplicable that "throughout his long circumstantial narrative" he does not register a single instance of a paschal pardon, if one had ever been granted.[52]

The fact is that there was no such custom, and the *privilegium paschale* is "nothing but a figment of the imagination."[53] Among the somewhat despairing attempts to find corroboration in Jewish sources for its existence, only one deserves allusion: "prisoners who were promised to be released from prison on Passover eve" are included among the persons for whom, though absent, the Passover sacrifice is offered,[54] and the fact that there is such a category of prisoners is said to prove that there was also a custom to free prisoners on Passover eves.[55] The reference to prisoners due for release does not, in fact, suggest that a general release took place on that particular day: it concerns only individual prisoners who happened to have been promised freedom on that day, and the rule is limited in terms to promises made by Jewish authorities, as promises made by other authorities could never be trusted.[56] In another context, we find mention of prisoners due for release in the interval between the first and last days of a feast:[57] this, too, is not to be taken as pointing to any customary discharge during that particular spell but just as the reasoning for the rule that what other people must do before the feast prisoners so discharged might do during it. While, then, there is no support for the view that Jewish law recognized any custom of freeing prisoners on the Passover, we do find in Roman law, at the time of the later emperors, the custom of pardoning criminals (*indulgentia criminum*) on the feast of Easter: a decree of the year 367 provides that "on account of the day of Easter which We celebrate in the depths of Our hearts," all prisoners shall be released except those "guilty of sacrilege against the Imperial Majesty, of crimes against the dead, sorcerers, magicians, adulterers, ravishers, or homicides";[58] a decree of the year 370 says that "the celebration of Easter demands that We pardon persons now tormented by the unhappy expectation of judicial investigation under torture and the fear of punishment. But consideration must be shown for the decrees of the ancients so that We may not rashly permit to escape punishment the crime of homicide, the disgrace of adultery, the outrage of high treason, the evil of magic, the treachery of sorcerers, and the violence of rape."[59] In 385 the decree already speaks of "the pardons which We are accustomed to grant . . . as soon as the day of Easter arrives."[60] It will be observed that these Easter pardons required legislation by the hand of the emperor, and that capital offenses, and, in particular, offenses of a treasonable character, did not enjoy the grace. In pre-Christian times, however, the festival would surely not have evoked imperial indulgences, although we hear of clemency and pardon vouchsafed on occasions of great imperial victory or triumph.[61] The later Easter remissions may echo the custom reported in the Gospels, but the Gospels had no valid tradition to rely upon in reporting it.

10. It was not the provincial governor, but solely the emperor in person, who had the power to grant pardons. For a governor

to usurp that imperial prerogative would be an offense under the *Lex Julia,* tantamount to treasonable excess of powers.[62] No governor in his senses would risk being called to account for exceeding his powers and being prosecuted for a treasonable felony, just to curry favor with the native population. Nor is there any evidence to sustain the theory that the emperor had especially authorized Pilate to grant annual pardons.[63]

It has been sought to identify Barabbas and detect a link between him and Jesus, and it has been speculated that the evangelists had access to some tradition of his existence which may have furnished the clue for their tale of the *privilegium paschale.*[64] These speculations seem irrelevant to our purpose: whether Barabbas existed or not, and whatever link there may have been between him and Jesus, the fact still is that there was no law or custom to release a prisoner on Passover, and that the people had no choice of a prisoner to be let go; if a Barabbas was indeed released by Pilate that day, the people had no hand in it—any more than they had in the conviction or crucifixion of Jesus. They were never confronted with the necessity to choose between Jesus and Barabbas, and hence made no choice; and just as they had no reason or occasion to present themselves at the governor's *praetorium* for the purpose of exercising any right or option in connection with any paschal pardon, so they had none to be there for any other object, the trial of Jesus included.

The figure of Pilate, as it appears in the Gospel reports of the Barabbas episode, deserves another glance. The evangelists would have their readers believe that a Roman magistrate, who was, as we know from Philo and Josephus, a remarkably tough character and notorious for his contempt of the Jews,[65]

acted as a veritable weakling, devoid alike of dignity, efficiency and spirit. Convinced that Jesus was the innocent victim of the malice of the chief priests, Pilate, instead of acting with the dignity and firmness that became a Roman magistrate, backed by military strength, and dismissing the charge against Jesus, is depicted as resorting to subterfuge. Thus, he is represented as clutching at the opportunity afforded by the custom as a means of saving Jesus, when he had himself the authority and the power to dismiss the charge. But that is not all. When the chief priests encounter his subterfuge by causing the crowd to demand the release of Barabbas, he is reduced to asking weakly of the crowd, "Then what shall I do with this man whom you call the King of the Jews?" (Mark 15:14). It is well to appreciate fully the incredible situation that Mark's statements imply. Here was a Roman governor, supported by an efficient military force, who, convinced of the innocence of a prisoner accused of sedition by the Jewish authorities, resorted to an otherwise unknown custom in order to do what he knew was right, i.e. release him. His subterfuge being frustrated, he then asks the crowd, which is apparently controlled by the chief priests, what he is to do with the prisoner. . . . If he had indeed resorted to the alleged custom to save Jesus, then Pilate must have been not only incredibly weak but also unbelievably stupid. For, if Jesus was the pro-Roman pacifist that Mark makes him out to be, surely Pilate must have realized what the decision would be, were the crowd given the choice between Jesus and a patriotic leader such as Barabbas, who had struck at their Roman oppressors. And then there is the question of the release of Barabbas. According to Mark, the outcome of Pilate's amazing conduct was that he condemned to death one whom he knew to be innocent, and released a popular resistance fighter, probably a zealot, who had just proved how dangerous he could be.[66]

I am content to be able to quote, and adopt, this analysis of a distinguished Christian theologian, Professor S. G. F. Brandon, who is not suspect of overstating his case.

Not only do the evangelists fail to show any intelligible reason why Pilate should have been so very much interested to save Jesus, except perhaps for the dream of Pilate's wife, reported in Matthew, to which we shall revert, but on top of that, while depicting him as a good-natured and merciful man, who would not be a partner to any harm done to the guiltless Jesus, they all have to end the story with Pilate "delivering" Jesus for crucifixion without any ostensible reason shown for his unforeseen change of heart. Their tendentious point of view impelled them so to construct it that blame for the crucifixion of Jesus was shifted from the shoulders of the Roman governor squarely onto the shoulders of the Jews. But the tradition that Jesus was, in fact, tried and sentenced by Pilate and crucified by Roman authorities was too solidly entrenched to be set aside and substituted by a simple tale of a trial and execution by the Sanhedrin. So some account had to be given of what had taken place at the notorious trial before Pilate, but processed in such a manner that Pilate would appear blameless of the upshot. We said that the first step in the processing was to assign the Jews, whoever they might be, an active and decisive part in the trial, if not as accusers, then as holders of the *privilegium paschale,* or if not in any official capacity, then at least as the noisy and clamorous multitude expressing the *vox populi:* and we have shown that not only could they not have performed any of the assignments, but, in all probability, not one of them could even have been present.

We must now inquire into what actually did happen at the trial, and, to that end, will start from the premise that Pilate, the judge, was neither particularly good-natured nor particularly ill-disposed, that he was neither in favor of Jesus nor in any way biased against him. If this premise gives overmuch credit to the Pilate of whose real character, as will be remembered, we have rather devastating testimony, it would, nevertheless, be only fair to assume that even a cruel and usually choleric man would, in his exercise of judicial functions, be able to check and restrain himself. And as against the testimony of the historians, we still have the glorification of Pilate by the evangelists, to which, in all the proven circumstances, no more kindly concession can be made than to suppose that he performed his duty as judge properly and efficiently and would not be a respecter of persons but would proceed and conduct himself in accordance with due law and procedure.

All the Gospels are agreed that the proceedings before Pilate opened with the governor addressing to Jesus the question, "Art thou the King of Jews?" (Matt. 27:11; Mark 15:2; Luke 23:3; John 18:33) . This would suggest that it was on that specific charge that Jesus was to stand trial: the absence of a report of any formal charge does not mean that none was preferred. The arrest of Jesus by a Roman cohort the night before presupposes that a charge had been framed, and the availability of the Roman governor early in the morning to hold trial can be explained only if the charge was known beforehand. The first question addressed by the court to the accused at the opening of the trial, if it did not refer to mere formalities, would naturally bear some relevance to the charge preferred against him, and the conclusion is that Jesus was charged before the Roman governor with pretending to be king of the Jews without being appointed or recognized as such by the emperor.

Conclusive proof that Jesus was charged on that count is furnished by the inscription of the words *Rex Judaeorum*—King of the Jews—on the cross whereon he was crucified. All the Gospels testify to this inscription (Mark 15:26; Matt. 27:37; Luke 23:38; John 19:19), if with slight variations. It was the law in Rome that in public executions the offense of which the convict had been found guilty was to be inscribed on the cross, so that all spectators would be aware of the lot of its perpetrator: *titulus qui causam poenae indicat*, a title indicating the cause of punishment.[67] In the Gospel According to John, the chief priests are reported to have begged Pilate, "Write not, The King of the Jews; but that he said, I am King of the Jews" (19:21), that is, that the offense of which Jesus was convicted was not that he actually was a king of the Jews, but only that he claimed to be. Pilate's reported refusal to change the wording—"What I have written I have written" (19:22) —could be interpreted theologically as an implied recognition by Pilate of the truth of Jesus' claim, but, interpreted literally, simply means that the inscription sufficed as it stood. We also find similar forms of public announcement of the *causa poenae* when the punishment was not death, for instance, when the hands of a thief had been cut off and he was made to go about wearing an explanatory placard;[68] and we see the *titulus* similarly displayed when a man accused of practicing Christianity was obliged to circle the amphitheater, in which the governor was to hold his court, with a placard upon him proclaiming, "This is Attalus the Christian."[69] In every instance, the inscription pointed to the charge on which the man had been, or was to be, tried, and it had to suffice to convey to the onlookers what the offense was for which he had been, or was about to be, punished.

Under Roman law, a claim to be king of a province under Roman rule was tantamount to insurrection and high treason: it was, by the *Lex Julia maiestatis* originally enacted by Caesar in 46 B.C. and re-enacted by Augustus in 8 B.C., a capital offense known as *crimen laesae maiestatis*,[70] the crime of causing injury to the majesty of the emperor. This injury comprised not only treason proper but also all insurrections and uprisings against Roman rule, desertion from Roman forces, usurpation of powers reserved to the emperor or his nominees, and all acts calculated to preju-

dice the security of Rome or of the emperor or of Roman govern-
ments in the provinces.[71] The definition of the offense, if indeed
it can be called a "definition," is so wide as to include practically everything that the emperor or a governor might consider
harmful to the interests of Rome or of himself: we find even senators and consuls beheaded for slight contempts of the emperor or
jokes about him, and a man was once executed because on election day a herald had inadvertently described him as emperor-
elect instead of consul-elect.[72] Because it was so all-embracing,
it became customary for prosecutors, for the sake of precaution, to
add to other charges of criminal conduct one of *laesa maiestas,*
which could in any event be established easily: thus the proconsul
of Crete was charged with embezzlement, but a charge of a treasonable offense was superadded, being "in those days supplementary to all indictments";[73] and an offense as "widespread between
men and women" as adultery was framed as treasonable so as to
make it capital.[74] Persons suspected of a treasonable offense
could be tortured until or unless they admitted the crime,[75] a
further good reason why suspects on some other ground were also
charged with something treasonable.[76] The crime of *laesa
maiestas* was, in fact, devoid of any legal limitation and did not
lend itself to strict definition.[77] The generally accepted formula
was that the *Lex Julia maiestatis* took in both the offenses expressly mentioned in it and such others as would demand severe
punishment "in order to avenge lawlessness,"[78] a formula omi-
nously reminiscent of penal laws in certain totalitarian systems
today.

It was in the emperor's power, and in his only, to nominate
any "king of the Jews." He had done so before, in the case of
Herod, and would do so again, in the case of Agrippa. But nomination save by the emperor, including self-nomination, would
amount not only to usurpation of the imperial powers but also
to a denial of the emperor's sovereignty, quite apart from the potential insurrection and defection that it implied. Manifestly, any
such rebelliousness called for condign punishment "in order to
avenge lawlessness," meaning, to uphold Roman rule and authority. For the commission and completion of the offense, it
would not matter whether the royal pretender acted in isolation
or already had followers among the people; but the offense would

be graver, and he must be regarded as much more of a threat, if he had succeeded in raising active support. Jesus' royal reception upon his arrival in Jerusalem, the great crowds of enthusiastic Jews surrounding him always—these things cannot have been hidden from Pilate, so that, in the governor's eyes, the kingly pretensions of Jesus were not a matter lightly to be dismissed.

There is yet another aspect of the *Lex Julia* to be observed: among the offenses which it lists is that of the failure of magistrates or judges, including provincial governors, to exercise their jurisdiction: the emperor's mandate to administer justice was regarded as binding them, too, to do so in every case that came before them, and to decline or neglect to try criminals, for instance, would signify contempt of the emperor's command.[79] When a man was suspect of actual treason or insurrection against the emperor, or of attempting or making overt preparations for it, it would have been equally treasonable of the governor not to prosecute, try, and punish him according to law: the governor was not only competent to try him but under obligation to. It is true that a Roman citizen accused of a capital offense was entitled to demur to trial by the governor and to ask to be heard by the emperor in Rome: thus Paul claimed to be judged "at Caesar's judgment seat" (Acts 25:10) as a Roman citizen (22:25–26), and though the governor might have acquitted him (26:32), he was duly sent to Rome (27:1). But when the accused was a native like Jesus, or a Roman citizen who did not claim his privilege of trial in Rome, the governor had no choice or discretion: if a charge under the *Lex Julia* had been preferred, he must proceed with the trial.

For the purpose of exercising their capital jurisdiction, the governors of the provinces were vested with the *ius gladii*, the right of the sword, that is, the imperial right to pass and carry out capital sentences.[80] There is no evidence for Mommsen's assertion that the governors of Judaea, unlike the generality of provincial governors, had no *ius gladii*:[81] not only the trial of Jesus but many other trials by governors reported in the New Testament and by Josephus discount it. The *ius gladii* was, in fact, inherent in the governor's terms of appointment, and there was no need to confer it expressly: it is the right to govern, where necessary, by force, and, as we noted, the governor in effect wielded his powers of government even in the exercise of his criminal jurisdiction. This equally explains the rule that the *ius gladii* is personal to the governor and cannot be delegated by him to anybody else, including local courts,[82] so much so that any purported delegation would in itself, as an unauthorized conferment of imperial powers, be treasonable.[83]

In recapitulation: the law was that when a Jew, not being a Roman citizen, is charged with contempt of the emperor or other treasonable offense under Roman law, he must be tried by the Roman governor; and the charge of claiming to be king of the Jews, without seeking or obtaining the prior fiat or approval of the emperor, is one such treasonable offense. When a man stands trial on a charge of that kind, three ways are open to the governor: he can find him guilty and sentence him *(condemnatio)*; he can find him not guilty and acquit him *(absolutio)*; or he can find the case not proven and ask that further evidence be adduced *(ampliatio)*.[84] We know that he could, and would, resort to torture to extract a confession,[85] even when the testimony of witnesses was available; we shall discuss this point in greater detail below. Only in one case was neither torture nor testimony required, namely, when the accused confessed, pleaded guilty, of his own accord.[86]

To the governor's question, "Art thou the King of the Jews?," Jesus replied, "Thou sayest it" (Mark 15:2; Matt. 27:11; Luke 23:3; John 18:37). Does this amount in law to a plea of guilty? Some scholars think that it merely implied a refusal by Jesus to answer to the charge,[87] amounting to neither a confession nor a denial. Others hold that it implied a denial; in other words, Jesus told the governor, *you* say that I am king of the Jews, but I do not say so at all;[88] this seems to be borne out by the governor's instant reaction, if only according to the Gospel of Luke: having heard the reply, "Thou sayest it," Pilate found "no fault in this man" (23:4).

Doubtless Jesus might have been less equivocal, and it is suggested that he advisedly chose to be vague—or the evangelists advisedly made his answer vague—so as to enhance the mystery of his mission.[89] At all events, on the face of it the answer appears not only to lack denial, but even to convey an admission in very polite and reverent syllables. The phrase "you said it," or "as you say," is not unknown even in modern speech as a mode of affirmation; and in the Aramaic and Hebrew of those times it was in regular and widespread use,[90] more especially as an acquiescent reply to embarrassing questions put by persons in authority.

Had Jesus desired to deny the charge, nothing would have been easier for him than to return Pilate a clear, unambiguous no: I am not king of the Jews, nor did I ever pretend to be. But Jesus did not wish to deny it at all: in his eyes, and on his lips, that must mean disavowal of a mission in which he firmly and sincerely believed. It is most significant that, according to John, Jesus did not content himself with the formal "Thou sayest it," but went on at once to say that his kingdom was not of this world: "if my kingdom were of this world, then would my servants fight, that I should not be delivered to the Jews: but now is my kingdom not from hence. . . . Thou sayest that I am a king. To this end was I born, and for this cause came I into the world, that I should bear witness unto the truth" (18:36–37). While the words here put into the mouth of Jesus clearly date from the much later period in which the Fourth Gospel was written, it is highly probable, all the same, that Jesus did add a word of explanation to his admission of kingship: his kingdom was not of this world, and therefore he was not the sort of king that Pilate might imagine. If he did, it becomes instantly plausible that he pleaded guilty: he was king of the Jews, not in a politico-secular but only in a theologico-moral sense, and the heavenly kingdom to which he laid claim was not identical with, nor in any immediate and practical sense dangerous to, the political kingdoms on earth, the Roman empire included. As one legal writer has pointed out, his reply was in the nature of "confession and avoidance": It is true that, as you say, I am king of the Jews, but the meaning which you attach to "kingdom" has nothing in common with mine; I am not a king in the sense that your emperor is, but a king *sui generis*, and my kingdom is beyond anything of which your laws would take cognizance.[91] On the assumption that Jesus did, indeed, take this stand, let us see how Pilate could have reacted.

In Roman thinking, as contrasted with Jewish, there was no clear distinction between secular and divine kingdoms: while the Jews set as king over them "one from among their brethren," whose heart may not be "lifted up above his brethren" and who is subject to all God's laws and commandments as is every other citizen (Deut. 17:15–20), the Roman king and emperor becomes, ex officio so to speak, God himself. It is not that, for their deification, the emperors needed any divine origin or revelation or authorization by deities other than themselves: they were experts at self-deification, and for that pretentious accolade could rely on precedents going back to Julius Caesar. Practically speaking, the purpose of deification was to secure absolute submission and obedience and the popular veneration that would normally be accorded only to the gods. Throughout the great law codes, emperors are still referred to, or refer to themselves, as "immortals," their palaces and bedchambers are spoken of as "sacred," their acts of legislation and codification as "consecrations" by their "most sacred names."[92] Not only offenses directed at their persons or at their rule and sovereignty, but also those against their private property, were classified as *sacrilegia*;[93] people who spoke in derision of the emperor were dubbed "irreligious,"[94] and to slander him was decried as an impiety.[95] Yet real sacrilege, such as the slandering of the gods, was not a punishable offense: the gods could be trusted to deal adequately with their own slanderers unaided.[96] The laws enacted by the emperors were their weapons for the vindication of their own divinity. A claim by any mortal within the empire to a competitive, and a fortiori an exclusive, divine title, could not be entertained or suffered by the emperor: he was the divine ruler to the exclusion of all others.

While, therefore, from the viewpoint of Jesus' Jewish line of thought, the messianic implications in his claim to a heavenly kingdom were perfectly legitimate, by the yardstick of Pilate's Roman concepts his claim to divine backing for his kingdom, and a divine mission transcending all earthly limitations, must have made matters much worse: here was a man who pretended not only to be king of a handful of people in a remote province, which was troublesome enough as a potential source of unrest and insurrection; a man who, for his rule, needed no "servants" to fight for and protect him, or any identifiable people to govern; his was *the* kingdom of heaven, and "every one that is of the truth heareth" his voice (John 18:37); there was no other "true" kingdom of heaven but this; his was world-wide and universal. In this arrogation of a monopoly of divine truth and of the "kingdom" representing and enforcing it was implicit a denial of the true divinity of any other kingdom, including that of the Roman emperor, which would not last a moment were it not for the imperial "servants," the armed forces of Rome, fighting for and protecting it. "Everybody that is of the truth" hears my voice, not the emperor's. Pretensions such as that smack of treason all the graver by not being confined either politically or geographically, and by professing to be divinely inspired and divinely enjoined.

According to John, when Pilate heard Jesus say that his kingdom was not of this world, he asked him a second time, "Art thou a king then?" (18:37), which seems to show that Pilate himself entertained doubts whether, in speaking of "kings," both understood the term in the same sense. If Jesus pretended to some transcendental and mysterious mission, limited to purely ideological or theological theories and exercises, maybe what he called his "kingdom" was really of no concern to the governor. To make sure what it was, he put his question again: was it, indeed, a "king" in the political connotation of the word that Jesus claimed to be? And Jesus answered, "Thou sayest that I am a king" (*ibid.*), not just "Thou sayest it," but "Thou sayest rightly that what I am is really a king," though, as I said before, my kingdom is not of this world. Pilate had now got the affirmation that he had asked for, and the emphasis placed by the evangelist on the addition of the words "that I am a king" is index that the phrase "Thou sayest it," employed by the previous Gospels, had always been understood to convey an affirmation.

By admitting that he was king of the Jews, Jesus had effectively pleaded guilty to the charge of being one: there was no least doubt that his kingship, whatever it was, had not been authorized by the emperor. The admission would have sufficed in law to convict him there and then; but the Gospels are unanimous in reporting that Pilate did nothing of the sort. Not only are the Jews—chief priests, elders, multitudes, all the people—reintroduced to perform their function of inducing Pilate, against his better judgment, to have Jesus crucified, but two of the Gospels interrupt the narrative of the trial to interpolate extraneous episodes—one of Pilate's wife telling him her last night's dream, another of the trial being referred to Herod Antippas. Let us first consider these interludes.

Matthew reports that when Pilate "was set down on the judgment seat, his wife sent unto him, saying, Have thou nothing to do with that just man: for I have suffered many things this day in a dream because of him" (27:19). While the dream won her a posthumous canonization, it does not appear to have made an impression upon her husband. It is hard to believe that the wife of the governor would dare to descend upon him in the midst of a court session: the report that "his wife sent unto him" suggests that the dream was communicated to him by a messenger. But if the evangelist goes out of his way to have dream and warning conveyed to the governor during the trial, we would expect that it would turn out to have been for a specific purpose. The governor himself is already represented as wishful to have Jesus acquitted or pardoned; the dream and warning of his wife could only have fortified him in his feeling of Jesus' innocence. But, so far from taking heed, he gives the "multitude" a choice between Jesus and Barabbas, of which the upshot is realization that he can "prevail nothing" (27:24). The belief in dreams as unmistakable media of celestial revelations and forebodings was so common and natural in those days as to invest them with an ominous reality, and nobody not unbalanced would lightly dismiss a dream as nonsense. His wife's dream had been urgently delivered to him, with not only its stern warning not to have anything "to do with this just man," but also a confirmation of his own inclinations: how, in all conscience, could Pilate not react straightway and set Jesus free?

It may be assumed that he was no less amenable to the impact of portentious dream than his contemporaries, and, moreover, would not casually disregard a dream of his wife's only to be reproached over and over again, in the way of marital relations, if and when it came true. No explanation is offered by the evangelist for Pilate's flouting of the dream; we are not even told whether, and how, he reacted when told of it. It has been suggested that his wife may have told it to him in the morning, before he went into court, and that it was the true cause, from the very start of the trial, of his being so favorably disposed toward Jesus; but if that was what happened, the evangelist would presumably have placed the story before the commencement of the trial and not in the middle of it. Her communicating the dream to her husband only after the trial had begun is explained by some scholars as owing to her recognizing the prisoner in the dock as the man whom she saw in her dream: "no doubt she was watching the proceedings from some convenient part of the building";[97] but if she did watch, and did actively interfere, it is difficult to understand why she acquiesced when her communication patently failed to impress the governor.

The real reason why the story of the dream was interposed by the evangelist was suggested, more than a century ago, by David Friedrich Strauss: the Romans of that time attached so great an importance to dreams that no tale was considered complete without a dream augury in it: "Who would not, reading of the warning dream of Claudia Procula—the legendary name of Pilate's wife—be reminded of the dream of Calpurnia, the wife of Caesar, in the night before his assassination, and her warning to him not to leave the house that day; and who would not be able to form his own judgment of the Gospel story, taking into account the common vogue and taste of the time on the one hand, and the evangelist's personal predilection for imaginative dreams, apparent already from his childhood accounts, on the other?"[98] That there was some "personal predilection" on the part of the author of the Gospel According to Matthew appears to be confirmed by the omission of the whole dream interlude from the later Gospels of Luke and John and by the absence of anything of the kind from the prior Marcan version. In any case, and whether or not Pilate's wife had dreamed that night and had communicated her dream to her husband, and whatever it may have been, the episode, for our purposes, is irrelevant, for even according to Matthew it in no way affected the course or outcome of the trial.

There may be some connection between the story of the dream and the tale, also found only in the Gospel According to Matthew, that Pilate "took water, and washed his hands before the multitude, saying, I am innocent of the blood of this just person: see ye to it" (27:24). We shall treat this more fully later;[99] enough here to say that if his wife's dream had convinced Pilate that Jesus was a "just" man and innocent of the charges laid against him, he may have desired to make peace with the gods by solemnly declaring his own innocence and placing the whole burden of responsibility on Jewish shoulders. Even though, under Roman law, he may have had to convict Jesus on his plea of guilty, in the eyes of the gods, who had laws of their own, that technical guilt by mortal standards might not have affected Jesus' being, and continuing to be, a "just" man; so, to please everybody, Pilate proceeded according to formal law, convicting and sentencing Jesus while relieving himself of any moral responsibility at the same time. In this way, perhaps, we can explain the absence from the Gospel account of any reaction by Pilate to his wife's dream and his failure to heed her warning, as well as the ceremony reported of taking water and washing hands, an obvious ritual in all likelihood intended to placate the gods.

The second episode to be considered is recounted only in the Gospel According to Luke. We are told that when Pilate had heard that Jesus was a Galilean, he concluded that he "belonged unto Herod's jurisdiction"; and since Herod "himself also was at Jerusalem at that time," he sent him to Herod for trial (23:7). Herod Antippas was "tetrarch" of Galilee, and while his official residence was Tiberias, he would—like all Jews—make pilgrimages to Jerusalem thrice in the year, once at Passover. "And when Herod saw Jesus, he was exceeding glad: for he was desirous to see him of a long season, because he had heard many things of him; and he hoped to have seen some miracle done by him. Then he questioned with him in many words; but he answered him nothing. And the chief priests and scribes stood and vehemently accused him. And Herod with his men of war set him at nought, and mocked him, and arrayed him in a gorgeous robe, and sent him again to Pilate" (23:8–11). The evangelist records, in a postscript, that from that "same day Pilate and Herod were made friends together: for before they were at enmity between themselves" (23:12); but we are left in the dark as to the cause of their enmity and what it was that suddenly made them "friends together."

To start with, there is plain difficulty with regard to the timing. Luke reports that the meeting of the council of the Jews took place only "as soon as it was day" (22:66). If we allow an hour for the meeting, and half an hour for bringing Jesus from the high priest's house to the *praetorium,* Pilate could have commenced his trial only half an hour before the third hour. We are told that "it was about the sixth hour," when Jesus had already been on the cross for some time, certainly for several hours, that he died (23:44–46). In the brief space available, it would be hard enough to account for the proceedings which took place, even according to Luke, before Pilate himself; also to squeeze into it the proceedings before Herod seems impossible, even on the altogether unfounded assumption that Herod resided in one and the same palace in Jerusalem with Pilate, and that no time was lost in transporting Jesus to and fro.

Indeed, many scholars deny the historicity of Luke's account of proceedings before Herod,[100] and there are good reasons to doubt the tradition, apart from the difficulty of timing.

Pilate, we recall, sent Jesus to Herod only after himself declaring that he had found "no fault in this man" (23:4). The impression is created that Pilate had acquitted Jesus, but had given in to the clamor of the multitude in view of the lingering possibility that, while innocent of any offense under Roman law, he might be guilty of an offense whereof the Jewish tetrarch could take cognizance. We have seen that there could not, lawfully, be any delegation of the governor's powers inherent in the *ius gladii* to a tetrarch or to anybody else,[101] and in view of the reported enmity between Pilate and Herod, it is the reverse of likely that Pilate would have conferred any gubernatorial jurisdiction on Herod. But, by Roman grant, a tetrarch exercised capital—and, indeed, unlimited—jurisdiction within the province under his rule, in Herod's case, Galilee, not in respect of matters justiciable by Roman emperor or governor, but in respect of all others. While this jurisdiction flowed from Roman law, from the title conferred by the emperor, it did not have to, and could hardly, be exercised in accordance with that law: in fact, it did not matter to the Romans what substantive law their puppet kings applied, or whether they exercised their jurisdiction in person or appointed law courts for the purpose. Pilate's acquittal of Jesus would not, therefore, preclude the tetrarch's convicting him and putting him to death, if not for the offense of which he had just been acquitted, then for any other. And by surrendering Jesus to Herod, Pilate would attain two ends at once: he would give in to the Jews, not by convicting Jesus against his better judgment, but—with good riddance to them and their importuning—by sending them and Jesus on to Herod: let Herod see whether there was any-thing wrong with Jesus.

It is, in this connection, of moment that, while the other Gos-pels do not specify the "accusations" brought against Jesus by chief priests and elders, Luke does: first, they accuse him of "per-verting the nation, and forbidding to give tribute to Caesar, say-ing that he himself is Christ a King" (23:2) ; second, that "He stirreth up the people, teaching throughout all Jewry, beginning from Galilee to this place" (23:5). The two first charges osten-sibly refer to offenses under Roman law: forbidding to give tribute to the emperor and pretending to be a king himself would be treasonable under the *Lex Julia*. The third, of "teaching throughout all Jewry," might, however, be regarded, prima facie, as an offense whereof the Jewish rather than the Roman authori-ties should take cognizance. Without it, Pilate would lack cause to transfer the case to Herod, and so it provides a convenient way out of the whole affair. It may be noted, parenthetically, that neither before Pilate nor before Herod do we hear any charge preferred corresponding to those allegedly brought against Jesus before the council of the Jews that morning, namely, that he was the Son of God (22:70). While this is easily explained as far as the trial before Pilate is concerned, since the pretension to divine origin without political implications would be an offense for the Jewish religious authorities to deal with,[102] and not one triable under Roman law, still, when they all appeared before Herod, the Jew, there was no slightest reason why they should not have explained to him, in so many words, that Jesus had already stood that morning before the Sanhedrin, had pretended to be the Son of God, and been found guilty "of his own mouth" (22:71). Had they done so, they could have impressed upon Herod that, Pilate having referred the whole case to him, it was now for him to execute a judgment already handed down by the most authorita-tive Jewish tribunal. But they just "stood and vehemently accused him" (23:10), and we know not of what.

We hear that Herod had been desirous to see Jesus for a long time (23:8). Could it be that Pilate knew that? Perhaps he thought that by delivering Jesus into his hands he could do Herod a service which would eventually be acknowledged favorably by

the emperor, of whose intimate relations with Herod we have
some evidence;[103] and are we not informed by the evangelist
that, by this sending over of Jesus, the enmity between Pilate and
Herod was ended and they became friends (23:12)? But, in the
first place, Herod did no harm to Jesus, but returned him to
Pilate, which he is unlikely to have done if he had really been
interested in getting hold of Jesus; it was certainly not just to
mock him and array him in gorgeous robes that Herod wanted
him so urgently; and by returning him to Pilate unscathed, the
tetrarch indubitably disappointed the "chief priests and scribes."
In the second place, Pilate knew of the friendship between Herod
and the emperor, and of the enmity between Herod and himself:
by transferring the trial of a case of *laesa maiestas* to him, Pilate
would have laid himself open to being denounced by Herod to the
emperor, and why should he take that risk?[104]

It would appear, therefore, that the story of the transfer of the
trial to Herod was an intrusion by Luke, the same Luke who afterward lets all "the kings of the earth" stand up and "rulers" gather
together against Christ: "for, of a truth, against thy holy child
Jesus, whom thou hast anointed, both Herod, and Pontius Pilate,
with the Gentiles, and the people of Israel, were gathered together" (Acts 4:26–27). We already know that, for the evangelists,
Pontius Pilate was less than enough to bear responsibility for
Jesus' death; for Luke, or his contemporaries or the public for
whom he wrote, it seems that the Jews were not adequate either:
they had to be joined by "the Gentiles," and the Gentile ruler
had to be joined by the Jewish king, so that it could be said that
all the world stood up against Jesus. The "Gentiles" may have
been the Roman soldiers who, we are told, mocked Jesus (Luke
23:36); and the role ascribed to Herod was also in the main confined to mocking (23:11): it could be a somewhat passive role,
because the burden of blameworthiness would anyway have to rest
on the Jews, not on the Romans or their puppets. Thus it was that
Herod could have Jesus returned to Pilate, and the trial before
Pilate could continue, as if no interlude with Herod had happened at all: it is true that Pilate was apparently told that Herod
had found no fault in Jesus (23:15), but, instead of accepting
that finding as sufficient and welcome cause to acquit and dis-

charge Jesus, as he himself had earlier intended to do, he again "called together the chief priests and the rulers and the people" and started the trial all over again (23:13).

Since the Herodian interlude changed neither the course nor the outcome of the trial before Pilate, we might regard it as for our purposes immaterial, like the interlude of the dream of Pilate's wife. But we have observed, among the charges which Luke describes as put forward by the chief priests and the people, one that, on the face of it, seemed to be within the cognizance and jurisdiction of the Jewish tetrarch rather than the Roman governor; and the inference is that when "the chief priests and scribes stood and vehemently accused him" before Herod (Luke 23:10), Jesus was charged with this Jewish offense rather than with the Roman ones. Still, Jesus answered nothing (23:9), presumably to display his contempt for Herod, his rejection of him and of his judicial competence. When, earlier in the morning, he was questioned by the council of the chief priests and scribes, that is, by the Sanhedrin, he had made reply (22:67-70), which was, in pointed contrast, a recognition of its right to judge him. But having stood mute before Herod, and the charges against him having not been proven either by his own confession or by independent evidence, Jesus could scarcely have been found guilty by Herod of any offense. Now it must not be assumed that such judicial considerations would have prevented Herod from having Jesus put to death or thrown in jail: we are told that when John the Baptist reproached Herod for having married his brother's wife, "he shut up John in prison" (3:20), and there is no mention that John was first duly tried and convicted. The reason why Herod desired so much to see Jesus was, it now transpires, that "he was perplexed, because that it was said of some, that John was risen from the dead; and of some, that Elias had appeared; and of others, that one of the old prophets was risen again. And Herod said, John have I beheaded: but who is this, of whom I hear such things? And he desired to see him" (9:7-9). At long last, Herod—or so we are told—had got this man Jesus in his grasp: not only had the Roman governor personally sent him and delivered him into his jurisdiction to do with him as he thought fit, but "the chief priests and scribes" were vehement in indicting him and dissociating themselves from him. What could have been simpler for the tetrarch, or more natural, than to seize this wonderful opportunity for getting rid of this possible reincarnation of the man whom he had beheaded? He needed no formal proof of guilt, no formal conviction or sentence: he could do to Jesus as he had done to John, with the difference that the killing of John must have stirred popular aversion, while the killing of Jesus would, it seemed, meet with the approval of "the chief priests and scribes" and their followers. But, instead, Herod "arrayed him in a gorgeous robe, and sent him again to Pilate"! Not to a Pilate of whom Herod could be sure that he would eventually convict and crucify Jesus, for Jesus had been sent to him in the first place precisely because Pilate had found no fault in him, and Herod maybe would, but to a Pilate who had already decided that the case was within Herod's jurisdiction, so that, by sending Jesus back to him, Herod would disobey Pilate's order!

The charges specified in Luke, of which Pilate would take cognizance, were, first, that Jesus perverted the nation and forbade the giving of tribute to Caesar, and, second, that he pretended to be king. Pilate chose the second and asked Jesus only, "Art thou the King of the Jews?" (23:3), presumably on the view that if he admitted this graver indictment, the minor one might be taken as merged in it. There were, according to Luke, other charges which Pilate may have held to be within Herod's jurisdiction; but these must have fallen away when Herod sent Jesus back without finding "fault" in him. The only charge which Jesus answered affirmatively was of his kingship of the Jews; and it was on that charge alone that he could be convicted.

It is true that we also find explicit charges in the Gospel According to John; but there they are not brought forward at the outset of the trial, but only in the course of the proceedings; they are not placed before the accused, that he may plead thereto, or before the court as the subject matter of evidence to be tendered and arguments to be heard in due process; they are rather presented by way of warnings and threats addressed to the governor, lest he acquit Jesus and discharge him. Thus Pilate is said to have been "the more afraid" when he heard the Jews say that Jesus had "made himself the Son of God" (19:7–8); and his "fear" appears to have become final and conclusive when "the Jews cried out, saying, If thou let this man go, thou art not Caesar's friend:

whosoever maketh himself a king speaketh against Caesar"
(19:12). While, for the reasons which we have given, it is out of
the question that "the Jews" attended the trial before Pilate
or, if they did, would have dared to speak to Pilate as they are
here reported as doing, it may well be that the considerations
which the evangelist puts into the mouth of the Jews, though not
coming from them at all, were in the mind of the governor. It is
true that "whosoever maketh himself a king speaketh against
Caesar," and true that Caesar would hardly understand, or forgive, a governor who would let an accused man go free after he
had expressly pleaded guilty to "speaking against Caesar." In the
circumstances, Pilate had no alternative but to convict Jesus,
as he must himself readily have seen. The Roman public, for
whom the Fourth Gospel was written, fully comprehended that
such royal presumptions, amounting to contempt of the emperor,
could not go unpunished: Pilate's action in convicting and crucifying Jesus would, therefore, be promptly understood; but since
the moral guilt had to be thrust unarguably upon the Jews, it had
to be the Jews who, by argument or warning, brought home to
Pilate the necessity of a conviction. That, over and above his
royal pretensions, the Jews also advised Pilate of the heavenly
pretensions of Jesus only made matters worse and the offense
much graver and more reprehensible still.[105]

But since Pilate had, in effect, no option save to convict Jesus,
and Roman readers familiar with Caesarean sensitivity must have
known that perfectly well, the author of the Gospel According
to John resorts to a desperate expedient to make the Jews blame-
worthy for the death of Jesus after all. Pilate is said to have sat
on the judgment seat, as if preparing to deliver final judgment
(19:13); he had Jesus brought forth, "and he saith unto the Jews,
Behold your King!" (19:14). When they, again, exclaimed,
"Away with him, away with him, crucify him!," Pilate first asked,
"Shall I crucify your King?," and, when he had their answer, "We
have no king but Caesar" (19:15), delivered Jesus "unto them
to be crucified. And they took Jesus, and led him away" (19:16).
In other words: Pilate did not condemn Jesus, or order him to be
crucified; he delivered him to the tumultuous Jews, for them to
crucify him. The majesty of the emperor was vindicated: Jesus
would, in due course, be executed, but no Roman hand would

have shed his blood; the wise and discerning governor could be represented, to later generations of Romans, as having pierced the secret of Jesus' divinity or as having, from first to last, recognized his innocence; and that, notwithstanding, Jesus was crucified in the end was due not to any act or decision of the governor, but solely to the cruelty and blindness and obduracy of the Jews. This might have been a story plausible and acceptable to Roman readers, for while they naturally knew that the Romans executed alien criminals by crucifixion, they need not have known, and most probably did not know, that the Jews never executed anybody by crucifixion, and so could have taken the story at face value. There would still be the serious flaw that it was, after all, by decision of the Roman governor that Jesus was delivered to the Jews: he could have saved Jesus by refusing to hand him over to his persecutors. Indeed, if Pilate had wished to spare Jesus, he could have jailed him for the time being; he could have acquitted him; or he could have transferred his trial to the emperor at Rome, in that way, moreover, saving the face of the affronted emperor. He chose none of these courses, but to surrender Jesus to the Jews, knowing full well what his fate would then be, and to represent him, in these circumstances, as innocent of shedding Jesus' blood is more than human ingenuity could devise. That the author of the Gospel of John, as distinct from his readers, knew the truth that Jesus could have been crucified only by the Romans and not by the Jews is clear from the report that it was "the soldiers" who carried out the crucifixion (19:23), an inconsistency which a more attentive editor might have avoided.

In Luke it is reported that when "the chief priests and the rulers and the people" had made their choice of Barabbas to be released and Jesus to be crucified (23:21–23), "Pilate gave sentence that it should be as they required" (23:24), and having let Barabbas go, "he delivered Jesus to their will" (23:25). This statement is not as explicit as that in John to the effect that he delivered Jesus to the Jews "to be crucified": it might be interpreted to mean simply that his sentence corresponded to the will of the Jews, namely, to release Barabbas and to condemn Jesus. It is evident from the report in Luke, too, that the crucifixion itself was carried out by Roman soldiers (23:36–37), and mention is even made of the centurion who commanded them (23:47). But the emphasis, also in Luke, on the fact that it was "to the will of the Jews" that Pilate delivered Jesus, and that his soldiers would never have been instructed to crucify him had it not been for "the will of the Jews" is, of course, intended to serve the set purpose of exonerating Pilate and incriminating the Jews.

Matthew reports that when Pilate had released Barabbas, he ordered Jesus to be scourged, and then "delivered him to be crucified" (27:26). That it was to Roman soldiers that Jesus was delivered is plain from the next verse: "Then the soldiers of the governor took Jesus into the common hall, and gathered unto him the whole band of soldiers" (27:27). Everything that follows is done by these soldiers, including the crucifixion itself (27:35) and the setting up of the *titulus* over Jesus' head (27:37); and it is only after they had reviled him (27:39–40) that "the chief priests, with the scribes and elders" come into the picture again, also mocking him (27:41).

Similarly in Mark, the earliest of the Gospels, Pilate is reported to have been "willing to content the people," and, therefore, to have freed Barabbas to them and then "delivered Jesus, when he had scourged him, to be crucified" (15:15), whereupon "the soldiers led him away into the hall, called Praetorium; and they call together the whole band" (15:16); and once more everything that follows is done by them alone, with "the chief priests" introduced as joining the soldiers in mocking Jesus only after his crucifixion (15:31).

The Synoptic Gospels rightly and accurately show that the Jews took no part in the crucifixion, and we may look upon the admission in John that Roman soldiers had crucified him (19:23) as indicative of a general consensus that the crucifixion was verily carried out by Roman troops under the supreme command of the governor. While mention is made in Luke (23:24) of a "sentence" pronounced by Pilate, it is significant that none of the Gospels actually quotes or describes the judgment or sentence; all speak of Jesus being "delivered" to be crucified: "all the evangelists are at pains to avoid putting on record the passing of a death sentence by the Roman" governor.[106] There can, however, be no doubt that a "sentence," as in Luke, was actually given: the soldiers would not have crucified Jesus, or, for that matter, the two "malefactors" crucified together with him, without a formal directive from the governor. That a judgment must have been so delivered has been concluded by some scholars from the fact that Pilate had sat on the *sella,* the "judgment seat" (Matt. 27:19; John 19:13), whence, normally, judgment was pronounced.[107] Again, the reticence to record the fact and tenor of the judgment can be explained only by the tendency of the evangelists to absolve him of responsibility for the crucifixion, as if, indeed, by throwing up his hands in despair, succumbing to the hysterical clamor of the crowd, and abdicating his own judicial and gubernatorial duties, he could have quitted himself of responsibility, either moral or legal.

The truth is that Jesus was sentenced to death by the Roman governor, on his plea of guilty, and in accordance with Roman law. He could not have been "delivered to the Jews," for crucifixion or at all, not only because Jews were not allowed to attend the trial and could not have asked that he be delivered to them, but because no Roman governor would tolerate Jews interfering or intervening in a trial conducted by him, or carrying out a death sentence pronounced by him or taking part in its carrying out. It had been a Roman trial, resulting in a Roman sentence, carried out by Roman executioners.

The story of it would have been simple and straightforward were it not for the fact that the evangelists, for their theological and political purposes, had to shift the guilt for the death of Jesus to the Jews. For that purpose, they had to invest the Jews, whoever they were, with an impertinence toward the governor, and an influence upon him, that are so unrealistic and so unhistorical as to verge on the ridiculous; and they had to divest the governor of his last shred of dignity and all sense of responsibility. The end product is a conglomerate of true traditions and figments of the imagination, in which the legal issues are inextricably confused and the characters and traits of the actors unrecognizably perverted.

Little did Pilate know that the trial that he held, and the crucifixion that he ordered, that morning, would go down in history as among the most momentous events in the life of mankind. "He would have been very much surprised if he had been told that the poor little Jew who appeared before him that day would cause his own name to be handed down in an immortal story."[108] He did nothing to deserve his fame—just another routine trial of a stubborn and foolish Jew; nor did he do anything to deserve to be slanderously misrepresented as so inept as to allow himself to be made a tool in the hands of contemptible natives and do their bidding against his own better judgment. He had arrived at his own judgment, and pronounced it, and would see to it that it was punctually carried out. Whether anybody acclaimed it or protested against it was of no concern to him. If he happened to be wrong, so much the worse: there was no court of appeal to set him right. If he had been right, so much the better: he did not care a whit that one Jew less was alive. For the sake of good administrative order, he would make a routine report to the emperor[109] of the trial that he had held and the sentence that he had passed, probably as one item among many in a monthly return, and that would be the end of the matter.

7 THE SCOURGING

Jesus was not only crucified: before his crucifixion, according to the Gospels of Mark, Matthew, and John, he was scourged or tortured. The version in Mark and Matthew is that when the Roman governor "had scourged Jesus, he delivered him to be crucified" (Mark 15:15; Matt. 27:26). According to John, Pilate scourged Jesus in the course of the trial (19:1), before he brought him out to face "the Jews" again (19:4–5). Luke also mentions scourgings, not, however, as facts which had happened, but as alternative proposals of punishment: "I will chastise him and release him" (23:16), or "I have found no cause of death in him; I will therefore chastise him and let him go" (23:22).

We also find that the Roman soldiers "spit upon him, and took the reed, and smote him on the head" (Matt. 27:30; similarly Mark 15:19), after Pilate had delivered Jesus to be crucified, but before the crucifixion. Luke did not adopt this version: according to him, the soldiers mocked Jesus, but even that only after crucifixion (23:36); nor is any such maltreatment at the hands of the soldiers reported in John.

Under Roman law, scourging, as a matter of course, was included in every sentence of death,[1] and it is commonly assumed

that the scourging of Jesus formed part of the capital punishment inflicted on him.[2] If we had only the tradition of Mark
and Matthew, this assumption might be justified, though even
there the scourging precedes the handing over for crucifixion—
that is, possibly, the formal sentence of death. But the Johannine
tradition, that Jesus was scourged independently of any sentence
of death and long before it was passed, raises doubts whether the
correct interpretation of the report in Mark and Matthew should
not also be that the scourging and the crucifixion were independent of each other. That the soldiers smote Jesus and spat at
him after the passing of sentence may perhaps be taken as a
description of the scourging which formed part of the capital
punishment, for they acted as executioners in any case (Mark
15:24; Matt. 27:35) ; this would require any earlier scourging to
be accounted for otherwise than as an adjunct to the crucifixion.
Pilate's order that Jesus be scourged may, then, have to be interpreted as issued in addition to the death sentence eventually
passed, and for other purposes; and the sequence of events would
thus be that, in pursuance of that preliminary order, Jesus was
scourged, and only after the fact and the result of that scourging
had been reported did Pilate proceed to give his final verdict.

If this construction, based on the Johannine tradition, is sound,
the question at once arises for what purpose Pilate ordered the
scourging. Did he really inflict this kind of suffering upon a man
in whom he had found no fault at all (John 18:38) , only to impress "the Jews" with the spectacle of his misery and humiliation?
It has been said, and is generally believed, that Pilate's words to
the crowd, "Behold the man!" (John 19:5) , were meant to convey
that of a man looking like that and so anguished nothing evil
and dangerous, nothing royal and pretentious, could reasonably
be apprehended;[3] or that the sight of a bleeding and abject Jesus
would stir the pity of the onlookers and move them to desist from
their bloodthirsty clamoring.[4] To that end, we are told, did
Pilate scourge Jesus. Then the "soldiers platted a crown of thorns,
and put it on his head, and they put on him a purple robe, and
said, Hail, King of the Jews! and they smote him with their
hands" (John 19:2–3) , and in that guise Jesus was brought forth
by Pilate "that ye may know that I find no fault in him" (19:4) ,
no fault in a preposterous and laughable pretender like this! But

the wholly unexplained fury of "the Jews" was so blind, so callously merciless, that, beholding the tribulation and absurdity of this—forsooth!—"king," they would again do naught save chant their sickening refrain, "Crucify him, crucify him!" (19:6). And Pilate, so far from being surprised or discomfited by his failure to induce them to more humane reaction, and himself drawing the only possible conclusion from that selfsame tribulation and absurdity by acquitting the preposterous "king" and letting him go free, is described as entirely willing to give in to the hardhearted and predatory "Jews," if only they carry out the crucifixion themselves (19:6).

If, indeed, the scourging had no object than to make it possible for a tormented and wretched Jesus to be exhibited to the crowd, the Lucan tradition that it was to be inflicted by way or in lieu of punishment would appear much more reasonable than, and preferable to, the Johannine that it was just another interlude in the trial, just one more incident in the protracted negotiations between the Roman governor trying Jesus in his palace and a furious throng outside. We have given our reasons for dismissing as unrealistic and absurd any notion of the governor commuting to and fro, jumping up from his bench and running out to confer with "the Jews," to be rebuked and chided by them time and again, and eventually doing their cruel bidding against his own better judgment. We are constrained to dismiss as no less unrealistic and absurd the notion that the governor would inflict torture with the sole aim of presenting a bloodied and pain-racked victim to the throng without, and seeking to excite their compassion of charity: not only would no Roman governor put any man to torture with any such purpose, but none would exhibit the victim to awaken either sentiment; if he did, it would be solely as a deterrent. Scourging could deter the masses if it were by way or in lieu of punishment: Pilate might have found Jesus' unlawful royal pretensions too silly and unreal to be taken seriously at all, and would, therefore, punish him by torture and scourging as a rueful warning not to indulge again in illicit activity or imagining. And if that were the course that he took, he might well have displayed the vexed body of Jesus to show the people that even seemingly preposterous claims or aspirations to royalty would be visited with harsh and degrading corporal chastisement.

The Lucan tradition, however, was that the torture, though considered by Pilate as a possible course, was not in fact inflicted by him, either by way or in lieu of punishment, or at all. It would be difficult, in the circumstances, to adopt the *ratio* given by Luke for a scourging which, by his own account, never took place, the more so as the Gospels are agreed, and there can be no doubt, that the punishment meted out to Jesus was his crucifixion. Assuming, then, on the authority of the Gospels of Mark, Matthew, and John, that there was some scourging, we must look for grounds for it other than punitive. A pointer to the direction in which to look might be found in a feature common to the Lucan and Johannine traditions, that the scourging was, or was intended to be, employed by Pilate as a favor shown to Jesus, whether, according to Luke, as a way of remitting the death penalty or, according to John, as a means to arouse the pity of "the Jews." If we take it that, by ordering Jesus to be scourged, Pilate had, indeed, in mind an attempt to change the course of the proceedings to his advantage, we must ask ourselves what could possibly be made to happen, by having him tortured, that could bring about this turn for the better. He had already admitted to pretending to the kingship of the Jews and thus pleaded guilty to the charge; the court had no option but to convict him on his own plea of guilty unless he would, in time, retract it, or could, again in time, be made to. After his plea of guilty, there was no need or opportunity to call for witnesses or other evidence to prove the charge; but if he were allowed to retract his plea, that need and opportunity would at once arise, and the outcome of the trial would depend on the credibility and weight of the proofs available. If, in fact, any doubt had entered his mind as to the guilt of Jesus, his plea of guilty notwithstanding, the course that Pilate might have taken would be to get him to retract the plea and then see whether the charge was sufficiently supported by believable testimony. Before the scourging, Pilate renewed at least twice (John 18:33, 35, 37) his questions to Jesus, whether he was king, and what he had done, but Jesus would say nothing to go back on his original admission. On the contrary, he made his final plea of guilty in answer to the last question (18:37). When Pilate had failed in his alleged appeal to "the Jews" to choose Jesus as the man to be pardoned on Passover (18:39–40), he "therefore took Jesus, and scourged him" (19:1), manifestly in an ultimate or further essay to save him.

It has been said that the scourging ordered by Pilate at this stage of the proceedings could have had only one purpose—to strengthen Jesus' plea of guilty by extracting a detailed confession of his pretensions and misdoings under torture.[5] As we shall presently see, the use of torture to extract confessions was, indeed, permissible and widespread; but why should the governor want to obtain a more detailed confession than the one that Jesus had already volunteered? There is no mention anywhere of accomplices to be tracked or other particulars to be disclosed, and it can hardly be assumed that the governor was overwhelmingly curious to be acquainted with superfluous minutiae of Jesus' teachings and pretensions. And if that had been the purpose of the scourging, some report as to the result of the torture, whether disclosures were made by Jesus, and which, would surely have been forthcoming.

According to Luke, the scourging of Jesus did not take place because "the chief priests and the rulers and the people" (23:13), present there, objected—"crying out all at once" (23:18) and being "instant with loud voices" (23:23) that he be crucified. The trend of the whole story in Luke would suggest that it was not so much the scourging to which they objected as the release of Jesus, even though he were first scourged. And since Pilate— or so we are given to understand—was not "allowed" by the throng to release Jesus, he also abstained from chastising him; and since he could not chastise him, as he desired, he refrained from freeing him, too. The idea that Pilate offered or entreated the people to content themselves with seeing Jesus punished with a penalty lighter than death[6] is too farfetched to be seriously entertained: it is not to be conceived that a Roman governor would delegate his sentencing power to a horde of obstreperous natives, or share it with them. And why should he punish Jesus at all if he had found him not guilty? Or, if he had found him guilty of a non-capital offense, why is that offense not mentioned and described? The pretension to being king of the Jews, at any rate, was a capital offense. It has been argued that Luke may have mistaken the scourging which went with every execution for a separate and alternative punishment,[7] as though the judge had discretion in a capital offense to inflict the penalty either of death or of scourging; but if Luke made that error, there is nothing to suggest that Pilate could make it. It is not astonishing that the Lucan tradition did not commend itself to the author of the Gospel of John; what in Luke was but a wish expressed by Pilate, but not realized, in the version of the fourth evangelist became actual fact; scourging in the course of a capital hearing was a feature of Roman criminal procedure with which he must have been familiar.

The law was that, in cases of offenses under the *Lex Julia maiestatis,* torture was to be used not only, as with other offenses, against slaves and aliens, but also against citizens and notables, without distinction.[8] Generally, however, it would serve only as a means to extract confessions from the accused, or make recalcitrant witnesses talk or wavering ones incriminate the accused.[9] Where the case had been proved, whether by the accused's confession or by testimony, this "procedural" torture would normally be dispensed with, in view of the "punitive" sort which would anyhow accompany the capital punishment. On the other hand, it would appear that torture was so standard a part of trials for *laesa maiestas* that the distinction between cases in which it was genuinely required and those in which it was not any longer necessary became rather shadowy, particularly in the eyes of laymen. In later times it became synonymous with interrogation (*quaestio*),[10] and we find that where interrogation of the accused under torture had failed to produce a confession, the accuser himself would be questioned on the rack until he admitted that his charge had been false.[11] An element of torture in the course of a trial of this kind would, therefore, be regarded as almost a routine matter; not to employ torture in the process of it would be an exception to the general rule.

It ought to be kept in mind that the offense with which Jesus was charged was not that he had already established his "kingdom," but that he professed to be king, that is, to be destined and qualified to establish a kingdom one day. He believed in his divine mission, and there was no need to employ torture to extract a confession. But it appears—as we observed in a previous context —that if, in spite of his destiny and qualification, he had agreed not to pursue his aspirations, he could scarcely have been convicted of treason. It may have amounted to a felony even to make preparations for future treasonable doings, but not necessarily a capital felony. The trial of Jesus took place at a time when it was still open to him to unburden himself of responsibility for the capital offense, if only he would disavow his royal pretensions thenceforth. It is true that the Roman governor's criminal jurisdiction had also for its purpose to deter the local inhabitants from hatching anti-Roman plots, or nursing ambitions or illusions of independence or salvation; but that could be effectively done by persuading any conspirator or aspirant openly to renounce his policy as erroneous and punishable and submit to the majesty and unassailable authority of the emperor. From the point of view of Roman colonial policy, it might even have seemed the wiser way to get popular leaders to make avowals of loyalty rather than to create venerated martyrs by crucifying them.

In the circumstances, it is not impossible that Pilate ordered Jesus to be scourged to extract not a second confession but a renunciation of his claims. If, under torture, he promised that he would no longer give play to his royal pretensions, Jesus might have been spared crucifixion, and Pilate have been satisfied with scourging as sufficient punishment of boasts now proved empty and harmless. We have evidence of flogging and scourging inflicted as a separate punishment for noncapital offenses,[12] for instance, a slave's disobedience of his master's bidding. Pilate may have thought that if the torture did not work, no harm would have been done—from his point of view—in trying; a person accused under the *Lex Julia maiestatis* was meet to be tortured in any event, for whatever purpose.

In this light, the Johannine story takes on a new meaning. Except for the Barabbas interlude, the scourging follows the question which Pilate addressed to Jesus, "What is truth?" (18:38): to show Jesus how relative and variable truth is, Pilate resolves to attempt to bring about a change, by the practically infallible means of torture, in Jesus' own concept of it. If he cannot persuade him by words that there is no absolute truth in this world, perhaps he will by torture. In the opinion of the governor, the argument with this stubborn pretender must have lasted much too long already.

The same interpretation would lend itself to the story in the Gospels According to Mark and Matthew: Pilate ordered Jesus to be scourged, to try to make him renounce his pretensions; when Jesus had been scourged but would not recant, he "delivered" him to be crucified, that is to say, sentenced him to death on the cross. In this way, the fact that scourging preceded the "delivery" for crucifixion is readily and reasonably explicable.

That torture is reported in the Gospels, and particularly in the Fourth, to have been used against Jesus must also be viewed against the background of what the evangelists knew of Roman trials of Christians in their own times: it appears that whenever a man was brought to trial on a charge of being a Christian, he was first tortured to coerce him into abjuring the faith. We hear, for instance, of a Christian tutor, Ptolemy, whom the city prefect had manacled and tortured lengthily after he admitted his Christianity; it was when, after the torture, he had reasserted his faith, that his execution was ordered.[13] In a letter which we have already quoted, written by Pliny during his governorship of Bithynia to the emperor Trajan, the methods of interrogating persons arraigned for practicing the Christian faith are described as follows:

> I interrogated them whether they were Christians; if they confessed it, I repeated the question twice again, adding the threat of capital punishment; if they still persevered, I ordered them to be executed. . . . Those who denied they were, or had ever been, Christians, who repeated after me an invocation to the gods, and offered adoration with wine and frankincense to your image . . . and who finally cursed Christ— none of which acts, it is said, can those who are really Christians be forced into performing—these I thought it proper to discharge. Others at first confessed themselves Christians, and then denied it. . . . They all worshiped your statue and the images of the gods, and cursed Christ. . . . [In a particular case] I judged it the more necessary to extract the real truth, with the assistance of torture . . . but I could discover nothing more than depraved and excessive superstition.[14]

While a scrupulous distinction is drawn between interrogation under threat of capital punishment and interrogation under torture, the second mode was resorted to freely whenever it was thought essential or expedient. It is noteworthy that Pliny was regarded by his Christian contemporaries as one of the most merciful and just of governors,[15] yet even he would not hesitate either to apply torture "to extract the real truth" or promptly to execute any accused person who would not forswear Christianity. In his reply to Pliny, the emperor wrote that it was "not possible to lay down any general rule which can be applied as the fixed standard in all cases of this nature . . . when these people are found guilty, they must be punished; with the restriction, however, that, when the party denies himself to be a Christian and gives proof, by adoring the gods, that he is not, he shall be pardoned on the ground of repentance, even though he may have formerly incurred suspicion."[16] This exchange of letters has been dated between the years 111 and 113,[17] that is, exactly synchronous with the Gospel According to John; and the procedure ascribed to Pilate in the trial of Jesus is very reminiscent of Pliny's in the trials of Christians: first, the twice-repeated questions, whether the accused was what he was charged with being, and then an attempt to make him pay homage to the emperor, if necessary by applying torture, either that he would "repent," and could be pardoned and discharged, or, if he would not, he must die.

We need not go into the psychological question of what might have been Pilate's motive in ordering Jesus to be scourged—whether it was purely or mainly altruistic, to make him recant and save his life, or whether Pilate's sadistic traits found an outlet in torturing before sentencing him. He may have regarded the torture as part and parcel of the procedure to be followed in trials of this kind, and he certainly was sufficiently callous not to give a second thought to the agony involved. The possibility of so framing it as to make it appear a favor that he had been gracious enough to accord Jesus may have been a further inducement.

In the conduct of criminal trials, neither the emperor nor a governor was bound by any fixed rules of procedure: how to proceed, whom and how to interrogate, whether or not to have recourse to torture, were all matters within the free discretion of each.[18] The restrictions incident on lower investigative officers, such as tribunes and centurions, who were not allowed to question Roman citizens under torture (Acts 22:25), did not affect the governor,[19] and if he was empowered to interrogate Roman citizens under torture, certainly he could apply torture to natives. This exceptionally wide discretion was not far short of an invitation not to neglect any good opportunity to order a scourging.

Whether the scourging of Jesus found its way into the Gospel reports on the strength only of their authors' personal knowledge of the like ordeal inflicted on Christians standing trial in Rome, or whether there was a valid tradition that Jesus did undergo scourging by order of Pilate, any torture applied before conviction and sentence must be clearly distinguished from the flogging attendant on execution, after conviction and sentence. The first was in the nature of a probative measure: it was designed to secure proof, either of guilt or of repentance; the second was purely punitive in nature. The first may be much more cruel, and cause more ache and suffering, than the second: for while probative torture may be applied, and stepped up, until the desired result is attained, the second is but a demonstration of vindictiveness and derision, and may be perfunctory. Of the flogging that accompanied the crucifixion of Jesus, we are given some, however scant, particulars (Mark 15:19; Matt. 27:30); of the scourging before his conviction, we have absolutely none.

But while the Gospels do not enlighten us as to what scourgings or tortures Jesus was subjected to, we know from Roman sources what the treatment normally was of those accused of *laesa maiestas*.[20] Disregarding its extreme cruelty, it was most efficacious, and it became so firmly entrenched in the system of law enforcement that we find it employed on a large scale not only in imperial Rome but also in the medieval Church.[21] In the later empire, torture was also used as a blend of interrogation and punishment, against civil servants who embezzled official funds or otherwise abused their offices, for instance;[22] or against overseers and even senators who, being entrusted with the distribution of food rations, had taken overgenerous helpings for themselves;[23] or such "enemies of the human race" as wizards, fortunetellers, magicians, and astrologers.[24]

In comparison with this kind of "self-supporting" torture, the chastisement accompanying the capital penalty might be described as mild, though it was severer in cases of crucifixion than in other modes of execution. A convict led from his cell to his place of execution was beaten (*flagellatio*) and mocked all the way,[25] whether to let the general public share in carrying out the execution[26] or to amplify its deterrence. And besides the buffeting and the mockery, a man about to be crucified had to bear his cross on his back all the way, his hands bound to the transverse bars, usually stripped, only his head covered.[27]

We hear that when Jesus was led away to be crucified, the Roman soldiers "spit upon him, and took the reed, and smote him on the head" (Matt. 27:30; similarly Mark 15:19); and then, "after that they had mocked him," they "put his own clothes on him" (Mark 15:20; similarly Matt. 27:31). Not only was he not naked, but he was given his own garments to wear, in preference to the "scarlet robe" in which they had earlier attired him so as to mock him (Mark 15:17; Matt. 27:28). And as they started to take him away, "as they came out, they found a man of Cyrene, Simon by·name: him they compelled to bear his cross" (Matt. 27:32; similarly Mark 15:21 and Luke 23:26). To be sure, the fourth evangelist has set aside the tradition that Simon bore the cross: in John we read that Jesus bore his cross himself (19:17); but in view of the unanimity of the three first evangelists, we may be justified in adopting the tradition of the Synoptic Gospels, the more so as it is generally accepted. It would, then, appear that not only were Jesus' hands not bound to the beams of the cross, but he had not even to bear it himself. We do not know whether he was spared the burden because his strength had failed him after the scourgings that he underwent,[28] or if he was originally of weak constitution and hence too infirm to shoulder so weighty a load;[29] what we do know is that the soldiers must have taken pity on him, if not when they smote him on the head and mocked him, at least when they led him away. They may have thought that by smiting and deriding him they had mishandled him enough, and could now forgo some of the sadistic pleasures which law and custom granted them.

Looking, however, at the reported particulars of the mockery, we find that Jesus was led into a hall where "the whole band of soldiers" were gathered, and there "they stripped him, and put on him a scarlet robe. And when they had platted a crown of thorns, they put it upon his head, and a reed in his right hand: and they bowed the knee before him, and mocked him, saying, Hail, King of the Jews! And they spit upon him, and took the reed, and smote him on the head" (Matt. 27:27–30; similarly Mark 15:16–19). This sounds like the story not of an actual flogging but of how the legionaries made sport of this odd and mirth-provoking

"king": if Jesus suffered, it was from the taunts rather than from the blows, from the assault rather on his dignity than on his body. It is the report not of a torture that caused physical scars, but of a heckling that caused anguish of the mind.

Moreover, even if we accept the report in John that Jesus was "scourged" (19:1), no dependable tradition or information exists that there were any aftereffects, wounds, or other external injury, which the soldiers would at once have seen. If Jesus had been tortured with the normal Roman thoroughness, his body would have shown patent signs of it: he would have bled profusely, have scarcely been able to stand on his feet, certainly been unable to confront the governor and address him freely (19:11). And if that, or anything like it, had been his state after the scourging, the evangelist would surely have made no secret of it: much more than Pilate could have desired to arouse the pity of "the Jews" at beholding the tragic and tormented Jesus, the evangelist yearned to arouse the perpetual compassion of the whole world at the pangs which the scourging brought. Some scholars think that because the torture was commanded by the Roman governor and could not be laid at the door of the Jews, the evangelists—true to their tendentious purpose—passed over Jesus' hurt in silence. Others have found their reticence in so grievous a matter a praiseworthy and "remarkable restraint," as if, rather than stirring the emotions of their readers "by dwelling on the sufferings of Jesus," they understated their case.[30] Others, again, have opined that torturing was so commonplace and widespread at the time that everybody for whom the evangelists wrote needed no telling what were the effects and how the victims looked, so that details were unnecessary.[31] But all these surmises are in the nature of afterthoughts to clarify an inexplicable omission. I would rather follow the theological doctrine that if the evangelists did not describe the pitiable condition of a scourged Jesus, it was because there was none, and that he was in fact unscathed, his outward appearance unchanged. But while some theologians hold that this was by grace of a divine miracle,[32] intervening either to prevent the torture from harming Jesus or to dispel at once any harm done, we must seek a more rational explanation: if Jesus' looks were untouched and unchanged, it would appear that the scourging was so light and superficial as to print no outward marks. Perhaps it was the same soldiers who scourged Jesus (John 19:1) and who mocked him (John 19:2-3; Mark 15:20; Matt. 27:31) :[33] for some reason or other, they restrained themselves and did not use that measure of violence which legionaries were apt to use in scourging suspects or convicts, and particularly slaves and aliens.[34]

Any proof that may be required for this thesis is furnished by the story of Simon of Cyrene. Normally the convict would be bound to the bars (the *furca*) of the cross and whipped along on his way to the place of crucifixion; it was already a matter of grace or indulgence if he was allowed to carry only the crossbeam (*patibulum*) and was not bound to it.[35] The *patibulum* would be nailed to the stake which stood permanently at the place of a crucifixion, thus forming the cross; the convict could be bound, or nailed, to the *patibulum* either before starting on his way or on arrival at the place.[36] There is no doubt that, as a matter of law, the carrying of at least the *patibulum* was an integral part of the punishment, and no condemned person could be relieved of it,[37] so much so that there are scholars who dismiss the entire tale of Simon as unhistoric, something that never happened and could not happen.[38] A compromise has been suggested, and generally accepted, that Jesus did carry the *patibulum* himself for part of the way, until he collapsed beneath its sheer weight, whereupon the soldiers asked a passer-by, who chanced to be Simon, to relieve him of the *patibulum* and bear it for him. The solution is based on ancient Christian tradition and is said to reconcile the seemingly contradictory Gospel reports: on the one hand, Jesus bore his cross himself, as reported in John (19:17) ; on the other, it was borne by Simon, as reported in the Synoptic Gospels. If this theory is accepted, Jesus will have undergone the added grief of bearing his cross, and even have succumbed under the burden, while Simon the Cyrenian still performed the service which the Synoptic Gospels ascribe to him. One cannot, however, avoid speculating why no Gospel has a single word to suggest that Jesus did break down under the oppressive freight; why John did not adopt the tradition that Jesus was relieved of the burden, though only after collapsing; and why the Synoptic Gospels time the incident with Simon at the very moment "as they came out" of the judgment hall (Matt. 27:32; Luke 23:26) and know nothing of the tradition that Jesus bore his cross himself for some part of the way. It is all the more perplexing, since the bearing of the cross, and the suffering that it meant, undoubtedly had great theological significance.

Ancient theologians have maintained that the authors of the Gospel of John suppressed the true and, even to them, well-known tradition of Simon of Cyrene, for the reason that it had given rise to a gnostic-heretical doctrine that it was Simon, and not Jesus, who had been crucified:[39] the man who carried the *patibulum* on his back would, as a matter of course, have been taken by the executioners in attendance at the place of crucifixion—who need not have been identical with the military escort on the way there—as the man to be crucified; and thus it was that Simon died on the cross and Jesus was saved. If Simon could be represented as nonexistent, or, at least, as never having borne the cross or as absent from the crucifixion, he could not very well be taken for the man who was crucified. But it seems that the doctrine in question was first propounded by a certain Basilides who lived long after the Gospel of John was published.[40] Another theory is that the fourth evangelist could not, or would not, believe that Jesus would not faithfully practice what he had himself often preached: bearing one's cross and denying oneself were the *sine qua non* of belonging to his disciples (Matt. 10:38; 16:24; Mark 8:34; Luke 14:27), and the evangelists, therefore, spurned the notion that he could have permitted anybody else to bear his cross for him.[41] Yet it was Jesus' admonition to "any man" who desired to follow him, "let him deny himself, and take up his cross, and follow me" (Matt. 16:24), that may have prompted the authors of the Synoptic Gospels to provide the story of Simon: here was a man who denied himself and bore the cross—the exemplar to be followed by all who would join the Christian faith.[42] By common consensus, however, that admonition seems to have been put into the mouth of Jesus by the evangelists who wrote under the impact of his crucifixion: the notion of bearing the cross as a feature of adherence to Christianity, or as a prerequisite of that adherence, is only an echo of Jesus' own crucifixion[43] and could not have been spread by him in his lifetime. It has been pointed out that the expression "bearing one's cross" or "carrying one's cross on one's shoulders" is also found in talmudic literature,[44] and may, therefore, already have been a metaphor in common usage in the days of Jesus; but all the sources where it occurs are of a much later period, and it is not impossible that the employment of it, even by Jews and in Hebrew, is an indirect, and certainly undesired, result of the crucifixion of Jesus. In this connection, it is of interest that the phrase appears as a comment on the story that Abraham took the wood of the burnt offering "and laid it upon Isaac his son" (Gen. 22:6), a story that—some scholars think—may have influenced the fourth evangelist to let Jesus bear his cross as Isaac bôre the wood for his own sacrifice.[45]

The probability that the author of the Gospel of John, out of theological motives of their own, discarded the Synoptic tradition of Simon of Cyrene and replaced it by the assertion that Jesus bore his cross himself is only heightened by the fact, already noted, that he took some liberty with other, and not the least important, details of the crucifixion story as well: while the other three Gospels are unanimous and reasonably unambitious in reporting that the Roman soldiers were in charge of all the crucifixion proceedings, from the moment of Jesus' "delivery" by Pilate until the very end, John reports, or insinuates, that he was delivered to the Jews, that the Jews led him away, and that "they" crucified him (19:16–18), a report so palpably wrong that the evangelist is at once caught contradicting himself (19:23). But, it being the Jews who led Jesus away, it was only natural that he should have to bear his cross himself: surely "the Jews," brutal archenemies of his as they are portrayed, would not grant him relief of the burden, the less so as the law required that he bear it. It is almost axiomatic that if the author of the Gospel of John saw fit, for politico-theological reasons, to substitute "the Jews" for the Roman soldiers who led Jesus to his crucifixion, he cannot have had many scruples about letting him, for ethico-theological reasons, bear his own cross.

Legally speaking, it was, of course, flatly forbidden to ask an innocent passer-by to bear a convict's cross for him: that meant transferring part of the sentence to be served by the convict to a wholly blameless outsider. But it is submitted that the credibility of the report is not affected by the illegality of the facts reported: where, in a criminal matter involving capital punishment, proceedings are reported in which competent judges, learned in the laws, not only entirely disregarded the substantive law to be applied by them, but also infringed all rules of statutory procedure —such a report, we have said, is not worthy of credence, especially if the judges concerned are generally known to be formalistic and conscientious in enforcing the law. It is different with men like the Roman soldiers who led Jesus to his crucifixion, untutored and simple folk who act either in conformity with orders expressly given to them or according to their own momentary instincts and inclinations: their disregard of legal niceties may be readily believed and in itself proves nothing. Even assuming that, when leading Jesus away, the soldiers were under the command of an officer who knew the law, and that they would not act without his approval, it is not improbable that in this particular case he would have approved: when the letter of the law is skirted to relieve the accused and make things easier for him, the illegality is, naturally, much less reprehensible than when it is transgressed in a manner detrimental to him; and the infliction of suffering and chastisement on the convict as he went to his crucifixion was, anyway, to a large extent left to the discretion of his guards and executioners. As nobody would quarrel with them over any excess of torture administered, so, presumably, nobody would find fault with them if they chose to exercise self-restraint and did not exhaust their powers of castigation.

This self-restraint presupposes that, for some reason, the soldiers and their officer pitied Jesus. Perhaps they were impressed with his reaction, or lack of it, to their sneers, or had been instructed to hasten the crucifixion. Whatever the reason, although Jesus had to bear his *patibulum* himself, and would, in the normal course of events, have been compelled to, when they chanced upon Simon of Cyrene, who was, as Christian tradition has it, only too willing to oblige, they gave him the cross to carry. There is, after all, nothing to astonish us in this willingness: any Jewish passer-by, meeting a unit of Roman soldiers escorting a Jew to crucifixion, would, instinctively, without waiting to be asked, at once volunteer to perform this last act of compassion. And to Roman soldiers it would barely matter which Jew bore the cross, so long as they had not to do it themselves.

To sum up: if the Roman governor had, indeed, before sentencing Jesus, ordered him to be scourged, as is reported in John and hinted at in Mark and Matthew, he was probably scourged, but not tortured as severely as in the normal Roman practice respecting persons accused of *laesa maiestas,* or of professing the Christian faith, but so lightly and superficially as to leave no visible outward signs. Jesus may have been given several blows or strokes, not with a view to extracting further confessions of guilt from him, but solely with a view to compelling or inducing him to express regret and repentance and to promise that he would no longer air royal pretensions. As he was spared the torture conventionally wreaked on persons charged with the same crime, so was he spared the scourging and suffering that usually accompanied crucifixion: not only was he not divested in nakedness, but he was given his own garments when led to the place of crucifixion; not only was he not required to carry his *patibulum* himself, but the usual beatings (*flagellatio*) on the way were not his portion either. All that we know attests that he was allowed to go freely and without further molestation: it seems that his escorts had spent their energy and viciousness in the preceding lampoon, or were husbanding their strength for the exertion to follow.

8   THE CRUCIFIXION

Jesus was brought to a place called Golgotha, meaning "the place of the skull" (Matt. 27:33; Mark 15:22; John 19:17), in the Lucan tradition rendered as Calvary (23:33), where, it seems, Roman executions were usually carried out. He was not the only prisoner to be led there that day—with him were two others (John 19:28), who are described in Mark and Matthew as *lestai,* wrongly translated in the King James Version as "thieves," for it signifies bandits or brigands[1] (Mark 15:27; Matt. 27:38), and described in Luke as *kakourgoi,* criminals[2] or "malefactors" (23:33). It has been suggested that both were probably rebellious zealots, sentenced to death for their part in a recent insurrection in Jerusalem.[3] Whatever their antecedents, the fact that they were put to death by crucifixion proves that, like Jesus, they were convicted by the Roman governor of a capital offense under Roman law.

It was widely believed, and has latterly been reasserted,[4] that the Romans had no monopoly of crucifixions, and that the Jews, even before the Roman occupation of Judaea, had adopted the mode from Persian patterns. The belief may rest on the Johannine tradition that it was the Jews, and not the Romans, who crucified Jesus; and we have shown that this tradition is controverted in the Gospel of John itself (19:23). But it is currently reinforced by arguments and evidence from Jewish sources, giving it the appearance of a scientific discovery rather than a traditional belief, and though some of the arguments have by now been conclusively refuted,[5] the penological and lego-historical problems involved are yet to receive the attention which they deserve. And the question is not just of penological or legal interest; that a tradition which originated in a tendentious misrepresentation can be, and is today being, resurrected and vindicated under a show of impartial scholarship renders critical vigilance indispensable.

Much of the confusion is due to faulty terminology. It so happens that the modern Hebrew usage for "to crucify," *tselov*, is the old Aramaic word for "to hang": wherever the Bible speaks of hanging (Hebrew: *taloh*), the authoritative Aramaic translation is *tselov*,[6] from which it has quite unwarrantably been concluded that all biblical hangings were crucifixions. In fact, the Hebrew *tselov* is derived not from the Aramaic at all, but from another Hebrew root, *shelov*, which has the sense of fixing or bracing wooden planks or beams to each other,[7] while the Aramaic *tselov* in all likelihood comes from the Assyrian *dalabu*, "causing pain or distress."[8] It is true that in Assyrian there are at least two other words for hanging,[9] of which derivatives also occur in Aramaic,[10] and it has been said that, wherever these other words are used, the intention is to convey the notion of extrajudicial hangings, whereas judicial hangings are rendered as *tselivot*.[11] But one can infer nothing from the fact that the Hebrew "hanging" is rendered *tselov* in Aramaic, and that *tselov* in Hebrew means "to crucify": the identity of the Hebrew word for "to crucify" and the Aramaic word for "to hang" is more apparent than real. The distinction in Hebrew between "to hang" (*taloh*) and "to crucify" (*tselov*) is postbiblical and occurs for the first time in talmudic sources; biblical Hebrew, in contrast to Aramaic, does not know the word *tselov*, either for "crucifying" or at all; and even assuming—though not admitting—that the Aramaic *tselov* could have borne the meaning of crucifying, too, that would purport only that the Aramaic translators of the Bible held that in biblical language no distinction could or need be made between hanging on the cross and hanging on the gallows. It may, indeed, be that neither the Hebrew *taloh* nor the Aramaic *tselov* connotes any particular mode of hanging, and that the mode employed in a given case had to be discovered otherwise than from the word used for "hanging." There is no such difficulty with the talmudic sources, in which hangings as such are expressly differentiated from hangings carried out "in the way (or: mode) practiced by the government,"[12] a plain allusion to the special form of hanging practiced by the Roman governor's forces, namely, crucifixion. The phrase "in the way practiced by the government" in itself already conveys an undertone of strangeness, as if one wished to dissociate oneself from an alien and exotic method and had no room for it either in one's laws or in one's language.

The Hebrew *tselov*, "to crucify," is found once in the Dead Sea Scrolls. The verse, "The lion did tear in pieces enough for his whelps and strangled for his lionesses" (Nah. 2:12), is in the Commentary on the Book of Nahum interpreted as follows: "This is the young lion who wrought vengeance on them that sought smooth things, and crucified all of them on the same day; such a thing had never happened before in Israel, for it is written, he that is hanged is accursed of God" (Deut. 21:23). I have rendered the word *tsalav* in the text as "crucified"; most translators render it as "hanged alive."[13] On the assumption, then, that we must conclude from the use of the term *tsalav* that the sense to be conveyed is hanging by crucifixion, we find the commentator reporting not only that there was a Jewish "lion" who revenged himself on his enemies by crucifying them, but also that such a thing as hanging by crucifixion had never before happened in Israel. And it could not ever have happened before, because, from the Jewish point of view and by the most ancient Jewish tradition, hanging alive, by crucifixion or otherwise, was an "affront to God" and a defilement of the holy land.[14] A majority of scholars believe that the "young lion" was Alexander Jannaeus, king of the Jews, whom Josephus reports as ordering the death of eight hundred Pharisees and their wives and children, while he and his concubines caroused and reveled in the spectacle: the eight hundred were "crucified," and their wives and children "slaughtered" before their eyes.[15] Another suggestion is that the reference is to a killing of sixty of the elders of Israel, said to have been the act of a priest named Elyakim, who was a collaborator with the enemy,[16] but the expression to describe the killing is "slaughtered," not "crucified," and the text affords no evidence of hanging or crucifixion. Alexander Jannaeus, however, if Josephus is to be believed, had to hang his victims alive, because he wanted them, before expiring on their crosses, to behold the atrocities done to their beloved ones. Conjecture as we may what took place and who the "young lion" was that crucified his adversaries, all that can be learned from this Essene comment on Nahum is that the crucifying had left so indelible an impression in the minds of the common people, when once it had occurred, as not to be forgotten or forgiven, for it was unheard of in the annals of Israel and was in conflict with all custom and tradition.[17]

The modes of execution which we find prescribed or described in the Bible are stoning (Deut. 17:5, *et al.*), burning (Lev. 20:14, *et al.*), hanging (Josh. 8:29, *et al.*), and slaying (Deut. 20:13). For reasons into which we shall presently inquire, the mishnaic codifiers dropped the hanging and added "strangling."[18] As far as biblical hangings are concerned, a distinction is necessary between hanging alive and hanging after execution: there is no biblical law which prescribes hanging, as such, as a proper way to inflict death; all recorded instances of hanging are factual reports, not legal prescriptions. There is, however, an explicit law providing for hanging after execution: "If a man has committed a capital offense, and is put to death,[19] thou shalt hang him on a tree: his body shall not remain all night upon the tree, but thou shalt in any wise bury him that day, for he that is hanged, is accursed of God; that thy land be not defiled, which the Lord thy God giveth thee for an inheritance" (Deut. 21:22-23). Executions had to take place in the late afternoon,[20] so that the corpse was taken down from the "tree" straight after the hanging, before sunset.[21] So far from being a demonstration of triumph over the wrongdoer and of rejoicing at his death,[22] it was rather a formal, and hurried, compliance with the scriptural injunction to let all the people see "and fear, and do no more presumptuously" (Deut. 17:13) and to pillory the offender against the sun (Num. 25:4); public deterrence was, understandably, a main purpose of all punishment. "He that is hanged is accursed of God" has been authoritatively interpreted to mean that "it is a curse before God to hang a man":[23] while, to deter potential offenders, it may be a dire necessity that convicts be hanged and publicly displayed, there can be no worse calamity in the eyes of God than to have to hang a fellow man. Reluctance to hang offenders, even after statutory execution, eventually led to a reform of the law: while biblical law did not distinguish between capital offenses with respect to the post-mortem hanging, it was later laid down that this hanging was to be confined to idolaters and men who had cursed God, pronouncing His ineffable Name: of such it could properly be said that they are hanged for cursing God, and when hanged are accursed of Him.[24] As a matter of law, therefore, hanging was never more than hanging after death, and hanging after death was ultimately reserved for idolaters and blasphemers.

As to the reported instances of hanging alive, it is submitted that they are all either non-Jewish or nonjudicial or both, and that there is no case in the Bible of a Jewish judicial execution by hanging alive. Examples of non-Jewish hangings are those ordered by Pharaoh, king of Egypt (Gen. 40:22), Ahasuerus, king of Persia and Media (Esther 7:10; 9:14), and the Philistines (II Sam. 21:9), all of whom may be presumed to have acted in conformity with their own laws and customs. Wherever we find Jews hanging men alive, it is in the course of wars or in warlike operations: Joshua hanged the king of Ai on a tree (Josh. 8:29), but even then he "commanded that they should take his carcass down from the tree as soon as the sun was down" (ibid.). We also find Joshua hanging five men after a previous execution by slaying (10:26). When David ordered the execution of the murderers of Ishbosheth, his enemy, they were first slain, then their hands and feet were cut off, and finally their bodies were suspended over the pool in Hebron (II Sam. 4:12). The injunction to "hang up before the Lord against the sun" (Num. 25:4) any who had bowed down to alien gods has been correctly understood not as directed to judicial organs, but as a call to a warlike, wholly nonjudicial, operation;[25] it is, anyhow, open to grave doubts whether the term here used, hoqa, actually stands for "hanging"; the better opinion would favor a sense of pillorying.[26]

Biblical law thus knew hanging only as a means of deterrence after execution had taken place and death had supervened in some other mode: hanging was not then used to put a convict to

death. It is only in subsequent periods that we find hanging alive
as a form of execution imported into Jewish law from foreign
sources. The most important evidence of this is in the Book of
Ezra: in a decree ascribed to the Persian king, Cyrus, we read
that "whosoever shall alter this word, let timber be pulled down
from his house, and, being set up, let him be hanged thereon; and
let his house be made a dunghill for this" (Ezra 6:11). The timber to "be pulled down from his house" could, of course, be made
as well into a gallows as into a cross; but it is said that the decree
had the effect of introducing the Persian mode of execution into
Israel, and that that mode was exclusively crucifixion.[27] First,
however, while records exist of crucifixion in Persia, it does not
follow that it was the one and only kind of execution in vogue
there: hanging and crucifixion alike may have been known and
practiced. And, second, not a solitary instance is chronicled of a
judicial execution carried out in ancient Israel in the manner authorized by Cyrus or in exercise of the specific power conferred by
him. We know from biblical sources (viz., the Book of Esther)
that the Persian king would hang his convicts "upon the gallows"
(Esther 8:7, *et al.*), and from other sources that Persian kings
would crucify their victims.[28] Even assuming, then, that crucifixion could be regarded as a—or the—Persian way of execution,
the mere fact that the Jewish authorities then subject to Persian
suzerainty were empowered to apply it, particularly for offenses
under Persian law, such as disobedience to the royal "word,"
would not in itself mark any change in Jewish law or in the competence or practice of the Jewish courts as such. Nevertheless, it
is said that we have here a "reception" of Persian law, attested by
the Bible itself, and it is this "reception" which is called in proof
of the contention that crucifying had become a Jewish mode of
execution.

Another instance is provided by the Aramaic translation of the
Book of Ruth. The translation is posttalmudic,[29] and hence several centuries later than the events with which we are concerned.
Ruth's words, "When thou diest, will I die" (Ruth 1:17), were
hermeneutically taken to mean that, among the other prescripts
of Jewish law, Ruth also took upon herself those relating to capital punishment: as if she had said: In all the ways that you may be
put to death under your laws, I, too, shall be ready to be put to

death.[30] This interpretation is rendered in the authoritative Aramaic version as follows: "Naomi told Ruth, we have four legal modes of execution, namely, stoning, burning, slaying, and hanging; whereupon Ruth said, in whatever way you will die, I will die." Is it that in posttalmudic times the mishnaic tradition of strangling[31] had fallen into oblivion, and one of strangulation by hanging substituted for it? Or had there been another reform in the meantime, with the archaic mode of strangling replaced by the more merciful hanging? Or ought the text to be dismissed out of hand as an obviously erroneous statement of law by an ignorant layman? One conclusion at any rate, I think, may fairly be drawn from the substitution, namely, that, as in strangling, so also in the hanging here mentioned, death is caused by strangulation, and, as regards the physiological cause of death, there would then be no difference between hanging and strangling.[32] But in that case it would follow that the hanging here referred to cannot have been crucifixion, because in crucifixion, as we shall see, death is not due to strangulation at all.

Admittedly, hangings were carried out by Jewish authorities, or on their initiative, at one time or another during talmudic and posttalmudic eras; but it is submitted, and will be shown, that all of them were executions by strangulation, in which the condemned man died of suffocation and which might properly be classified, therefore, as "strangling." Crucifixion, on the other hand, is the one and only mode of hanging in which death is due not to suffocation but to exhaustion or exposure or other causes of which we shall speak. Thus in normal hangings death is instantaneous, whereas in crucifixion it may be delayed for hours and even days. If normal hanging may be regarded as a reasonably humane mode of execution, because of its instantaneity, crucifixion must be deemed utterly inhumane, if only because of its protractedness. What the two modes have in common is really nothing but the name: execution on the gallows and execution on the cross are equally referred to as "hangings." Even the crucifixion of Jesus is described in the New Testament as hanging, and his cross as the tree whereon he was hanged (Luke 23:39; Acts 5:30; 10:39).

The most notorious of Jewish hangings is that reported to have been decreed by Simon ben Shetah (2d century B.C.): eighty witches were hanged on a single day in Askalon.[33] The story, which is from a later period, goes that a scholar had a dream in which his dead master told him that the great Simon ben Shetah would have to suffer the pangs of hell because of women witches rampant in Askalon, against whom the law was not being enforced.[34] When Simon heard that, he promptly enforced the law, whether with the help of eighty young men whom, according to the story, he enlisted for the purpose or through other executioners. The historicity of this wholesale hanging has been challenged,[35] but if it did, in fact, take place, the question arises whether it was a result of judicial proceedings or an emergency measure undertaken on the personal responsibility of Simon, acting not as a court of justice but as an executive authority. The second possibility is bespoken by the fact, commented upon in the Talmud,[36] that rules of procedure and evidence were disregarded, yet Simon was known to insist, in his judicial capacity, on strictest compliance with all formalities and in particular the rules of evidence,[37] as well as by the fact that according to law these women should have been stoned, not hanged.[38] Thus it became well established Jewish tradition that Simon's action was of emergent character, and it has been held that "no law may be inferred from emergency measures."[39]

While we have no information of the particular "emergency" which prompted Simon to do what he is reported as doing, we certainly know the law, which is that to incur the death penalty, the witch, or the sorcerer, must have committed a real and overt act of witchcraft or sorcery, and the act been proved by at least two eyewitnesses; merely claiming the talent to practice witchcraft, even performing feats of sleight of hand or juggling to make people believe in one's possession of magic capacity, is not enough.[40] At the same time, to claim the talent to practice witchcraft is also forbidden,[41] though not, strictly speaking, a criminal offense. If the witches of Askalon had not yet committed any real and overt acts of witchcraft proper which could be proved against them, but had purported to own supernatural powers and made people believe it, the authorities responsible for upholding public order and religion may well have felt called upon summarily to put a stop to this perilous trickery, the more so as it apparently threatened to become endemic, if as many as eighty women held themselves out as practicing witchcraft in a small town like Askalon.[42] Had the women been stoned, the false image might have been created of a regular execution following a regular trial; they were advisedly hanged, so as to demonstrate that they had forfeited their lives, although they could not be brought up to Jerusalem for trial and execution in due course of legal process. Such an extrajudicial forfeiture of life might, in the eyes of men like Simon ben Shetah, be justified by the divine command "Thou shalt not suffer a witch to live" (Exod. 22:17) or "There shall not be found among you a witch" (Deut. 18:10), commands directed not to the witch as prohibiting her craft, but to the citizen and, a fortiori, to the leaders of the community, enjoining them not to suffer the presence or activity of a witch in their midst, whether she has been or can be prosecuted judicially or not. This wide, but still literal, interpretation of the divine behest was invoked until late in the Middle Ages throughout Christendom to justify the persecution of witches.[43] The action of Simon against the witches of Askalon had to be swift to be successful: if word got around of the steps planned against them, they were likely to disappear. Therefore, he ordered the action completed on one day, even if it meant employing eighty executioners. And because execution had to be quick, hanging was the method, the speediest way of causing death. The witches would never have been crucified, because that would have entailed slow, protracted, and painful death.

Witches were not the only offenders that might be done away with even without due process of law: a similar license appears to have been allowed by law in respect of certain idolaters and temple desecrators caught *in flagrante delicto*,[44] and, some scholars say, in respect also of inciters to idolatry so apprehended.[45] But nowhere is there indication that death had, in any of these cases, to be inflicted by hanging; on the contrary, we find that in one case the mode prescribed or authorized was slaying by the sword, copying the "zealous" act of Phineas, who took "a javelin in his hand" and killed the offender *in flagrante* (Num. 25:7–8, 11).[46] To modern minds this kind of dispensation with due process of law may be odious, but for the ancients the example of Phineas had kept its full splendor. In the words of Philo Judaeus, a contemporary of Jesus: "Rightly are all those who are imbued with virtuous zeal, entitled to inflict the punishment [on idolaters caught *in flagrante*] without dragging them before a court or a council or other authority; they are qualified by their hatred of evil and by their love for God . . . and they may be convinced that in that moment they are councillors, judges, commanders, assemblymen, prosecutors, witnesses, laws, even the people as a whole—all in one and at the same time."[47]

It follows that the hangings of Simon ben Shetah lend no support to the theory that hanging was an approved and common mode of Jewish execution. It was resorted to only when legitimate judicial modes were not legally available, or, possibly, also for the purpose of showing that the execution was nonjudicial. It was selected as an emergency mode for the reason that it led to a quick and relatively painless death; hence it could not have been hanging by crucifixion, on a cross, for that was as lingering as it was painful, but only hanging on a stake or gallows, where death was due to strangulation.[48]

How lingering and painful was death by crucifixion is revealed in the Gospels themselves.[49] The Gospel tradition fixes the hour of Jesus' crucifixion as the third (Mark 15:25), and when we take into account all that is said to have happened that morning, first in the palace of the high priest, then the escorting of Jesus to the *praetorium*, then the trial before Pilate, and finally the taking of Jesus to the place of execution, this was the earliest possible hour to fix. In the sixth hour, we are told, that is, when Jesus had already been on the cross for three hours, "a darkness was over all the earth" (Luke 23:44; Mark 15:33; Matt. 27:45), and three hours later, in the ninth hour, Jesus cried out in anguish, "My God, my God, why hast thou forsaken me?" (Matt. 27:46; Mark 15:34), or, "Father, into thy hands I commend my spirit" (Luke 23:46). Jesus survived on the cross for six hours.

Matthew tells that vinegar mingled with gall was given to Jesus to drink, but when he had tasted it he would not drink (27:34); according to Mark, it was wine mingled with myrrh, "and he received it not" (15:23). From Luke we know that "there followed him a great company of people, and of women, which also bewailed and lamented him" (23:27), and they would of a surety have followed him all the way to Golgotha. Combining both traditions, it may, I think, be permissible to infer that it was the women accompanying Jesus on his way to execution, and attending him in his last hours on the cross, who brought the wine and begged him to drink: it was an ancient Jewish custom that a condemned man, when led to the place of execution, had to be given a draft of wine with incense in it, "in order that he may lose his mind," that is, become unconscious; and it was "the dear women of Jerusalem who volunteered and brought the wine" and offered it to him.[50] This custom is told in the Talmud in connection with convicts about to be stoned, and stoning, too, as practiced in talmudic times, ends in a very swift death, not as the slow extremity of crucifixion. But, manifestly, if "the dear women of Jerusalem" saw to it that even a man about to die by stoning should be anesthetized against excess of pain, a fortiori would they be solicitous of one facing crucifixion; and if they did their act of grace to a man about to die by judgment of the Jewish court, with even greater compassion would they minister to one sentenced to death by the enemy governor. Jesus did not drink the wine, and his consciousness was awake throughout the six hours that he hung upon the cross.

According to Mark and Matthew, Jesus was silent all the time and did not speak until the sixth hour, when he gave up his spirit, but Luke and John report that he uttered. At the moment of crucifixion, he said, according to Luke, "Father, forgive them; for they know not what they do" (23:34), and when the "malefactors" who were crucified with him addressed him, he said to one of them, "Verily I say unto thee, To day shalt thou be with me in paradise" (23:43). According to John, when Jesus saw his mother and his disciple standing by, he said to his mother, "Woman, behold thy son!" and to the disciple, "Behold thy mother!" (19:26–27), and went on, "I thirst" (19:28). We are not concerned here with the theological implications of this or that utterance attributed to Jesus; suffice it to note the tradition, common at least to Luke and John, that while he was upon the cross he did speak, and his words could be heard.

We find in Roman sources, too, that men lived on for long hours on the cross, and spoke as they hung there. It is reported, for instance, of the Punic king Bomilcar, crucified by an exultant proletariat, that as he hung on the cross he addressed the crowd in chiding: his words are said to have been so moving that the remorse and pity of the people were stirred, but when he fell silent, he breathed his last.[51] And the emperor Claudius once expressed a desire to witness a crucifixion, of which he had heard as being the most ancient form of execution: *more maiorum*,[52] whereupon several convicts were one day crucified before his eyes, and when he had gazed on them for many an hour, he became impatient or weary and ordered that they be killed.[53]

On one important question, penologically, the Gospels are mute: whether Jesus was nailed to the cross or bound to it. It appears that it was normal Roman practice to bind the convict to the cross by ropes,[54] not nail him to it. But it is ancient Christian tradition that Jesus was nailed to the cross: the earliest text to mention nails piercing the hands of Jesus is the story of the Doubting Thomas (John 20:25); Paul speaks metaphorically of "the handwriting of ordinances that was against us" as nailed by Jesus to the cross (Col. 2:14); and Justin Martyr seems to be the first to speak of nails through the feet.[55] The fact that Jesus expired on the cross after some six hours had passed forcefully sustains the tradition that he was nailed, not bound: the nailing opened wounds in his flesh, and he must have lost much blood, greatly hastening death. If only bound, he might have endured yet a while, even several days.[56] The theory that he was taken down from the cross still living,[57] and its recent elaboration that this stratagem had been contrived by him beforehand,[58] also presuppose binding in the first instance; it must have been known that nailing, with its inevitable aftermath of hemorrhage, would bring death speedily. A victim nailed to the cross may die of weakness induced or aggravated by loss of blood and complications of open wounds. A victim bound may die of hunger or thirst, or of inclemency of weather, or, especially at nights, by attack of vulture or jackal, none of them causes normally predictable. How the end of crucifixion could differ from one case to another is illustrated by the story of Josephus, who, finding three of his friends crucified, asked the emperor to pardon them: when they were taken down, two died, and only the third survived.[59]

The tradition that Jesus was nailed to the cross, not bound to it, has further corroboration in Jewish legal sources. Certain provisions of the purification laws in the Talmud are based on the premise that persons crucified not only stayed alive for a length of time but lost blood throughout.[60] What is more, the "nail from the cross" (or the "nail from the crucified") is mentioned in the sabbatical laws as a medical appliance, and, as such, some authorities allow it to be carried on the Sabbath.[61] Medical opinion of the day seems to have been divided as to the use for which this nail ought to be recommended: there were those who thought it infallible in reducing swellings and inflammations;[62] others preferred it as a cure of nettle stings;[63] a later medical pundit insists on prescribing it for treatment of thrice-recurring fever.[64] But an assertion that all this superstitious nonsense imported from the heathen (the "Emorites") should not be clothed with statutory sanction was eventually voted down, on the view that the sabbatical laws must take cognizance of everything that the physicians may, at one time or another, accept as therapeutically useful.[65] That belief in the remedial efficacy of such nails was indeed an importation from Rome, presumably together with the cross itself, is highly probable: they seem to have been applied in Rome to treat epileptics,[66] and even to check the spread of infectious and epidemic diseases.[67]

The legal significance which Jewish canons assigned to nails of the cross, and to blood lost on it, suggests not only that the Romans in Judaea crucified by nailing, not binding, the victim to the cross, but also that such crucifixions were not uncommon. Crucifixion was, indeed, the only mode of execution "practiced by the government" of Rome in Judaea,[68] and it was practiced extensively enough. In the year 4 B.C., the Roman governor, Varus, ordered some two thousand Jewish underground fighters to be crucified in the mountains of Jerusalem;[69] after the crucifixion of Jesus, we find the governor Tiberius Alexander sentencing Jacob and Simon, sons of Judah the Galilean, to death by crucifixion;[70] within a few years, a second wholesale crucifixion of zealots was ordered by the governor Quadratus.[71] Then came Felix, who outdid his predecessors by crucifying not only rebels and zealots, but also any citizen suspected of collaborating with them,[72] and who succeeded him, on one single day had 3,600 Jews crucified, or killed on the way to the cross.[73] The emperor Titus bade that the prisoners taken during the siege of Jerusalem be crucified on the walls of the city, and day after day five hundred perished thus; the soldiers, Josephus reports, had to twist the wretched victims into the most gruesome postures, "as their number was very large, and there was no room for the many crosses, and not crosses enough for the many bodies."[74] It may be deduced, then, that crucifixion was not only the judicial mode of execution practiced by the Romans in Judaea, but also their non-judicial and quasi-military manner of dealing punitive death; and in view of the multitudinous crucifixions recorded by Josephus, it is hardly to be wondered at if the fate of crucified persons gave rise to legal problems of all kinds and those problems, again, to intricate discussion.

Apart from the context of purification and sabbatical ordinances, we find such discussion mainly in the laws of marriage and divorce. When a woman who has been married desires to remarry, she has first to adduce evidence that her husband has died; and the fact that he has been seen hanging on a cross is not in itself evidence of death.[75] The reason given for this rule is that "a rich matron might still come along and redeem him"[76]—another indication of how long the victim may linger on the cross before death comes. But there is a positive side to this: the longer life lasts, the brighter the prospect of ultimate redemption. We are entitled to infer that the wealthier matrons among the "dear women of Jerusalem," who, as we read, attended crucifixions, time and again succeeded in bribing Roman soldiers or officers to have a still-breathing victim taken down from the cross. If witnesses had beheld wild animals or vultures attacking the men on the cross, their testimony would be accepted as proof of death provided that the parts of the body seen to be so attacked were vital ("the parts where the soul goes out") ;[77] this points to the fact, seemingly established by experience, that death upon the cross not seldom was the result of rending by birds or beasts of prey. There is, as well, some evidence that not a few Roman emperors regarded crucifixion as only the prelude to throwing the corpse to the beasts.[78]

In the ensuing talmudic exegesis, it is said that people, places, and times differ from one another: one man dies more quickly because of his obesity, the other more slowly, being strong and athletic; in one place, where it is cooler, men will hold out longer than in another, where it is hot and dry; and physical suffering is easier to bear in winter than in summer.[79] No general rule can, therefore, be laid down for the length of time, or even minimal and maximal lengths of time, that a man can stay alive on the cross. But it is provided that where three days have elapsed after crucifixion, evidence is no longer admissible, not because it could reasonably be assumed that the victim was still alive, but because his features would no longer be recognizable, so that the witnesses cannot be relied upon to identify the man whom they saw hanging unless there are other means of identification.[80]

Another rule provides that if a man crucified speaks from the cross and orders a bill of divorcement to be written to his wife in his name, his injunction is to be complied with: his body may have become weak, but his mind is presumed still to be sound.[81] The same rule applies where he did not speak but nodded his head in agreement to the question whether he wished the bill written.[82] The object in writing such a bill is to avoid the trouble of proving death: the wife would be allowed to remarry not as a widow but as a divorcee.

The "dear women of Jerusalem" were wont, as we saw, to try to render unconscious the men about to be crucified, and so spare them pain and torment. Jesus would have none of their ministrations, and did not sip the drink which they held out, nor, it appears, did the two convicts crucified together with him. Both, like Jesus himself, were fully conscious throughout: according to Luke, one said to him, "If thou be Christ, save thyself and us" (23:39), and the other rebuked him, "saying, Dost not thou fear God, seeing thou art in the same condemnation? And we indeed justly; for we receive the due reward of our deeds; but this man hath done nothing amiss" (23:40–41). According to Mark and Matthew, the two who were crucified with Jesus joined the others present in reviling and railing at him (Mark 15:32; Matt. 27:44). Though Jesus said nothing, there is no doubt that he heard the abuse: his ignoring of it was not a sign of weakness or of indifference, but deliberate. When he sees fit to retort, his voice rings out: one of the two says, "Lord, remember me when thou comest into thy kingdom" (Luke 23:42), and Jesus bows down to him: "Verily I say unto thee, To day shalt thou be with me in paradise" (23:43).

We are concerned with the phenomenological rather than the theological implications of this story. From the theological point of view, differing explanations have been offered to give the triple crucifixion some deeper meaning: the commonest is that already propounded by Mark, that Scripture had to be fulfilled, he that "hath poured out his soul unto death" was to be "numbered with the transgressors" (Isa. 53:12; see Mark 15:28), a prophecy which, in a Lucan tradition, had been made by Jesus himself the evening before (Luke 22:37). This tendency to make events occur so as to demonstrate that Scripture fulfilled itself in Jesus we shall find in other happenings reported as taking place at or instantly after the crucifixion; but just as it is, of course, possible that the events were framed to fit Scripture, so it is equally likely that they did take place and that scriptural verses were afterward invoked to point the desired theological moral. Fulfillment of a scriptural prophecy by a particular event would not in itself render that event improbable, even in the eyes of rational nontheologians; but where a reported occurrence is in itself, on objective grounds, improbable, its reporting may well be due to the theological proclivity to see Scripture realized. It was, for example, pointed out a century ago that the report of the "chief priests" (Mark 15:31) with "the scribes and elders" (Matt. 27:41) and the "rulers" (Luke 23:35), not to speak of the common folk around, mocking and reviling Jesus while he hung on the cross, could have been inserted into the Gospel story for only one purpose, namely, to affirm that Jesus verily underwent all that the Psalmist had foretold: "All they that see me laugh me to scorn: they shoot out the lip, they shake the head, saying, He trusted on the Lord that he would deliver him: let him deliver him, seeing he delighted in him" (Ps. 22:7–8). Jesus was being ridiculed identically: "He trusted in God: let him deliver him now, if he will have him" (Matt. 27:43). It simply will not bear belief that priests or scribes or elders or rulers or any commoner should mock and curse a fellow Jew hanging on a Roman cross, whatever his crime was. Hence the theory that Scripture had to be fulfilled;[33] and that, by the same stroke, the Jews could be presented as the cruel and inhuman creatures, lacking the least decency, and true to the vileness of character portrayed throughout the Passion story, was only a further and more welcome ground for arranging that Scripture fulfill itself.

The crucifixion was bad enough without all this execration, and

the evangelists need not have tried to make it worse to aggravate
the ordeal of Jesus. They may, in their days in Rome, have witnessed crucifixions where the mob was licensed to vilify the victim
and people gave free rein to their baser instincts; or the normally
concomitant scourgings may have impressed them as the kind of
consequential vulgarity that had to be provided in the story of the
crucifixion of Jesus no less. But irrespective of all attendant excesses, crucifixion was known in Rome as the gravest and cruelest
death (*summum supplicium*) ,[84] originally practiced in the more
barbarous and less gentle ages of bygone ancestors (*more
maiorum*) ,[85] and kept on only as a mode of putting slaves and
aliens to death, or for the most heinous crimes.[86] Tacitus reports
a debate in the Roman senate, where a member protested against
its infliction, arguing that "it is not what a depraved criminal
may deserve, that we ought to inflict on him: in the days of an
enlightened ruler and of a senate unfettered by precedent, hang-
man and cross and ropes should be abolished, and punishments
provided for in the laws that can be inflicted without cruelty by
the judges and that will not disgrace this generation."[87] There
was no echo of this lonely voice, but it shows how much, even
then, more liberal and progressive Romans recoiled from the use
of crucifixion. The general horror that it existed can be felt in
the names given to appurtenances of it: the victim was made to
stand on an "unhappy" plank (*infelix lignum*) and was hanged
on an infamous beam (*infamis stipes*) .[88] Though other manners
of execution practiced in Rome were not distinguished for any
humaneness, this was, as Cicero put it, the most cruel and terrible
penalty (*crudelissimum et teterimum supplicium*) :[89] it was, as
has recently been remarked, "the acme of the torturer's art."[90]

It is significant that in the Gospel According to John we find
no report or mention of any insult or mockery hurled at Jesus by
Jews in general or by the chief priests present (19:21) in particular. It is the Jews who are represented by the fourth evangelist
as leading him away for crucifixion (19:16) , and, at least by insinuation, as crucifying him (19:18) . There could be no plainer,
no more unmistakable, indication that the fourth evangelist was
determined to outvie his predecessors in blaming and branding
the Jews. All the same, he gave up the Marcan tradition of their
tirades against Jesus on the cross, though Matthew and, to a less

extent, Luke had adopted it. To be faithful to his tendentious purpose, he should have been quick to take it up and exploit it to the hilt. Be it noted that, as far as concerns the mockery of the Roman soldiers, John follows the tradition of the Synoptic Gospels, though he places it at a somewhat earlier stage (18:2–3) : the more remarkable, surely, that he knows nothing of any mockery by the Jews. To suggest that he did not mention this or that reviling because he "ignored the details which he regarded as merely accessory"[91] fails to do justice either to the dramatic quality or to the anti-Jewish bias of the Johannine accounts. And the hypothesis that John felt that for his account he had no need to speak of it, because his account had been "stripped of any element of proof from prophecy,"[92] is disproved by at least two instances of Scripture fulfilled recorded in John (19:28, 36). Either, then, John had a tradition of his own, which taught him surely that the Jews had not mocked Jesus, or he chose to pay no heed to the report of the Synoptic Gospels because of its inherent incongruity. Some scholars maintain that John must have been present in person at the crucifixion of Jesus and reported what had actually happened there, and in particular the exchange of words between Jesus and his mother and the disciple (19:25–27), as an eyewitness who heard them spoken and beheld the speakers;[93] that would be all the more reason to prefer his account of the events to that of the other evangelists and to discard, as he did, their tale of Jewish mockery and abuse. It seems that Luke had similar scruples: while his "rulers" sneered at Jesus, "the people stood beholding" (23:35), refraining, strangely enough, from participation in what, according to Mark (15:29) and Matthew (27:39), must have been a public pastime.

Evident though the incongruity of the Marcan account is, it is argued that there will always be people to derive "some sickening pleasure in the sight of the tortures of others, a feeling which is increased and not diminished by the sight of pain," and that "the cross represented miserable humanity reduced to the last degree of impotence, suffering and degradation,"[94] and hence a welcome target of popular contumely. This kind of ready-made psychology ignores, once again, the peculiar position of the Judaean Jews under Roman dominion: it is totally out of the question that the average, that is, the not particularly depraved, common man, seeing a compatriot crucified at the hands of the detestable Romans, would or could so have demeaned himself as to stop and pour vituperation on the hapless head of the victim, his own neighbor and fellow citizen and tribesman. If he could do nothing to hearten or comfort him, he might stand there mute, seeking at least to convey sympathy by his mere presence, but would never open his lips to hurt him. I do not think that any idiosyncratic Jewish trait need be invoked to establish this: the same might be said of any nation under foreign rule that has preserved a remnant of national pride and solidarity, and is not utterly devoid of elementary kindliness. However pleasurable the sight may be to perverts of a body writhing in agony, or motionless and impotent, no perversion will withstand the pressure of public opinion and the threat of clandestine vengeance by zealots; and the first and slightest attempt at "amusement" at Jesus' expense would have been energetically and efficaciously suppressed on the spot. Even on the unwarranted assumption that among the Jews were some who had had a hand, or an interest, in the execution of Jesus or in doing away with him otherwise, the imagination boggles at the thought that, having won their presumably secret purpose, they would now parade their triumph or satisfaction in public: on the one hand, they would have to fear the scorn of the masses, who would not lightly pardon so fatal a case of collaboration with the enemy; on the other, not only possible pangs of conscience, but simple common and sober prudence, would prompt them to hold back and stay home. Nor can they be supposed to have come to the scene of the crucifixion in an endeavor to quiet their guilty consciences in a bedlam of noisy jeers and rude insults: for if they really did regret what they had done to Jesus, they could still try to save him, and if Pilate had in truth been as reluctant as the evangelists make him out to be to see Jesus crucified, there must have been some chance still of obtaining a pardon from him before Jesus died. In short, everything speaks for the accuracy of the Johannine tradition that no chief priests and no elders, no scribes or rulers, and no Jews, whoever they may have been, cursed Jesus or mocked him after his crucifixion: all who were present were stricken dumb, in grief and bitter disappointment.

Another Johannine tradition has it that when Jesus knew "that all things were now accomplished," he said from the cross, "I thirst" (19:28). "Now there was set a vessel full of vinegar: and they filled a sponge with vinegar, and put it upon hyssop, and put it to his mouth. When Jesus therefore had received the vinegar, he said, It is finished: and he bowed his head, and gave up the ghost" (19:29–30). We do not hear who "they" were that put the drink to Jesus' lips. Luke reports that the soldiers who had mocked him came to him and offered him vinegar (23:36); but there is no mention of Jesus accepting it. According to Mark and Matthew, when Jesus had cried out, "My God, my God, why hast thou forsaken me?," of some of them that stood there, "one ran and filled a sponge full of vinegar, and put it on a reed, and gave him to drink" (Mark 15:35–36; Matt. 27:46–48); and when Jesus had taken from the drink, he "yielded up the ghost" (Matt. 27:50; similarly Mark 15:37). Here we have a tradition that in some form is common to all Gospels; and it is not without interest for our inquiry.

We can dismiss the Lucan version that the drink was offered to Jesus by the Roman soldiers, if only because Luke here is a sole dissenter. The other evangelists are unanimous in reporting that one or more from among the bystanders fetched the drink and gave it to Jesus; John says so not expressly but by reasonable implication. Whether it was on hearing the cry or sigh of Jesus, or on their own impulse, they brought him vinegar: not water, which would have quenched his thirst, or wine, which might have robbed him of his senses, but vinegar, which neither relieves thirst nor anesthetizes. They had brought it for Jesus to drink, knew that it worked to hasten death, and that, indeed, was what they proposed to do and shorten his agony. A medieval writer assures us that "according to certain people, the fact of drinking vinegar under conditions such as these, is apt to hasten death, or so it is said."[95] This cautious assurance is reminiscent of a talmudic debate whether vinegar has or has not a quality of refreshment: those who gainsay this allow its drinking on fast days, even on the Day of Atonement; those who hold that it refreshes forbid its drinking then.[96] Still, it may have the quality of speeding death where dissolution has set in, even though it may also be "refreshing"; and we do find it said that any drink, whatever its nature, would be apt to speed death in those circumstances.[97] Most scholars, however, are agreed that the evangelists chose vinegar as the draft offered to Jesus not because of any inherent virtue but, again, to make scriptural prophecies come true, as, for instance, "in my thirst they gave me vinegar to drink" (Ps. 69:21).[98] The Psalmist decries the giving of vinegar as wholly inept to quench thirst, but on that day people evidently thought that the drink which they offered Jesus would relieve him of his torment and bring him peace.

The episode lends further weight to the view that the people present, so far from wishing to harass Jesus and vilify him, were single-minded in purpose—to lighten his sufferings as best they could. Of course, the evangelists would not, or could not, admit that in so many words, and, clinging to their policy, put into the mouths of the people such phrases as would be bound, in the reader's eyes, to empty their deeds of all merit. That they had no valid tradition of what was actually said by the people may be inferred from the inconsistencies of the Gospel stories. According to Mark, the man who had run and brought the vinegar to Jesus said to him, proffering it: "Let alone; let us see whether Elias will come to take him down" (15:36). This, it would seem, was a little too much even for Matthew: that man was not the mocker, for he at least would be consistent; but "the rest said, Let be, let us see whether Elias will come to save him" (27:49). The fourth evangelist dismisses the Marcan version, even as moderated by Matthew, as either unreasonable or unnecessary: his story is straightforward, that when Jesus had said, "I thirst," they gave him of the vinegar, of which there was there already "a vessel full"; and when Jesus "therefore had received the vinegar, he said, It is finished" (John 19:28–30). The words "There was set a vessel full of vinegar" (19:29) imply that the vinegar was always kept available and handy at the place of crucifixion, and that what "they" did to Jesus "they" would do to any person dying on the cross, from compassion, to be sure, and not in ill will. Luke, we recall, lets the Roman soldiers administer the vinegar to Jesus, and they, confessedly, "mocked him" before offering it to him, and at once said to him: "If thou be the king of the Jews, save thyself" (23:36–37): we have already expressed our doubts as to the acceptability of the Lucan version that the vinegar was offered to Jesus by the Roman soldiers; but, having before him the Marcan story that those who

did so mocked him at the same time, it is not at all surprising that
Luke scouted the notion that they could have been Jews, and replaced them by the Roman soldiers.

The Gospel According to John goes on to tell that "The Jews
therefore, because it was the preparation, that the bodies should
not remain upon the cross on the sabbath day, (for that sabbath
day was an high day,) besought Pilate that their legs might be
broken, and that they might be taken away. Then came the
soldiers, and brake the legs of the first, and of the other which
was crucified with him. But when they came to Jesus, and saw
that he was dead already, they brake not his legs: But one of the
soldiers with a spear pierced his side, and forthwith came there
out blood and water" (19:31–34). It was only after this episode
that Joseph of Arimathaea "besought Pilate that he might take
away the body of Jesus" (19:38). In contradistinction, Mark
reports that "when the even was come, because it was the preparation, that is, the day before the sabbath, Joseph of Arimathaea
. . . came, and went in boldly unto Pilate, and craved the body
of Jesus. And Pilate marvelled if he were already dead; and calling unto him the centurion, he asked him whether he had been
any while dead. And when he knew it of the centurion, he gave
the body to Joseph" (15:42–45). If the Johannine version is to
be accepted, the Jews came to Pilate and told him that Jesus had
not yet died, and for those tidings Pilate would not have required
confirmation from the officer commanding his troops, because the
time elapsed since the crucifixion would not ordinarily have been
long enough for death to supervene. The petition which the Jews
desired to make of the governor was that he order the legs of the
crucified to be broken: it was the eve of Sabbath and Passover,
and the bodies should not be allowed to hang on the crosses after
sunset; and the breaking of their legs would hasten death. The
Jewish delegation which presented itself to the governor and submitted this plea must have left Golgotha while Jesus was still
alive; otherwise it was pointless. In other words, when the delegation was absent pleading with Pilate, the people who had stayed
behind heard Jesus say, "I thirst," and gave him of the vinegar.
And Jesus must have died before the delegation came back with
Pilate's commands. If the Marcan version is to be accepted, the
whole incident of the breaking of legs is imaginary, because if it

had really happened Pilate would not have expressed wonderment that Jesus had already died and have verified the information by questioning his centurion. This particular difficulty would not arise according to the Gospels of Matthew and Luke, for there Pilate is not reported as voicing surprise at Jesus' death (Matt. 27:58; Luke 23:52).

While, according to Mark, the governor was amazed that Jesus should already be dead, according to John he agreed to have the death hastened. The breaking of legs is not, nor is it meant to be, an extra torment: it is the *coup de grâce*, intended to bring the sufferings to a swifter end. The Jews who besought Pilate to have Jesus' legs broken are, however, reported to have acted not out of pure compassion but so that they might perform their religious duty and bury him before sunset. As far as Pilate was concerned, there was no objection whatever to letting the bodies hang on the crosses throughout the night and for days and nights to come; on the contrary, it was, as we have seen, the well-established Roman custom to expose the victims on the crosses, even after death, to jackal or vulture: to be devoured and dismembered by "the fowls of the heaven and the beasts of the earth"[99] was regarded as a supplementary and particularly degrading punishment, which was the condemned man's deserts, and of which he could be relieved only by an act of grace. By ordering the legs of the crucified men to be broken, Pilate in effect conceded waiver of some of the punitive incidents of crucifixion, and as the waiver was represented to him as a matter not of grace or mitigation but rather of religious observance, he saw no reason to refuse it.

It is true enough that Jews were strictly forbidden to let a corpse hang overnight "upon the tree" (Deut. 21:23), a prohibition which, although by the tenor of the law applying only to persons executed for capital offenses under Jewish law and by sentence of a Jewish court, was certainly enforced—perhaps by analogy—in respect of persons executed by sentence of a non-Jewish court as well. The approach of the Sabbath and feast day only lent a special urgency to what was a binding duty in any circumstances. If burial had to be finished before sunset on any working day, then it must be exceptionally hurried on the eve of a festival day, when people had to purify themselves in time to attend temple services, if they were to have sufficient leisure after the interment to prepare for the feast. Now, if it had really been the Jews who brought pressure upon Pilate, on this of all days, that Jesus be crucified, how could it be that in all probability they did not know that his death might be delayed until after sunset? From practical experience, to which the aforementioned rules of Jewish law bear ample witness, they must have been aware that days would often pass until a man died on the cross: if, nevertheless, they cried out for the crucifixion of Jesus on that very morning, it must have been in the knowledge that the night and the feast would be likely to supervene before he died, and that they would have to let him hang on the cross overnight and during the feast. It would seem that they did not care. One might say, of course, that "the Jews" who clamored for Jesus' crucifixion were not identical with "the Jews" who asked Pilate to have his legs broken; but then there is no differentiation between this and that kind of "Jews" in the Gospel of John. If, for instance, the Jews who besought Pilate to hasten Jesus' death were friends or disciples of Jesus, the evangelist would surely have said so, just as he made no secret of the particular personal relationship of Joseph of Arimathaea to Jesus (19:38; similarly Luke 23:50–51; Matt. 27:57; Mark 15:43). If any differentiation were permissible between the categories of "Jews," it would be consequential to distinguish between Jews learned in the law, and conscious of their religious duty, who would see to due compliance with the rules in respect of the prescribed daylight burial of the executed man and the proper keeping of Sabbath and feast days, and other Jews who, on the eve of Passover, allegedly had nothing better in their minds than to give vent to hysterical clamor for the crucifixion of Jesus.

Moreover, if "the Jews" who desired to bury Jesus before nightfall were the same as "the Jews" who had cried out for his crucifixion, another query would arise. We read in John that the Jews "went not into the judgment hall, lest they should be defiled; but that they might eat the passover" (18:28). If, then, they desired to keep themselves pure for the evening's ritual repast, how is it that they were prepared, in the afternoon, to defile and sully themselves by burying the dead? Whether it would have defiled or sullied them to enter the judgment hall is open to the gravest doubts, but that it would to take part in a burial is incontestable

(Num. 19:11–14). Either they had no compunction about uncleanness in the morning, in which case they would have entered
the judgment hall, or they had the strongest compunction about
it in the afternoon, so shortly before the commencement of the
feast, in which case they would have taken no steps enabling
them to bury Jesus before the feast began. The truth is that in
the morning, as we have shown, they did not enter the judgment
hall, not for fear of being defiled, but for entirely different reasons
beyond their control; and in the afternoon they were gladly prepared to become unclean, if only they could bestow on Jesus and
his fellow convicts the last favor and honor of a proper Jewish
burial.

It has been suggested that the episode of the breaking of the
legs owes its *raison d'être* to the conclusion which the evangelist
wished to reach: "For these things were done, that the scripture
should be fulfilled, A bone of him shall not be broken" (19:36).
It is only a "lamb without blemish" (Exod. 12:5) that is fit for
Passover, as a sacrifice to God, and it is "without blemish" that,
on the sanctification of Passover, Jesus would make his ultimate
sacrifice to God. "Neither shall ye break a bone thereof" (Exod.
12:46) is an enlargement of the basic injunction to choose a lamb
without blemish; but that the breaking of bones was singled out
for special mention as spoiling the immaculacy of the paschal
lamb plainly suggests that unbroken bones are the cardinal
attribute of a flawless lamb. However usual the breaking of bones
may have been with lambs prepared for a meal or a sacrifice, you
would not normally break the bones of a man; and the fact that
the legs of Jesus were unbroken would have been without significance, and would not have lent itself to any possible comparison with the unblemished sacrificial lamb, were it not for the
report of the breaking of the legs of the two convicts crucified
together with Jesus, or for the general knowledge of a custom of
breaking the legs of convicts hanging on the cross. It is after the
legs of those two others had been broken that the miracle occurred
of Jesus left intact: God took his spirit when he was still without
blemish, his sacrifice was thus made perfect, as of the paschal
lamb, and his "precious blood," spilled on the cross as was the
blood of "a lamb without blemish and without spot" upon the
temple altar, would redeem the sins of men (I Pet. 1:19).

"When they came to Jesus, and saw that he was dead already, they brake not his legs; But one of the soldiers with a spear pierced his side, and forthwith came there out blood and water" (John 19:33–34). This thrust, entailing, as it evidently did, the opening of a wound, would at first sight appear to nullify all the endeavors to leave Jesus intact and "without blemish"; but it may be that anything done to his body after death could no longer diminish his faultlessness, for it was at the moment of death that the sacrifice without blemish ascended to heaven. Or it may have been considered no less important than fulfilling the Scripture's "A bone of him shall not be broken" (19:36) to realize another prophecy of Holy Writ, namely, "They shall look on him whom they pierced" (19:37). The sentence is taken from a prophecy of Zechariah (12:10) in which God promises to "pour upon the house of David, and upon the inhabitants of Jerusalem, the spirit of grace and of supplications: and they shall look upon me whom they have pierced, and they shall mourn for him, as one mourneth for his only son, and shall be in bitterness for him, as one that is in bitterness for his firstborn. . . . In that day there shall be a great mourning in Jerusalem. . . . And the land shall mourn, every family apart" (12:10–12). The words "and they shall look upon me whom they pierced" are taken out of context in their quotation in John (19:37), and it may not be amiss to restore them to their place: the sight of the pierced—whoever he may be[100]—will cause general mourning and lamentation in Jerusalem; there will be no family and no household left unafflicted; that this prophecy was truly fulfilled in the death of Jesus is to be shown by the fact that his side was "pierced." As we established, a sense of general affliction there undoubtedly was, and there can be little question that the lamentation and mourning over Jesus were common and widespread throughout Jerusalem. But the authors of the Gospel According to John does not seem to have been sufficiently aware that the prophecy of a deep and universal affliction at the death of Jesus had anyhow come true, regardless of any "piercing."

It has been argued that, physiologically, the story of the piercing cannot be sustained, as blood and water would not come out together from a pierced corpse, certainly not so as to be discernible by the naked eye.[101] The whole story was seemingly inserted for the sake of fulfillment of the scriptural prophecy, not on the strength of any valid tradition of an actual happening. And what is true of the piercing would in all probability be true of the breaking of legs: that unsubstantiated tale, too, might have been written into the Gospel According to John for the very same reason. The blood and water issuing were interpreted as symbols of the Eucharist and of baptism,[102] as Jesus is said to have come "by water and blood" (I John 5:6) ; and this, for the evangelist, must have borne a special meaningfulness, since he insists on the veracity of the eyewitness on whose "record" he relies (John 19:35) . But even that insistence has been found to fall short of counterbalancing the fact that these incidents, and the presence of mother, disciple, and eyewitness at the crucifixion, are not mentioned by the earlier evangelists: if this had been based on any sound tradition, the Synoptic Gospels could never have passed over them in silence.[103]

Nonetheless, it is submitted that the fourth evangelist may well have possessed information, or a sound tradition, of the breaking of the legs or bones of the two particular convicts, or of crucified convicts in general. We find that the emperor Augustus had the legs of one of his secretaries broken, for divulging official secrets;[104] and Tiberius did likewise with men who would not be indecently used by him.[105] These were instances of separate punishment, but we also find the breaking of legs as incidental to crucifixion,[106] not necessarily only as a means of speeding death, but also as a prelude to the actual crucifixion.[107] In contrast to the drawing of water and blood by the piercing of Jesus' side, for which there is no precedent or parallel, the breaking of legs appears to be in line with regular usage, and, if for this reason only, the Johannine tradition that the Jews asked Pilate to order the breaking of the legs of the convicts on the crosses cannot be dismissed offhand. It is not without interest that, while Pilate was asked to order his soldiers to break their legs and seems to have done so, no such plea had been made to him as to the piercing of the side of Jesus: it was "one of the soldiers" who, on his own prompting, as it appears, drove in the sword (19:34) , and it is not clear from the record whether he wanted to make sure that Jesus had breathed his last or whether it was just another act of insult and reviling. Even, therefore, if it had happened at all and was not invented merely to have Scripture fulfilled, it would have no bearing on the role in which "the Jews" were cast.

It is "the Jews" (19:31) who are expressly credited with beseeching Pilate to hasten death by the breaking of legs. It is, needless to say, quite out of tune and out of context to find "the Jews" given the merit of humanity or kindliness: it might have dovetailed much more neatly into the general picture if Pilate himself had been fathered with the original will to cut short the sufferings of Jesus on the cross, whereupon we would, as a matter of course, expect the Jews to protest loudly and insist that his sufferings be intensified and protracted; the more distressful and the lengthier, the better. If, relentless persecutors and crucifiers of Jesus as they were depicted to be, the Jews asked Pilate that Jesus' legs be broken, surely they must have been urged by evil motives: maybe it was not at all to speed his death and abridge his pain, but to add to his torment and suffering, and the breaking of legs would certainly inflict anguish enough. It has, accordingly, been suggested that the Jews used the "preparation" for the approaching Sabbath as a pretext only, making it appear to Pilate as if they were concerned with hastening Jesus' death, whereas in truth they were out to aggravate his misery, to cause him greater hurt and ache; and the gullible Pilate, in his ingenuousness, yielded to their suasion and benignly condescended to confer on Jesus this last grace.[108]

If our thesis is correct that the Jews loved Jesus and identified themselves with him, and that, at the sight of what he had to endure, their love could not but gain depth on this—his last—day, and that neither they nor any of their leaders had a say in his prosecution or condemnation, then it becomes plausible that when they saw him in agony on the cross, fluttering between life and death, they ran to the governor, entreating of him a word to his officers that would bring death without further heart-rending pause. The rapid nearing of the holy feast was, as we have said, a welcome argument to put to Pilate; but that fact must have weighed on the mind of Jesus as heavily as on the minds of the onlookers: Jesus was the last person to wish or agree that the Sabbath be desecrated for his sake or the festal night profaned by letting a crucified man—the "curse of God"—hang overnight without burial. It was because they all knew of Jesus' own susceptibilities in the matter that the Jews were all the more anxious that the ultimate honors of the dead be paid to a beloved brother before the Sabbath entered.

If, on the other hand, it were true that the Jews had demanded the crucifixion of Jesus that very morning, and that Pilate had given in to them reluctantly and against his better judgment, not only would those same Jews not have dared now to come to him with this plea, but he would never have acceded to it had it been made: he would still harbor a grudge against them, and their further, and now altogether inconsistent, importunity could only arouse his fury and extinguish his last flicker of patience. Moreover, they would themselves have foreseen that, as likely as not, they would not be allowed to quit his palace unharmed. If the Jews did in fact beseech Pilate to hasten Jesus' death by ordering his legs to be broken, then this was the one and only time that they confronted the governor in the matter of Jesus: the one and only errand respecting Jesus that any Jews essayed to Pilate was an errand of mercy and compassion.

The story, common to all the Gospels, that the Roman soldiers who had crucified Jesus "parted his garments, casting lots upon them, what every man should take" (Mark 15:24; similarly Matt. 27:35; Luke 23:34; John 19:23), also preached fulfillment of a scriptural prophecy, namely, "They part my garments among them, and cast lots upon my vesture" (Ps. 22:18). There is authority for the contention that it was the right of the executioners in Rome to appropriate the convicts' garments,[109] but no such custom is reported in Judaea. As only Jesus' garments, and not those of the two convicts crucified with him, were divided among the soldiers, it would seem that the story had no purpose save fulfillment of Scripture, the more so as his garments were not outstandingly valuable, made of one piece of unseamed cloth (John 19:23) and apparently humble enough.

We find such special treatment again accorded to Jesus, in preference to his fellow convicts, in the matter of burial. We are told that Joseph of Arimathaea "craved the body of Jesus" (Mark 15:43; Matt. 27:58; Luke 23:52; John 19:38), but said nothing about the bodies of the others. By Jewish law and custom, it was to be expected that he would do the two the act of grace that he did Jesus. It may, of course, be that he did not, in fact, dis-

criminate, but buried all three, but that the evangelists did not
mention it, simply because the fate of the two was no longer
relevant to their story. We may assume that Joseph, described as
a disciple of Jesus (Matt. 27:57; John 19:38), followed Jesus'
teaching: "If ye love them which love you, what reward have ye?
do not even the publicans the same? And if ye salute your
brethren only, what do ye more than others? do not even the
publicans so?" (Matt. 5:46–47); and that what he did for the man
whom he loved he did, no less, for strangers whom he knew not.

While the Jews who went to Pilate to ask him to hasten Jesus'
death are shrouded in anonymity, the name of the Jew who
begged Pilate's permission to bury him has been preserved for
eternal fame. Joseph of Arimathaea (in Hebrew: *Haramati,* or
of the highlands) is said to have been a member of the Sanhedrin
(Mark 15:43; Luke 25:50), and some scholars theorize that he was
personally known to the evangelists and served them as source
of primary information[110]—which can be neither proved nor disproved; but if the evangelists, or any of them, had firsthand intelligence from him of what took place at the meeting of the Sanhedrin the night before, they would certainly not have withheld
their source, any more than they withheld his name in the burial
episode. But it would also have to be anticipated that had this
Joseph, this disciple of Jesus, taken part in a meeting of the
Sanhedrin such as the Gospels describe, he would have spoken
up and tried to exert some influence on the course of events; or
if he reported the proceedings to the evangelists, that he would
at least have asserted that he had done everything in his power
to avert the tragedy. As far as we are concerned, we may safely
accept the tradition that this disciple of Jesus, like other disciples
and followers of his, was a member of the Sanhedrin and attended
the session in the high priest's home the night before; but if he
did report to any evangelist what had transpired, he did not—
alas!—succeed in persuading them to transcribe his report in the
Gospels. What—as we believe—had really taken place at the session
is, assuredly, in total consonance with the membership in the
Sanhedrin, and with the presence, of Joseph of Arimathaea as
well as of any other disciple and follower or sympathizer of
Jesus, at the meeting.

A recent writer has suggested that Jesus and Joseph were parties to a conspiracy: Joseph agreed to administer a drug which would keep Jesus alive but give him the appearance of death; then he would ask permission to take him off the cross, and pretend to bury him; and after a few days Jesus would rise again as if resurrected.[111] So far from subscribing to a theory which would, in effect, incriminate both Jesus and Joseph, if not legally, then at least morally and theologically, we prefer to content ourselves with the simple and very human story told in the Gospels, that Joseph was a friend and follower of Jesus who volunteered to bury him, and did bury him in his own land, before nightfall, in the finest of Jewish custom and tradition.

The Roman law was that a convict, after execution, might not be buried:[112] we have seen that the crucified, in particular, were left on the cross until beasts and birds of prey devoured them.[113] Guards were mounted on duty at the cross to prevent kinsfolk or friends from taking down a corpse and burying it; unauthorized burial of a crucified convict was a criminal offense.[114] The emperor or his officers might, exceptionally, grant kinsfolk or friends authorization to bury the convict,[115] and what in Rome was the imperial prerogative was in a province the right of the governor. What Joseph of Arimathaea asked of Pilate was, therefore, nothing unusual, nor is Pilate reported to have made any difficulty in granting his wish. We know from Josephus that the Jews were always very solicitous and particular about burying their dead, and those especially whom Roman crucifixions had killed,[116] and it would appear that they sought and got special burial permits in each individual instance. It is unarguable, however, that had it really been the Jews who petitioned Pilate to crucify Jesus or anybody else, and even had Joseph of Arimathaea not been one of them, the governor would have entertained their later petition for permission to have him taken off the cross and buried: if the governor had, indeed, "delivered" Jesus to the Jews for crucifixion, he would not now "deliver" him to them for burial. And it is highly improbable that he would have recognized Joseph of Arimathaea as having abstained from the persecution of Jesus that morning: these Judaeans were all much of a muchness in his eyes.

Jesus was buried in the grave which Joseph had dug on his own land (Matt. 27:60; Luke 23:53; John 19:41), proof that he was not regarded as a convict executed by a judgment of a Jewish court, which, indeed, he was not—we know that convicts executed by order of the Jewish court must be interred in a cemetery set aside for that special purpose and known as the court's grave-yard.[117] The law was that private persons were not allowed to bury such convicts, and that no one might mourn them, whereas convicts executed by order of the Roman governor had to be buried and mourned like any person who had died a natural death.[118] It would not matter of what offense a convict had been found guilty by the Romans: that it was a Roman court which had sentenced him was enough to entitle him to the benefits of Jewish burial and traditional Jewish mourning. So his mother and Mary Magdalene sat down at the side of Jesus' grave and mourned (Matt. 27:61; Mark 15:47), until the Sabbath came, after timely readying of the spices and ointments for his body (Luke 23:56); everything was done in "the manner of the Jews" in burying their own dead (John 27:40). It was Jewish custom to clothe the dead in white linen,[119] and so Jesus was "wound in linen clothes" (John 19:40), "fine linen" bought by Joseph (Mark 15:46). He was buried and mourned and honored as every Jew would have been who, like him, had been the victim of persecution by the Roman oppressors. It was in a garden that he was laid to rest, near the place where he had been crucified; and in the garden was a new sepulcher "wherein was never man yet laid" (John 19:41): that was the last resting place that Joseph had chosen for his master and teacher, and he would make sure that the homage befitting the great dead of Israel would be accorded in full. Joseph did his simple duty, as one Jew to another, and that he was not alone in doing it is attested by John (19:39), who here again brings in Nicodemus, the Pharisee (3:1), and who, for that matter, could properly have brought in all the "Pharisees" of Jerusalem to join hands in paying Jesus their farewell respects.

PART THREE

The Aftermath

9 PETER AND PAUL

Luke reports that after the death of Jesus his disciples, the apostles, organized themselves into a group and started to spread the new faith. Their main spokesman, Peter, is said to have reproached "the men of Judaea and all ye that dwell at Jerusalem" for having "taken" Jesus and, "by wicked hands," crucified and slain him; hearing which the people were "pricked in their hearts," deeply troubled, and afraid (Acts 2:14–37). Again, after miraculously healing the lame, Peter reminds "the men of Israel" of Jesus, "whom ye delivered up, and denied him in the presence of Pilate, when he was determined to let him go. But ye denied the Holy One and the Just, and desired a murderer to be granted unto you. . . . And now, brethren, I wot that through ignorance ye did it, as did also your rulers" (Acts 3:12–17). Luke, author of the Acts, is here found true to Luke, author of the Gospel: the utterances here ascribed to Peter do not add to our knowledge or appraisal of the facts as reported in the Lucan Gospel. But it will be remarked that already, at the very beginning, Peter is reported as exploiting the crucifixion of Jesus as a skillful device to arouse the guilt feelings of the masses, and as succeeding in pricking their hearts.

It appears that the activity of Peter and the other apostles soon came to the attention of the Jewish authorities. Diverging from Jesus, the apostles took their stand on a belief in the resurrected Christ as Saviour from sin and iniquity: "let all the house of Israel know assuredly, that God hath made that same Jesus, whom ye have crucified, both Lord and Christ" (Acts 2:36). Concerning the resurrection, it is said that the Sadducees, who, as will be remembered, denied all afterlife, were "grieved that they taught the people and preached through Jesus the resurrection from the dead" (Acts 4:2); but even among the Pharisees, who accepted an afterlife, were many to whom the story of the resurrection of Jesus was unbelievable and, from the point of view of Jewish orthodoxy, potentially dangerous. We hear that Peter and the other apostles were taken into custody one evening (4:3), and the next morning the "rulers, and elders, and scribes" (4:5), as well as the high priest and many of his "kindred" (4:6), gathered together in Jerusalem, a description which would once more fit a gathering of the Great Sanhedrin. From the sequence of events, it appears that the Sanhedrin was not convened that day to hold a trial; indeed, it was manifestly not a Small Sanhedrin that did meet and would have been competent to try a criminal case,[1] and the purpose seems to have been an inquiry into questions of religion. The apostles were asked, "By what power, or by what name, have ye done this?" (4:7), a question faintly reminiscent of that addressed to Jesus long before: "By what authority doest thou these things, or who is he that gave thee this authority?" (Luke 20:2; similarly Matt. 21:23 and Mark 11:28). But while Jesus himself had taught as one having authority (Mark 1:22) and might, therefore, be asked for his credentials,[2] the apostles had, it seems, not relied on any authority of their own, but professed to represent some "power" neither known to the authorities nor recognized by them. Peter replied that if he had succeeded in performing the miracle of healing the lame, it was "by the name of Jesus Christ of Nazareth, whom ye crucified, whom God raised from the dead, even by him doth this man stand here before you whole. This is the stone which was set at nought of you builders, which is become the head of the corner. Neither is there salvation in any other: for there is none other name under heaven given among men, whereby we must be saved" (Acts 4:10–12). On hearing this pronouncement, the members of the Sanhedrin consulted with each other privately: "What shall we do to these men? for that indeed a notable miracle hath been done by them is manifest to all them that dwell in Jerusalem; and we cannot deny it" (4:16). As we have seen, wonder-workers, especially in the realm of medicine, were not infrequent in Jerusalem at the time, and could always attract considerable numbers of admiring followers: to put such miracle-men out of action, or persecute them, would be likely to anger the people, and that, as we know, was the last thing that the Sanhedrin would care to do. Still, this kind of deification of Jesus, and the "power" of universal salvation attributed to him, came perilously near to apostasy and ought to be stopped by every means. So the Sanhedrin decided "to let them go, finding nothing how they might punish them, because of the people" (4:21); but they "commanded them not to speak at all nor teach in the name of Jesus" (4:18), and threatened them (4:21) that if they persisted in so doing, they would be punished.

Heedless of the warning, Peter and the other apostles continued to teach and preach "with great power," giving "witness of the resurrection of the Lord Jesus" (Acts 4:33), and, whether by teaching and preaching or by working "many signs and wonders among the people" (5:12), were able to add "multitudes both of men and women" of new believers in the Lord (5:14). This is said to have aroused the wrath of the high priest "and all that were with him, which is the sect of the Sadducees" (5:17). It may be that the Sadducees are singled out because, in the event, it proved to be a Pharisee who moved the Sanhedrin to overcome any "indignation" that it might feel at the disobedience of the apostles; but we are safe in assuming that such "indignation" as there was need not have been confined to Sadducees. The high priest, presumably in his capacity as president of the Sanhedrin, decided to take action and had the apostles arrested (5:18). After their miraculous escape from prison (5:19–24), they were found teaching the people in the temple (5:25), where they were taken into custody, the people protesting so vigorously that the arresting officers feared that they might be stoned (5:26). Peter and the other apostles were brought before the council, this time, it would appear, a Small Sanhedrin summoned to conduct a trial and presided over by the high priest. The charge upon which they were to be tried emerges clearly from the opening question of the high priest: "Did not we straitly command you that ye should not teach in this name? and, behold, ye have filled Jerusalem with your doctrine, and intend to bring this man's blood upon us" (5:28) : in other words, we bade you not to teach in Jesus' name, and you have disobeyed us, and are in contempt of the Sanhedrin; and as if it were not enough that you deify this man, you even accuse us of crucifying him (4:10). Peter's reply is that when the command of a human agency collides with the command of God, "We ought to obey God rather than men" (5:29) ; and then comes at once the reiteration of the previous indictment: "The God of our fathers raised up Jesus, whom ye slew and hanged on a tree" (5:30). The author reports that "When they heard that, they were cut to the heart" (5:33). Now the defense that a divine command must always have precedence over a human was perfectly valid and reasonable, and could hardly cut the members of the Sanhedrin to their hearts; it was another, perhaps still arguable, matter whether the overriding divine command had really been given or was only a pretext, and that would and could be gone into in the due course of the trial. "They were cut to the hearts," not by this line of defense but by the repeated indictment, or insinuation, that they had had a hand in the crucifixion of Jesus.

The high priest and the members of the Sanhedrin present at the trial of Peter and the other apostles had been present at the night meeting in the house of the high priest in the matter of Jesus: they knew how Jesus had found death, who had crucified him, and what exactly had preceded his tragic end. It is not at all surprising that their bitter "indignation" should be due not only to the flagrant disobedience and contempt shown by Peter and the other apostles respecting the orders of the Sanhedrin, but also to the fact that they "intend to bring this man's blood upon us": no contempt could be worse than that implicit in blaming the Sanhedrin—of all people!—for the death of Jesus. Unquestionably, the endless public repetition of charges against the Sanhedrin, however unfounded, as if it were responsible for the crucifixion of God's chosen Christ, was calculated to undermine, among the ignorant masses, any respect and loyalty which the council still enjoyed. But undermining sanhedrial authority was, for the apostles, indispensable to establishing an authority of their own; and as the crux of the new faith that they preached was the crucifixion and resurrection of Jesus, no better or more damaging weapon could have been invented by them, to make people detest the Sanhedrin and with it all established authority, than the slander of responsibility for the crucifixion.

The first reaction of the members of the Sanhedrin, on hearing Peter's words, was that they ought to put him and his accomplices to death (Acts 5:33). Again, it cannot have been the defense pleaded by Peter, that he defied the Sanhedrin only because he had to obey God, which made them "take counsel to slay them" (5:33): the injunction to obey God rather than kings and other worldly authority (Deut. 17:19–20) is much too deeply planted in Jewish legal consciousness to be deemed a spurious or vexatious plea, lightly to be dismissed. If Peter had said nothing more than that, the discussion which did eventually take place would have ensued forthwith; but with Peter taking up the high priest's complaint that he intended to bring Jesus' blood upon the Sanhedrin, and reiterating his previous slanders, it was only natural that the members should react as they are reported to have done: if we want to uphold sanhedrial authority, and protect ourselves from slanderous sedition, we must take some dramatic step to gag these people once and for all; if admonition, threat, and command are of no avail, what alternative is there but to put them to death? And no less natural might it appear to be that people who found themselves again and again branded in public with the wanton murder of an innocent, nay, a holy, man should lose their patience and self-restraint; and if they were judges themselves, who not only took no least part in the murder but went out of their way to save the man's life, it would be strange if they did not take effective action to vindicate their good name.

However "natural" all that may be, these men, being judges, did not, in the event, yield to instinct and inclination, but acted in accordance with the law. It was not a capital offense in Jewish law to slander the Sanhedrin, or to charge it, or any of its members, with murder, even publicly; hence neither Peter nor the other apostles could be capitally convicted and put to death for accusing the Sanhedrin of complicity in the crucifixion of Jesus. To bring such a false charge became a capital offense only if committed by a witness in the trial of the person so charged by him, and only if it resulted in the conviction of the accused: "if the witness be a false witness, and hath testified falsely against his brother; then shall ye do unto him, as he had thought to have done unto his brother. . . . And thine eye shall not pity: but life shall go for life" (Deut. 19:18–21). But so long as the charges, however untrue, were leveled only in the streets and market places, or even in the temple and assembly halls, so that they could not result in a judicial sentence to death, the maximum penalty which the slanderer could suffer was flogging;[3] and, indeed, we find that Peter and the other apostles were flogged, as the outcome of this trial, by sentence of the court (Acts 5:40). Nothing, however, came of the "counsel" which the members of the Sanhedrin took to have them put to death (5:33) : that would have been against the law.

It was at this stage of the proceedings, when the members of the Sanhedrin were still debating whether capital punishment was not merited, that "one in the council, a Pharisee, named Gamaliel, a doctor of the law, had in reputation among all the people" (5:34), took the floor. Rabban Gamliel, as he is known in the Jewish sources, was not only a Pharisaic member of the Sanhedrin but the leading and outstanding legal and religious authority of his time: in the absence of the high priest he presided over the Sanhedrin,[4] and would normally be the first and most authoritative spokesman for the Pharisaic majority. Luke must have known a reliable tradition that it was Gamliel who had intervened and taken the lead in the trial of Peter: he could not be suspected of crediting any Pharisee, or, for that matter, any Jew, with a pro-Christian attitude unless he had substantial evidence in support of it.[5] The sense of the speech ascribed to Gamliel is so very much in harmony with what we know from other sources of his teachings and his character that the report of his intervention might be said to confirm the historicity of the very trial itself.

While that sense is authentic, wording and content give rise to some difficulty. The speech starts with a general and introductory admonition to "Ye men of Israel," to "take heed to yourselves what ye intend to do as touching these men" (5:35) ; but it then goes on to recount past history: "For before these days rose up Theudas, boasting himself to be somebody; to whom a number of men, about four hundred, joined themselves; who was slain; and all, as many as obeyed him, were scattered, and brought to nought. After this man rose up Judas of Galilee in the days of the taxing, and drew away much people after him: he also perished; and all, even as many as obeyed him, were dispersed" (5:36–37). The events in question could not have been mentioned by Rabban Gamliel, because they took place long after the trial of Peter and the other apostles. We know of a certain Theudas who pretended to be a messiah and attracted an "enormous multitude of people who followed him to the River Jordan"; the Roman governor Cuspius Fadus detached a company of calvarymen, who killed many of them and took the others captive; Theudas himself was beheaded, and his head brought to Jerusalem.[6] This was in the year 45, more than a decade after the trial of Peter.[7] As for Judas of Galilee, we have no information that he himself had been killed; we know only that his two sons were crucified by sentence of the governor Tiberius Alexander, whose term began in the year 49.[8] It is true that we hear of the underground operations of one Judas the Galilean at the time of the census (A.D. 6),[9] and Gamliel might also have had information, which has not come down to us, of his execution;[10] as it may equally be that the Theudas of whom Gamliel spoke was a different person from the Theudas of Josephus. But the preferable opinion seems to be that the author of the Acts, who knew of the executions reported in Josephus, put them into the mouth of Gamliel in disregard of the anachronism involved,[11] his readers being anyway unable to check the historical data.

That it was these particular instances which the author of the Acts saw fit to turn into the words of Gamliel is not without significance. First, "it is notable that the author of the Acts was led to depict an eminent rabbi as seeking to evaluate Christianity in terms of the movements of Judas of Galilee, the founder of Zealotism, and Theudas. We can only wonder whether he was prompted to do this in the light of some tradition that did connect them together."[12] Second, and for the purpose of our inquiry more importantly, the movements of both Judas and Theudas were directed against Roman oppression, and were fought by the Romans: if Judas "perished," it was at the hands of Rome, just as his sons were crucified by sentence of a Roman governor, and as Theudas was beheaded as a Roman captive by Roman soldiers. Neither Judas or his followers nor Theudas or his were ever tried or sentenced by the Jewish courts; if they "perished" or were "slain," it was without the concurrence of the Jewish authorities and by a Roman use of force aimed no less at the Jews in general than at the individual victims. Whether or not any other connection existed between the movements of Judas and Theudas and that of the Christians, one similarity at least, suggested by Gamliel's speech, is certain, and that is that Jesus, like Judas and Theudas, was not tried and sentenced by a Jewish court, but came to his death at the hands of the hateful Romans, by Roman action and for a Roman cause.

Had Gamliel wished to allude to apostates tried and sentenced by the Sanhedrin for inciting to idolatry and suchlike offenses of a religious nature, he could easily have done so:[13] but the allusion would have been irrelevant, because Jesus had not been so tried or sentenced. It was only occasions of Roman prosecution and execution that were apposite; and the point which Gamliel wanted to make was that even where a Jewish leader had been executed by the Romans, his followers would be scattered and fall into oblivion unless God willed it otherwise. It might have been expected that execution by the Romans would have the effect of raising the dead leader to the rank of a saintly martyr, thus strengthening the ties between his followers and their determination to persist in their cause, but all such expectations, however reasonable they appeared to be, would come to naught if God willed it so. That all the followers of Judas of Galilee "were dispersed" appears to be an error of fact: we well know, and Rabban Gamliel knew, that the zealots did not disperse, but multiplied in numbers and intensified their underground activity after the death of their founder, Judas; but Luke may not have known it, and his error does not take away from the point that he desired Gamliel to make: if Judas' followers did not disperse but persisted and multiplied, it was a sure sign of God's will, too.

This, then, was Gamliel's conclusion: "And now I say unto you, Refrain from these men, and let them alone: for if this counsel or this work be of men, it will come to nought: But if it be of God, ye cannot overthrow it; lest haply ye be found even to fight against God" (5:38–39). As far as the future of the Christian

movement as such was concerned, this was—and was accepted as—
a conclusive answer: should the movement continue to exist and
flourish, that would in itself be proof enough of its being willed
and blessed by God, and any human effort to "overthrow" it must
prove futile; on the other hand, if you are right, and if this movement is not willed by God but is an affront to Him, you can be
sure that He will not let it endure and thrive. Anyhow, and whatever the future—or God—may hold in store for them, the men
now standing trial before you cannot be punished for the views
which they propagate and the doctrines which they preach: insofar as those views and doctrines are mistaken and heretical, God
will not countenance them, but will consign them to limbo. Intrinsically, therefore, there is nothing in them, be they ever so
unorthodox, that would be punishable in law,[14] even by the minor
penalty of flogging.

But Peter and the other apostles, though acquitted of charges of
apostasy and any others connected with the preaching of their
new faith ("they commanded that they should not speak in the
name of Jesus, and let them go," 5:40) , were "beaten" (*ibid.*) ,
that is, sentenced to be flogged. Rabban Gamliel had not said a
word about the second part of the high priest's indictment, that
they "intend to bring this man's blood upon us" (5:28) , to which
Peter had virtually pleaded guilty by his reiteration that "you
slew" Jesus and hanged him on a tree (5:30) . One can only speculate why it should have been passed over in silence by Gamliel: the
opinion may perhaps be ventured that he regarded it as beneath
his dignity, and beneath the dignity of the Sanhedrin, to waste
any words on so impertinent a slander. There could be no doubt
that vilifying the Sanhedrin and the "rulers of the people" (Exod.
22:28) was a criminal offense, punishable by flogging;[15] and, that
offense having been committed in the face of the court, and before
that again and again in public, in the temple (3:15; 4:10) , the
Sanhedrin could hardly ignore it. So it did what the law required
it to do: it inflicted the punishment of flogging (Deut. 25:2-3) on
the slanderers, and left it at that. We hear that Peter and the
other apostles, after that castigation, rejoiced "that they were
counted worthy to suffer shame for his name" (5:41) , as indeed
they very well might, seeing that an advocate as inspired as Rabban Gamliel had taken up their cause, and their defamation of

the Sanhedrin had not provoked a more drastic and more painful reaction. It is an ancient Jewish rule of ethics that, when insulted, you should not retort, and that, even while listening to abuses, you should keep silent.[16] That is what the Sanhedrin did when Peter aired his disgraceful calumny that it had slain Jesus and hanged him (5:30).

The words reported of the high priest that Peter and the other apostles intended "to bring this man's blood upon us" clearly mark the resentment which the accusation stirred in him. Nor can the author of the Acts have intended, by that choice of words, to convey anything but such resentment. Now, if Jesus had been tried by the Sanhedrin and convicted of a capital offense under Jewish law, a reproach of having slain and hanged him could not have been resented; rather, if the Sanhedrin had failed to see Jesus executed, after he had been duly tried and convicted of a capital offense, it could rightly have been charged with violating the law: once a sentence had been finally pronounced, the Sanhedrin had no discretion but was in duty bound to ensure that the execution was carried out promptly.[17] To be credited as having slain and hanged a convicted criminal would be a compliment and no insult, and from the Sanhedrin's point of view it could make no difference that he might be considered innocent by his admirers and followers and of the highest moral or spiritual excellence. The charge that his blood was upon them, the members of the Sanhedrin, would not then have left any impression: had it not been upon them, they ought to consider themselves guilty of a grave dereliction of their judicial duty: "And thine eye shall not pity" (Deut. 19:21). The resentment of the high priest, as well as of his fellow judges (5:33), shows, therefore, that everybody present was fully aware that Jesus had not been tried by the Sanhedrin or convicted of any capital offense under Jewish law: it is in these circumstances that Peter's charge that the Sanhedrin had slain and hanged him assumes its slanderous character.

Whether Peter did actually utter, and repeat, this charge as the Acts reports or whether it was Luke who put it into his mouth without any valid tradition of actual utterance is not for us to decide, and a decision would not, for the purpose of our inquiry, be very material. What is important and significant is that, if made, the charge, so Luke holds, was hotly resented and flatly rejected;

and it is from this resentment and rejection that we may draw our conclusions. It is noteworthy that in the Epistles ascribed to Peter there is not a syllable of blame for the Sanhedrin as respects the death of Jesus: he asserts his witnessing of Jesus' sufferings (I Pet. 5:1), that Jesus, like the "lamb without blemish and without spot," was "foreordained" by God to become the costly sacrifice by which mankind was to be redeemed (1:18–20), and freely took this sacrifice and suffering upon himself (2:21). If, physically, Jesus was put to death, spiritually he was made alive (3:18). His tribulations should serve as an example: "let none of you suffer as a murderer, or as a thief, or as an evildoer, or as a busybody in other men's matters. Yet if any man suffers as a Christian, let him not be ashamed" (4:15–16), and "as Christ hath suffered for us in the flesh, arm yourselves likewise with the same mind: for he that hath suffered in the flesh hath ceased from sin" (4:1). No mention is made of the Jewish authorities, which may be accounted for by the fact that the Epistles are addressed to people outside Judaea (1:1). Yet there are express exhortations to obey "governors," "kings," and those that are "sent for the punishment of evildoers" (2:13–14), in spite of anything that they might have done to Jesus.

James, the eldest brother of Jesus, and, like Peter, an eyewitness of what happened after his trial, addressed himself in his Epistle to the "rich men," whose "riches are corrupted" (5:1–2), who "have lived in pleasure on the earth and been wanton" and made themselves fat for the day of slaughter (5:5). It was they whom he accused of having "condemned and killed the just; and he doth not resist you" (5:6). James was described by Paul as one of the pillars of the faith (Gal. 2:9): he was, as from the year 44, the head of the Christian community in Jerusalem,[18] and must have been informed of exactly what had happened to Jesus: nevertheless, not only is there no mention in his Epistle of Jewish responsibility for the death of Jesus, but he himself was an observant Pharisee all his life,[19] however ardent a Christian he had become. The Pharisees, described by Josephus as "the most fair-minded of the citizens and the most diligent in their respect for the law," are reported by him to have protested vehemently to the Roman authorities when, in the year 62, a Sadducean high priest "of bold and violent character" convened the Sanhedrin and had James and others tried for "breaking the law"; they were convicted and stoned for their contumaciousness.[20] It does not matter whether their objections were against the unilateral act of the high priest in convening the Sanhedrin, or the apparently wholly Sadducean composition of the court, or the nature of the charge and the cause for conviction, or the insufficiency of evidence or irregularities of procedure, or against all these things; the fact that they complained—even though they had nobody to complain to except the Roman governor—is proof enough that from the Pharisaic point of view James should and could not have been convicted, any more than Peter. But the Sadducees and the Sadducean high priest seem, for some reason unknown to us, to have borne a grudge against James, one deep and flaming enough to make them resolve to be rid of him. It would be reasonable to assume that there was a connection between James's imprecations against the rich and the Sadducean rancor against him; that he now went so far as to accuse these "rich men" of having "condemned and killed the just," of having crucified Jesus, might have been the last straw. James may, of course, have meant to address the Romans when he spoke to the corrupt that live in pleasure and wantonness, rather than the Sadducees; if this was what he intended, his charge that the Romans had condemned and killed Jesus was only the simple and obvious truth. And that it was, indeed, the Romans against whom his diatribe was directed appears to follow from the ensuing consolation, "Be patient, therefore, brethren, unto the coming of the Lord" (5:7; and cf. 5:8–11). The authenticity of the Epistle of James is, however, contested.[21]

A contemporary source more important than the Epistles of Peter and James are those attributed to Paul, now commonly taken to have been written two or three decades after the death of Jesus,[22] when most of his contemporaries were still alive (cf. I Cor. 15:6). While Paul was not in Jerusalem when the events took place that led up to Jesus' death, it is conceivable that he had firsthand information from persons who had been present. It is true that his Epistles probably underwent editorial changes before incorporation, about a century later, into the canon of the New Testament,[23] but the same applies, with the same probability, to the other Books of the New Testament, and inconsistencies between them were nevertheless allowed to abide.[24] Judging from his Epistles themselves, I would submit that he had no reliable briefing or firsthand testimony of Jewish initiative or part in the trial or crucifixion of Jesus. Only once do we find him writing in terms that the Jews killed Jesus: he wrote to the Thessalonians that they "also have suffered like things of your own countrymen, even as they have of the Jews; who both killed the Lord Jesus, and their own prophets, and have persecuted us; and they please not God, and are contrary to all men" (I Thess. 2:14–15). The context indicates that the word "killing" is used somewhat allegorically: what the Jews are doing to all their prophets, including the Lord Jesus, is just one instance of their general attitude and behavior of displeasing God and being "contrary to all men." The next verse says that the Jews "forbid us to speak to the Gentiles that they might be saved," and their interference with our missionary activities in this way makes full "the measure of their sins": trying to prevent us from preaching to the Gentiles is the culmination of all their sins, the killing of Jesus and their prophets included. It would appear, therefore, that this sort of "killing" was spiritual rather than physical. The least that can be said about this Pauline outcry is that it is grossly exaggerated: just as the Jews did not really "kill" any of their own prophets, so they did not "kill" Jesus.[25]

In an earlier Epistle, we find Paul writing that Jesus had been crucified by "the princes of the world" (I Cor. 2:8). "Princes of the world" might be an epithet for Roman governors, but is certainly not a fitting description of Jews, or even of their elders and priests. It has been said that the plural form points to Pilate and the Jews together;[26] but however flattering, from the Roman point of view, this conjunction may be for the Jews, they would hardly, even in such a bracketing, be described by Paul as princes, let alone as princes of the world. We incline to the opinion that the Greek term here used, *archontes,* is to be interpreted as meaning spiritual as distinct from the earthly princes who, according to one school, were evil demons acting under order from Satan,[27] or, according to another, good spirits doing God's will.[28] We find the expression "prince of the world" on the lips of Jesus himself, saying that he saw him coming but had no power over him (John 14:30); the allusion here, too, is doubtless to a spiritual power. The interpretation of *archontes* as spirits would mean that they directed the actors and so left them no discretion: in terms of responsibility, this would discharge the actors, whoever they were.

This also falls into line with a still earlier Pauline pronouncement that God Himself condemned Jesus to die (Rom. 8:3), treating Jesus as if he were sin personified. By Jesus' death, God delivered the world from sin—surely a divine purpose, worthy of divine action. And if no blame can possibly attach to an ommiscient and omnipotent God for allowing Jesus to die on the cross, logically no blame could attach to the instruments that God chose and directed to attain His own ends. The cross now becomes a symbol of salvation (Gal. 6:14), not of pain and suffering; and Jesus' death, rather than the tragic outcome of judicial murder, becomes propitiation of the remission of sin and of the faith in righteousness (Rom. 3:25).

Paul's theory starts from the premise that Jesus, though he had died, was yet living (Acts 25:19): his message is that the cross whereon Jesus was crucified became thereby the symbol of life. But the "preaching of the cross" (I Cor. 1:18) is "unto the Jews a stumbling-block, and unto the Greeks foolishness" (1:23), at least so long as they are not "called" and converted to the faith (1:24), for those who do not believe in the resurrection, the cross must always be meaningless as a symbol of faith (15:12–19). They are the "unworthy" who, if they presume to eat his bread and drink his wine, representing Jesus' body and his blood, "shall be guilty of the body and blood of the Lord" (11:27), as "guilty" as can humanly be.

As Jesus' death, and the cross as the instrument of it, were thus "foreordained" by God, no criminal liability can cling to anybody who carried out God's will, Jews or Romans; and as the death was but a prelude to Jesus' true and eternal life, there could have been no murder. But while this is clearly Paul's position in his Epistles, we need feel no surprise that, in the Acts, we find words ostensibly spoken by him which would fit Luke's well-known stand. There he is reported as saying that "they that dwell at Jerusalem and their rulers" have condemned Jesus, thereby fulfilling the words of "the prophets which are read every sabbath day. . . . And though they found no cause of death in him, yet desired they Pilate that he should be slain" (Acts 13:27–28). The reason why the Jews did so is declared to be "because they knew him not" (*ibid.*) . We recall that the "rulers" had already appeared in Luke as those who were active at the trial and who "desired" Pilate to have Jesus crucified (Luke 23:13; 24:20) ; now Luke again makes Paul speak of the "rulers." That Luke's "people" (23:4, 13) or "multitude" (23:1) are now replaced by those "that dwell at Jerusalem" has no particular import: perhaps Paul is designed to stress that it was the Jerusalemites only, and not Jews from other places, of whom Paul himself was one, who were in any way to blame. But note well that Luke here has Paul assert that all that the Jews did to Jesus they did to have "fulfilled all that was written of him," and Luke is the only evangelist who, in his Gospel report of the crucifixion, does not even once allude to the fulfillment of Scripture! That the Jews fulfilled prophecies by condemning Jesus just because "they knew him not," and presumably did not know or remember the actual prophecies either, seems to imply that had they known Jesus, they would not have condemned him: Jesus would not have died, and the prophecies would be unfulfilled. Or, equally, had they but known or remembered the prophecies, they would not have condemned him, for they would not have wanted the prophecies to come true with Jesus, of all men, and, once more, he would not have died. Since, however, the prophecies had to come true, and since Jesus— if only to rise again—had to die, it seems a good thing that the Jerusalemites turned out to be so unknowledgeable: whatever and whoever they were, at any rate they were chosen as God's instrument to bring about the eschatological end for which the world had been waiting. And "when they fulfilled" all that they had been chosen and "foreordained" to do, they took Jesus from the cross and buried him; thus Luke, through Paul, confirms a tradition which we have already recognized as valid. But the Jews had found "no cause of death" in Jesus: quite the opposite of what is alleged by Luke in his Gospel account (22:71) , here it is said that they desired Pilate to slay Jesus, not because he had been found worthy of death, but, on the contrary, despite his not having been found worthy of death, and only so that God's will might be done.

Nor should it be overlooked that, among the many speeches of Paul recorded in the Acts, his address in the synagogue of Antioch (Acts 13:14 ff.) is the only one with a reference to the cause of

Jesus' death. Before the people at Jerusalem (22:1–21), before the Sanhedrin (23:1–6), before the Roman governor (24:10–21), and before King Agrippa (26:2–27), he intrudes no slightest insinuation of sanhedrial or Jewish complicity in the condemnation or crucifixion. Not only does he, unlike Peter, not indict the Sanhedrin directly, but even in pleading his case before the governor, where the Sanhedrin was his adversary, he said not a word about sanhedrial responsibility for the death of Jesus, although it must have been in his interest to incriminate the Sanhedrin and absolve the governor's predecessor, the one to show that his own persecution was but part of a system which had started with Jesus, his master and mentor, and the other to ingratiate himself with the governor, who would not, we may guess, think much of a religion or school founded by a man convicted of a capital offense under Roman law and duly crucified. The silence imputed to Paul is the more significant, as Luke had here another admirable opportunity to establish Jewish responsibility for the death and crucifixion of Jesus, and Roman innocence of it, by seemingly most credible evidence: if he let this splendid chance slip by, it must have been because of an awareness of traditions as to the real contents of Paul's speeches. If any conclusion at all is permissible or necessary from a statement in one exceptional speech, and an ambiguous one at that, surely a conclusion may fairly be drawn from the fact that in none of the many of his speeches is there mention of any blame to be attached to the Jews for the death of Jesus.

It has been said that Paul had no interest in the historical Jesus: his interest was centered on the eschatological Jesus, and consequently the human causes of Jesus' death were regarded by him as irrelevant.[29] Even so, Paul would scarcely have identified himself with the Pharisees ("Men and brethren: I am a Pharisee, the son of a Pharisee," Acts 23:6) if he believed that they had wronged and persecuted Jesus, with the Jews ("I also am an Israelite, of the seed of Abraham, of the tribe of Benjamin," Rom. 11:1) if it had been the Jews who had caused Jesus to be crucified. "God forbid" the thought that God may have "cast away his people" (ibid.): in God's own time, they will all be saved (11:26), Jews and Greeks alike (1:16). The general belief in resurrection was already common to Paul and the Pharisees (Acts 23:9); now they had only to share, as well, his belief in the resurrection of Jesus, and its eschatological significance, and they would partake of salvation. All of Paul's exhortations to the Jews were dictated by love, and a sense of belonging; there was never in them the tiniest element of grievance or rancor: if, indeed, he saw in the Jews the murderers of Jesus, that would be almost impossible to explain.

No one disputes that Paul's was a principal role in bringing about the final and, it seems, unbridgeable rift between Jews and Christians.[30] But Paul, unlike the evangelists, did not provoke the Jews' animosity by stigmatizing them whether as deicides or at all; the truth is that he never gave up hope that "all Israel shall be saved" (Rom. 11:26) and God's mercy extend to them all (11:32) ; Jesus was himself a Jew who had come down to earth to be their "merciful and faithful high priest" and "to make reconciliation for the sins of the people" (Heb. 2:17) . The difference of theology or of particular tenets of faith is not in itself a cause for enmity or strife: Paul's theology was one of salvation, of forgiveness of sins, of liberation from the shackles of law and ritual (cf. Heb. 10) ; it had nothing but benefits and blessings for those who embraced it; it held out nothing but bliss to those yet to be won over. Any kind of a priori hostility would seem incompatible with the a priori acceptance of nonbelievers, and the express invitation to such to partake of "salvation." The rift between Pauline Christianity and the Jews is in no sense inimical:[31] it is one between two different religions, and if it turned out to be unbridgeable, it was because the Jews could not accept the new creed or understand many of its tenets, and because they would not forsake the faith of their fathers or agree to be delivered from "the shackles of law and ritual." If, for reasons of their own, or because of their blindness (Rom. 11:25) , they would not partake of the salvation offered, so much the worse for them: they might then be an object of pity, and God's mercy should be entreated for them, but neither their blindness nor their stubbornness has warranted hatred. If, throughout history, the general and official Christian attitude toward Jews has differed from that toward other non-Christians, that is no reflection of theological or doctrinal divergencies, but mirrors only the bigotry and prejudice grafted onto Christian hearts by the portrayal of the Jews, in the

Gospels, as the murderers and crucifiers of Jesus.[32] This portrayal is the work of the evangelists, and they did not start to delineate it until at least four decades had elapsed after Jesus' death. The great apostles preceding them knew nothing of any such murder, and were far from indoctrinating any such ill will.

10 HIS BLOOD BE UPON US AND OUR CHILDREN

The forebodings of the high priest in the trial of Peter, that there was intent that the blood of Jesus was to be "brought upon us" (Acts 5:28), were to be verified soon enough. It fell to Matthew to accomplish it, and he did so with a fatal efficacy that he would himself hardly have anticipated.

The Great War (66–70) had ended with a Roman destruction of the temple and city of Jerusalem. When it began, most of the Christians left Jerusalem: they had been forewarned "by means of an oracle given by revelation to acceptable persons there";[1] many settled in Pella, east of the Jordan, and many joined the new communities in Rome or in Alexandria. Mark lived and wrote in Rome; Matthew lived and wrote in Alexandria. Mark had already damned the Jews unreservedly with responsibility for Jesus' death: his concern had been to whitewash the Roman governor, to represent him as finding no fault at all in Jesus, to explain away the glaring antithesis between Jesus' crucifixion by the Romans and his innocence under Roman law. This tradition, as we saw, was taken over by Matthew; but while Mark wrote with his eye on the Romans, Matthew wrote with his eye on the Jews. Alexandria must, at that time, have been the largest Jewish community on earth: Josephus reports that when anti-Jewish pogroms broke out there during the Great War, fifty thousand Jews were killed.[2] Tension ran high not only between Romans and Greeks on the one hand and Jews on the other, but also, in ever mounting degree, between Jews and Christians: whether it was that the Jews were angered by the disloyalty of the Christians who had forsaken Jerusalem upon the outbreak of the fighting and now saw in them not only dissidents in matters of religion and transgressors of the law but also traitors to the national cause, or that the Christians regarded the destruction of the temple as proof not only of divine wrath and the final alienation of God's love from His originally chosen people, but also of "the fulfilment of Christ's prophecy and a confirmation of their belief that the scepter had passed from Israel to the Church."[3] While Matthew, who also lived in the Roman empire, had no interest whatever in discarding the Marcan tradition of Roman innocence in the crucifixion of Jesus or in detracting from it, his purpose in putting the blame on the Jews, apart from making them the scapegoat for absolution of the Romans, was, more particularly, to furnish the Jews themselves with conclusive testimony that the destruction of the temple, and the whole disaster that had befallen them, was divine punishment for the murder of Jesus. The moral of this divine lesson could only be that the Jews would now either see the light and become Christians or else, if they persisted in denial of Jesus Christ, bare themselves to ever recurring manifestations of divine displeasure. Conversely, those already become Christians would draw encouragement and confidence from the speed and severity of God's punishment of stiff-necked deicides. But to justify that punishment in appearance, nay, even to present it as inescapable, Jewish guilt must be firmly established: some people might say that it was not enough to have just a section of the Jews, priests or elders, for example, saddled with responsibility: guilt had to be placed on the nation as a whole, as warrant for a penalty of such universal dimensions. Or others might say that it was not enough to saddle the Jews with only indirect responsibility: they may have been instigators and procurers, but the crime itself was ultimately committed by Roman executioners; and had not the governor truckled to the Jews, Jesus might still be alive. These were considerations which had to be wiped out, and as that could not be done by arguments, it had to be done by unequivocal "facts."

Accordingly, we find Matthew—and Matthew only—adding to the Marcan account the following seemingly factual report: "When Pilate saw that he could prevail nothing, but that rather a tumult was made, he took water, and washed his hands before the multitude, saying, I am innocent of the blood of this just person: see ye to it. Then answered all the people, and said, His blood be on us, and on our children" (27:24–25).

Before we examine the details of this story, certain exegetical theories have to be disposed of. It has been said, for instance, that the words "his blood be on us" are not necessarily to be interpreted as a Jewish avowal of guilt for the crucifixion of Jesus, but simply as an assertion by the Jews that they are satisfied of his guilt, so that Pilate might safely proceed to condemn him.[4] In other words: the Jews did not admit or assume any responsibility for the crucifixion: that responsibility would always be the Roman governor's and rest with him alone; what they did was only an attempt at persuading him that the execution of Jesus was amply justified on data which they had investigated carefully and whose validity and reliability they could attest. In fact, their exclamation, "his blood be on us," was nothing else and nothing more than was always said of witnesses for the prosecution testifying in criminal trials: it was the law that before their evidence was taken they were warned by the court in the following terms: You should know that criminal proceedings differ from civil proceedings: in civil cases a man can make good any damage that he may have caused, by paying, but in criminal cases his blood and the blood of his children, until the end of the world, will hang on you.[5] It would appear, then, that the blood of a convict put to death was invariably said to "hang" on the witness on the strength of whose testifying he had been found guilty, whether the evidence had been true or false: if it had been true, there could be nothing wrong or bad in the blood of the convict hanging on the witness; only if it had been false would this blood, wrongly shed, cry unto God (Gen. 4:10). Since, in the case of Jesus, the Jews were satisfied in their own minds that his guilt had been conclusively determined, they could unhesitatingly declare, "his blood be on us," as though they had been witnesses testifying against him.

Another theory is that, so far from being an incitement to Pilate to proceed with Jesus' crucifixion, the words in reality were meant as a warning to him not so to proceed: instead of saying, stop, you are shedding innocent blood, they said, stop, if you shed this blood, we shall not be able to answer for it.[6] Protagonists of this theory find it supported by the fact that, grammatically speaking, the words in the original Greek are used not in the future but in the present tense, as if the Jews were saying, we are all shedding this blood if you crucify him, and we do not want to shed it; if we have so far only cried, let him be crucified! (27:22), now that you have washed your hands and declared the innocence of "this just person," we are no longer willing to have his blood shed, for it would be tantamount to shedding our own.

All these, and some similiar, theories are desperate and hopeless attempts to take the most pungent stings out of the Matthean story. It has been said that in recent times, with the inception of searches for biblical authority for a better and friendlier relationship between Jews and Christians, these words in Matthew have become a *crux interpretum*,[7] being, as indeed they are, a formidable obstacle on the path toward ecumenical accord, and immense efforts are being made to overcome the difficulties to which they give rise. It is submitted that this purpose, however laudable it may be, cannot be achieved by depriving the words of their natural meaning; nor is it an admissible mode of interpretation to assign a meaning to them which they cannot bear either in logic or in grammar. We have to accept and appraise the story as it is; and once having described the background against which it was framed, we are prepared for the worst implications. We may, and shall, have to dismiss it as unhistorical and fictional, but assuming that the things happened and the words were uttered as the story tells, we cannot get around the implications by shutting our eyes to the purport that was meant to be conveyed.

The true sense of the words "his blood be (or is) on us" is simply this: if this man, as you say, is innocent, and if, by crucifying him, as we desire you to, you will indeed shed innocent blood, then his blood shall be claimed from us, we shall be answerable for it, and you will be free from responsibility. Pilate had said to the people, or so the story goes, that he was innocent "of the blood of this just person," and had told them, "see ye to it"—

you brought him here, you insist on his condemnation, you want his blood shed, well and good: it is your responsibility, not mine. Whereupon the people at once agreed: nothing could be more reasonable than that those who clamored for the crucifixion should undertake responsibility for it, the more so as the actual executioner, Pilate, had professed to give in to the clamor against his will and contrary to his better judgment. So "all the people" answered: Be not troubled, his blood will not be upon you at all; God in heaven is our witness that we are taking his blood upon ourselves, here and now; and if it be innocent blood that is being shed, God will discover and visit us with it.

The phrase "his blood be on me or on my head" is a form of locution frequently found in biblical Hebrew to signify acceptance of responsibility if death should occur. The *locus classicus* is the scriptural exhortation, "That innocent blood be not shed in thy land, which the Lord thy God giveth thee for an inheritance, and no blood be upon thee" (Deut. 19:10) : by failing to prevent the shedding of innocent blood, you take that blood upon yourself; "and the land cannot be cleansed of the blood that is shed therein, but by the blood of him that shed it" (Num. 35:33) . When Joshua's men had made a pact with Rahab that her kin should be spared and not killed by the invading army of the Israelites, they said to her: "Whosoever shall go out of the doors of thy house into the street, his blood shall be upon his head, and we will be guiltless; and whosoever shall be with thee in the house, his blood shall be on our head, if any hand be upon him" (Josh. 2:19) . That is to say, they assumed full responsibility for the death of any of Rahab's folks that stayed in her house and did not go forth from it, even if death came not by the kinsmen's own fault but by "any hand"; but for any such person killed beyond her house they would not be answerable, even if they themselves were the killers: his blood would be on his own head, not on theirs. Again, when the man who killed Saul had confessed his deed, though he had killed the king at Saul's own behest, David exclaimed: "Thy blood be upon thy head, for thy mouth hath testified against thee, saying, I have slain the Lord's anointed" (II Sam. 1:16) , for the confession sufficed to establish the killer's blood guilt. Similarly, innocence may be protested in the phrase "I am pure from the blood of all men" (Acts 20:26) , a declaration that the blood of no man is upon me or my head. When Jeremiah stood charged before the court of priests, he warned them: "But know ye for certain, that if ye put me to death, ye shall surely bring innocent blood upon yourselves, and upon this city, and upon the inhabitants thereof" (Jer. 26:15). That is how Pilate would have been cautioned, if indeed the intention had been to prevent him from crucifying Jesus.

While the use of the phrase "his blood be on us" would, therefore, be quite natural on Jewish lips, and its meaning clear and unambiguous, the preceding words of Pilate, and more particularly the washing of his hands, are so Hebrew and so un-Roman in character that they cannot, in reason, be attributed to him at all. It is biblical law that "if one be found slain in the land which the Lord thy God giveth thee to possess it, lying in the field, and it be not known who hath slain him," then the elders of the nearest city "shall wash their hands" over a heifer and say, "Our hands have not shed this blood, neither have our eyes seen it. Be merciful, O Lord, unto thy people of Israel, whom thou hast redeemed, and lay not innocent blood unto thy people of Israel's charge. And the blood shall be forgiven them. So shalt thou put away the guilt of innocent blood from among you . . ." (Deut. 21:1–9). The washing of hands is here a manifest demonstration of innocence that the hands are clean of any blood that has been shed; but the symbolic washing of hands and the pronouncement accompanying it, "Our hands have not shed this blood, neither have our eyes seen it," follow the discovery of the man slain, and do not precede the slaying. When blood had already been shed, one could declare one's innocence and ignorance of the crime, and wash one's hands of it, but when blood is about to be shed, no amount of washing of hands can wipe away complicity in the shedding, unless one does everything in one's power to prevent it. By washing his hands and protesting his innocence before delivering Jesus up for crucifixion, Pilate could not, either in law or in logic, free himself of responsibility for what happened afterward: by the shedding of blood that supervened, his clean hands would be tainted once more.

Still, the analogy of the washing of hands after discovery of the body of a slain man, the establishment of innocence and the freedom from responsibility secured by it, must have served the author of the Gospel of Matthew as precedent for the course of action which he depicts Pilate as taking. The washing of hands, in a context of declaration of innocence of bloodshed, was familiar enough to Jewish readers, and the risk might perhaps safely be run that they would not go into legal details and differentiate between the washing of hands before and after the event. But what the average Jewish reader would not know—and possibly the author of the Gospel of Matthew did not know it either—is that this kind of symbolic ceremony was unknown and unfamiliar to Romans:[8] while a Jewish dignitary might be imagined to wash his hands and declare his innocence of bloodshed, a Roman governor would never do the like, because the whole rite and its symbolism were strange and meaningless to him. If the Jewish readers of Matthew accepted—and could be expected to accept—the story of Pilate's washing his hands, it was because they grasped its symbolism instantly and instinctively and would not pause to render themselves an account of the fact that what was self-understood for them was outside the cognizance and understanding of other peoples.

In Rome, however, readers must have been better informed. They would have known that no Roman governor would ever commit the folly of washing his hands in public before "multitudes" of natives, and demean himself to make a solemn declaration of his innocence, as if they were his judges—and in respect of an official act which he was about to perform in the exercise of his gubernatorial authority and imperial power! The idea was too absurd to be offered to an erudite public. It made no sense at all, because the ceremonial symbolism involved in the act was unintelligible to them, and what was left of outward act and speech, after taking away the symbolism, was so derogatory of the dignity and standing of a Roman governor that the policy of presenting Pilate in as favorable a light as possible would be gravely jeopardized. Nothing more predictable, then, than that the authors of the Gospels According to Luke and to John should decide to omit the tale. However decisive and momentous the self-arraignment of the Jews, "his blood be upon us and our children," must have been for the later evangelists as well, they would forgo its advantage and prefer to do without it, if only not to bewilder their readers with the description of behavior so un-Roman-like, so un-governor-like, and so senseless on the part of Pilate. Bearing in mind that Mark, the first evangelist, had no tradition of a washing of hands by Pilate or a self-arraignment of the Jews, and that the story appearing in Matthew had been rejected by the third and fourth evangelists, we are safe in assuming, with the concurrence of a good many outstanding contemporary scholars,[9] that there is no valid tradition whatsoever behind the Matthean report.[10]

The anonymous author of an apocryphal Gospel wrongly attributed to Peter[11] found a highly original way to solve the riddles of the report. The first of the extant fragments of this Gospel starts as follows: "But of the Jews none washed their hands, neither Herod nor any of his judges. As they would not wash, Pilate arose. And then Herod the king commanded that the Lord should be marched off, saying to them, What I have commanded you to do to him, do ye."[12]

It will be remembered that, in a Lucan tradition, Pilate had transferred the trial of Jesus to Herod on hearing that Herod was in Jerusalem and that Jesus was a Galilean, subject to the king's jurisdiction (Luke 23:7). But while Luke recounts that Herod sent Jesus back for trial before Pilate (23:11), the apocryphal Gospel assumes that he accepted the transfer and that all subsequent proceedings, up to and including sentence, were conducted under the presidency, and hence under the responsibility, of Herod alone. Joseph of Arimathaea is there described as "the friend of Pilate and of the Lord," and when "he came to Pilate and begged the body of the Lord for burial," Pilate had to send to Herod to beg the body from him; "And Herod said, Brother Pilate, even if no one had begged him, we should bury him, since the sabbath is drawing on" (Gospel of Peter 2:3–5). Pilate is portrayed as a friendly observer who, if he but could, was ready to do anything to save Jesus from his fate, but was powerless to interfere with the course of Herodian justice: even for the favor of permission of burial he had to address himself to Herod and could do nothing of his own accord. If those had truly been the facts, Pilate would automatically be relieved of all responsibility for Jesus' death: Jesus would have been tried and sentenced by a Jewish court presided over by King Herod, in whom the governor had expressly vested due jurisdiction. Still, it appears that the washing of hands, reported in Matthew, was too material an episode to be left out of even this radically different story; and as the anonymous author seems to have known that this manner of rite was typically Jewish, he tried to build it into his narrative as a Jewish and not a Roman mode of conduct. Thus it is that the washing of hands is now given the function of determining the innocence of the accused in the Jewish court: whoever thought him innocent would rise and wash his hands; those who thought him guilty would stay seated and refrain from performing the rite. Pilate, though not himself one of the judges, did—if we may conjecture what was in the part of the fragment that, regrettably, has not survived—perform it according to Jewish court custom, as expressive of his opinion that Jesus was innocent: it seems that, since he was present in court, Herod and the judges extended him the courtesy of an invitation to take part in the ceremonial voting. But then "neither Herod nor any of his judges" washed his hands, and a clear majority had thus voted to find Jesus guilty; where-upon "Pilate arose," the proceedings being at an end, and the court could not rise until the governor had withdrawn. It is no-table that while the ceremony of the washing of hands is thus retained and duly judaized, the Jewish self-arraignment is lost sight of, unless it, too, was recorded in another, lost, part of the fragment: perhaps there was no longer any need of this self-ar-raignment, since the responsibility for sentencing and crucifying Jesus had now been laid, fairly and squarely, on Herod and his Jewish court, to the exclusion of the Roman governor and any-body else.

It would be supererogatory to emphasize that there never was any such custom in a Jewish court of judges voting for acquittal by washing their hands. But the very ingenuity of the construction points up the dilemma in which the chroniclers found themselves: there was this Matthean story of Pilate's washing his hands and declaring his innocence, and the ensuing self-arraignment of the Jews; and there was the hazard that all this contriving to fix the entire responsibility on the Jews might well be undone by the im-probability, if it were not the impossibility, of Pilate's behaving in the fashion reported. To put aside the whole story, as Luke and John did, was too facile an evasion, and it may have been considered impolitic to sidestep the problem at the price of forfeiting so persuasive and conclusive a warrant for holding the Jews liable as would be their own voluntary declaration of liability. So the problem was tackled; and the upshot was a series of progressively more fanciful and more improbable inventions.

However we construe the facts set down, there are questions which do not admit of satisfactory answers. First, not only would Pilate not declare his innocence to a Jewish crowd, but the cry of the Jews, "his blood be upon us," would make no impression upon him. Here sat—virtually—a Roman viceroy, trying a man whom he thought innocent: how could a hysterical protestation of subject Jews assembled in the courtyard, venturing to accept responsibility for what he, Caesar's proxy, was about to do, change his mind? Not only was this "acceptance" of responsibility an effrontery, bordering on criminal contempt, but it also amounted to a presumption of judicial authority, as if the crowd knew better than any judge, and an imperial one at that, where innocence lay and where guilt. Had Pilate been a merciful and forgiving judge, he might have shrugged off this hysteria with a smile and proceeded to deliver his verdict as befitting; but we know him to have been choleric and implacable, so that the natural reaction to be expected of him would be a thunderous and uncompromising chastisement of this type of meddling. To envisage him seated meekly on his throne, doing neither the one nor the other, but spiritlessly succumbing to the hectic impertinence of a Jewish crowd is to conjure up the most absurd and least historical of spectacles.

Second, however impetuous the volunteering spirit of that crowd, the responsibility for his acts and decisions would anyhow be Pilate's alone in the final analysis. He could not delegate it, and it was not to be lightened by somebody else collaterally sharing it. If Jesus was innocent, and Pilate so found yet ordered his crucifixion in spite of it, he could not rid himself of responsibility for judicial murder by the plea that a second party had assumed it. The Jewish self-arraignment was, from start to finish, legally and politically, worthless and wasted, and however relevant it was to become morally and theologically, in the ears of Pilate it must have sounded as just so much senseless garrulity.

Third, we do not know who the Jews were that took the responsibility upon themselves: on whose heads, on the heads of whose children, was the blood of Jesus to be? Matthew informs us that it was "all the people" who said, "his blood be on us, and on our children" (27:25). It is claimed that the word "all" was used advisedly, to give to "the people" immeasurable weight and importance;[13] but "all" the people can hardly have gathered in a square which, at a very generous estimate, could hold no more than a thousand.[14] Who, then, were the people present? Did they cry out in unison, or did some cry out and others not? What was their authority to accept liability for Jesus' blood? Had anyone sent them there and empowered them to call down his blood upon their heads and upon the heads of their children? If so, who was it, and what was the fount of the sender's authority so to empower them? Was it the chief priests and elders that "persuaded the multitude" (27:20) to assume responsibility for "all the people"? If so, why did they not assume it directly themselves? And whence came the authority of "chief priests and elders" to be answerable for "all the people" or to induce the multitude to be? Even granted that such a cry was uttered in the hearing of Pilate by several hundred Jews, nothing in that assumption of fact would justify our regarding it as the unsolicited self-arraignment of the Jewish people in totality, binding and execrating its generations until the end of days.

Fourth, responsibility for a given deed or act is assigned not by virtue of any declaration purporting to assume it, but by objective standards: it would lie where it objectively and truly lay, regardless of the circumstance that certain volunteers, who were not genuinely responsible, had taken it on themselves. The situation is not quite like that in which an accused person pleads guilty though he may be innocent: for some reason of his own, he is taking upon himself the consequences of his plea rather than the hardships of a trial. Yet, even in such a case, his real "guilt" may be, and may remain, a matter of doubt and speculation, however justified in law his punishment. As far as real "guilt" is concerned, the exclamation "his blood be upon us" could be of probative value only if it were made on the strength of facts objectively established and in accordance with them; if those facts did not warrant assumption of responsibility by the volunteers, then the exclamation ought to be deemed, and dismissed, as a spontaneous and impulsive outburst, born of incitement or emotion and owing nothing to rational deliberation.

Nevertheless, these words, put by Matthew in the mouths of "all the people," have been interpreted and accepted, all down the ages, as a reasoned admission by the Jews of premeditation and malice aforethought in the killing of Jesus. Tertullian (about 155–225) wrote that Jesus was killed "by the whole community of the synagogue of Israel: for when Pilate wanted to release him, they clamored before him, his blood be upon us and our children."[15] None of the many other charges leveled at the Jews in the Gospel stories has been held so obdurately against them as unassailable proof of guilt and responsibility for the crucifixion as has this exclamation of theirs, "his blood be upon us and our children." Adapting the words of King David which we quoted, it was said of the Jews that their own mouth has testified against them, saying, the blood of Jesus is indeed upon their heads (cf. II Sam. 1:16). And just as Abel's blood, that crieth to God from the ground, fell upon Cain, his murderer, and Cain's punishment was to be "a fugitive and a vagabond in the earth" (Gen. 4:12), so the Jewish people, on whose head was the blood of Jesus, were to be fugitives and vagabonds in the earth, bearing the murderers' brand wherever they went.[16]

It is natural enough and theologically justified that the dispersion of Jewry, and all the manifold adversities that befell it at the hand of God, should have been looked upon by Christian observers as a divine retribution which it must have amply deserved: "Jews are beheld scattered through the whole world, that they have been punished on no other account than for the impious hands they laid on Jesus."[17] Indeed, the sight of God's punishment awarded to the Jewish people might well harden such observers in the belief that guilt for Jesus' death did in fact attach to them. Some of the Fathers of the Church, appearing to content themselves with the penalty that a just and all-knowing Deity had thought fit to inflict on the Jews, insisted that it was, now, for Christians only to "preach to the Jews with a spirit of love," not "for us to boast over them as branches broken off," and that the faithful should "say to them, without exulting over them, Come, let us walk in the light of the Lord" (Isa. 2:5).[18] But many others evidently felt that God had not brought punishment enough, and that it was the duty of the Church to offset His clemency by persecuting the Jews in whatever way possible: for "their odious assassination of Christ, there can be no expiation, no indulgence, no pardon; vengeance is without end; and Jews will live under the yoke of servitude for ever."[19] As self-confessed deicides, it needs little arguing that they are the scum of mankind: "lustful, rapacious, greedy, perfidious bandits," "inveterate murderers, destroyers, men possessed by the devil," whom "debauchery and drunkenness have given the manners of the pig and the lusty goat; they are impure and impious, and they know only one thing, to satisfy their gullets, get drunk, to kill and maim one another"; indeed, they surpass "the ferocity of wild beasts, for they murder their offspring and immolate them to the devil."[20] They must be oppressed and tormented wherever and whenever Christians find them, and the pious that have conversed with them solely so as to win them over to the true faith will be reproached on Judgment Day, God saying to them, "Depart from me, because you have had intercourse with my murderers."[21]

Whether this divine ratification of the Jewish self-arraignment was too obvious to be ignored or misunderstood, or whether the unfriendly bearing of Jews toward them had awakened in Christians a hostility which, for its violent outbreak, sought or needed "absolute" proof that the Jews had been culpable, the fact is that by a voluntary and intentional self-imposition of responsibility for the death of Jesus, as reported in Matthew, the Jews brought upon themselves a measure of vengeance and castigation without parallel in the annals of the world and, as it would seem, not yet exhausted. There is no virtue in surmising what would have happened if Matthew had eschewed the idea of tacking Jewish self-arraignment onto the gamut of innuendoes and allegations of Jewish guilt which the several Gospel reports had already transmitted: as likely as not, persecutions and vengefulness would have been no less. What is so fantastic about the self-arraignment of the Jews is that it was held out to be, and was represented as being, a species of power of attorney whereby the Jews—that is, all Jews—irrevocably authorized all Christians to make them and their children, generation after endless generation, suffer retribution for the blood of Jesus. It was said to be some sort of divine judgment which the Jews brought upon themselves and their descendants, and that the Roman governor had been chosen by God to perform the divine service in which that judgment was passed.[22] Now and to all eternity, each one was bidden to execute God's vicarious verdict. What would have been a usurpation of divine right of punishment became the mandatory discharge of the divine will: having vowed the vow unto the Lord that Jesus' blood be upon them and theirs, and having bound their souls thereby, the Jews were by divine law inescapably committed to paying for Jesus' blood with their own lives and the lives of their scions (cf. Num. 30:2); and the believers "considered themselves called to assist the Almighty in effectuating his 'curse', and free to indulge their hostilities with a divine seal of approval."[23]

There is yet another, no less disturbing, aspect of the story of Jewish self-arraignment: it was the Lucan tradition that however active the Jews may have been in bringing about the condemnation and crucifixion of Jesus, they might still have acted out of ignorance or delusion. Luke makes Peter say to the people that although they had killed Jesus (Acts 3:13–14), "I wot that through ignorance ye did it, as did also your rulers" (3:17). And in the Gospel According to Luke, the famous saying is ascribed to Jesus: "Father, forgive them; for they know not what they do" (23:34). It is not to be excluded that Luke abandoned the Matthean tale of the self-arraignment of the Jews because of the contradiction that it involved between their not knowing what they were doing and a purposeful assumption of full responsibility. Attention has been drawn to the fact that the verse with Jesus' prayer to God to forgive the Jews is missing from several manuscripts of the Gospel of Luke,[24] because, it may be inferred, editors and copyists alike found the tenor and sense of the prayer irreconcilable with the guilt and responsibility to which the Jews themselves are said to have confessed. There is a world of difference between accusing a man of a deed done out of ignorance and charging him with one done deliberately and with acceptance of complete responsibility for it: in our case, it is the difference between an indictment of judicial error and one of premeditated murder. Jesus himself had asked God to forgive them that had crucified him, and it would seem axiomatic that his followers should join in his prayer and, where called upon, practice the same forgiveness themselves. But no. We find the Fathers of the Church and innumerable believers in Jesus Christ, throughout the ages, disavow his example and renounce his teaching. So far from accepting the premise that the Jews did not know what they were doing and therefore, if for no other and better reason, forgiving them, these Christians have predicated that the Jews were self-confessed and wanton murderers and deicides, never, by divine injunction, to be forgiven. If Jesus' prayer, and his own forgiveness, had justification and made sense so long as the premise of Jewish error and ignorance was accepted, once that premise had to be surrendered neither prayer nor forgiveness was justifiable or reasonable. The Lucan and Pauline tradition of divine pardon of any Jewish sin involved in the crucifixion was to be rivaled, if not replaced, by the Matthean tradition of Jewish guilt and an eternal curse laid on the Jewish people, and it was the Jewish self-arraignment invented by Matthew that became the theological, or pseudo-theological, basis of never-ending persecution and tyranny.

The fact that the Jews, whoever they were, could in no wise have spoken the words which the Gospel of Matthew imputes to them, and that the episode of the washing of hands could never really have taken place, lends one more tragic touch to the disastrous and total misconception of the Jewish role in the trial of Jesus. Not only did "the Jews" not arraign and execrate themselves before Pilate, or solemnly undertake responsibility for what Pilate would do to Jesus, but they were not even present at the trial; and when Pilate came out of the *praetorium* where the trial had been held, it was only to announce the final sentence of crucifixion. But "history" was to be that "the Jews" had caused the death of Jesus and, what is more, had of intent assumed the full responsibility for it and delivered themselves and their children, voluntarily and unconditionally, to everlasting affliction.

11 THE ACTS OF PILATE

Nicodemus the Pharisee, twice mentioned in the Gospel According to John as a friend of Jesus (3:1 and 19:39), is said, "after the passion of the Lord upon the cross," to have recorded in the Hebrew language all that he had seen and heard "concerning the conduct of the chief priests and the rest of the Jews." The record has been lost, but one "Ananias, an officer of the guard, being learned in the law," had made a search "for the reports made at that period in the time of our Lord Jesus Christ, which the Jews committed to writing under Pontius Pilate," and he assures us that he "found these acts in the Hebrew language, and according to God's good pleasure translated them into Greek for the information of all those who call upon the name of our Lord Jesus Christ."[1] This version, which Ananias himself dates in the year 425, was discovered about a hundred years ago, and since then several manuscripts of it have come to light, each slightly differing from the other. Opinions are divided whether Ananias was not really the author of this record himself, or found earlier reports which he did translate: some scholars think that the documents on the trial of Jesus before Pilate, which are mentioned in the First Apology of Justin, about 150, are identical with the records of Ananias; others hold that Epiphanius, writing in 375, had knowledge of it,[2] but we would opine, preferably, that the date of composition is uncertain and cannot be surely established.[3] It decidedly was not written by Nicodemus, or any other eyewitness, or later than the year 425.

Like all apocryphal Gospels, this so-called Gospel of Nicodemus, with the Acts of Pilate as its major part, must have been written to supplement the Gospel accounts "on points where they did not entirely satisfy either the curiosity or the imagination of the faithful,"[4] or, we might add, with special reference to the Acts of Pilate, where the information in the Gospel reports did not tally with such knowledge and experience as authors versed in the law, like our Ananias, possessed of Roman legislation and procedure. But let us, at the outset, comment that there is a sharp rift of appraisal as to the legal acumen of our author: while one outstanding theologian has maintained that he gives us a true and accurate picture of the legislation and procedure in force in Rome and the Roman provinces overseas at the time of his writing,[5] a no less distinguished historian pillories him as woefully unlettered in Roman law, whether of his own time or any.[6] We are concerned not so much with the author's legal or other qualifications as with his efforts to bring sense into the story of Pilate's attitude to Jesus. It is—as we shall show—crystal clear that while starting from the premise, and maintaining throughout, that the account of the Canonical Gospels must be followed in substance, it strenuously endeavors to explain away some of the incongruities that we have already disclosed, by introducing into the trial new happenings not previously recorded; that he felt this to be necessary is no less interesting than the manner in which he went about accomplishing the task that he had set himself.

Instantly following the Prologue, we find the Jewish council assembled, presumably in the council chamber, and the outstanding participants are mentioned by name, such as Annas, Kaiaphas, and—behold!—Gamaliel. We are not told what went on, but it appears that as a result of the meeting the members

came to Pilate accusing Jesus of many deeds. They said: "We know that this man is the son of Joseph the carpenter and was born of Mary; but he says he is the Son of God and a king. Moreover he pollutes the sabbath and wishes to destroy the law of our fathers." Pilate said: "And what things does he do that he wishes to destroy it?" The Jews say: "We have a law that we should not heal anyone on the sabbath. But this man with his evil deeds has healed on the sabbath the lame, the bent, the withered, the blind, the paralytic, and the possessed." Pilate asked them: "With what evil deeds?" They answered him: "He is a sorcerer, and by Beelzebub the prince of the devils he casts out evil spirits, and all are subject to him." Pilate said to them: "This is not to cast out demons by an unclean spirit, but by the god Asclepius." The Jews said to Pilate: "We beseech your excellency to place him before your judgment-seat and try him." And Pilate said: "Tell me, how can I, a governor, examine a king?" They answered: "We do not say that he is a king, but he says he is." And Pilate summoned his messenger and said to him: "Let Jesus be brought with gentleness" (I,1–2).

Jesus, in this account, was not in the custody of the high priest or of the Jews, nor had he been arrested at all. Judas had not betrayed him, but was, presumably, following Jesus, attentive to his teachings. The Jews in council had decided to indict Jesus before the Roman governor. But what had they against him? That he "polluted" the Sabbath and wished to "destroy," that is, to reform, "the law of our fathers," may well have enraged the council, if he indeed had done so; but it knew that charges such as these could carry no weight with Pilate: for him, there could be nothing reprehensible or criminal in breaking the Jewish day of rest or in trying to amend the antiquated and barbarous ordinances of the natives. While not hiding the fact that the real reason why the Jews accused Jesus was that he transgressed Jewish law and, at least by implication, denied sanhedrial authority, our author makes them add a further charge, for the benefit of Roman susceptibilities: "he says he is the Son of God and a king." But when these Acts were written, Jesus had long been raised to sonship of God, though, to judge from the Synoptic Gospels, he himself had never expressly claimed anything of the sort; the slight anachronism would pass unnoticed by the readers. The pretension to kingship, however, is a charge common to all Gospel accounts; and it was only good Roman tradition that a real king should claim to be divine and of godly descent. Our author was perspicacious enough to know that Pilate would never have accepted charges of transgressing Jewish law as sufficient cause to issue a summons; so he makes him ask the accusers what exactly

Jesus did by way of altering or breaking the law: his specific conduct might divulge an act on which an indictment could be framed even under the Roman code. Their reply that "by evil deeds" he had achieved good results, namely, healed the seemingly incurable, would make little impact on Pilate either: he was accustomed to all sorts of wonder-workers who performed similar miracles—by associating not with demons and devils, but with the god Asclepius, patron of physicians. So only the charge was left that Jesus pretended to be a king of divine lineage, and that, of course, was an offense of which the governor must take cognizance. Before issuing a summons, however, he would make sure: perhaps this king was not a mere pretender, but one of the tribal chieftains in whom this exotic province could well abound: and adjudication between the rival claims of local satraps was a matter for the emperor rather than for a governor. It may also be that Pilate was first made to give jocular expression to his skepticism as to the seriousness of the charge by asking, "How can I, a governor, examine a king?" thus providing an early opportunity for an already well-established answer, originally deferred until after the crucifixion: "Write not, The King of the Jews; but that he said, I am King of the Jews" (John 19:21).

Our author must have taken it that the Jews could no longer exercise capital jurisdiction in their own courts. Instead, he reproduces, later on, the verses from John in which Pilate said to the Jews, "Take him yourselves and judge him by your own law," and they replied, "It is not lawful for us to put any man to death" (III,1; John 18:31). Significantly, however, we find him adding, without authority from John, a further question by Pilate, to which the Jews have no reply: "Has God forbidden you to slay, but allowed me?" showing that what they had spoken of was not so much formal jurisdiction as Jewish abhorrence of bloodshed and the alleged Roman indifference to it.

Jewish wrath, to be strong yet reasonable enough to warrant a charge before the Roman governor, had to flow out of Jesus' defection from Jewish law and religion. In Jewish eyes, the action launched by Jewish leadership to accomplish Jesus' trial and hanging could be vindicated only—or so our author thought—by establishing that his ongoing activity did, in effect, endanger the maintenance of authority according to Jewish law. That is why the old disputes between Jesus and the Pharisees about healing on the Sabbath are now being disinterred: there seemed no good reason why all the evangelists should have gone to such lengths in describing them unless they played their fatal role in the ultimate disaster. From the Jewish point of view, as contrasted with Pilate's, a sorcerer in league with Beelzebub, who went further and ventured to lay down the law and grant arbitrary and unauthorized dispensations from compliance with God's commands, must be silenced and done away with, if only for reasons of self-preservation. It will be remembered that there is no mention of any such "accusation" by the Jews in the Canonical Gospels. Before the Sanhedrin the charge—if any—brought against Jesus was blasphemy, and before Pilate it was pretending to be a king. No reference whatsoever to his many breaches of Jewish law, whether by healing on the Sabbath day or by failing to wash his hands or by not fasting or by taking it upon himself to reform the divorce laws—none, either at the meeting of the Sanhedrin or in the proceedings before Pilate. But our author seems to have felt that without a fundamental cleavage between Jesus and the Jews torn by irreconcilable differences of loyalty and belief, any sanhedrial action against him is still unelucidated and appears unreasonable —as indeed it would be—and since he had no other or better reasons for cleavage than were adduced by the evangelists for the earlier clashes between Jesus and the Pharisees, he made the best of them. He could hardly have been aware that the alleged clashes could never in fact have taken place and that the differences of opinion and approach were mostly in the nature of afterthoughts. Nor had he any real knowledge of the measure of importance which would be attributed under Jewish law to such sins as healing on the Sabbath, and in matters of Jewish law the ignorance of his readers corresponded to his own. He could, therefore, safely hazard his particular choice of charges against Jesus: Jewish animus was plausibly explained in that way, whatever Pilate's reaction to the charge turned out to be.

He seems to have known that Pilate would not hold a trial unless a charge had first been presented to him: that on the strength of it he would also issue a summons or a warrant of arrest, cause the accused person to be brought before him by his own officers, his "messengers," and then "examine" him on the charge. But he either did not know or disregarded the provision of Roman law that the accuser had to be an individual and could not be a group or body of persons, while, at the same time, it was essential for his purpose that the Jews, as represented by their highest authority, the Sanhedrin, be involved in the trial: it would be useless to make an individual Jew, be he the high priest in person, responsible for what was to befall Jesus. So Pilate is recorded as entertaining a collective indictment, without raising any formal objection, but in instructing his messenger to bring Jesus before his court, he is said to have admonished him to treat the prisoner "with gentleness," which may, perhaps, be interpreted to mean that on the face of it he did not consider the charge serious enough to warrant the shackling of Jesus or his being conveyed forcibly to the court. Or it might be seen as Pilate's first inkling of a true divinity in Jesus, whom he durst not now treat rudely.

So far from manhandling Jesus, the messenger is reported, at great length, to have done him reverence, "and taking the kerchief which was in his hands, he spread it upon the ground, and said to him: Lord, walk on this and go in, for the governor calls you" (I,2) ; called upon to justify himself to the governor, he answered that all the people had given ovations to Jesus, so he thought that he must be a Lord (I,3-4). When "Jesus entered in, and the standard bearers were holding the standards, the images of the emperor on the standards bowed and did reverence to Jesus" (I,5). The Jews protested to Pilate against the standard bearers, but when he reproached his ensigns, they made reply: "We are Greeks and servers of temples, and how could we reverence him? We held the images; but they bowed down of their own accord and reverenced him" (*ibid.*). For assurance, Pilate replaced the standard bearers by twelve sturdy Jews and told the Greeks that "if the standards do not bow down when Jesus enters, I will cut off your heads." Thereupon Jesus was brought into the *praetorium* again, and again the standards bowed down and did reverence to him (I,6).

Pilate is thus confronted with clearly perceptible manifestations of divinity. His own messenger, who is unlikely to be lightly swayed by the fanaticism of provincial barbarians, is so deeply affected as to feel compelled to pay this prisoner the respect due to a royal or holy personage, and, what is more, the images of the emperor himself, that is, of divine and deified majesty, bow down and do reverence to Jesus. To a Roman mind, such as Pilate's, this kind of miraculous revelation must have been almost conclusive proof of the divinity of Jesus, or at least a celestial quality or association in him. It is in our memory that no comparable revelation in the trial before Pilate is reported in any of the Canonical Gospels: our author rightly felt that, without a miracle, Pilate's attitude toward Jesus, as described, cannot be clarified or comprehended. It is because Pilate must have realized, or feared in his heart, that Jesus was, indeed, a divinity of whatever description or character that he insisted on discharging him, being anxious to avoid all involvement in his death: you can never know—we can imagine his thoughts—how and when these gods—even though of merely local origin and minor standing—may strike to avenge themselves. He had only to behold the miracle to be thoroughly frightened; or in the language of our more reticent author, "when Pilate saw this he was afraid, and sought to rise from the judgment-seat" (II,1) .

And while he was still thinking of rising up, his wife sent to him saying, have nothing to do with this righteous man, for I have suffered many things because of him by night. And Pilate summoned all the Jews, and stood up and said to them: You know that my wife fears God and favors rather the customs of the Jews, with you. They answered him, yes, we know it. Pilate said to them: See, my wife sent to me saying, have nothing to do with this righteous man, for I have suffered many things because of him by night. The Jews answered Pilate: Did we not tell you that he is a sorcerer? Behold, he has sent a dream to your wife! (II,1) .

The story of the dream of Pilate's wife is taken from Matthew (27:19) , but now the ensuing discussion is amplified. Pilate must have regarded the dream as a further confirmation of his misgivings, and that, to be sure, is why the story of it is inserted here, at this early stage: here was a god who not only performed miracles but also appeared in dreams. From what Pilate says to the Jews, it seems that his wife had become enamored of Jewish customs and therefore, it was to be expected, particularly susceptible to Jewish deities. The dream of such a woman must surely impress the Jews: if his own fears could be dismissed by them as heathenish superstitions, hers would of a certainty be recognized as prompted by true piety. But the Jews were to disappoint him sorely: not only was his wife's dream not divinely inspired, but it actually afforded further proof of Jesus' diabolical machinations. We told you, they said, that he was just a sorcerer, and now you see that he has succeeded in bewitching your wife.

The developing situation must have embarrassed Pilate greatly. He had good reason to apprehend that the miracles which he had seen with his own eyes did point to Jesus' godhead, yet these Jews might be surmised to be familiar with their own deities, and if they were adamant that Jesus' powers were devilish and not divine, he ought not to discredit their insolence lightly, for it was common knowledge that miracles could be worked by devils and demons as well as by deities. He could make the mistake of his life if he left a man who was in league with the devil free to rampage at large, especially since the man had already demonstrated that he was powerful enough to compel even the image of the emperor to bow down to him, but it might also be a calamitous blunder to lay hands on a god and call forth his inescapable vengeance. In the circumstances, a wavering and undecided Pilate need not astonish us.

The natural thing for him to do was to turn to Jesus and inquire how he reacted to the charge that, whereas he professed to be a god, he was in reality a sorcerer. But Jesus would not answer (cf. Matt. 27:14; Mark 15:5), saying only, "each man has power over his own mouth, to speak good and evil; they shall see to it" (II,2). So the Jews "saw to it," and said to Jesus that he was "born of fornication" (II,3). A long and loud discussion followed on whether or not Jesus was so born: twelve men, listed by name, stood up and declared, "We deny that he came of fornication, for we know that Joseph was betrothed to Mary, and he was not born of fornication" (II,4). Whereupon Annas and Kaiaphas told Pilate that the twelve were proselytes who should not be believed; and on Pilate's asking, "What are proselytes?" they advised him that they "were born children of Greeks, and have now become Jews." This infuriated the twelve, who protested that they were "not proselytes, but children of Jews and speaking the truth," and added that they had all been present at the betrothal of Joseph and Mary (*ibid.*).

And Pilate called to him these twelve men who denied that he was born of fornication, and said to them: I put you on your oath, by the safety of Caesar, that your statement is true, that he was not born of fornication. They said to Pilate: We have a law not to swear, because it is a sin. But let them swear by the safety of Caesar that it is not as we have said, and we will be worthy of death. Pilate said to Annas and Kaiaphas: Do you not answer these things? And Annas and Kaiaphas said to Pilate: These twelve men are believed that he was not born of fornication. But we, the whole multitude, cry out that he was born of fornication, and is a sorcerer, and claims to be the Son of God and a king, and we are not believed (II,5).

It seems that birth of fornication was, at least in the eyes of the Jews, inconsonant with divine, messianic, or royal qualification. To impute such birth to Jesus was to say that his claim to royalty or other distinction was ruled out by illegitimacy. Pilate, we sense, readily understood, and accepted, this Jewish aspect of the matter, though he could not have been unaware that in Greek and Roman concept illegitimate birth was no bar to divinity or royalty, even if it was a serious disadvantage in the lower strata of society. Still, he is said to have gone into the question with remarkable thoroughness. First, he tenders an oath to the twelve who testify to Jesus' legitimacy, and though the oath administered is secular, "by the safety of Caesar," they refuse to take it, with the prevarication that they are not allowed to swear even to the truth.[7] Hearing that, and taking it for granted that if Jewish law prevented the twelve from taking an oath, the elders and priests would undoubtedly refuse likewise, Pilate did not trouble to tender the oath to them, although the twelve suggested that he do, perhaps insinuating that Annas and Kaiaphas were not as observant and pious Jews as they claimed to be. In the event, he was faced with contradictory statements, one that Jesus was born of fornication, the other that he was born in wedlock, and neither confirmed on oath. The possibility that there was truth in the allegation of illegitimacy could not, therefore, be dismissed; and the fact that it was the high priest and the elders who maintained it may have lent weight and credibility to their affirmation, and thus substantiated their charge of false royal pretensions.

It is inferable that our author knew that among the disparagements devised by Jewish sages of the third and fourth century to discredit Jesus was the allegation that he was a child of adultery: his mother, Miriam Magdala, was said to have given birth to him while married to one Papos ben Yehudah, but he was the offspring of her illicit intercourse with one Pandira or Pentera.[8] It is hardly surprising that the Christian doctrine of Jesus as son of God should have given rise to slanders of illegitimacy and even bastardy in the camp of the unbelievers and the skeptics, and the allegation that Jesus was "born of fornication," which the priests and elders are said to have advanced, is much less scurrilous than the one made around the time of our author's writing, that he was a child of adultery. For the purpose at hand, it was enough that birth of fornication be alleged: the purpose was served if, in the eyes of Pilate, he could be proved to be disqualified from any claim to royal status or dignity.

Again, the interpolation of this legend of Jesus' birth is our author's own handiwork: there is not a word in any of the reports of the Canonical Gospels to suggest that Pilate showed the faintest interest in the incidents of Jesus' birth. Furthermore, our author must have perceived the need to enlarge on the reports for greater plausibility, or, even if the unauthorized professions of royalty were an offense per se, irrespective of the legitimacy or otherwise of the pretender's birth, that would not necessarily be so with a profession of divine descent or divine inspiration, backed as it was by proof of successful and impressive working of miracles: such a claim, they may have thought, might well fail because of the claimant's illegitimate birth. But illegitimacy had not been conclusively established; all that may have been ascertained was that, from their own subjective point of view, the priests and elders could perhaps not have admitted Jesus' claims, if any, to divine descent or divine inspiration, by reason, *inter alia,* of the circumstances of his birth.

Having "sent out the whole multitude" and privately consulted with the twelve who had testified for Jesus, Pilate was "filled with anger" on learning from them that the priests and elders wished to kill Jesus only because he healed on the Sabbath day: "for a good work do they wish to kill him? And they answered him: Yes" (II,6). Whereupon Pilate is said to have gone out of the *praetorium* and to have negotiated outside with "the Jews" precisely as reported in the Gospel According to John (18:30–31), with the added question, "Has God forbidden you to slay, but allowed me?" (III,1). As no further answer was forthcoming, Pilate re-entered the *praetorium* and had the exchange of question and answer with Jesus that is reported in John (18:33–38); then he came out to the Jews again and announced that he had found no fault in Jesus. "The Jews said to him: He said, I am able to destroy this temple and build it in three days. Pilate said: What temple? The Jews said: That which Solomon built in forty-six years; but this man says he will destroy it and build it in three days" (IV,1).

This transposition of the charge resting against Jesus for his words anent the destruction and rebuilding of the temple, from the Gospel report of the nocturnal meeting of the Sanhedrin (Mark 14:58; Matt. 26:61) to the report of the trial before Pilate, may have been intended to cure an inexplicable omission by Mark and Matthew. Our author had no difficulty here, as he had refrained from reporting what had gone on at the meeting. But Pilate is said to have been unmoved by the fresh charge, and may have scouted it as ridiculous or trivial. Thus, the reference to this Gospel charge seems to answer no discernible purpose in the present context. And indeed, as if no fresh charge had been put forward, Pilate proceeds to make his pronouncement: "I am innocent of the blood of this righteous man; see to it yourselves. The Jews replied: His blood be on us and our children" (IV,1; cf. Matt. 27:24).

But while, according to Matthew, Pilate's declaration of innocence and the Jewish self-arraignment are the last stages of the trial, followed by the instant freeing of Barabbas and the delivery of Jesus for scourging and crucifixion (27:26), in the report of our author they are just another episode in the course of the trial: even though the Jews volunteer to take the blood of Jesus on themselves, he is not delivered to them, for crucifixion or to any other end. But their ominous self-arraignment must have made a deep impression on Pilate, and our author obviously intended that it should: Pilate interrupts the trial and calls the elders and priests and Levites (!) to him to talk to them "secretly." And this is what he has to say: "Do not act thus; for nothing of which you have accused him deserves death. For your accusation concerns healing and profanation of the sabbath" (IV,2). The priests and elders had known all along that infringements of the Sabbath were not a sufficient charge to bring before the Roman governor; nor would they admit that it was only profanation of the Sabbath which had driven them to these extremes against Jesus. It had been suggested to Pilate by the twelve witnesses that the violations of the Sabbath were in reality the only reason for the persecution of Jesus, and he had to guard himself against falling into the trap laid for him by spurious charges of which, prima facie, he had to take cognizance, but which were not the true motives for the Jewish wish that Jesus be tried and hanged. So he put it to the Jews that their real aim was one which was of no concern to him, and he added his good counsel, to let the man go. But "the elders and the priests and the levites answered: If a man blasphemes against Caesar, is he worthy of death or not? Pilate said: He is worthy of death. The Jews said to Pilate: If a man blasphemes against Caesar, he is worthy of death, but this man has blasphemed against God" (*ibid.*). It does not matter whether the blasphemy alluded to here is the claim to divinity or the words about the destruction and rebuilding of the temple: neither, as we have seen, amounts to blasphemy in any legal or technical sense. But Pilate would not know that; and as motivating the measures taken by the Jews against Jesus, the vindication of an offended God, no less—and, indeed, even more—than the vindication of an affronted emperor, must have been amply sufficent even in his eyes.

We are then told that the governor "called Jesus to him and said to him: What shall I do with you? Jesus answered Pilate: As it was given to you. Pilate said: How was it given? Jesus said: Moses and the prophets foretold my death and resurrection. The Jews had been eavesdropping and heard, and they said to Pilate: What further need have you to hear of this blasphemy?" (IV,3).

We need not dwell on the inherent improbabilities of this story of secret consultations first with the priests and elders and then with Jesus; and of the Jews "eavesdropping" yet unreprimanded when they disclosed the offense by offering comment on what they had illicitly overheard. They had now found a new "blasphemy" to rely upon: Jesus' insistence that he was the one of whom it had been prophesied that he would die and be resurrected. In the Canonical Gospels, too, Jesus is reported as making similar state-

ments (Matt. 16:21; 20:18–19; Mark 9:31; 10:33–34; Luke 9:22),
but he made them to his disciples, not to Pilate. The evangelists
may have thought that if Jesus told Pilate that he wished to die
so that the prophecy might be fulfilled and he would rise again,
the governor would have nothing to answer for if he acceded to
his wish, nor could any possible blame attach to the Jews or whoever had instigated the Roman proceedings. But they also knew
that Pilate would scarcely have given in to such a preposterous
wish: he would have sent Jesus away, perhaps imprisoned or
scourged him (cf. Luke 23:16), and not only would the object
of Jesus have been thwarted, but the Jews would be allowed to get
off scot-free. What the evangelists advisedly refrained from writing, our author advisedly put in: when Pilate was secretly talking
to him, Jesus consoled him: you do as was "given" and foreordained to you; even by putting me to death, you do only God's
will and need have no pangs of remorse, for my death will be
transitory, and I shall be resurrected. Not that Pilate must needs
have believed it, but whether he believed it or not, Jesus' words
were a clear moral discharge for him, whatever he eventually decided. It was quite different with the eavesdropping Jews: not
only did they not believe in Jesus' pretensions, but they seized
upon his words as further proof of his blasphemous proclivity,
and so far from being morally discharged from responsibility for
their part in the ultimate event, they are all the more guilty for
their disbelief and for turning divine revelation into criminal
blasphemy.

Pilate could not see any "blasphemy" in the utterance of Jesus:
"If this word is blasphemy, take him, bring him into your synagogue, and judge him according to your law. The Jews answered
Pilate: It is contained in our law, that if a man sins against a
man, he must receive forty strokes save one, but he who blasphemes against God must be stoned. Pilate said to them: Take
him yourselves and punish him as you wish. The Jews said to
Pilate: We wish him to be crucified. Pilate said: He does not
deserve to be crucified" (IV,3–4).

As will be remembered, this statement of Jewish law is not
exact. Even a blasphemer against God is punishable with strokes
only, so long as he has not pronounced the ineffable Name (Lev.
23:15–16). If Jesus' offense had been blasphemy alone, he could

not have been stoned, because he had not pronounced the Name. It should not be assumed that our author knew these niceties of Jewish law but misstated it for an ulterior purpose: he may have thought, in good faith, that the Jews held Jesus guilty of such blasphemy as under Jewish law was punishable with death. Even then, they would not put him to death themselves: they "wish him to be crucified," that is, to be executed by the Romans. The Johannine version, that the Jews had no capital jurisdiction or power to execute capital judgments (John 18:31), is—for the second time—rejected by our author: first he makes Pilate ask, "Has God forbidden you to slay, but allowed me?" (III,1), suggesting that, as we have already seen, it was not a matter of formal jurisdiction; and now he makes Pilate, on hearing from the Jews that under Jewish law Jesus is liable to stoning, authorize them expressly to take him "and punish him as you wish." This authorization leaves open the possibility that although, in general, capital jurisdiction could not be exercised by the Jews, in this particular case the governor saw fit to allow an exception to the rule, vesting them with all requisite power "to punish him as you wish"; but there is no reason—and our author adduces none—to suppose that in the case of Jesus the rule was relaxed and special dispensation given. It is much more logical to suppose that as far as offenses under Jewish law were concerned, the Jewish courts could anyhow, and in any case, punish as they wished. Pilate is bound, therefore, to have wondered why, in this particular case, the Jews insisted on refraining from the exercise of their own jurisdiction and on Jesus' being punished by the Roman governor and under Roman law. To be able and ready to punish him, Pilate had first to be satisfied that he had, indeed, committed an offense under Roman law; the blasphemy of which the Jews spoke was certainly not such an offense, and as matters stood at that moment, the governor was not persuaded that Jesus did "deserve to be crucified."

So the trial is allowed to drag on. First, Pilate draws the attention of the Jews to the fact that "he saw many of the Jews weeping," whence he concludes that not all the Jews want Jesus to die. To his further question, "Why should he die?" he gets the answer, "Because he called himself the Son of God and a king" (IV,5), and we are back at the original indictment under Roman law.

It is at this point that witnesses for the defense come forward. There is Nicodemus himself, making a long speech, with a winding-up reminiscent of Rabban Gamliel's speech in the trial of Peter (Acts 5:38–39), that all those who did "signs which were not from God" perished anyhow, they and their believers: "And now let this man go, for he does not deserve death" (V,1). Then comes a procession of men and women testifying that they had suffered from incurable diseases and that Jesus had healed them. Under cross-examination by the Jews, some of them admitted that the healing had been done on a Sabbath day. The Jews objected to the evidence of women being heard, because "we have a law not to permit a woman to give testimony" (VII,1), which was true enough, but rightly disregarded by the governor, because in his court he applied the Roman and not the Jewish law of evidence. As far as the testimony of Nicodemus was concerned, the Jews objected that it was not reliable, because he had become a disciple of Jesus and spoke "on his belief" (V,2). Finally, "a multitude of men and women" came forward and said, "This man is a prophet, and the demons are subject to him." Pilate asked them, "Why are your teachers also not subject to him?" whereto they replied that they did not know (VIII,1). The issue of the case for the defense was that Pilate turned again to "all the multitude of the Jews," and once more he asked, "Why do you wish to shed innocent blood?" (*ibid.*).

For Pilate, the logical inference from the evidence that he had heard, and from the impressions which he had gained and had expressed, should have been to acquit Jesus and dismiss the court. There is no reasonable or other explanation here, any more than in the Canonical Gospels, why he did not. He is here said to have turned to Nicodemus and the twelve witnesses and to have said to them that "the people are becoming rebellious," and then to have asked them: "What shall I do?" (IX,1), a question unthinkable as coming from the Roman governor, and even less conceivable as coming from a judge and addressed to defense witnesses. At all events, they had no sager advice for him than this: "Let them see to it," which was nothing new or helpful. The inspiration suddenly came to Pilate himself. Calling again "all the multitudes of the Jews," he reminded them of "the custom that at the feast of unleavened bread a prisoner is released" to them: "I have in the prison one condemned for murder, called Barabbas, and this Jesus who stands before you, in whom I find no fault. Whom do you wish me to release to you? But they cried out: Barabbas! Pilate said: Then what shall I do with Jesus who is called Christ? The Jews cried out: Let him be crucified! But some of the Jews answered: You are not Caesar's friend if you release this man, for he called himself the Son of God and a king. You wish therefore him to be king and not Caesar" (*ibid.*).

So our author could not do without the story of Barabbas and the *privilegium paschale:* at the time of his writing, the Easter amnesties were already well established, and the Barabbas incident, so notorious from the Canonical Gospels, could not be left out. But it does not fit into his story at all. If this was indeed a sudden inspiration of Pilate as to how to solve his dilemma, he should have announced that in conformity with his custom he would free Jesus in Passover pardon; he must have known beforehand that, if he gave them a choice, the Jews would not pick on Jesus. The question "What shall I do then with Jesus who is called the Christ?" is taken from Matthew (27:22) and is much less plausible here than it already is there. Our author must have sensed the incongruity and inappropriateness of the tale in his context: not all the Jews cry out, "Let him be crucified"; some prefer to warn the governor, at precisely this juncture, that the freeing of Jesus would be interpreted as an act of disloyalty toward the emperor, a warning which our author has taken over from John (19:12). But while, according to John, the warning had an instant effect and Pilate at once sat down in the judgment seat to pronounce sentence (19:13), our author presents it as disposing only of the idea of pardon: it concludes the Barabbas episode and opens the way for the trial to continue.

Pilate is reported to have become "angry." He said to the Jews: "Your nation is always seditious and in rebellion against your benefactors." When the Jews asked, "What benefactors?" Pilate proceeded to remind them of their history ("As I have heard"), how they always rose up against God Who had chosen them from all peoples and showered on them miraculous boons without number; and he ended his speech, saying, "And now you accuse me of hating the emperor!" (IX,2).

And he rose up from the judgment seat and sought to go out. And the Jews cried out: We know as king Caesar alone and not Jesus. For indeed the wise men brought him gifts from the east, as if he were a king. And when Herod heard from the wise men that a king was born, he sought to slay him. But when his father Joseph knew that, he took him and his mother, and they fled to Egypt. And when Herod heard it, he destroyed the children of the Hebrews who were born in Bethlehem (IX,3).

When Pilate heard these words, he was afraid. And he silenced the multitudes, because they were crying out, and said to them: So this is whom Herod sought? The Jews replied: Yes, this is he. And Pilate took water and washed his hands before the sun and said: I am innocent of the blood of this righteous man. You see to it. Again the Jews cried out: His blood be on us and our children (IX,4).

Then Pilate commanded the curtain to be drawn before the judgment seat on which he sat, and said to Jesus: Your Nation has convicted you of claiming to be a king. Therefore I have decreed that you should first be scourged according to the laws of the pious emperors, and then hanged on the cross in the garden where you were seized. And let Dysmas and Gastas, the two malefactors, be crucified with you (IX,5).

That the Roman governor regarded himself as a benefactor of the Jews under his rule is highly probable, as it is that he found it characteristic of the Jews always to rebel against their benefactors. In the way that our author has built up his story, it did verily seem like a small uprising if the Jews, for all the governor's exhortations to the contrary, insisted so loudly that their demands be met. But Pilate is not made to crush insurrection, as would have been the natural thing for him to do; he is said to have given in to the Jews in defeat, which is the last thing that one would expect him to do. Our author knew all this as well as we know it, and so, as a last-minute solution, he furnished Pilate with an acceptable ground for convicting Jesus: Herod had sought to kill Jesus at birth (Matt. 2:16) because he had been told that the king of the Jews was to be born (2:2), and since Herod believed what "the wise men from the east" had read in the stars, Pilate had no cause to doubt their wisdom or astrology. There was, then, something in the assertion of the Jews that here was a man who aspired to kingship if, already at his birth, kingship had been predicted for him by competent astrologers. That King Herod had thought fit at the time to forestall this prospective usurpation of royal power and had gone to the length of ordering all new-born sons to be killed could only have fortified Pilate in his con-clusion that this kingship was a serious business, and not to be trifled with.

But, in the eyes of our Christian author, to find Jesus guilty of pretending to be a king was not what Pilate ought to do. Jesus had to be crucified, not by a reasoned and well-founded sentence of the Roman governor, but at Jewish instance and on Jewish responsibility. So Pilate is made to do two things so that this pur-pose may be achieved: first, he washes his hands in innocence (cf. Matt. 27:34), and the Jews reiterate their self-arraignment; and then, pronouncing judgment, he says that not he, the Roman governor, but "your nation," that is, the nation of the Jews, has convicted Jesus of claiming kingship. We recall that at the outset the council of the Jews was represented as acting as accusers; here the Jewish "nation" is represented as acting as the convicting court. That in fact the Jewish "nation" did not so act is patent from the whole sequence of events described in the trial report, and the words "your nation has convicted you" can have no other meaning, no other purpose, than to burden the Jews with a responsibility that, in law or fact or logic, they would not have to carry. And, as concerns the washing of hands, the story in Matthew had presumably already become common property, and it was too good to be shelved, however misplaced it might seem in the context. That the self-arraignment of the Jews which fol-lowed, "his blood be on us and our children," appears here for the second time during the trial plainly attests the paramount significance which our author and his Christian contemporaries must have attached to it and its implications.

Observe that, as distinguished from the stories of the Canonical Gospels, this trial report mentions no confession or admission ("Thou sayest it") by Jesus, so that conviction could not, here, have been founded on a plea of guilty, for no such plea is alleged. But, again in contrast to the Canonical Gospels, evidence was taken for both prosecution and defense, although no clear line is drawn between what the Jews "cried out" or "said" as accusers and what they testified. The whole narrative is so constructed as to warrant eventually conviction for kingly pretensions: that for tendentious purposes the conviction is shifted onto the shoulders of the Jewish nation is beside the point.

The sudden, terminal appearance of the "curtain" which Pilate commanded "to be drawn before the judgment seat on which he sat" is of particular interest for our inquiry. It has been authoritatively described as an "absurdity"[9] and led as proof that our "author has no knowledge of how trials were actually conducted."[10] It is certainly true that if the "judgment seat on which he sat" was outside the *praetorium,* under the open sky, there could have been no curtain; but the preceding paragraph (IX,3) , saying that Pilate "rose up from the judgment seat and sought to go out," shows that the judgment seat was in the *praetorium;* otherwise, he would have sought to re-enter the palace from the courtyard where he had presumably been sitting. But if the proceedings took place within the *praetorium,* then there had to be a curtain, the *velum,* to shut off the courtroom (the *secretarium*) from the adjoining premises; and as we saw, the curtain would be lifted whenever the governor desired to admit into the court a person or persons from outside.[11] So far from proving that our author had "no knowledge of how trials were actually conducted,"[12] I think that his mention of the curtain establishes that he knew that governors usually held trials in a *secretarium* within the *praetorium,* that is, *in camera* and not in public, and that, by lifting the *velum,* they could at will allow the admission of waiting persons, whether to give evidence or to present arguments or for any other purpose approved of by them. He evidently assumed that so long as "the Jews" and the several witnesses were permitted to address the governor, and were questioned by him, the curtain had been lifted, and it is curious that Pilate should have ordered it drawn just when he was about to give final judgment, our hypothesis having been that even where the trial had been held *in camera,* judgment would always be pronounced in public.[13] But after ordering the curtain drawn, Pilate is said not to have delivered judgment but to have turned to Jesus, saying, "Your Nation has convicted you of claiming to be a king," which sounds like an explanation or apology offered to Jesus personally rather than a formal sentence. The next words, "I have decreed that you should first be scourged," and so on, and "let Dysmas and Gastas, the two malefactors, be crucified with you," may have constituted the formal sentence, spoken not to Jesus in private, but pronounced in public. The conclusion that the entire proceedings took place within the *praetorium* and not outside is fortified by the report that after this pronouncement of sentence "Jesus went out from the *praetorium*, and the two malefactors with him" (X,1).

Our author was, then, in the unenviable position of knowing that a Roman governor would hold trial only within the *praetorium*, with the curtain drawn, so that apart from specially authorized persons no one could enter and be present, and at the same time of being under compulsion, in loyalty to tradition and to Christian partisanry, to embroil the "Jews," and the more Jews the better, in the instigation as well as the outcome of the trial, so that they had to be present at it. Reproducing the Johannine account of the exchange of questions and answers with the Jews, he must have thought it only natural also to adopt the Johannine version that Pilate went out to them (III,1; John 18:29), with this difference that whereas, according to John, he went out to them three further times (18:38; 19:4, 13), here he goes out but once more (IV,1). With our author, however, the rule is that Pilate "calls" or "summons" into the *praetorium* those Jews whom he wishes to hear or question, a procedure which, while it was unknown to John, would conform much better to what we know of the usual judicial practice: he summoned "all the Jews" (II,1); he "called to him Annas and Kaiaphas" (II,4) or the twelve witnesses (II,5), the elders and priests (IV,2) or Jesus (IV,3); and, having heard them, "sent" them "out" again (II,6; IV,3). One may marvel at the possibility of "all the Jews," or "the whole multitude," being crowded within the *praetorium* which, however large a courtroom it may have been, could hardly contain "multitudes," or one may draw one's own conclusions as to the real size of the "multitudes" from the fact that they could be all fitted into a regular courtroom. Parenthetically, our author wisely relinquishes the Johannine theory that the Jews would not enter the *praetorium* for fear of defiling themselves: he knew the usual procedure, that the governor would hold his court in the *praetorium* and summon to him there any persons wishing or required to attend, and, consequently, no Jews could be involved in the outcome of the trial who were not ready and willing to enter the *praetorium*. What he seems to have misconceived is that the governor would never summon undefined "multitudes" of people or admit them into his court: he might have summoned the people named as having acted as accusers (I,1), but not all the "priests, elders, and levites" as an indeterminate whole; but, then, our author had to concede to Gospel tradition that it was the undefined "Jews," or the scarcely more closely defined "chief priests, elders and scribes," who were to have ultimate responsibility for the crucifixion of Jesus thrust upon them.

However uncompromising his finality in this ascription of guilt, if only on the strength of their recurring self-arraignment, "his blood be on us and our children," it must in fairness be said that our author distinguished himself by charity toward the Jews and by an optimistic confidence, reminiscent of Paul but surpassing him, in their salvation in the end. His Acts of Pilate do not finish with the condemnation and crucifixion of Jesus, or even with his resurrection, as do the Gospels; he continues to describe at length what happened in the councils of the Jews afterward. While the Jews first imprisoned Joseph of Arimathaea for burying Jesus, and dismissed as heretical and unbelievable the many testimonies that came before them of Jesus' reappearance on earth and his ascent to heaven, it appears at the last that, persuaded by Joseph, Nicodemus, and three rabbis from Galilee, the "priests and the levites and the rulers of the synagogue," including Annas and Kaiaphas, withdrew their objections and accepted Jesus as "the Lord's doing, marvellous in our eyes" (Ps. 118:23). And all the people, led by them, joined in praising the Lord God and singing, "Blessed be the Lord Who has given rest to the people of Israel according to all His promises"; and after "this hymn of praise, they all departed, every man to his house, glorifying God. For His is the glory for ever and ever. Amen" (XVI,7).

12 NON-CHRISTIAN SOURCES

The most compelling argument that can be advanced against the theory propounded in this book is that it finds no support in the Jewish, that is, in the talmudic, sources. A meeting of the Sanhedrin during the night of Passover or on the Passover eve, for the purpose of rescuing a young Jewish messianic aspirant and popular teacher and preacher from trial and crucifixion by the Romans, would—or so it might be assumed—have in all probability been reported. Even if those who took part in the meeting could be expected to keep it secret and its purpose undisclosed so far as the Romans were concerned, there was no need or warrant for such reticence among the Jews themselves; on the contrary, if the Sanhedrin had failed in its efforts to spare Jesus a Roman trial and crucifixion, the interested priests and elders might at least have gained some profit, in the clashes of internal politics, from publicizing how they had gone out of their way to save him. And, in that case, the likelihood was that an account of the happenings would have found its way into the Talmud or the Midrashim.[1] And even if we do not reckon with politically inspired publicity, the fact alone that the Sanhedrin assembled at that particularly unusual time for that particularly exceptional

298 | THE TRIAL AND DEATH OF JESUS

purpose would have been justification enough for including at least some allusion to the proceedings in the talmudic reports. It has been said that it ought to be inferred from the complete silence of the talmudic sources that no such nocturnal session of the Sanhedrin actually took place.[2]

This reasoning *e silentio* may, at first sight, appear to be reinforced by the existence of talmudic passages which, so far as they touch on the trial of Jesus, tend to confirm the Christian tradition of a Jewish Trial and to upset any theory of the Sanhedrin being convened for another and variant purpose. The following is the text of a Baraitha[3] which is the most important of these passages:

On the eve of Passover, Jesus (of Nazareth) was hanged. For forty days, a herald went out before him, crying aloud: Jesus is going to be stoned for having practised sorcery and for having enticed Israel and led them astray; let anybody who has something to say in his defence, come forward and defend him. Nobody came to defend him, so they hanged him on the eve of Passover. Ulla asked: Do you think that he was one in whose favor defenders should have been called? Was he not an enticer, to whom the Divine command applied, thy eye shall not pity him, neither shalt thou spare him (Deuteronomy 13, 8–9)? But (they replied), with Jesus things were different, because he was close to the government.[4]

It will be observed that Jesus is here said to have been accused of sorcery, a charge of which we have found traces in the Gospels also (Matt. 9:34; 12:24; Mark 3:22; *et al.*), though not in connection with the trial. At about the time when this Baraitha may have been written, the first half of the second century, we find Justin Martyr writing in his Dialogue with Tryphon Judaicus that the Jews saw in Jesus a sorcerer.[5] But the only sorcery that could possibly be laid at the door of Jesus was the performance of miraculous feats in healing the sick; and while—as we have seen alleged in the Acts of Pilate—those who had been treated and cured by Jesus might have been forthcoming as witnesses for the defense, no such person would be willing to testify against him; and it is at least doubtful whether the "Pharisees," who were eyewitnesses to these wonders, would have been willing to admit that Jesus had wrought true miracles. The evangelists must have had good reasons, and doubtless valid traditions as well, if they were so careful to exclude sorcery, and the association with Beelzebub, from the charges brought against Jesus either before the San- hedrin or before the Roman governor. Even the Acts of Pilate which, as will be recollected, mentions Jesus' fraternizing with demons and devils in the bill of indictment, does so not by way of a separate charge of sorcery but only as negating Jesus' divine descent or inspiration. The report that Jesus was accused of sorcery may well imply that the Jesus of this passage is identical not with Jesus Christ but with another Jew of that name who was indeed convicted of that offense.[6]

Apart from sorcery, Jesus is said to have been charged with enticing Israel and leading them astray. This is a grave offense, if not the very gravest known to Jewish law: it means enticing another to "serve other gods, which thou hast not known, thou, nor thy fathers; namely, the gods of the peoples which are round about you" (Deut. 13:6–7), idols of wood or stone, as the heathen worship.[7] It does not have to be affirmed that Jesus never preached idolatry: everything that he taught and said, he did in the name of the one God in heaven, the Jewish God, and it was his whole purpose to bring the people nearer to this, the true and only God. His preaching and teaching may have run counter to those of the established leadership of the day, and even, perhaps, have con- stituted this or that crime, but it could not, by any stretch of the imagination, be regarded as enticement to idolatry. Again, an- other Jesus, of whom we know that he had been convicted of enticement to idolatry,[8] may have crept into our story, and Jesus Christ have been mistaken for him.

It is true that the punishment for sorcerers as well as for enticers to idolatry was death by stoning,[9] and the herald of our Baraitha announces that Jesus is to be stoned. But in the opening sentence and in speaking of the execution, the Baraitha says that Jesus was not stoned, but hanged; and we know that Jesus Christ was not stoned, but hanged, whereas, had he been convicted by a Jewish court of sorcery or of enticement to idolatry, he would, and should, have been stoned. Some scholars think that the intro- duction of the element of stoning into the passage is an attempt to justify the condemnation of Jesus from the Jewish point of view, and that the fact that Jesus was not stoned but crucified "was too firmly fixed by tradition for the talmudic writers to go so far as to say that he *was* stoned."[10] Others have attempted to explain away the contradiction by suggesting that the stoning had to do with the sentence of the Jewish court, and the hanging with the crucifixion by the Romans;[11] or that the hanging mentioned was not the mode of actual execution, but the biblical post-mortem hanging for purposes of deterrence (Deut. 21:22–23), that is to say, that they stoned him first and hanged his corpse afterward.[12] But all these explanations are in the nature of hindsight, and none is consistent with the text of the Baraitha: on the face of it, the passage speaks of an execution by hanging by order of a Jewish court, and the announcement of a forthcoming execution by stoning precedes it.[13]

There are other incongruities, too. The story that the herald went forth for forty days, appealing for witnesses, reflects a rule of law that after sentence had been passed on an accused, a herald had to go out before him when he was led from the court to the place of execution and announce: "This man A, son of B, is about to be stoned for having committed the offense C, and the witnesses D and E have testified against him; let anybody who can testify in his defense come forward and testify"; if any defense witness then came forward, the condemned man would be returned to court, and on the strength of the new testimony, the sentence might be reversed.[14] But the procedure must take place as soon as sentence was passed, and the sentence had to be executed on the same day, before the sun went down:[15] the ritual of sentencing, and the call for further defense witnesses, had to be so drawn out that there would be the briefest possible interval between the termination of the legal process and the act of execution; any postponement of that act was deemed a delay of justice which the condemned man should not suffer.[16] The longest spell that could conceivably be allowed for the after-sentence appeal for defense witnesses was a few hours: if the court had delivered its verdict in the forenoon, the herald would circle around on his errand until late in the afternoon; and that may often have been long enough for him to present the accused, and to make his prescribed announcement, in every street and market place of the city. But it is out of the question that an execution should be put off for forty days to give potential witnesses for the defense an opportunity to speak; not only would the court not be in session all that length of time, but it would have been regarded as highly unfair and, in fact, quite unlawful to keep the condemned man in interminable suspense between verdict and death. The only departure that we find from this rule is the case of the "rebellious elder," whose execution, according to one opinion, had to be carried out in Jerusalem during one of the three great festivals, when people from all over the country were gathered in the city, so as to perform the command, "And all the people shall hear, and fear" (Deut. 17:13), even if it entailed postponement of the execution by several weeks. But one inclines to the view that the bidding, "And all the people shall hear," might be performed with equal propriety by notifying the people that an execution had taken place: it sufficed that they all hear of the execution, not necessarily behold it.[17] With sorcerers or enticers to idolatry, however, nobody ever suggested that it was permissible to delay their execution until the next great festival at Jerusalem, or for forty days, or at all.

There could be a link between the forty days of our Baraitha and the period which elapsed after the council meeting reported in the Gospel According to John (11:47) until the Passover eve which was "nigh at hand" (II:55). It may well be that the writers of the Baraitha knew of the Johannine tradition that there had been a meeting of the Sanhedrin a few weeks earlier, in which the judges had taken "counsel together for to put him to death" (II:53), and that they desired to occupy the interval of time between the alleged resolve to put Jesus to death and the giving of effect to it by utilizing it for action in favor of Jesus and to his advantage. Or perhaps the authors of the Gospel According to John knew of the talmudic report of the herald and his announcements for forty days, and predated accordingly the presumptive sanhedrial decision. One way or another, the two stories do not match: by the Gospel of John, the council meeting was not a court session, but highly conspiratorial; in the Baraitha, the herald could not have undertaken his task except after a formal session of the court and a resultant formal sentence. It has been opined that the forty days announcements were inserted in the Baraitha to provide an answer to Christian charges that in the case of Jesus the Sanhedrin acted with undue precipitancy and without adequate thought.[18]

Finally, there is the very pertinent question of Ulla (about 280–300) : the law is that the rule whereby a herald calls for defense witnesses once sentence is passed is inoperative in convictions for enticement to idolatry. In respect of all other offenses, if a man were acquitted, and witnesses then came forward to testify against him, they would not be heard or the acquittal ever be rescinded. But if it was acquittal on a charge of enticement to idolatry, and new witnesses for the prosecution could afterward be found, the case would be reopened and the verdict might be set aside.[19] Conversely, with all other offenses, defense witnesses would be called for and heard even after conviction; but with conviction for enticement to idolatry, no defense witnesses would be invited or heard thereafter, and execution would follow automatically, all because of the biblical injunction, "Neither shall thine eye pity him, neither shalt thou spare . . . him" (Deut. 13:8–9). The reply given to Ulla's question is the most surprising of all: the case of Jesus was different because he was "close to the government." Though he was convicted of the heinous crime of enticement to idolatry, it appears to have been enough for the convicted man to have had near connections with the "government" for defense witnesses to be canvassed and, if forthcoming, presumably to be heard, and for the "pity" which was denied to others convicted of the same offense to be shown to him. And not only would the defense witnesses be called for on the day when sentence was passed, but being "close to the government" seemingly warranted a radical deviation from the standard practice, that is to say, advertising for such testimony for as much as forty days after the pronouncing of sentence. The "government," *malkhut,* means here, as in every occurrence of the word in the Talmud, the non-Jewish or Roman government, and it has yet to be explained why Jesus should have been "close" to it. Even assuming that during the Roman occupation, and out of fear of Roman reprisals, the Jewish courts may have accorded special indulgence to accused persons who enjoyed the protection of Roman authorities or Roman officers, why, in logic or expediency, should they extend particular favors in the matter of calling for defense witnesses after sentence, of all things? They might have withheld prosecution; they might have laid down a punishment lighter than the law prescribed; they might have relaxed all manner of rules of law and procedure, if tangible benefit could thereby be conferred on the accused. But why should they have engaged, as an exceptional concession, in the almost invariably unavailing effort to find new witnesses for the defense? Not only would the accused gain nothing, but his protectors, the Romans, might reasonably see in this kind of "partiality" a deceitful and insolent pretense of differentiation.

Our Baraitha is not the only passage in the Talmud that tells of a hanging on Passover eve. In another, we hear of a certain Ben Satda, or Ben Stada, a resident of Lod (Lydda), who is said to have been hanged on that eve.[20] He, too, had been convicted of enticing to idolatry, and his case is discussed in the context of an exception to the rules of evidence applicable in such cases exclusively, namely, that the charge may be proved by the testimony of *agents provocateurs,* and not obligatorily by independent and spontaneous witnesses.[21] This exception is being justified, like that to the rule of calling for further defense witnesses, by the biblical injunction, "Thine eye shall not pity him"; and the saying goes that the more cruelty you show toward an enticer to idolatry, the more mercy you show to the community at large.[22]

Two points stand out in this summary of the case of Ben Satda: one, that while, as an enticer to idolatry, he should have been stoned, he is reported as being hanged; the other, that, of all days, it was on the eve of Passover that they hanged him. It should, therefore, cause little wonder that this Ben Satda should have been identified with Jesus, on the assumption that both the Ben Satda report and the earlier Baraitha refer to Jesus Christ. Later talmudic scholars have obligingly contributed a pseudo-etymological theory that Satda, meaning something like adulteress, was the nickname of Jesus' mother;[23] others argue that she was so called after an ancient goddess of that name.[24] But all this is vain theorizing, and the parental Satda furnishes no slightest clue to identification.

Nor are the coincidences of mode and date of execution in any way conclusive. As to the mode, we find a variant of the report in other early sources, namely, that Ben Satda was stoned and not hanged.[25] It has been suggested, not without cause, that the text may have undergone revision to align it to the Baraitha on Jesus, and that the original, and veracious, report had it that the man had, indeed, been stoned, as was the law. And as to the date, the variant lacks all reference to the eve of Passover as the day of execution, and it is arguable, then, that if hanging had been substituted afterward for stoning so as to make the report fit, the eve was likewise interpolated subsequently with the same object.

Two further factors render the identification of Ben Satda with Jesus extremely unlikely.[26] First, Ben Satda is said to have stood trial and been put to death in Lod, whereas Jesus stood trial and was crucified in Jerusalem and, as far as our knowledge goes, had never visited Lod. The second and more determinant point is that the report of the Ben Satda case would not have merited entry in the talmudic texts at all were it not for the exception to the rules of evidence which it exemplified: the emphasis is not on what happened to Ben Satda, but on the prearranged planting of witnesses whose testimony would normally be inadmissible, but was tolerated when the charge was enticement to idolatry. Not only is there no imaginable nexus or similarity between the divergent modes of proof employed in the cases of Ben Satda and of Jesus, but it is just the report of the planting of witnesses that lends an appearance of authenticity and truth to the Ben Satda story, supporting as it does a rule which went into the law books and kept its place in them.

We have reliable information of another "Jesus," a disciple of Joshua ben Perahya, three to four generations before the time of Jesus Christ.[27] This one became an apostate, and we are told that Joshua ben Perahya "rejected him with both hands"[28] as an enticer to idolatry. In some of the manuscripts, he is described as "Jesus of Nazareth" as is, too, the Jesus of our Baraitha in some of the manuscripts. That the disciple of Joshua ben Perahya could not have been identical with Jesus Christ is unarguable: he lived, as we said, about a century before him. Still, being Jesus by name and an enticer to idolatry by his works, he was eagerly identified later on with Jesus of Nazareth, as well by the authors and editors of the talmudic texts as by—and this is even more significant—the book censors of the Church. If the Baraitha on Jesus and the reports on Ben Satda and on the disciple of Joshua ben Perahya have anything in common, apart from the charge of enticement to idolatry, it is that none could win the imprimatur of the censors: none was allowed inclusion in the editions of the Talmud sanctioned for printing and publication. We owe our knowledge of the passages to the lucky, but illicit, survival of a few uncensored manuscripts which were published only recently.[29]

But we do not know whether the ecclesiatical scrutineers suppressed the reports of the trial and execution of Ben Satda and the disciple of Joshua ben Perahya because they had themselves interpreted them as referring to Jesus Christ, or because they may have had inkling of an authentic Jewish interpretation according to which the passages did refer to Jesus Christ, or could possibly be held to. The adding of the epithet "of Nazareth" was certainly of Jewish origin, and in the Baraitha as well as in the story of Jesus, the disciple of Joshua ben Perahya, the sole purpose of the interpolation must have been to make it plain that the passages did, in fact, relate to Jesus Christ. It is possible that the Church's censors only accepted this apparent Jewish interpretation *ex abundanti cautela:* it was always wiser to suppress a passage which might be licensed for publishing than to permit publication of one that ought to be suppressed. So they decided to eliminate everything which might conceivably be suspected of the remotest relationship to the trial and crucifixion of Jesus Christ.

The censors appear to have done a very thorough job of work. The sages of the Talmud are bound to have possessed much knowledge of the life of Jesus and of details of his teachings and, just as surely, were not hesitant to express their displeasure at them in their academies and assembly houses. Yet we find few references to Jesus in the Talmud; and it is an open question whether such allusions—which may be supposed to have been unfavorably critical in all cases—had been removed, even before the Church's censors had a chance to appraise them, because the Jews themselves foresaw and feared their censure or were stifled by Christian ukase.[30] Whatever the answer, while any anticipated or actual censorship by the Church of derisive and derogatory remarks about Jesus and his teachings is easily understandable, it is difficult to follow why fault should be found with reports which, on the whole, could only provide evidence—and from Jewish mouths—to authenticate the Gospel stories on his trial and crucifixion. The Gospels report a trial by the Jewish court, and so does the Baraitha; the Gospels insinuate Jewish responsibility for the crucifixion, and the Baraitha accepts it for the hanging at least. Moreover, while the

Gospels admit that the Roman governor had something to do with the trial and crucifixion, the Baraitha does not mention Pilate at all, as if he had, indeed, been wholly innocent of this blood! The only apparent cause for Church disapproval of the Baraitha could have been its saying that defense witnesses had allegedly been sought for Jesus, or it might be its assertion that Jesus had been "close to the government." But the terms of reference of the censors were to expunge everything "offensive against the Christian religion,"[31] and what can there be offensive against the Christian religion in remarking that Jesus was close to the government or that defense witnesses had been summoned? My submission is that the true reason for suppressing the passages was that Jesus was represented in them as an enticer to idolatry and a sorcerer, characterizations that could, and must, have been looked upon as insulting. Since the Gospels report charges against Jesus quite different from enticement to idolatry and sorcery, such characterizations were a libelous Jewish falsehood and should be taken out of the texts. As a consequence, every report in the Talmud of a trial for either of those crimes that could by any construction be linked up with Jesus was methodically obliterated.

We have already remarked that the charge against Jesus of enticing to idolatry was totally inept: he practiced no idolatry and certainly did not preach it, and there is nothing in any of the talmudic sources preserved to us—except for the one Baraitha —to suggest that he ever did either of these things. Jewish converts to Christianity are referred to in the Talmud as *minim*,[32] meaning apostates, but never as idolaters, and while the epithet of apostate was not altogether complimentary, to call them idolaters would have been regarded, even by the outraged orthodox, as undeservedly abusive. We may naturally expect, then, that the describing of Jesus as idolater and sorcerer would be thought by Christians to be a grave affront: the more so as he is said to have been convicted, and not acquitted, of such disgraceful charges.

Later savants of the Talmud, however, had to wrestle with, by then, well-established traditions that a "Jesus" had been hanged on the eve of Passover for enticing Israel to the worship of idols and for the commission of sorcery. They knew, of course, that Jesus Christ had been crucified on that eve, they knew of the miracles which he had wrought, they knew him as founder of a new religion which now threatened and endangered their own. They were no historians; they did not pretend to give exact renderings of historical events any more than did the evangelists in their time. They were single-minded in a determination to strengthen and vindicate what they believed to be the true faith, to safeguard observance of Divine Law and adherence to ancient tradition; to those ends, they would not for a moment shrink from denigrating and scoffing at the new and apostatical creed which, by all accounts, Jesus Christ had founded. So it was only natural for them to identify the "Jesus" hanged on a Passover eve for enticement to idolatry and for sorcery with the Jesus crucified on a Passover eve for—as they surmised—founding a new religion: mayhap, the judges of those bygone days had verily found him guilty of idolatry on the evidence presented to them, and the fact that their own Christian contemporaries were no idolaters would not in itself cancel out the possibility of idolatrous tendencies and teachings on the part of their erstwhile prototype. And what stronger and more telling argument could there be against the new religion than the circumstance that its begetter had been a sorcerer and an enticer to idolatry?

It thus came to pass that the Baraitha, speaking of a Jesus, was amended to speak of Jesus of Nazareth, that the Jesus taught by Joshua ben Perahya was likewise made a man of Nazareth, and that Ben Satda was taken to be identical with Jesus the son of Mary. We do not know how many men of the name were tried on charges of enticement to idolatry or sorcery; what we do know is that none of them was Jesus Christ. It could be that the Baraitha refers to the disciple of Joshua ben Perahya, or to Ben Satda, or to a third Jesus of whom there is no other record; it is not beyond the bounds of probability that either of the first two was, or both of them were, "close to the government"—which Jesus Christ was not—and by that closeness enjoyed special treatment: of the affiliations of the other namesakes of Jesus we know nothing, and all or any of them might well have qualified for the particular grace accorded to the well connected. And all or any of them might have lived in Lod and there stood trial, and not—as did Jesus Christ—in Jerusalem.

If neither the Baraitha nor the Ben Satda report has any bearing on the proceedings against Jesus Christ, we must conclude that no talmudic record of any such proceedings exists, that is to say, either was never made or, if made, was so effectively suppressed, whether by talmudic editors or extraneous censors, that not a vestige of it had survived. I have touched on the probability that some such chroniclings must have been set down at the time; the likelihood now suggests itself that such as were have been irretrievably lost. If that be so, then the nonavailability of talmudic evidence to support one theory or another of what actually happened at the trial of Jesus, and before it, becomes irrelevant. But it can, at any rate, be safely averred that there is no reliable or authentic talmudic tradition which is inconsistent or incompatible with the theory which we have developed. From the point of view of sources in the Talmud, the matter is *res integra,* and we are left to look for other sources.

The first and earliest record to which one would instinctively look for information is the writings of Josephus. He had appointed himself annalist of Jewish history in general, and in particular the events preceding and during the Jewish War with Rome; and his known devotion to detail and his concern for precision seemed to guarantee that he would furnish us with all the information that we would require. He was born a few years after Jesus' death, and from his early youth had applied himself to the study of Jewish history and of the trends and doctrines circulating within the Jewish religion of his day, the tenets of Pharisees, Sadducees, and Essenes, and he cannot but have come across the new Christian teachings and become familiar with them. That Christianity was a familiar feature of Rome, where he wrote, will become apparent in the extracts that we are about to quote from Tacitus and Suetonius. In Josephus' *opum magnum,* the *Antiquities of the Jews,* on the heels of the report of the putting down by Pilate of a Jewish uprising provoked by the government's misappropriation of temple funds, we find the following passage:

About the same time came Jesus, a wise man, if one can call him a man at all. For he was a performer of miracles and the teacher of all men, who received the truth with joy. He attracted many Jews and many Greeks. He was the Christ. Pilate sentenced him to die on the cross, having been urged to do so by the noblest of our citizens; but his followers did not forsake him, for he appeared to them on the third day, being alive again, just as God-sent prophets had predicted this and a thousand other miracles concerning him. And up till now the people of the Christians, who are named after him, have not disappeared.[33]

There is only one other allusion to Jesus in the works of Josephus: in a report of the trial of James, that apostle is referred to as "the brother of Jesus who was called the Christ."[34]

There is an apt comment that if the passage on Jesus had been written by Josephus in the very words in which it has been preserved, then "it would be necessary to conclude that he was himself a Christian; for the suggestion that Jesus was more than a man, and the assertions that he was the Christ and had risen from the dead on the third day, could surely not have been made by one who did not share in the Christian faith."[35] We know, however, that Josephus, however disloyally he may have behaved toward the Jewish nation, never became a Christian. Indeed, an early Christian writer, Origen (about 185–255), expressly declares that Josephus did not believe in Jesus as the Christ,[36] and the reference to James as being the brother of one "who was called the Christ" is given as proof that Josephus saw in Jesus not the real but only a so-called Christ.[37]

It would follow that the passage could not have been written by Josephus. To salvage some of its authenticity, it was suggested that the typically Christian verbiage had been interpolated afterward by a Christian editor,[38] so that the part of the report to be attributed to Josephus himself would be what is left after cutting out the characteristically Christian phrases. The text, as amended by a French scholar, would then read:

At this epoch there appeared Jesus, called the Christ, an able man and worker of miracles who preached to people who were eager for something new, and he led astray many of the Jews and also many Greeks. Although, when he was denounced by some of the chief people among us, Pilate condemned him to be crucified, those who loved him (or whom he had deceived) from the beginning did not cease to be attached to him; and today the sect is still in existence, which, calling itself after him, is known as Christians.[39]

It will be seen that, excisions apart, some changes are made in the text: for instance, "led astray" replaces "attracted." Our scholar must have felt that if Jesus was just an able preacher and miracle-worker, no reason was visible why he should be denounced, or why the governor should sentence him to death. If he was the Christ—that is, if he claimed messianic authority—the rejection of his claim and the desire to uphold Jewish religious and Roman secular authority might explain these measures against him; if he was not, some other explanation would surely have been implied by Josephus. The expression "led astray" is wide and vague enough to imply it and, at the same time, not too radical a departure from the word used in the original text: people can be "led" by being attracted to a leader, and it depends solely upon the eye of the observer whether or not they are led "astray."

All this, however, is guesswork. Some scholars maintain that the whole passage was interpolated, and that the master manuscript of Josephus had no mention of the trial and crucifixion of Jesus;[40] others think that from the preceding and following passages and from what we know of the views and purposes of Josephus, a reconstruction of his true report could be attempted and accomplished, using, of the language preserved, only such locutions as are identifiably Josephian.[41] For our part, we content ourselves, negatively, with the conclusion that the passage in question, as it has come down to us, cannot have been authentic; once it is established that at least some of the phrases in it were interpolated by a Christian editor, no part of it can confidently be regarded as the composition of Josephus, and the whole is suspect. It is immaterial whether the interpolation put the passage in the place of something that Josephus did write but is now lost, or whether fragments of what he wrote are preserved in our text: it is demonstrably not feasible to differentiate clearly between what stemmed from Josephus and what did not. Thus, the alleged denunciation[42] of Jesus by the noblest citizens may be an intrusion, too, or it may be genuinely Josephian; with no objective and reliable criterion to determine which it is, it can prove nothing.

The passage, as it stands in our texts, is quoted verbatim by Eusebius (260–340), who makes much of the fact that it is "a historian sprung from the Hebrews" who thus "furnished in his own writing an almost contemporary record" of what happened to Jesus.[43] It is significant that this should have mattered so greatly to the early Christians: Eusebius' eminent adversary, Porphyry, had just published his fifteen books against the Christians,[44] contending that Jesus had never lived and that the stories of his passion and resurrection were impossible doctrines which contradicted any true conception of God, and predicting that the new religion would soon perish because "it had no national basis and required blind faith."[45] Eusebius also mentions memoranda which, it appears, were published anonymously, and wherein Jesus was "blackened."[46] Now if the Jews themselves, the first and instant sufferers from Jesus' defection, not only admitted that he had lived and taught and worked miracles in their midst, but also that he had, indeed, been crucified and resurrected, heathen skeptics like Porphyry could be decisively silenced. It was, therefore, essential that an affirmation such as that which appears in our text of Josephus should figure in a book written by a Jew and, purportedly, from the Jewish point of view, and not for Jewish readers, but for the Romans and the Gentiles. Josephus fulfilled all these specifications perfectly, and Eusebius made the most of what he conveniently found in his book. That he could do so points to the interpolation dating back to before his time; as Origen had no knowledge of it, it is generally assumed that it was added in the latter half of the third century.

Since Josephus wrote mainly for a Roman readership in a city where, in his time, Christianity was hardly in good repute, and since his concern was to put the Jews in as favorable a light in Roman eyes as could be, it has been said that he "might have deemed it prudent not to remind his Roman readers that Judaea had produced Christianity in addition to all the other ills with which it had recently afflicted the Roman empire."[47] This consideration, however, would not apply unless Josephus had intended to write of Christianity in kindly terms; but if—as may reasonably be assumed—he would have written disparagingly, there could only have been all the more reason for him to show how the Jews, for once in harmonious accord with the Romans, did all that they possibly could to nip the new movement in the bud. He had a unique opportunity to stress not only the astonishing and highly intelligent foresight of the Jews, who from the start had known that the new creed was humbug, but also the wise statesmanship of the Roman governor who had at once discerned the merits of the Jewish charges against Jesus and sentenced an ominous "Christ" to crucifixion. It is no mystery, then, that Christian interpolators finding in Josephus' book an anti-Christian passage like that which we have conceived would be vitally interested in striking it out, and even less mysterious that, having decided to strike it out, they would replace it by one suited to their own purposes. It is true that in a Josephian report that the Jews had urged Pilate to condemn Jesus there was nothing that could do disservice to the Christian cause. On the contrary, if the interpolators had discovered such a report, they might be relied upon to let it stand intact and make the most of it; but Josephus himself would then be suspect of a tendentious purpose of his own: no less than the interpolators were at pains to put the blame on the Jews and whitewash Pilate, Josephus was at pains to assign the credit for the crucifixion of Jesus to Jews and Romans in equal shares. Indisputably, either tendency is calculated to falsify history.

Before we turn our backs on Josephus and his so-called *testimonium Flavium*, it is as well to glance at the Old Russian or Slavonic version of his book on the Jewish War, incorporating a long passage on Jesus which has not survived in the extant Greek rendering of it. The passage runs:

At that time also a man came forward—if it is fitting to call him a man. His nature as well as his form were a man's, but his showing forth was more than that of a man. His works were godly and he wrought wonder deeds, amazing and full of power. Therefore it is not possible for me to call him a man, but in view of the nature he shared with all, I would also not call him an angel. And all that he wrought through some kind of invisible power, he wrought by word and command. Some said of him: Our first lawgiver has risen from the dead and shows forth many cures and arts. But others supposed that he was sent by God. He opposed himself in much to the law, and did not observe the Sabbath according to ancestral custom. Yet he did nothing reprehensible nor any crime, but by word solely he effected everything. And many from the folk followed him and received his teachings; and many souls began to waver, supposing that through him the Jewish tribe would be freed from Roman hands. It was his custom often to walk outside the city, preferably on the Mount of Olives; it was there that he dispensed his cures to the people. And there gathered around him a hundred and fifty servants, and from among the people a great number. When they saw his power, and that he accomplished everything he wanted by word of mouth, they urged him that he should enter the city, massacre the Roman soldiers and Pilate, and rule over them. But he scorned it. Later, the leaders of the Jews obtained knowledge thereof and they convened with the high priest and said: We are powerless and too weak to withstand the Romans, like a bow that is bent. Let us tell Pilate what we have heard, and we shall have no trouble; if he should hear it from others, our goods may be confiscated, we may ourselves be beheaded, and our children may be exiled. So they went and informed Pilate. He sent his men, who killed many of the people, and they brought this miracle-worker before him. He interrogated him, and he found that he did good and not evil, that he was no revolutionary, and that he did not aspire to royal power; and he discharged him. For he had healed his wife who had been dying. He went to his accustomed place and wrought the accustomed works. And as an ever increasing number of people gathered around him, he won great reputation among them all. The teachers of the law were envenomed with envy, and they gave thirty talents to Pilate that he should kill him. Pilate took the money and gave them permission to carry their purpose into effect themselves. They seized him and crucified him, notwithstanding the laws of their ancestors.[48]

In the same manuscript mention is made, in another place, of the inscription on the cross on which Jesus had been crucified, that "Jesus the king had not reigned, but had been crucified by the Jews because he had predicted the destruction of the city and the ruin of the temple."[49]

Opinions as to the authenticity of this passage are sharply divided—they range from a belief in its Josephian origin[50] to its dismissal as a forgery and hoax,[51] with intermediate theories of interpolations into some original text,[52] of which the "projected attack on the Romans in Jerusalem which the latter anticipated and bloodily suppressed"[53] may or may not have formed a part. We must resign ourselves to concluding that there is no proof of Josephus' authorship of any portion of it, and that the uncertainty of date and authorship of its several components deprives it of any probative historical value.[54]

Subject to all due reservations on that point, it is nevertheless significant that we find that the anonymous miracle-worker, doubtless to be identified as Jesus,[55] is acquitted and discharged by Pilate after being denounced to him by "the leaders of the Jews" and by the high priest as an evildoer, a revolutionary, and an aspirant to royal power. When Pilate established that he was a doer of good and not of evil, and not a revolutionary or ambitious of kingship, in short, when he found no fault in this man, he did the only thing which he could in fairness be expected to: he acquitted him and set him free. The notion that he would, though finding no fault in him, enter into negotiation with "the Jews" and entertain their uncontrollable clamor that he be crucified is apparently too absurd for the author of our passage to adopt it, notwithstanding the Gospel reports with which he must have been acquainted. In fact, if Pilate had found no fault in Jesus, he could by no manner of means have sentenced him, or otherwise permitted his execution, so long as he exercised his judicial functions with due regard to law and procedure, and no amount of Jewish hysterics, in threatening or uproar, could possibly have deflected him from that course. There was only one thing—or so the author of our passage not unreasonably imagined—which could so induce Pilate, and that was a bribe. The "thirty pieces of silver," which, according to the Gospel tradition, were the reward of Judas for his betrayal (Matt. 26:15), now become the bribe paid to Pilate for his misprision. Again, a Gospel tradition which appears so farfetched—the betrayal by Judas, as we saw, being as unnecessary as it was improbable—is adapted and reformulated to fit in with a factual situation in which it becomes eminently tenable. Still, Pilate is said not to have ordered his own men to crucify Jesus, but to have permitted the Jews themselves to be the crucifiers: this sudden and ultimate lapse into gross irrationality can be understood and must be forgiven in the light of the overriding and dogmatic compulsion to brand the Jews as deicides incontrovertibly. It had to be the Jews that crucified Jesus, not just by clamoring for his crucifixion or even by taking upon themselves, by word of mouth, the responsibility for his blood, but in actuality and by their own hands doing the fatal deed. And this in spite of[56] the law of their ancestors that a man is never to be executed by crucifixion; or, perhaps, in spite of the law of their ancestors that a man is never to be executed unless by sentence of a competent court. Not only—according to this account—was there no sentence, and no trial, of a Jewish court, but there was no trial and no sentence by Pilate either—just a "permission" to the Jews to do what they liked with Jesus; and it is an open question whether that permission had been required because Jesus was in Roman custody or under Roman protection—maybe because of his having healed Pilate's wife, or only to forestall a prosecution for his murder or for usurping official Roman crucifixion procedures. Indeed, the *titulus* said here to have been inscribed on the cross brings us back to typically Roman law and custom; and it is almost pathetic to observe that instead of inscribing on the cross the designaton of the offense committed, and no more, the Jews are reported to have written on it not only details of Jesus' offense but also that he had been crucified "by the Jews." Moreover, that the details of the offense comprise not only what Jesus had done—predicting the destruction of Jerusalem and its temple—but also what he had not: "Jesus the king did not reign," as though his claim to kingship was well established and not illegitimate, so that if he "did not reign," it was due solely to his murderous crucifixion by the Jews for making predictions which soon proved true in every case. The Roman *titulus* testifying to the offense of a criminal about to be crucified is thus transformed into a *titulus* testifying to the guilt of the crucifiers.[57]

The absence from this story of any mention of Jesus' proper name, his virgin birth, and his resurrection has prompted some scholars to hold that it was written by a Jewish apologist, other than Josephus, who wanted to satisfy his Jewish readers that Jesus had been rightly crucified by the Jews because he could, but would not, save them from Roman oppression, or because he was an impostor pretending that he could.[58] But this theory seems to overlook the cardinal fact that the story was compiled as an interpolation into the writings of Josephus or as a forgery of them, and that its author at any rate intended it to be taken for genuine Josephian writing. As a Jew, he would not necessarily have alluded to either the virgin birth or the resurrection or any other later Christian attributes of Jesus: that they were, ostensibly, referred to in the original passage in the *Antiquities* has already been construed as clear indication that Josephus, the Jew, could not have written it. Furthermore, that a Jewish apologist, of all people, would go to the extreme of taking the crucifixion out of Pilate's hands, where it had been placed forthrightly even by the Gospel reports, and making the Jews crucify Jesus themselves is just not credible: if a Jew did that, or were reported as doing it, it would be for purposes of self-arraignment rather than apologetics.

Whether it was by the working of inside or outside censors, or by the working of interpolators and editors, the fact abides that whatever reports may have been embodied in talmudic sources and in the writings of Josephus on the trial and crucifixion of Jesus are now no longer identifiable as such. And while the Jewish censors and editors who revised the talmudic texts centuries after the death of Jesus, at a time when Christianity had won its triumphs and Judaism was reacting in a spirit of disdain and derogation, did all that they could to defame and deride Jesus, and to cause him to be identified with all sorts of despicable criminals of different periods, the Christian interpolators would naturally eliminate everything offensive to Jesus and the Christian faith, and replace it by a spurious copy of Jewish self-arraignment and Jewish deicidal guilt. Talmudic denigrations of Jesus are as little reliable, and as unauthentic, as are the Christian interpolations. But while the denigrations have been robbed by efficient ecclesiastical censorship of much of their intended effect, the interpolations have been allowed, throughout history, to wreak disastrous havoc.

The catalogue of contemporaneous non-Christian reports of the trial and crucifixion of Jesus would not be complete without reference to two great Roman historians, Tacitus (55–115) and Suetonius (69–140). Both mention the Christians. Suetonius reports that during the reign of Claudius (41–54), Christus instigated the Jews to cause continuous disturbances, whereupon the Jews were expelled from Rome;[59] and during the reign of Nero (54–68), punishments were inflicted on the Christians, "a sect professing a new and mischievous religious belief."[60] The Christus who instigated the "Jews" cannot have been Jesus, because Jesus had died before Claudius ascended the throne; but that Jews were driven out of Rome in the reign of Claudius we also know from the Acts (18:2), and the instigator may have been either one of the Christians or a person bearing some similar private name.[61] It has been sought to prove that the name "Christus" was known in Rome as that of the founder of this "new and mischievous" religious sect from the celebrated passage in the *Annales* of Tacitus, reading:

> In order to destroy the rumors [that he had set fire to the city], Nero invented false charges against people who were hated for their abominations and who were commonly called Christians, and had the most appalling tortures inflicted on them. The author of that name was Christus who had, during the reign of Tiberius, been executed by Pontius Pilate, the procurator. Repressed for the moment, this detestable superstition broke out anew, not only in Judaea where it originated, but also in this city in which there flows from anywhere all that is horrible and shameful and is at once taken up. Those who confessed were tried first, and then multitudes of people were convicted on the strength of the testimony of those [who had confessed], not so much because of having committed arson, but because of hating mankind.[62]

The punishments which in the Suetonian report Nero inflicts on the Christians are obviously identical with the appalling tortures in the Tacitean; but it is only Tacitus who seizes this fortuitous opportunity to give not only the explanation of the origin of the name but also to recount the fate of the eponymous Christus at the hands of Pontius Pilate.

Serious doubt has been cast on the authenticity of this passage in Tacitus.[63] It has been said that he is the only pagan writer to use the name of Pilate at all,[64] not to speak of Pilate's role in the story of Jesus. This remarkable uniqueness among Roman historians of the pre-Christian era has led one scholar to opine that Tacitus took his clue from none other than Josephus,[65] with the incidental result that the authenticity of the contested passage in Josephus would be rendered much more credible; but this opinion has been conclusively rebutted.[66] A good many scholars hold the view that Tacitus' source was the writings of one or other early Christian writer,[67] if not the Gospels or the Pauline letters themselves. But there is the convincing rejoinder that there was no need at all to assume that Tacitus searched for a literary source: he may have had from hearsay the information which he then conveyed in the message. He had himself been governor of a province in which many Christians lived, and—like his friend Pliny[68]—would certainly have had to try many of them on charges of apostasy and disloyalty to the emperor; and from his interrogation of them, he would soon have elicited all that there was to know about the identity and end of the—however legendary—founder of their faith.[69] Possessing that information, it was only natural, and very much in line with the scholarly integrity for which Tacitus was famed,[70] that he sifted out of it, and rejected, what must have been untrue and unthinkable in his eyes, as, for instance, that the Jews—whom he presumably identified with the Christians anyway[71]—should have insisted on the crucifixion of Jesus even against the will and better judgment of the Roman governor, or that Jesus should have arisen again after death. He accepted, and recorded, only that part of the fate which in his appraisal must have been eminently reasonable, and hence probably true: namely, that the initiator of all this "detestable superstition," this "hatred of mankind," and the "abominations" connected with them was tried and crucified by the Roman governor in accordance with Roman law.

But the mere statement that Pilate, the procurator, had sentenced Jesus, the Christ, to crucifixion does not amplify our knowledge by anything of value. As distinguished, perhaps, from students of history, we do not need the authority of Tacitus for a proposition which we are in any event prepared to assume on the strength of the Gospel reports. And no inference can properly be drawn from the silence of Tacitus on each and all of the controversial issues.

The sum total of non-Christian sources on the trial and crucifixion of Jesus is, thus, nil. Whether by accident or by design, the way was wide open for a Christian monopoly of all records and reports and their channeling to such purpose as Christian policy and prejudice might dictate.

13 THE PERVERSION OF JUSTICE

Jesus' prophecy had come true: the temple was destroyed, and not one stone was left upon another (Mark 13:2; Matt. 24:2; Luke 21:6). Surely this was the divine retribution expected for the crucifixion of Christ, and surely God would not inflict unmerited punishment. What better, what stronger, evidence of Jewish guilt could there be? And mark—it is the Jewish people as a whole that is being punished, not just priests or elders or scribes: God's wrath has descended on all of them and on all their children—the very curse which they had, unbidden, called down upon themselves. Now their city was in ruins, their country ravaged, their nationhood dissolved, and they were scattered and dispersed far and wide, easy and natural target for endless torture and persecution. It was manifestly God's will, too, that their punishment should not be tied to time or space: so enormous was their crime that however perpetual, undefined, and immeasurable the penalties they had to endure, there could be no expiation of it. The agonizing requital must be suffered forever.

The Jews shared the conviction that the ruin of Jerusalem and its temple and the fragmentation of the Jewish people among the Gentiles were the sentence of God: if He sent evil, it must be deserved. We find in the Talmud a long list of sins and transgressions of which the contemporaneous generation had been, or was believed to have been, guilty and for which it was visited with divine retribution; and for hundreds of years discussions went on for what particular wrongdoing this, and for what the other, visitation may have been earned.[1] There was not, of course, among the many and manifold wickednesses of the generation, either the crucifixion of Jesus or the curse which the Jews had allegedly invoked upon themselves: in respect of all that was connected with the death of Jesus, the Jewish conscience was, at that time and ever after, clear and quiet. However much and however often, throughout the ages, the Jews have been bitterly reminded of their so-called guilt as deicides, their own self-judgment was unassailable: quite apart from their disbelief in the divinity of any human creature, not excepting Jesus, they could, in perfect good faith, reply to their adversaries that if a Jewish court of that time had, indeed, found Jesus guilty of a capital crime, he must be deemed to have been rightly convicted, and the court to have acted and adjudicated according to law and to the best of its knowledge and ability. And while it was perhaps not their business to deny that Jesus had been tried and convicted by a Jewish court, for they might, as regards this basic fact, have thought that they had to proceed on the assumption that they did not possess all the information which their adversaries had, they actually did deny that, too, and went so far as to assert that forty years before the destruction of the temple, capital jurisdiction was no longer exercised by Jewish courts, which could not, therefore, have tried Jesus in the year 30 on a capital charge.[2] What the Jews unfortunately failed to do was to meet their Christian challengers on the Christian premise and argue the case for Jewish innocence on the basis of an analysis of the Gospel reports themselves: but then the holy books of the Christians (*Sifrei Minim*), since the earliest talmudic times, have been strictly taboo and banned: not only would no Jewish scholar study them, whether out of intellectual curiosity or in a desire to obtain the necessary intelligence of the adversary's weapons, but there are even pronouncements in the Talmud that those books must be burned.[3] They must have been, and in some circles must still be, regarded as highly dangerous stuff indeed, much too dangerous to have lying around

in any Jewish home—an apprehension, I dare say, born of ignorance rather than of information.

The clear conscience of the Jews was to be of no avail to them,
and it became, in fact, totally irrelevant. From the earliest days,
Jewish guilt in the crucifixion of Jesus was made a convenient and
natural starting point for saddling the Jews with all sorts of other
real and imaginary murders. Thus, in apocryphal writings of the
first century, we already find the Jews, whether in general or in
the persons of their chief priests and elders, branded with the
wanton killing of Ananias and Cleophas, described as two friends
of Jesus; or with jailing Joseph of Arimathaea and then letting
him die or starve or, in another version, perish of poisoning; and
again, Longinus, the centurion who saw Jesus die on the cross
and said, "Truly this man was the son of God" (Mark 15:39;
Matt. 27:54), or—as seems somewhat more probable—"Certainly
this was a righteous man" (Luke 23:47), is said to have been put
to death in Rome by Pilate, whom the Jews had bribed to that
end, and his severed head to have been brought to Jerusalem in
proof of that murder. And Mary, mother of Jesus, is said to have
been burned to death by the Jews, Martha and Lazarus are said
to have been drowned by them in the sea at Jaffa, and Simon of
Cyrene naturally to be the first to be crucified by the Jews, having
done what Jesus ought himself to have done—borne his cross.[4]
Proved able and eager to murder even the Son of God, the Jews
would certainly not shrink from murdering his next-of-kin and his
followers; and thus, inveterate murderers that they were anyhow,
any unnatural death for which no other culprit could be found
might, automatically almost and at any rate conveniently, be
blamed upon them. So sure and soon enough, the Jews became
the standard scapegoat to atone for any violent and unpunished
Christian death: an urgent need of Christian blood for Jewish
ritual was not only the first, but also the most enduring, fabrica-
tion to provide a motive for the Jews' unquenchable bloodthirsti-
ness. In the due course of a logical and inexorable evolution, the
Jews were ultimately held responsible for all disasters and
calamities that befell the Christian world: these were no longer
divine punishments, but abominable Jewish crimes. Whenever
plague or pestilence broke out—and there were outbreaks in
plenty—it was always the Jews that had caused it, by poisoning

waters and pastures,[5] it being facilely forgotten that Jews drank from the same wells as Christians did, or by bribing and hiring lepers to spread diseases,[6] or by doing exactly what Jesus is said to have been charged with: entering into league with the devil and with malignant demons.[7] The fables of Jewish combinations of murder and magic, poison and sorcery, blood and ritual, aimed at the total destruction of Christendom, were "repeated often enough, in various guises, to indicate that they were quite generally believed."[8]

It is not only that Jewish guilt for the crucifixion of Jesus had virtually become a dogmatic article of faith; the typical characteristic of the Jews as deicides and hence as unbridled murderers has been so drilled into the consciousness of successive generations of Christians that modern elaborations of radical anti-Semitism have found fertile soil everywhere. As hatred of the Jews was—at least originally—motivated by a matter of faith, namely, the Gospel truth of Jewish guilt in which the faithful had unquestioningly to believe, it could not be countered by argument: any attempt at denying the Gospel truth merely provided another ground for detestation and abhorrence.

It is not our purpose to inquire from a theological point of view into the phenomena of Christian obloquy and torment of the Jews: the all too obvious discrepancy between the preachings of Jesus (cf. Matt. 5:44) and the teachings of Paul (cf. Rom. 9–11) and Christian practice throughout the ages sets problems which it is not for us to solve. But it is only fair to acknowledge, in this context, the remarkable and impressive ecumenical efforts of recent times, on the part of both Catholic and Protestant theology, to rectify some of the immemorial blunders which had become sanctified and had even found their way into the liturgy.[9] The Second Vatican Council, in its 1965 session, declared that the "Jewish authorities and those who followed their lead pressed for the death of Christ; still, what happened in His Passion cannot be charged against all the Jews, without distinction, then alive, nor against the Jews of today." Even this minimal and, indeed, self-understood decree met with considerable opposition, which goes to show how deeply ingrained are these prejudices. The decree implies that there cannot be, or ought not to be, any change as yet in the fundamental belief that the Jewish authorities in Jerusalem on the day of the crucifixion were, in fact, responsible for the murder of Jesus, an implication which not only perpetuates the fatal errors and misinterpretations of bygone ages, but also keeps intact the emotional basis, and the pseudo-ethical and pseudo-theological justification, for the traditional prejudice and animosity against the Jews.[10] Two thousand years may have elapsed, but the Jews of today still are, and claim to be, descended from the murderers of Jesus, and what is worse, so many choose to identify themselves with their ancestors, in lieu of repudiating and disowning them and their deeds: only they are at fault if the ill will is allowed to persist.

What we, as lawyers, are concerned with primarily is the phenomenon, never and nowhere more vividly and appallingly demonstrated than in the trial of Jesus, that the effect of judicial proceedings on the public mind and on public opinion, and public reaction to them, do not so much depend on their nature, or on what actually happened in the course of them, as on the manner in which they are reported and for what purpose. If that viewpoint holds good for contemporaneous reporting, it must a fortiori apply to reports written decades after the event, with no material but only oral traditions to rely on; and if it holds good, as well, for modern reporting with the aid of such mass media of information as the press, radio, and television, it must a fortiori apply to reporting in ages of antiquity with the aid only of the most primitive of means and resources. Most vulnerable, and hence most suspicious, of all are reports of the so-called historic trials: while judicial proceedings are normally reported for their own sake, that is, to give information of their conduct and purpose and of what actually happened at them, as soon as a trial has become "historic," the first and constant object of routine reporting is automatically replaced by conscious or subconscious evaluations *sub specie aeternitatis*. Only the legal historian might be interested in routine reports of long-past trials, but then he is *avis rarissima* even among lawyers. As far as the general public is concerned, reports of long-past trials must always look, for their justification, to some extralegal significance: apart from and independently of their purely legal content, they must have a contribution to make to political, social, religious, or cultural history. A legal historian may well exploit Plato's report of the trial of

Socrates, for instance, to enrich our knowledge of Athenian criminal procedure, but Plato never wrote it for the sake of preserving that kind of information: he wrote it because he regarded the conduct of Socrates at and after his trial, and the words which he addressed to his judges, as a practical demonstration of the Platonic philosophy; and it was this philosophy, and its proven practicability, which he desired to immortalize—and succeeded. Plato's example—and it could be multiplied—shows that even when the report of such a "historic" trial serves purposes other than trial reporting as such, it does not necessarily mean that facts would be suppressed, let alone falsified or misrepresented; but the idiosyncratic tendency and object of the report may clearly appear from the identity of the reporter or of the readers to whom it is addressed, or from the particular emphasis laid on one or the scant emphasis laid on another fact, or—especially where the report is not contemporaneous—from what is still remembered by the reporter and what has fallen into oblivion. For a proper appraisal of the validity and reliability of the report, the critical observer must always submit it to narrow scrutiny, first as to its object and tendency, and then as to the means and sources available to the reporter. That is what we have endeavored to do with the Gospel reports of the trial of Jesus.

As far as affects the identity of the reporter, one other point cannot be overstressed: the reporter may have wielded some special legal or religious authority, or may *post hoc* have been vested with it. That may, on the one hand, dissuade skeptics from raising doubts as to the accuracy of the report and, on the other, confer upon the report itself the authority of its author. It is common experience, even today, that a report appearing in a provincial and little-known paper is easily dismissed as untrustworthy, yet the same report, if published by a prestigious metropolitan journal, will be accepted by all and sundry as absolutely reliable: the provincial daily depends for its credibility on the goodwill and confidence of its individual readers; the mammoth competitor has the reputation, almost the postulate, behind it that everything it prints is true. The same distinction subsists between official law reports, which are known or presumed to be edited and compiled under judicial supervision, and private ones, whose reliability rests on the acumen and renown of the in dividual reporters; and, even more so, between law reports published by competent lawyers and those by journalists featured in the daily press. But it does not always work to the commendation of the authoritative reporter: in our particular inquiry, we have to do with the mischief which authoritative reporting may cause by the very reason of the authority with which it is clothed. Any false and misleading report, if published by legal or religious authority, or by way of governmental decree, will have to be accepted by any person subject to that authority or government as incontrovertible truth: either it is so accepted or the person repudiates not only the report but also the authority of the reporter. Normally, the authority which a person has acknowledged, whether voluntarily by his own persuasion, or by force of tradition or education, or as a concomitant of the political, social, or religious conditions of his life, will be strong enough to withstand any possible doubts or misgivings as to the accuracy of the particulars in any such report, and rather than giving way to his feelings of incertitude in respect of it, he will put his trust in the authority. The more ancient or sacrosanct the authority, the more inexpugnable will be the report: the longer people have believed in its truth, and the greater the number of people who have believed in its veracity, the more easily and the more firmly will it establish itself as incontrovertible truth in the minds of the generations that follow. Strange as it may seem to the modern observer, the presumption of truth is still considerably enhanced if fortified by antiquity and a concourse of co-believers. Thus it is that reports garbed in authority, however false and distorted they may be, "make" history: while the real, historical truth will be, unconscionably, forgotten, the fabricated but authoritative "truth" persists in indestructibility.

A most dangerous pitfall for the fair-minded reporter, and a technique of the simplest for the tendentious one, is overemphasis on the role played in a trial by the audience, or by spectators, or by the public at large. The proceedings are, or can easily be, misrepresented as if reactions or interferences by members of the public were a decisive factor in the outcome, not unlike the determinant part of the chorus in a Greek tragedy. Readers without training or experience in legal matters, and more particularly in days gone by, would not entertain the slightest suspicion as to the accuracy of a report that stressed either the favoring or the disastrous turn which public responses had given to the events. On the contrary, the more the role of the public is accented, the more self-complacently will the reader, himself a member of the public and a potential figure in a public trial, accept the report and enjoy it. Public responses, however, have, ordinarily, nothing to do with the legal aspects of the proceedings: the public is, as a rule, unconcerned about the law as such, and is disinterested in the significance to be attributed to this or the other procedural step toward the attaining of the ultimate result. What usually intrigues people is either the personality of the accused, or a sensational disclosure of facts hitherto unknown or unproved, or an item in the trial to which, under the conditions prevailing, some particular political or other importance adheres. But the livelier the public interest and the more rigorous and outspoken public participation in the trial, the graver the risk of overrating it; and the nonprofessional reporter as well as the untrained reader may be apt to think that raucous interference by the public, especially if not sharply halted by the judge, has had an influence on the outcome which, in fact, it could not have exerted. Furthermore, that sort of meddling in the course of a trial is likely to be mistaken for the expression of public opinion in general, of the true *vox populi*, whereas it may in truth be nothing more than spontaneous and haphazard explosions of casual, unorganized spectators. And if the report of a trial is made false and misleading by the innocent misrepresentation of the influence inhering in public reactions that have actually occurred, then to invent such a reaction solely for the purposes of the report, and to endow it with a virtual usurpation of judicial power, as if the judge had been ousted from his bench and stripped of discretion, will render the report unadulterated fiction, or, if it claims binding authority, sheer fraud.

All this has happened in the reporting of the trial of Jesus. The first reporters—if we disregard, as we must, the sparse and ambiguous sayings attributed to Peter and Paul—were the evangelists: neither they nor their readers troubled themselves about the legal or technical details of the trial or the legal purport of the events which were described. Their objective was theological and missionary, and their reports were intended and calculated to absolve the Roman governor of all responsibility for the crucifixion, though there was no escaping the initial premise that it was he who had ordered it to be carried out, and to place that responsibility squarely and solidly upon the shoulders of the Jews. It was with that purpose and that tendency in mind that their reports were written, but once those reports were canonized and elevated to the rank of Scripture, their purpose and their tendency faded from memory and they took on a sacrosanctity of their own. Such was the religious, ecclesiastical authority with which they were clad that it amounted to heresy to cast doubt on their factualness and accuracy. What had really happened was allowed—or caused—to fall into oblivion; what had been inexactly and tendentiously reported as having taken place became the Gospel truth and was made history. Never in the chronicles of mankind has a trial been so widely and so skillfully reported, and never was a false report invested with higher and more exalted authority.

The instant and direct effect of this untrue but hallowed report was twofold. First, its aim was accomplished—the Roman governor was depicted as a just and upright, if timid and ineffectual, judge; the Jews are shown to have manipulated him as a mere instrument to commit a murder which they had planned. Second, the outcome of the trial is represented as judicial murder: Jesus was crucified, not because he had been duly convicted either by the Jews or by the Roman governor, but because the Jews had conspired to kill him; and any convictions and sentences recorded against him were just sham proceedings, conducted for the sake of appearances, and in reality tantamount to an abuse of judicial process. In that representation, resulting in a judicial murder, the trial of Jesus has been branded as the worst "perversion of justice" that ever occurred,[11] the worst of all such perversions, because Jesus was the best of men, "certainly this was a righteous man" (Luke 23:47) , and deserved least of all to be convicted and crucified. It is, indeed, a commonplace by now to regard his crucifixion as the very exemplar of judicial murder, exhibiting, as it does, all the features that could possibly be imagined. While the "normal" judicial murder may be due to a mistake of the judge, made possibly in good faith, the cause alleged for the crucifixion of Jesus was no mistake, either of the Sanhedrin or of

Pilate, and certainly not a mistake made in good faith, but a coercion of the judge, by the bullying and bluster of frenetic and rebellious crowds, into knowingly perverting justice against his will and his better judgment, and, what is more, a coercion employed in pursuance of an antecedent conspiracy for the killing of Jesus. What the trial reports achieved was, in other words, not only the shifting of accountability from the Roman governor, where it belonged, to the Jews, who were wholly innocent, but also the transformation of a regular and routine trial, which in the ordinary way would end in justice being done, into a riotous upheaval of the masses, which could hardly end in anything but a miscarriage of justice.

The possibility that an injustice may have been done in the trial of Jesus is not open to doubt. But not every injustice amounts in law to a miscarriage of justice: a man may be innocent of the crime with which he is charged, and, from the moral standpoint, it would be highly unjust to inflict any punishment on him; still, if he chose to plead guilty to the charge, legal justice would require him to undergo the punishment as though he had committed the offense. The attitude of the law, to make every man the ultimate arbiter of his own fate by allowing him to admit or to deny his guilt, is assuredly consonant with human dignity and the individual right of self-determination. And a man may have perfectly valid reasons for pleading guilty to a charge of which he is in fact guiltless: it is a very common practice in petty cases, in which the time which would otherwise have to be wasted in court and the expenses which would have to be incurred bear no reasonable relation to the fine which a plea of guilt would attract; or a man may elect to take upon himself a penalty which must else be borne by another person whom he wishes to protect or whose identity he wishes to conceal; or a man will resolve to be tried and sentenced, whether or not he has committed an offense, so that he may earn the glory of martyrdom. If Jesus pleaded guilty to the charge brought against him before Pilate, it need not have been because he was, or thought he was, in fact guilty; it could well have been because he wanted his prophecies to come true (cf. Luke 9:22; John 17:11–13; et al.) .[12] Whatever his prompting, his deliberate plea of guilty was, as we have seen, sufficient in law to warrant his conviction. From the purely legal angle, once he pleaded guilty it ceased to matter whether he was in fact guilty or not; and while we offer no opinion, one way or the other, on the theory—recently expressed again with great force[13]—that Jesus had in actuality been an insurgent and was tried and convicted as such, we may take it that he had really done nothing to deserve capital or any punishment, and was sentenced solely because of the stand which he himself had chosen to adopt in his trial before Pilate. On that assumption, all the same, the crucifixion cannot be said to have been in the nature of judicial murder: on the contrary, it was the carrying out of a sentence passed in the due course of justice. The stand which Jesus chose to adopt may have been suicidal, and tragically to be deplored. It may have been morally or tactically ill advised. But no error of judgment on Jesus' part can reflect upon the justice administered by Pilate.

While, as we say, the "perversion of justice" in the trial and crucifixion of Jesus has been given the character of prototype and forerunner of many a subsequent judicial murder, not enough attention has so far been directed to the fact that the perversion of truth and justice in the reports of the trial was the first and has been the persistent cause not alone of judicial and quasi-judicial murders and torments without number, but of mass murder and persecution on an unprecedented scale. I dare say that the reporters themselves, who, after all, wrote primarily for the propagation of their faith, could never have envisioned what untold and unspeakable sufferings they were conjuring up by the tale of their fictitious accounts. Perversion of truth in a trial report has this in common with judicial murder, that just as perverted justice, even if eventually redressed, cannot bring a hanged convict to life again, so perverted truth, however it be corrected afterward, cannot give breath a second time to the multitudes murdered on the grim strength of it. And if, and so long as, they are allowed to abide in their crookedness, perverted justice and perverted truth are only too likely to be ruinous to innocent lives.

Had the impact of the Gospel reports of the trial of Jesus been confined to the religious sphere, as their authors presumably desired and contemplated, thus serving, like the reports on the life and teachings of Jesus, to edify the faithful and to recruit and teach the uninitiated, it might perhaps be argued that it would not be the concern of legal, possibly as distinct from religious, historians to inquire into their precision and reliability. Or if they had not been armored in impregnable authority, professing to set down, in a binding manner that was impervious to all challenge, the truth of the facts as they actually happened, the legal historian might have disregarded them and consigned them to the limbo of legendary and unverifiable tradition. But when, in reliance on such accounts, acts of vengeance and persecution are perpetrated which are, owing to the sacrosanctity superimposed on the reports, approved and encouraged under the color of religious law, then they are no longer documents of religious import only. All prejudice and hatred which conduce to persecutions and unlawful discriminations are—especially nowadays, with the growing awareness of human rights and of the reprehensibility of racial and religious partiality—a matter for the lawyer, no less than for the educator or the sociologist, to examine. If a prejudice which still has its baleful effects in our time is rooted in distant history, it is surely imperative for the legal historian to step in and provide practicing lawyers, as well as educators, sociologists, and others, with the information needed to combat and excise that prejudice. And the imperative becomes almost categorical if, even in our present age, eminent lawyers come forward and promote the Gospel stories to the rank of authentic law reports: it is in the face of such pseudo-scientific legal scholarship that protests must be lodged and issues marshaled in the right perspective.

The trial of Jesus is part and parcel of Jewish legal history. Not only was Jesus a Jew who lived and taught and fought and died among his people in Jerusalem, but the Sanhedrin, the Great Council of the Jews and their highest court, is said to have taken a part in the events which led to his trial and crucifixion. The question what exactly was the part, if any, which the Sanhedrin took in those events is of the greatest possible interest to the historian of Jewish law. That the trial before the Roman governor was conducted under Roman law and according to Roman procedures adds further interest to the problems involved: the law and procedure applied by the occupying power in Judaea in those days is surely also integral to Jewish legal history. If Jews in general, and Jewish legal historians in particular, have sorely neglected the trial of Jesus, it is because of a traditional but wholly unreasoning eschewal of study of the New Testament and the dearth of pertinent Jewish sources. This unhappy omission has cost Jewish legal history the information to be derived from this most noteworthy of all the reported trials of the period, and it has, besides, engendered an apathetic indifference to the authenticity ascribed to the Gospel reports of the trial and the conclusions to be drawn from them. In the event, the allegation of Jewish responsibility for the crucifixion of Jesus was allowed to stand practically uncontested, if we discount the many apologetic and defensive efforts to limit it to contemporaneous Jews, or to certain individuals among them, or to the high priest and his clique of collaborators with Rome. It is a depressing thought that it should be Jewish canon, with its ban on New Testament study, that has so long delayed an independent and unbiased legal inquiry into the trial of Jesus; however much in arrear the inquiry may be, neither its problems nor its results will have lost any of their actuality.

Hundreds of generations of Jews, throughout the Christian world, have been indiscriminately mulcted for a crime which neither they nor their ancestors committed. Worse still, they have for centuries, for millennia, been made to suffer all manner of torment, persecution, and degradation for the alleged part of their forefathers in the trial and crucifixion of Jesus, when, in solemn truth, their forefathers took no part in them but did all that they possibly and humanly could to save Jesus, whom they dearly loved and cherished as one of their own, from his tragic end at the hands of the Roman oppressor. If there can be found a grain of consolation for this perversion of justice, it is in the words of Jesus himself: "Blessed are they which are persecuted for righteousness' sake: for theirs is the kingdom of heaven. Blessed are ye, when men shall revile you, and persecute you, and shall say all manner of evil against you falsely, for my sake. Rejoice, and be exceeding glad: for great is your reward in heaven" (Matt. 5:10–12).

NOTES

INTRODUCTION

1. Carmichael, *The Death of Jesus*, pp. 9–10.
2. Schweitzer, *The Quest of the Historical Jesus*, pp. 442 ff.
3. Powell, *The Trial of Jesus Christ*, p. 14.
4. MacRuer, *The Trial of Jesus*, pp. ix–x.
5. See: Winter, *On the Trial of Jesus*, p. 6; Dibelius, *Formgeschichte des Evangeliums*, p. 214; Dodd, *Historical Tradition in the Fourth Gospel*, p. 96, and *Interpretation of the Fourth Gospel*, p. 450. In the words of Craveri, *The Life of Jesus*, p. 391: "Historical accuracy cannot be claimed for the report of a fact to which none of the Apostles was a witness and which the Evangelists could only reconstruct, concerned as they were more for religious symbolism than for veracity."
6. Brandon, *The Trial of Jesus of Nazareth*, p. 116, remarks that Luke's professed access to reliable sources and his aim to present "an orderly account" of the events, stand "in apparent contrast to the records of Jesus' life that already existed" in the earlier Gospels. Peter, *Finding the Historical Jesus*, p. 36, notes that Luke's statement "of the trouble to which he went in the preparation of his Gospel . . . point[s] to the currency of statements at variance with those in the New Testament, and indicate[s] that at least some of the New Testament writers were anxious to show themselves reliable witnesses."
7. Bruce, *The New Testament Documents*, pp. 47–48, relies on John 21:24 for the proposition that Jesus' disciple John, son of Zebedee (cf. Matt. 4:21), was an eyewitness to the crucifixion and resurrec-

tion (John 21:2, where "the sons of Zebedee" are mentioned) and the author of the Fourth Gospel, and finds that the "internal evidence" reveals him as "an author who was an eye-witness of the events he describes." He quotes, to the same effect, Olmstead, *Jesus in the Light of History*, at pp. 206 and 248, and Sayers, *The Man Born to Be King*, pp. 28–33. As will be shown, the "internal evidence" indicates that the Fourth Gospel was written neither by an eyewitness nor by any person "thoroughly conversant with Jewish customs" or "intimately acquainted with Jewish laws" (Bruce, *ibid.*, p. 49) . We have Luke's testimony to the effect that John was, at least in the eyes of the men learned in the law, "unlearned and ignorant" (Acts 4:13) , a testimony which tallies with John's authorship of the Fourth Gospel better than any undeserved reputation of legal erudition. The view that the author of the Fourth Gospel was not John the Apostle or any other eyewitness to the events there described is maintained by Lietzmann, *History of the Early Church*, Vol. I, p. 233, who says that the author was not "an eyewitness of a historical event, but the God-inspired interpreter of a supra-historical process"; and if he had any knowledge of Jewish laws and customs, it was only of such laws and customs as prevailed at the time and place where he lived (p. 226) . Goguel, *Jesus and the Origins of Christianity*, Vol. I *(Prolegomena to the Life of Jesus)* , pp. 150–151, held it to be "impossible that this Apostle could have composed the Fourth Gospel: (i) because this book at the very earliest dates from the last decade of the first century and cannot therefore be the work of John son of Zebedee who died as a martyr in 44; (ii) because the theology of the Fourth Gospel represents a stage in the evolution of Christian thought which is later than Paulinism; (iii) because the Fourth Gospel is not the work of one hand, but is a compilation of different elements." These (and additional) arguments to refute the authorship of John the Apostle, as well as the considerations which can be adduced in favor of such authorship, are reviewed at length by Dodd, *Historical Tradition in the Fourth Gospel*, pp. 10 ff., who arrives at the conclusion that the question of authorship is "incapable of decision" (p. 16) ; but we may agree with him that "the question of authorship is not as important for the problem of historicity as has been supposed. Even if it were certain that the work was by a personal disciple, we could not proceed directly to the inference that his account is a transcript of the facts, or that he intended it to be such" (p. 17) . A very early commentator had already observed that John, "aware that the physical facts had already been recorded in the Gospels, encouraged by his pupils and moved irresistibly by the Spirit, wrote a spiritual Gospel" (Clement, quoted by Eusebius, *Historia Ecclesiae* VI 14) . As Eduard Meyer said in *Ursprung und Anfaenge des Christentums*, Vol. I, pp. 310–311, "The Fourth Gospel is a free creation of its author, who used his traditions only as the raw material which he entirely remolds. It can be regarded as a historical source only if and insofar as it would be possible to sift out the raw material and restore it to its original form" (my translation from the German). Attempts to sift valid traditions from otherwise unhistoric reports in the Fourth Gospel will repeatedly be made in this book.

8. A "problem of peculiar complexity" is "constituted by the fact that we have no direct access" to the relevant traditions: "The reason for this is well known, although its significance seems rarely to be appreciated. It is that the Christian community at Jerusalem, which was the Mother Church of the faith, disappeared so completely after A.D. 70 that none of its documents survived" (Brandon, *Jesus and the Zealots,* p. 148). As for the record which Nicodemus (cf. John 3:1 and 19:39) was traditionally believed to have made of the events he is said to have witnessed, see Chap. 11, *infra*.

9. Winter, *op. cit.,* pp. 2 ff.

10. Bornkamm, *Jesus von Nazareth,* pp. 12–13 (my translation from the German).

11. *Ibid.,* p. 20.

12. Sjoeborg, *Der verborgene Menschensohn in den Evangelien,* p. 214. In the words of another recent writer, "The documents at our disposal do not provide the careful historian with the material for a biography of Jesus. . . . A few of the major themes of his preaching, the general location of his activity, and the place and date of his execution at the hands of the Roman authorities are about all that the historian can discover. All the rest—from legends of his birth, through stories concerning his relationship with his disciples, to details of his arrest and execution—has come to us through the preaching of the early Christian congregations. This material was not intended to be documentary evidence of historical or biographical 'facts.' It was a story in the service of the Easter kerygma" (Van Buren, *The Secular Meaning of the Gospel,* p. 123).

13. Lietzmann, *op. cit.,* p. 223, in relation to the Fourth Gospel. See also Dodd, *The Interpretation of the Fourth Gospel,* who regards it "as being in its essential character a theological work rather than a history" (p. 444): "It is indeed inevitable that an episode which stirred men so deeply, and which (in Christian belief) possessed unique spiritual significance, should impose on its reporters the necessity of relating it to their most profound thoughts and feelings, and indeed to their ultimate beliefs about God, man, and the universe. For the Synoptic evangelists, that meant relating it to eschatological conceptions derived from Jewish religious tradition. For John, it meant relating it to more rational, and more universal, ideas" (p. 446).

14. Schweitzer, *op. cit.,* p. 88, shows that it was in 1782 that it was first demonstrated that Mark's was the earliest of the Gospels. This is by now generally accepted (see Goguel, *op. cit.,* pp. 136 ff.). That it cannot be dated before the year 70 or 71 has been painstakingly

and persuasively elaborated by Brandon, *Jesus and the Zealots,* pp. 222–242, and *The Trial of Jesus of Nazareth,* pp. 24–80. But the orthodox tenet, of course, always was, and still is, that the canonical order reflects the true chronology: orthodox tradition places the Gospel of Matthew, as the first and earliest, at about the year 44 (see, for instance: Bruckberger, *L'Histoire de Jésus-Christ,* p. 27). According to Augustine, Mark followed Matthew "as his lackey and abbreviator, so to speak" (*De Consensu Evangelistarum* I 4).

15. Goguel, *op. cit.,* p. 142, whose views are adopted in the text, says that the "composition of the Gospel of Luke may be placed between 72 (the date of the composition of Mark) and 90, a date to which the composition of the Acts of the Apostles, the second book addressed to Theophilus, does not seem to be posterior. We may fix the date of the redaction of this work about the year 85. The dependence of the Gospel of Matthew upon what we believe to be the second form of the Gospel of Mark gives us as the date of the composition the earliest that is possible, somewhere about the year 85. In my opinion it cannot be earlier than the year 90." There are, however, scholars who date the Gospel of Luke much later, on the assumption that Luke wrote with both the Gospels of Mark and Matthew before him: that would mean that it could not have been composed earlier than about the year 100, and some think it ought to be dated nearer 150 (see: Sandmel, *A Jewish Understanding of the New Testament,* pp. 190–191).

16. Lietzmann, *op. cit.,* p. 222, places the Gospel of John "at the beginning of the second century." Albright, *From the Stone Age to Christianity,* pp. 380–381, says that John was usually dated between 90 and 120 A.D., but that "radical members of the Tuebingen and the Dutch School thought that John was even posterior to 150 A.D., but they had very few adherents in this extreme position." Dodd, *Historical Tradition in the Fourth Gospel,* p. 424, writes that "most critics" are now persuaded "that a date later than 120 for the Fourth Gospel is virtually impossible, and that a date not far from 100, rather before than after, is reasonable." Eduard Meyer, *op. cit.,* Vol. III, p. 647, also dates the Gospel of John in the first or second decade of the second century.

17. *"Perduellio":* Mommsen, *Roemisches Strafrecht,* p. 575. And see Tertullianus, *Apologeticum* 24, 27, 28, describing the refusal by Christians to take the oath of loyalty to pagan gods as *crimen laesae Romanae religiosi* as well as *crimen laesae augustioris maiestatis.*

18. Bainton, *Early Christianity,* p. 21.

19. "The Gospel of Mark . . . was the product of the dangerous and perplexing predicament of the Christian community in Rome. . . . Designed to meet that predicament, the Markan Gospel is essentially an apologia" (Brandon, *The Trial of Jesus of Nazareth,* p. 79). And see Brandon's *Jesus and the Zealots,* Chap. 5 ("The Markan Gospel: An Apologia ad Christianos Romanos"), pp. 221–282, where the

point is extensively elaborated, with the conclusion that "the transference of responsibility for the Crucifixion from the Roman to the Jewish authorities was motivated by the apologetical purpose of the Markan Gospel" (p. 282).

20. Brandon, *Jesus and the Zealots*, p. 247.

21. While such "pious fraud" negatives historical reliability, the absence of any such pious fraud would not necessarily raise any presumption of authenticity: see Albright, *op. cit.*, p. 388.

22. Opinions on this are divided. Abrahams, *Studies in Pharisaism and the Gospels*, Vol. II, p. 57, maintains that the "synagogue had far less quarrel with Gentile Christianity . . . and Christianity as such was not the object of much attention, still less quarrel." This is certainly true for the first century; but in the second century, "bitterness mounted" (Baron, *A Social and Religious History of the Jews*, Vol. I, p. 245) ; and we have talmudic sources to indicate that Christians (*Minnim*) were looked upon with even greater disdain than idolaters, for the latter are apostates who did not know better, while the former are apostates who knew and should have known better: B Shabbat 116a. Still, the grave accusations raised against the Jews by such second- and third-century writers as Tertullian and Origen, for stirring up the pagans against the Christians by spreading false calumnies against them, were vigorously denied and refuted by a great number of "Apologies," several of them by Christian authors, who all wrote in the second and third century—"the century of the greatest Jewish unpopularity" (Parkes, *The Conflict of the Church and the Synagogue*, pp. 110–111). "If we compare the situation of the Jews and the Christians, we can see that it is probable that the Jewish attack on Christianity would be less violent than that of the Christians on Judaism. The Christians were claiming the promises in a book which was composed of promises and denunciations. The denunciations, therefore, must belong to the Jews. But they, on their part, were only compelled to adopt a negative attitude, the refusal to accept the Christian claim as to the person of Jesus, and though this naturally involved disputing His perfection and the two miraculous events concerned with His life, the Virgin Birth and the Resurrection, there is not much evidence in these first centuries that their attack went further" (Parkes, *ibid.*, pp. 114–115).

23. To the same effect: Baer, *Judaism in the Synoptic Gospels*, p. 136.

24. Goguel, *op. cit.*, p. 136.

25. Harnack, *The Sayings of Jesus, passim;* and see Bruce, *op. cit.*, pp. 38 ff.; Lietzmann, *op. cit.*, Vol. I, pp. 46 ff.; *et al.*

26. Lietzmann, *ibid.*, p. 47.

27. *Historia Ecclesiae,* III 39.

28. "There is nothing more negative than the result of the critical study of the Life of Jesus"—that is what Schweitzer (*op. cit.*, p. 398) testifies in conclusion of his *Quest of the Historical Jesus*. On the other hand, "We have reason to be grateful to the early Christians

that . . . they have handed down to us, not biographies of Jesus,
but only Gospels, and that therefore we possess the Idea and the
Person with the minimum of historical and contemporary limitations" (*ibid.*, p. 3) . The field has thus been opened wide to speculation and imagination, and there is no end to the "varied activities in
preaching, evangelizing, teaching, apologetics, and controversy"
which make for the incessant "action and reaction" on the Gospels,
even within the Church (Goguel, *op. cit.*, p. 136) .

29. Cf. Dibelius, *op. cit.*, p. 205. It must be conceded that, as James
Peter has put it, "When it is said of an alleged happening in the
past that it is 'possible,' the meaning is that the historian who makes
that statement concedes that this thing could have taken place;
whether it actually did, is another, though of course closely related,
question to be answered in the light of the information that he has
about it. When it is said that the alleged happening is 'impossible,'
the meaning is that the historian who makes that statement is applying criteria, not derived from the directly relevant data, to decide
that however unanimous the contemporary testimony (agreement
and early date being among the chief criteria respected by historians) , this thing just did not take place; the question of the statue
shaking its head . . . is a case in point. What appears as an objective signification of 'impossibility' is in fact what the majority of
historians (or perhaps all of them) consider to be impossible . . ."
(*op. cit.*, pp. 104–105) . To which I would add only the rider that
even if the majority of historians (or perhaps all of them) consider
it possible for the statue to shake its head, the external data and
criteria indicating the impossibility should prevail even over such
consensus.

30. Winter, *op. cit.*, p. 154.
31. *Ibid.*, p. 10.
32. See Goguel, *op. cit.*, pp. 61–69. For theories of the nonhistoricity
of Jesus, see: W. B. Smith, *The Pre-Christian Jesus;* J. M. Robertson,
Christianity and Mythology: The Historical Jesus, and *The Jesus
Problem—A Restatement of the Myth Theory;* Sadler, *Has Jesus
Lived on Earth?* and *Behind the New Testament;* Couchoud, *The
Enigma of Jesus;* and the writings of Bruno Bauer, Albert Kalthoff,
Arthur Drews, and other German writers of this school whose doctrines were summarized by Schweitzer (*op. cit.*, p. 156) as follows:
"The question which has so much exercised the minds of men,
whether Jesus was the historic Christ, is answered in the sense that
everything that is known of Him belongs to the world of imagination, the imagination of the Christian community, and therefore has
nothing to do with any man who belongs to the real world."
33. Rousseau, *Émile—Profession de Foi* (*Oeuvres Complètes*, 1846) ,
Vol. II, p. 597.
34. Bultmann, *Die Erforschung der synoptischen Evangelien*, p. 33.
35. Bultmann, *Jesus*, p. 10. The reason why we know nothing is that

"the Christian sources had no interest therefor, are fragmentary in character and overgrown by legends, and other sources do not exist" (*ibid.;* my translation from the German) .

36. *Ibid.,* p. 14. And see Bultmann's last exposition of the matter in his paper, "Das Verhaeltnis der urchristlichen Christusbotschaft zum historischen Jesus," in *Sitzungsberichte der Heidelberger Akademie der Wissenschaften; Philosophisch-Historische Klasse,* 1960, Vol. III, pp. 26 ff.

37. In the words of Schweitzer: "In order to find in Mark the life of Jesus of which it is in search, modern theology is obliged to read between the lines a whole host of things, and those often the most important, and then to foist them upon the text by means of psychological conjecture. . . . Whatever the results obtained by the aid of the historical kernel, the method pursued is the same: 'it is detached from its context and transformed into something different.' 'It finally comes to this,' says Wrede, 'that each critic retains whatever portion of the traditional sayings can be fitted into his construction of the facts and his conception of historical possibility, and rejects the rest.' " Schweitzer himself is far from subscribing to this kind of "modern theology": according to him, "All these things of which the Evangelist says nothing, and they are the foundations of the modern view, should first be proved, if proved they can be; they ought not to be simply read into the text as something self-evident. For it is just those things which appear so self-evident to the prevailing critical temper which are in reality the least evident of. all" (*op. cit.,* pp. 332–333) . While we derive consolation and encouragement from the fact that in proposing "conceptions of historical possibility" of our own, we are but following an honored tradition of very long standing, we shall indeed readily accept Schweitzer's challenge not to make any assumptions without first trying to prove them.

38. According to Winter (*op. cit.,* pp. 8–9) , the evidence in our hands is "far from complete. We have detailed accounts of Roman law in force at the time, but the rulings applied in outlying provinces were hardly identical with those observed *in Urbe* or in such senatorial provinces as had been under Roman administration for a relatively long period. We have ample descriptions of the injunctions of Jewish Law, yet these belong to a time posterior to that of Jesus. Some of the enactments regulating Roman judicial procedure were certainly applied in the provinces no less than in the capital city itself; some of the ordinances enumerated in the treatise Sanhedrin of the Mishna were already valid in the time of Jesus. Yet much latitude is given for surmises." Now as far as Roman law and gubernatorial practice are concerned, it will be shown that there is ample independent source material to warrant a reconstruction of the trial before Pilate, the scourging, and the crucifixion, as they could in fact and in law have taken place. And as for Jewish law, the ob-

jection that it was not "codified" until centuries after Jesus' death had been taken before (see: Klausner, *Jesus von Nazareth,* p. 464; Danby, "The Bearing of the Rabbinical Criminal Code on the Jewish Trial Narratives in the Gospels," pp. 51 ff.), but appears to me to be irrelevant: there can be no doubt that what was "codified" was existing law; and the mishnaic law in the field of criminal law and procedure incorporates rules which must be presumed to have been practiced at the period when criminal (that is, capital) jurisdiction was still actually exercised, and it was so exercised until the year 70 only (see note 43, p. 346, *infra*). To the same effect, see Abrahams, *op. cit.,* pp. 129 ff. As we shall see, the existence and contents of the relating "ordinances" of Jewish law have not been disputed by New Testament scholars; and the fact that according to the Gospel reports those laws were ignored or violated serves them simply as additional evidence that the proceedings in question were tainted with illegality. The same applies to such discrepancies as divulged between the Gospel reports of the trial before Pilate and what is known of Roman law and practices prevailing in Judaea at the time. To plead that our knowledge of contemporary law and practice is "far from complete" does certainly not afford an excuse from probing thoroughly into such information as we do have—the less so as that information can, indeed, be shown to be amply sufficient for our immediate purpose.

39. Some of my Israeli critics observed that the essence of my method was to subject the Gospel reports to some kind of quasi-forensic cross-examination, which was not a historical method at all (Tamir, in *Mi-Bifnim,* pp. 455 ff.). Be that as it may, the attempt to stage a trial in which the evangelists are cross-examined on their reports and testimonies, and in which expert evidence on Jewish and Roman law is adduced, has been made before in a very impressive manner by Goldin, *The Case of the Nazarene Reopened, passim,* at the conclusion of which the reader, qua jury, is asked to give his verdict as to whether there can be any Jewish responsibility for the death of Jesus.

1 . THE ROMANS

1. Josephus, *Antiquities,* 17,6,5.
2. Megillat Ta'anit, 21 (ed. Lurie, p. 161).
3. For a long list of Jewish grievances against King Herod, see Allon, *Mehkarim Betoledot Yisrael,* Vol. I, pp. 40–42.
4. Daniel-Rops, *Daily Life in the Time of Jesus,* p. 81.
5. Josephus, *Wars,* 2,3,4.
6. Josephus, *Antiquities,* 17,10,2.
7. *Ibid.,* 17,10,10.

8. Graetz, *Geschichte der Juden*, Vol. III, p. 252.
9. Tax demands in indeterminate amounts are mentioned in B Nedarim 28a. Taxation amounting to virtual confiscation is mentioned in B Sukkah 29b.
10. Tax collectors "standing in their own shoes" or "on their own feet": B Nedarim 28a.
11. M Nedarim III 4; T Nedarim II 2; B Sanhedrin 25b.
12. B Sanhedrin 25b.
13. B Shevu'ot 39a.
14. *Histories*, V 5 (Wellesley trans., p. 273).
15. *Ibid.*, V 4 (Wellesley trans., p. 273).
16. *Antiquities*, 18,3,1.
17. Josephus, *Antiquities*, 18,3,1, and *Wars*, 2,9,2.
18. Brandon, *Jesus and the Zealots*, p. 69.
19. *Antiquities*, 18,3,1.
20. *Wars*, 2,9,3.
21. *Antiquities*, 18,3,1.
22. Brandon, *Jesus and the Zealots*, pp. 70–71; *The Trial of Jesus of Nazareth*, pp. 36–37.
23. Josephus, *Antiquities*, 18,8,2–8. Konvitz, *Expanding Liberties*, p. 306, takes this to be "the first recorded instance of mass non-violent resistance"; in fact, it was at least the second.
24. Josephus, *Antiquities*, 18,8,2; Tacitus, *Annales*, XV 54; Philo, *Legatio ad Gaium*, 188, 203.
25. Hieronymus, Commentary on Matthew 24:15; Origen (Origines), Commentary on Matthew 22:15.
26. Schuerer, *Die Geschichte des juedischen Volkes im Zeitalter Jesu Christi*, Vol. I, p. 489, n. 145.
27. *Antiquities*, 18,3,2.
28. *Wars*, 2,9,4.
29. Brandon, *Jesus and the Zealots*, p. 76, n. 3.
30. Bultmann, *Geschichte der synoptischen Tradition*, p. 53, quoting Justinus and Hegesippus.
31. Cullmann, *Der Staat im Neuen Testament*, p. 9.
32. Morrison, *The Jews under Roman Rule*, p. 148.
33. Olmstead, *op. cit.*, pp. 148–149.
34. Thus: Klausner, *op. cit.*, p. 218, n. 106.
35. Brandon, *Jesus and the Zealots*, pp. 77–78, n. 4; Ben Chorin, *Bruder Jesus—der Nazarener in juedischer Sicht*, p. 195.
36. Brandon, *op. cit.*, p. 72 (quoting Philo, *Legatio ad Gaium*, 299–305).
37. *Ibid.*, p. 73.
38. *Ibid.*
39. Suetonius, *Tiberius*, 36 (Graves trans., p. 128).
40. *Ibid.*, 49 (Graves trans., p. 133).
41. *Ibid.*, 58 (Graves trans., pp. 137–138).
42. *Ibid.*, 59 (Graves trans., pp. 138–139).

43. Eusebius, *Historia Ecclesiae,* II 5, 7 (Williamson trans., p. 79) .
44. Graetz, *op. cit.,* p. 257; Schuerer, *op. cit.,* p. 492, n. 147.
45. See Chap. 6, *infra.*
46. *Legatio ad Gaium,* 301 (Smallwood trans. quoted by Brandon, *op. cit.,* p. 68) .
47. Winter, *op. cit.,* p. 53.
48. Eduard Meyer, *op. cit.,* Vol. I, pp. 202–203 (my translation from the German) .
49. *Antiquities,* 18,4,1.
50. *Ibid.,* 18,4,2.
51. Suetonius, *Tiberius,* 65.
52. Schuerer, *op. cit.,* Vol. I, pp. 492–493, n. 151; Vol. III, pp. 527–528.
53. "Man darf die Angaben der Evangelien ueber Pilatus nicht so verstehen, als habe sich dieser bei seiner wiederholten Weigerung, Jesus zu verurteilen, von Erwaegungen des Rechts und der Menschlichkeit leiten lassen. Was ihn dabei bestimmte, war vielmehr die von Philo und Josephus so sehr betonte Judenfeindschaft. Weil er die Juden verachtete und gern jede Gelegenheit wahrnahm, sie diese Verachtung spueren zu lassen, nahm er sofort eine Oppositionsstellung ein, als an ihn das Ansinnen gestellt wurde, den eingebrachten Gefangenen kurzerhand zu verurteilen. In seiner Schrift 'Legatio ad Gaium' schreibt Philo woertlich: 'Pilatus war nicht gewillt, irgend etwas zu tun, was den Juden gefallen haette' " (Blinzler, *Zum Prozess Jesu,* pp. 35–36) .
54. Brandon, *The Trial of Jesus of Nazareth,* p. 137, writes: "The historical realities of the situation are forgotten in portraying this dualistic drama, namely, that Pilate is the Roman governor, with supreme authority and the force to back it. . . ."
55. Josephus, *Wars,* 2,8,1 (as translated by Brandon, *Jesus and the Zealots,* p. 31) .
56. Cf. Midrash Bereshit Rabba, 24, 1.
57. B Babba Batra 8a; J Shevi'it IX 2.
58. Cf. Brandon, *Jesus and the Zealots,* p. 347.
59. It is reported of Rabbi Hanina the priest (a contemporary of Jesus) that he taught his disciples to pray for the welfare of the government, however alien it may be: M Avot III 2.
60. Olmstead, *op. cit.,* p. 215; Klausner, *op. cit.,* p. 437.
61. Roman decrees and proclamations were read by the people "with awe, fear, trembling and trepidation": Midrash Vayikra Rabba 27,6; and, whenever they could, they would tear them off and burn them: Midrash Bereshit Rabba 42,3; Esther Rabba 11; Tanhuma Shemini 9. See Lieberman, "Roman Legal Institutions in Early Rabbinics," pp. 7–9.
62. Eusebius, *Historia Ecclesiae* II 5,7 (Williamson trans., p. 79) .
63. B Avodah Zarah 2b.
64. Riessler, *Altjuedisches Schrifttum ausserhalb der Bibel,* p. 1015.

2 . CHIEF PRIESTS, ELDERS, SCRIBES, AND ALL THE COUNCIL

1. A manslayer had to remain inside the city of refuge until the death of the high priest; after the high priest's death he could return to his land: Num. 35:28. A high priest who had become impure or otherwise incapable of officiating would not be deposed, but would step back and have his *locum tenens* deputize for him—but it is he who would always be regarded as the only high priest in office: M Horayot III 4; M Megillah I 9; M Makkot II 6; M Yoma I 1.

2. Valerius Gratius, who governed Judaea from 15 to 26 and was the immediate predecessor of Pontius Pilate, deposed and appointed no fewer than four high priests: Josephus, *Antiquities*, 18,2,2.

3. M Sanhedrin I 5; T Sanhedrin III 4.

4. This illusion probably originated in the practical experience which they had when they succeeded, through the intervention of the high priest, in holding a census (Luke 2:1–3) to find out what the potential resources and revenues of this province would be: Josephus, *Antiquities*, 18,1,1. Though the Jews did not want to have anything to do with the census (*ibid.*), they eventually cooperated when the high priest urged them to do so. But as the Romans would presumably remember the good offices of the high priest in their behalf, so would the Jews remember that it was the Roman hired high priest who persuaded them, in the Roman and against their own interest, to collaborate with the enemy.

5. Brandon, *Jesus and the Zealots,* p. 65.

6. Josephus, *Antiquities,* 18,2,2; 18,4,3.

7. Stauffer, *Jerusalem und Rom im Zeitalter Jesu Christi,* p. 67; Brandon, *The Trial of Jesus of Nazareth,* p. 198, n. 196.

8. Schonfield, *The Passover Plot,* pp. 143, 149.

9. B Yoma 8b: "And as money was paid for the high-priesthood, the high priests used to be replaced every year." To the same effect: Sifrei Bamidbar 131. And see Graetz, *op. cit.,* p. 346; Klausner, *op. cit.,* p. 217.

10. Avot de-Rabbi Nathan I 5 and 13b, quoted by Finkelstein, *The Pharisees,* Vol. II, p. 764. And see Midrash Tanhuma Emor 6.

11. Finkelstein, *op. cit.,* p. 774.

12. Many talmudic and midrashic sources indicate that this may have changed after the destruction of the temple and the cessation of the high priesthood: several emperors and their emissaries are said to have negotiated and conversed with Jewish sages, and for theological disputations they may have chosen renowned scholars rather than active politicians. See Allon, *Toledot Hayehudim Beeretz Yisrael Bitekufat Hamishnah Vehatalmud,* Vol. I, p. 335, *et al.*

13. For a lucid and exhaustive exposition of these theories see Mantel, *Studies in the History of the Sanhedrin*, pp. 54–92.

14. Schuerer, *op. cit.*, Vol. II, p. 215; Franz Meyer, *Einige Bermerkungen zur Bedeutung des Terms Synedrion*, at p. 548; Allon, *op. cit.*, Vol. I, pp. 116 ff., and Vol. II, pp. 144–145.

15. Tchernovitz, *Toledot Ha-Halakha*, Vol. VII, pp. 217 ff.

16. For instance, that the high priest was not normally presiding, but could take the chair if he so wished, or even seize presidential authority autocratically: Hoffmann, *Der oberste Gerichtshof in der Stadt des Heiligtums*, pp. 37 ff. Or, that he was entitled to preside whenever there was on the agenda some subject matter which the rules or customs reserved for his chairmanship: Jelski, *Die innere Einrichtung des grossen Synedrions von Jerusalem*, pp. 37 ff.; Belkin, *Philo and the Oral Law*, p. 88.

17. Josephus, *Antiquities*, 18,2,1–2.

18. Winter, *op. cit.*, p. 39.

19. M Parah III 5.

20. Schuerer, *op. cit.*, Vol. II, p. 219, n. 14.

21. *Antiquities*, 19,8,1.

22. Kohut, *Arukh Hashalem*, Vol. VII, p. 89.

23. Dalman, *Aramaeisch-Neuhebraeisches Woerterbuch zu Targum, Talmud und Midrasch*, p. 360.

24. Stauffer, *Jesus—Gestalt und Geschichte*, p. 93.

25. Buechler, *Das Synedrion in Jerusalem und das grosse Beth-Din in der Quaderkammer des jerusalemischen Tempels*, pp. 41 ff., 221 ff.; Zeitlin, *Who Crucified Jesus?*, pp. 63–83, and "The Crucifixion of Jesus Reexamined," pp. 339–340 (*et al.*); Flusser, *Jesus*, p. 120; Franz Meyer, *op. cit.*, pp. 548–549.

26. Josephus, *Antiquities*, 15,6,2; 15,7,4.

27. Brandon, *Jesus and the Zealots*, p. 330.

28. M Sanhedrin XI 2; Sifrei Devarim 152.

29. Sifrei Devarim 153.

30. M Kiddushin IV 5; M Sanhedrin IV 2.

31. "Talmidei Hakhamim": M Sanhedrin IV 4.

32. Urbach, *Class-Status and Leadership in the World of the Palestinian Sages*, p. 15.

33. *Antiquities*, 18,1,4. And see Schuerer, *op. cit.*, Vol. II, pp. 197–201.

34. *Antiquities*, 18,1,3. Finkelstein, *op. cit.*, Vol. I, p. cxxxii, comments on this passage in Josephus as follows: "The description of the Pharisees in Josephus agreed fully with the implications of the talmudic writings. From both works the Pharisees emerge as a group which, accepting the Torah as the word of God and considering existence meaningful only so far as it provided opportunity for service to Him, adhered loyally to the rituals enjoined in the Scripture. The Pharisees followed a series of norms in which the word of Scripture was elaborated. They studied the word of the Torah and indulged in continuous contemplation of the right, in an in-

sistent search for the ethical life. They possessed a wide reputation for piety, tolerance, wisdom. This reputation clothed the Pharisees with enormous power used with remarkable self-restraint. They were loath to impose punishment for crime, and when compelled by evidence to do so, inclined towards leniency. They treated one another with great affection, and were generally mild and temperate to opponents. They despised present luxury, and sought instead to deserve future bliss. They realistically appraised the paradox of man's consciousness of freedom and of circumstances beyond his control, such as heredity and education, weighting his decisions. For generation after generation, this remarkable group, disciples of the prophets, labored, studied and taught in Jerusalem, to such effect that even Josephus (who had deserted their way of life) was stirred by profound admiration for the Pharisees and their achievements."

35. Allon, *Mehkarim Betoldot Yisrael,* Vol. I, pp. 26 ff.

36. Schuerer, *op. cit.,* Vol. II, p. 396. In the Pharisaic conception, "Judaea was regarded as Yahweh's holy land," and "the recognition of another lord than Yahweh—another lord who, though mortal, was worshipped as a god by his subjects," was an act of apostasy towards Yahweh (Brandon, *The Trial of Jesus of Nazareth,* p. 29).

37. Finkelstein, *op. cit.,* Vol. II, p. 619.

38. To the same effect: Lietzmann, "Bemerkungen zum Prozess Jesu II," p. 83; Juster, *Les Juifs dans l'Empire Romain,* Vol. II, p. 133; Burkill, "The Competence of the Sanhedrin," pp. 80–96; Winter, *op. cit.,* p. 88; Guignebert, *Jésus,* p. 567. And see note 44 and Chap. 6, *infra.*

39. Eduard Meyer, *op. cit.,* Vol. I, p. 199; Powell, *op. cit.,* p. 27; Olmstead, *op. cit.,* p. 229; Jeremias, "Zur Geschichtlichkeit des Verhoers Jesu vor dem Hohen Rat," pp. 145–150; Kilpatrick, *The Trial of Jesus,* p. 21; *et al.*

40. Schuerer, *op. cit.,* Vol. II, pp. 209–210; Blinzler, *Der Prozess Jesu,* p. 111, and *Zum Prozess Jesu,* p. 23; Stauffer, *Jerusalem und Rom im Zeitalter Jesu Christi,* p. 121; Koch, *Der Prozess Jesu,* p. 93; Kautsky, *Der Ursprung des Christentums,* p. 423; *et al.*

41. Cullmann, *op. cit.,* p. 30; Winter, *op. cit.,* p. 9. And cf. Bienert, "Von der Kollektivschuld am Tode Jesu," at p. 40.

42. Among those who hold that the Sanhedrin had no power to execute its capital sentences, opinions are divided, for instance, as to whether the Roman governor would order sanhedrial sentences to be executed as a matter of course or only as a matter of discretion; and it has been said that no sanhedrial sentence would be executed unless the offense was recognized as capital also under Roman law: von Mayr, "Der Prozess Jesu," pp. 215 ff. Some scholars regard the gubernatorial order as a sort of *fiat,* enabling the sanhedrial authorities to have their sentences executed by their own agents (thus apparently Brandon, *The Trial of Jesus of Nazareth,* p. 92; and *Jesus and the Zealots,* p. 254; Sherwin-White, *Roman Society and Roman Law in the New Testament,* pp. 32–43) ; others insist that

it was the Roman executioners who had to be employed for that purpose, and that the execution of sanhedrial sentences had to conform to Roman law and procedure (Doerr, *Der Prozess Jesu in rechtsgeschichtlicher Beleuchtung*, p. 62; Dibelius, *Jesus*, p. 115). The theory has also been propounded that the Sanhedrin was deprived by the Romans of all criminal—or at least capital—jurisdiction and retained competence only as an inferior tribunal charged with the issue of warrants of arrests, the conduct of preliminary inquiries, and the like (Klausner, *op. cit.*, p. 462; Jacobs, *Jesus as Others Saw Him*, pp. 140 ff.; Husband, *The Prosecution of Jesus*, p. 135; Danby, *op. cit.*, p. 75; Radin, *The Trial of Jesus of Nazareth*, pp. 227 ff.; Schmidt, *Die Geschichte Jesu*, p. 170). On the other hand, among those who hold that the Sanhedrin retained jurisdiction in criminal—or even capital—cases, there are those who think that sanhedrial sentences were appealable as of right, and the Roman governor sat as an appellate court (Dubnow, *Divrei Yemei Am Olam*, Vol. II, p. 220), and others who think that the exercise of sanhedrial jurisdiction in capital cases, or the convening of the Sanhedrin for capital trials, required the previous consent of the Roman governor (Zucker, *Studien zur juedischen Selbstverwaltung im Altertum*, p. 82; Lengle, *Roemisches Strafrecht bei Cicero und den Historikern*, p. 51). It is true that Josephus (*Antiquities*, 20,9,1) reports at least one instance in which a high priest applied for the consent of the Roman governor to convene the Sanhedrin for a capital trial; but it is submitted that no general rule can be derived from this single report. It is also true that, according to some Egyptian papyruses, local courts were sometimes employed by governors in Roman provinces overseas to conduct preliminary inquiries for them; but, in contradistinction to such reports from other provinces, there is no evidence whatever of any such practice ever having prevailed in Judaea. For the reasons given in Chap. 5, *infra*, the theory that the Sanhedrin ever served the Roman governor as an inquiring or arresting auxiliary organ must be dismissed as unfounded.

43. The talmudic tradition is that forty years before the destruction of the temple, that is, exactly in the year 30, capital jurisdiction was taken away from Israel; and we find this tradition in two versions, one Babylonian and one Palestinian. The Babylonian version (B Avodah Zarah 8b; B Shabbat 15a; B Sanhedrin 41b) is as follows: "When Rabbi Yishma'el, son of Yossei, fell sick, his disciples asked him to leave them some of the sayings of his father. He told them: forty years before the destruction of the House, the Sanhedrin was exiled and sat in a shop." This tradition gave rise to a discussion among scholars of later generations as to what were the implications of the Sanhedrin's exile and refuge in a shop. "Said Rav Nahman, son of Yitzhak, it means that they ceased to try capital cases. And why should they have ceased to try capital cases? Because they saw that the number of murderers increased to such an extent that they

could not cope with the trial work; so they said, we had better exile ourselves to another place (outside the temple precincts), in order not to be guilty of dereliction of our duties; for it is written, And thou shalt do according to the sentence which they of that place which the Lord shall choose shall show thee (Deut. 17:10) —an indication that it is that place only, and no other, at which jurisdiction may be exercised."

The Palestinian version (J Sanhedrin I 1) is as follows: "Forty years before the destruction of the House, capital jurisdiction was taken away. And in the days of Shimon ben Shetah, civil jurisdiction was taken away. Said Rabbi Shimon bar Yohai, Blessed be God, because I am not wise enough to judge." Another text gives the latter part slightly differently, that is to say: "In the days of Rabbi Shimon bar Yohai, civil jurisdiction was taken away. Said Rabbi Shimon bar Yohai, Blessed be God, because I am not wise enough to judge" (J Sanhedrin VII 1).

There is another, contradictory, talmudic tradition to the effect that capital jurisdiction ceased only when the temple was destroyed, that is, in the year 70 (B Sanhedrin 52b; B Ketubot 30a; Mekhilta of Shimon bar Yohai, Shemot 21,14). As capital jurisdiction had, according to Scripture, to be exercised within the temple precincts ("the place which the Lord shall choose"), the destruction of the temple amounted to an automatic abolition of such jurisdiction. But there are in the talmudic sources clear indications that, in fact, capital jurisdiction continued to be exercised after the destruction of the temple, even though "contrary to the Torah, because the situation so required" (B Sanhedrin 46a; *et al.*) —which renders any voluntary abandonment of jurisdiction long before the destruction of the temple highly improbable.

The Palestinian version, as will have been observed, speaks of the cessation not only of criminal but also of civil jurisdiction, whether in the days of Shimon ben Shetah—that is, about 150 years earlier—or in the days of Shimon bar Yohai—that is, about 100 years after the destruction of the temple. It is a well-established and well-documented (and not really contested) fact that civil jurisdiction did not cease at all, either before or after the destruction of the temple; and the conclusion would suggest itself that the mention of civil jurisdiction in this context might have for its sole cause the sigh of relief by Rabbi Shimon, "Blessed be God, because I am not wise enough to judge." Now, in another context, the same Rabbi Shimon bar Yohai is reported not to have been as modest as all that, but to have boasted that if there were two geniuses in this world, it would be his son and himself (B Sukkah 45b): if the adjudication of civil matters was a task too difficult even for a genius like him, surely civil jurisdiction must have been taken away from Israel! However that may be, it may safely be assumed that since civil jurisdiction had in actual fact not been taken away from Israel, so was the capital (or criminal) jurisdiction not taken away from Israel forty years before the destruction of the temple; and as in regard to civil jurisdiction the tradition is but a legend intended to provide the background for Shimon's blessing, so has the tradition in regard to the capital jurisdiction some extraneous cause or purpose. Such extraneous cause or purpose would presumably be common to both the Palestinian and the Babylonian tradition: it can be no accident that both traditions date the cessation of capital jurisdiction in the year 30, and the cause and purpose of the traditions must have some relation to that date. It is submitted that the tradition was established for the purpose of dissociating the Sanhedrin from any connection with the crucifixion of Jesus, which had taken place that very year: if, forty years before the destruction of the temple, the Sanhedrin no longer exercised capital jurisdiction, whether because of its exile to a shop or because the jurisdiction had "ceased," then it could not very well have tried or executed Jesus.

Yossei, the father of Yishma'el, in whose name the tradition (in its Babylonian version) is transmitted, belonged to the fourth generation of the Tanna'im: that is to say, he could not have transmitted it to his son earlier than about 100 years after the destruction of the temple. The interpretation by Rav Nahman, son of Yitzhak, that the exile of the Sanhedrin meant the cessation of jurisdiction in capital (that is, murder) cases, dates about 150 years later—about 250 years after the destruction of the temple: and whatever be the legal and logical merit of that interpretation, it is certainly quite worthless as historical evidence. (The Palestinian tradition of the "cessation" of capital jurisdiction appears to have been unknown in Babylonia, for otherwise there would not have been anything new or remarkable in the tradition transmitted on the sickbed by Yishma'el, son of Yossei; traditions or dicta not included in the Mishna were often unknown to scholars who had not heard them propounded: cf. B. Shabat 19b *et al.*) The reason given by Rav Nahman, or by scholars in the course of the discussion with him, for the exile of the Sanhedrin is not, as will be remembered, that the capital jurisdiction had anyway been taken away from it, and therefore there was no scriptural obligation for it to remain sitting within temple precincts, but that the number of the murderers had increased to such an extent that the Sanhedrin could no longer cope with its work load. While it may be quite true that, at that time, there was a considerable increase in violent crime in Judaea, it is wholly inconceivable that the Sanhedrin would, for that reason, abandon its jurisdictional powers, thereby virtually admitting to the Roman authorities that it was incapable of maintaining order and of performing its judicial duties. On the contrary, the Sanhedrin was vitally interested in proving that it was equal to any judicial or administrative functions that would be entrusted to it, and that the maintenance of peace and order within the Jewish population could safely be left in its hands. Any addition to its judicial work load would only have provided it with a fresh challenge to cope with it all the more efficiently and speedily; and the notion that the Sanhedrin could have given up in despair and relinquished its autonomous jurisdiction to Roman occupation forces and their courts is manifestly unreasonable and unhistorical (see also Graetz, *op. cit.,* Vol. III, p. 554).

Capital jurisdiction was, as a matter of fact, exercised by the Sanhedrin during the forty years preceding the destruction of the temple (for ample instances, see Winter, *op. cit.,* pp. 13–15; Schuerer, *op. cit.,* Vol. II, p. 209, n. 72; Zucker, *op. cit.,* p. 87; and cf. Josephus, *Wars,* 6,2,4; and Acts 4:1–22 and 5:17–42). We have independent evidence to the effect that during that period the Sanhedrin stayed within the temple precincts and did not go into exile, into any shop or at all: M Pei'ah II 6; Midrash Tanna'im, Devarim 26,13, while its exile into a "shop," when the temple had finally been destroyed, is vouched for also by another tradition: B Rosh-Hashanah 31a.

The period of forty years occurs first in the traditions ascribed to Shimon bar Yohai and to Yossei, father of Yishma'el—that is, in the second half of the second century. At that time, the Christians started to propagate their faith and to stress the differences between Christianity and Judaism, not only in matters of religion but also in respect of loyalty to Rome (Lietzmann, *History of the Early Church,* Vol. II, pp. 172–188), and the Gospels which blamed the Jews for the crucifixion of Jesus and whitewashed the Roman governor were given wide publicity. The Jews, who had (as will be shown in detail in Chap. 12, *infra*) no tradition or knowledge of their own of any sanhedrial trial of Jesus, found themselves in a situation in which they had to defend themselves: it was felt that it was not enough to dismiss the Gospel stories as lies; and it was thought that a tradition to the effect that at the time of the crucifixion the Jewish courts no longer exercised any capital jurisdiction might be a reasonable and acceptable argument in their defense, the fact being that Roman governors had, indeed, in several cases deprived local provincial courts of capital jurisdiction previously enjoyed by them (see Mommsen, *op. cit.,* p. 240). However reasonable or even conclusive this kind of argument may have appeared to them, it did not avail the Jews anything—whether because it did not appear reasonable to their persecutors, or because they knew that it was not historically true, or because they were not amenable to argument in any case. Needless to say, the fact that the tradition was unhistorical (and could easily be proved to be so) did not, on the other hand, deter any protagonists of Jewish guilt from relying on it to explain the delivery of Jesus by the Sanhedrin into the hands of the Roman governor instead of executing him itself. It is only in modern times that it is called in aid by liberal-minded scholars to exculpate the Sanhedrin; but since it is certainly unhistorical, it can serve neither exculpatory nor accusatory purposes.

44. Winter, *op. cit.*, pp. 10 and 154; Mantel, *op. cit.*, pp. 254–265; Juster, *op. cit.*, Vol. II, pp. 139–149. Notwithstanding the formidable and almost conclusive evidence to the contrary, it was recently stated that it can now be regarded as settled that the Sanhedrin had no power to impose capital punishment: Schneider, in *Novum Testamentum*, Vol. 12 (1970), p. 24, n. 3. And see note 38, *supra*.

45. M Sanhedrin I 5.

46. M Sanhedrin I 4. The statements of Stauffer, *Jerusalem und Rom im Zeitalter Jesu Christi*, p. 118, that all cases of apostasy (including cases of false prophecy, inducement to idolatry, blasphemy, and the like) had to be tried by the Great Sanhedrin of Seventy-one, is erroneous and not borne out by the references given, *ibid.*, on p. 158, n. 66.

47. *Antiquities*, 14,5,4.

48. M Sanhedrin I 5.

49. *Antiquities*, 20,8,8. Much capital is made of this report by Olmstead, *op. cit.*, p. 179, as well as by MacRuer, *op. cit.*, p. 40.

50. Brandon, *Jesus and the Zealots*, p. 114.

51. It is true that the activities of the zealots date back to before the time of Jesus; but when Josephus speaks of the zealots' reckless enterprise, soon to expand into "enormity," or of the many sufferings afflicted on the people as a result of "agitations" of zealot leaders, and of the large-scale "brigandage" and the "murders of many of the noblest men," he ascribes "personal greed" as a motive to zealots only, whom he decries as robbers and desperadoes, but nowhere implicates high priests or elders or scribes in any such misdeeds (*Antiquities*, 18,1,1 and 18,1,6). Josephus' aversion to the zealots has been explained as due to the conviction that they were to blame for the "ruin of Israel," and to his desire "to excuse his people to his Gentile readers, whose natural antipathy to the Jews had been greatly increased by their ferocious conduct during the war" (Brandon, *Jesus and the Zealots*, p. 36). In his description of the zealots' creed, however, Josephus makes it clear that "in all other matters" they agreed with the Pharisees (*Antiquities*, 18,1,6) —thus not only dissociating them, and any allegations of misconduct, from the priestly aristocracy, but also identifying their ideology with that of the great majority of the people.

52. Olmstead, *op. cit.*, pp. 179–180.

53. B Pessahim 57a; T Menahot XIII 21. The full text reads as follows:

> Woe to me from the house of Bo'ethos!
> Woe to me from their clubs!
> Woe to me from the house of Hanin!
> Woe to me from their whispers!

Woe to me from the house of Katheros!
Woe to me from their pens!
Woe to me from the house of Yishma'el, son of Phabi!
Woe to me from their fists!
They are high priests,
and their sons are treasurers,
and their sons-in-law are overseers,
and their servants beat the people with rods!

54. See Josephus, *Antiquities*, 19,6,2; 20,8,8; and Schuerer, *op. cit.*, Vol. II, pp. 218–219.

55. T Menahot XIII 22.

56. Thus, for instance, Zeitlin, "The Crucifixion of Jesus Re-examined," at p. 366.

57. There is an explicit rule in Jewish law that no man may endanger the life of another to save his own, nor may a single soul be surrendered, even though many may be in danger of their lives: M Terumot VIII 11–12; T Terumot VII, 20; J Shevi'it 35; B Sanhedrin 74a; *et al.* For an exposition of the origin and development of the rule, see Daube, *Collaboration with Tyranny in Rabbinic Law, passim*.

58. Josephus, *Antiquities*, 17,9,3, describes Judas and Matthew, the zealot leaders, as teachers of the law. *Ibid.*, 18,1,1, he reports that Judas was joined by a Pharisee by the name of Zadok. While "Judas clearly was the more important figure and was the better remembered," Zadok's "association is important, for it shows that Zealotism was not incompatible with the profession of Pharisaic principles": Brandon, *Jesus and the Zealots*, p. 54.

59. Stauffer, *Jesus—Gestalt und Geschichte*, p. 96, praises Kaiaphas for the masterly ingenuity with which he initiated the proceedings and brought them to the desired end; but there is nothing in the sources to warrant the elevation of Kaiaphas to the rank of a legal mastermind. See also Ben-Chorin, *op. cit.*, p. 193.

3. JESUS

1. For a notable exception, see Kuemmel, "Die Weherufe ueber die Schriftgelehrten und die Pharisaeer," at p. 146.

2. B Sanhedrin 25b. And see Chap. 1, *supra*.

3. See: Kee, "The Question About Fasting," p. 167.

4. M Ta'anit III 3–4.

5. M Ta'anit II 10.

6. Zeitlin, *Who Crucified Jesus?*, pp. 130–132.

7. Thieme, "Die religioes motivierte Judenfeindschaft," at p. 50, quotes a doctoral dissertation accepted in 1959 by the Papal Bible Institute in Rome, to the effect that, according to New Testament testimony, there was originally no enmity at all between Jesus and the Pharisees,

and that Jesus had himself been a promising and practicing Pharisee. Indeed, Jesus expressly acknowledges Pharisaic righteousness (cf. Matt. 5:20).

8. B Avodah Zarah 27b–28a; M Shabbat VI 10 and XIV 3–4; B Shabbat 108b–109a; T Shabbat VII 23. And see Mantel, *op. cit.,* p. 269.
9. B Eruvin 6b. The same rule applies also to private and commercial law: B Shevu'ot 48b; B Babba Batra 124a.
10. B Shabbat 21a and 126b. And see Wolfson, "How the Jews Will Reclaim Jesus," at pp. 27 ff.; and my "Prolegomena to the Theory and History of Jewish Law," at p. 51.
11. B Shabbat 73b; J Shabbat V 1. And see Boaz Cohen, "The Rabbinic Law Presupposed by Matthew 12,1 and Luke 6,1," pp. 91–92.
12. M Pei'ah IV 4 and 10; M Menahot X 3.
13. M Shabbat VII 2. And cf. Exod. 34:21: "in harvest thou shalt rest."
14. B Menahot 96a.
15. Cf. Exod. 16:29: "See, for that the Lord hath given *you* the sabbath."
16. Mantel, *op. cit.,* p. 271.
17. B Hullin 106a.
18. B Hagigah 18b.
19. Isa. 1:11–17.
20. The Zacharias whom Jesus refers to here is Zechariah, a high priest, stoned to death by order of the king for disobedience to royal orders to reintroduce idolatry (II Chron. 24:18–21). His father's name was Yehoyada, and Jesus himself would certainly not have mistaken that name.
21. T Shabbat VII 23. It is true that healing by "whispers" was expressly deprecated by some scholars: M Sanhedrin X 1.
22. B Sanhedrin 101a.
23. Josephus, *Wars,* 6,5,3. And see Bin Gorion, *Yeshu Ben Hanan, passim.*
24. Brandon, *Jesus and the Zealots,* pp. 332, 339.
25. *Ibid.,* p. 333.
26. Winter, *op. cit.,* p. 143; Carmichael, *op. cit.,* p. 112.
27. M Shekalim I 3. Some scholars hold that these money-changers were not private traders but temple officials: Baer, *op. cit.,* p. 133. For our purposes, this would make no difference, as even officials are not immune to corruption.
28. J Ta'anit IV 5. Some scholars opined that the booths and dovecotes were not on the Temple Mount but on the Mount of Olives, quite a distance away (Baer, *op. cit.,* p. 134, n. 40; Klausner, *op. cit.,* p. 433); but there is no valid reason to place the stalls elsewhere than on the Temple Mount, and recent excavations appear to confirm that they were there indeed, in the immediate vicinity of the temple entrance (I am indebted for this information to Professor Benjamin Mazar).
29. Olmstead, *op. cit.,* p. 91; Brandon, *Jesus and the Zealots,* p. 331.

30. To the same effect: Dalman, *Orte und Wege Jesu*, p. 309.
31. Brandon, Cullmann, Eisler, Carmichael, and others.
32. Brandon, *Jesus and the Zealots*, p. 333.
33. M Berakhot IX 5.
34. The theory that Jesus expelled newly arrived traders who formerly traded in the "shop" to which the Sanhedrin had just been exiled (Eppstein, "The Historicity of the Gospel Account of the Cleansing of the Temple," pp. 42–58) falls to the ground if the Sanhedrin had not in fact been exiled, to any "shop" or at all (see note 43, p. 346, *supra*). But the historicity of the whole temple-cleansing incident is strongly contested: see, for instance, Baer, *op. cit.,* at p. 135.
35. J Sanhedrin I 19. The rule was later changed, and only heads of schools could ordain.
36. We know of two scholars, Eliezer ben Hyrkanos and Yehoshua ben Hanania, who were both ordained by Yohanan ben Zakkai: J Sanhedrin I 2.
37. For a full treatment of the subject, see Daube, *New Testament and Rabbinic Judaism,* pp. 205–223.
38. Strack and Billerbeck, *Kommentar zum Neuen Testament aus Bibel und Midrasch,* Vol. I, pp. 860 ff.
39. M Sanhedrin XI 2.
40. B Sanhedrin 87a.
41. B Horayot 4a–b.
42. B Eruvin 13b; B Babba Metzia 59b.
43. Parkes, *op. cit.,* p. 22, writes that "a flood of messiahs sprang up in the first half of the first century A.D. The causes of emergence of so much messianic unrest have often been missed. It was not merely a reaction against the loss of national sovereignty. It was brought about by the fact that according to the calendar in use among the Jews at that time, the coming of the Messianic age was expected about the middle of the first century." And see Pickl, *The Messias, passim;* Silver, *A History of Messianic Speculation in Israel,* pp. 16 ff.
44. Parkes, *op. cit.,* p. 83.
45. Whether or not these prophecies were authentic utterances of Jesus is the subject of much controversy: see Brandon, *Jesus and the Zealots,* p. 269, n. 2. Recently, the case for their authenticity was taken up by Schonfield (*op. cit.,* pp. 86 ff.) , who opines that Jesus was able to specify beforehand who would act against him, by putting together scriptural indications as to the fate of the Messiah— as, for instance, Psalms 2:2: "The kings of the earth set themselves, and the rulers take counsel together, against the Lord and against his Anointed": the kings of the earth are the Romans, while the counseling rulers are the chief priests and elders.

A Czechoslovakian scholar, Ian Kamelsky, propounds in an (as yet unpublished) article on the trial of Jesus the theory that, having indeed uttered these prophecies, Jesus found himself in jeopardy of being indicted as a false prophet unless his prophecies came true (cf. Deut. 13:5 and 18:20–22); and the Sanhedrin found itself in the dilemma either of having him delivered into the hands of the Roman governor, so that his prophecies might be substantiated, or of having him executed as a false prophet; and it was in deference to Jesus and in recognition of his divine inspiration that the Sanhedrin decided to deliver him up.

The view, to which we subscribe, that these prophecies were never uttered by Jesus but were put into his mouth after the event, has been stated by Bornkamm (*op. cit.*, p. 162) as follows: "These prophecies of suffering are molded not so much upon the expectation of future happenings, as rather upon an experience looking back on the earthbound. . . . The Passion story of Jesus went into these prophecies in great detail. This means, from the point of view of tradition-history, that these words can hardly have been spoken by Jesus himself; they belong to a later stratum of tradition, in which the accomplished history of Jesus gave also to his words a new stature" (my translation from the German).

46. Flusser, *Jesus*, p. 117, and "Mishpat Yeshu," p. 110.

47. Zucker, *op. cit.*, p. 78, n. 1.

48. *Antiquities*, 18,5,2.

4. THE ARREST

1. The Greek terms used in the original are *speira*, meaning cohort, and *khiliarchos*, meaning tribune—both technical terms to describe Roman military units. See Winter, *op. cit.*, pp. 44 ff.; Brandon, *The Trial of Jesus of Nazareth*, p. 196, n. 156. Blinzler, *Der Prozess Jesu*, pp. 68 and 71–74, wrongly assumes that *speira* is the description of a Jewish military unit.

2. Schonfield, *op. cit.*, pp. 149, 137.

3. Schuerer, *op. cit.*, Vol. II, p. 266.

4. M Bikkurim III 3: "When they approached the city of Jerusalem, they sent a herald to announce their arrival and decorated their first-fruits; the *Pahot*, the *Seganim* and the *Gizbarim* would then go out to meet them: the more the people were that arrived, the more distinguished would be the delegation that met them. And all the tradesmen of Jerusalem would rise in their honor and greet them, Our brethren, men of distant cities, be welcome!"

5. T Horayot II 8–10: "A sage takes precedence over a king—for if the sage dies, he is irreplaceable, while, on the king's death, all Israel are eligible to the kingship. The king takes precedence over the high priest; the high priest over the priest allowed to don the sacral vestments; the priest donning sacral vestments over the priest in charge of wars (cf. Deut. 20:2); the priest in charge of wars over the *Segan*;

the *Segan* over the priest in command of the temple police; the temple police commander over the senior priest; the senior priest over the administrator (*Amarkal*); the administrator over the treasurer (*Gizbar*); the treasurer over the lay priest; the lay priest over the levite; and the levite over the common israelite. . . ."

6. Klausner, *op. cit.*, p. 466.

7. So also Winter, *op. cit.*, pp. 44–45.

8. Stauffer, *Jesus—Gestalt und Geschichte*, p. 91, writes that the chief priests and senators who, according to Luke 22:52, were present in person—"presumably in order to be available as witnesses or advisers, should any lego-religious incidents arise"—had brought along with them their house slaves or servants, "robust fellows, who had, for this nightly pursuit of criminals, equipped themselves with staves and swords (Mark 14,43; John 18,10)." Brandon, *Jesus and the Zealots*, p. 255, n. 3, after stating that by describing this force as *okhlos*, "Mark undoubtedly intends to give the impression that the Jewish authorities employed an armed mob," rightly concludes that it "is most unlikely that these authorities would have resorted to such an undisciplined body when they possessed an efficient military body in the temple police." Nor is it likely that the regular temple police would be reinforced, or would allow itself to be reinforced, by house slaves of priests or elders, the less so as they were already reinforced (as Stauffer admits) by the Roman cohort; and the resulting mass levy (*Massenaufgebot*) cannot reasonably be explained: its dismissal as "remarkable" (*auffaellig*) does not explain anything.

For similar "mob theories" in relation to the identity of Jewish "multitudes," see Chap. 6, *infra*.

9. Gellius 16,4; Livius, 7,25; 8,8; 26,28; 29,24; 43,12. And cf. Adams, *Handbuch der roemischen Altertuemer*, pp. 656 ff.

10. Goguel, *op. cit.*, Vol. II (*The Life of Jesus*), pp. 469, 498. Blinzler, *Der Prozess Jesu*, p. 69, assumes that the unit seconded for this purpose numbered 200 to 300 men only. Keim, *Die Geschichte Jesu*, p. 314, writes that the Johannine version cannot be correct, not only because the Romans had nothing to do with the arrest of Jesus, but also because "the levy of about five hundred men was a wholly impossible exaggeration."

11. Winter, *op. cit.*, p. 48; Goguel, *op. cit.*, Vol. II, pp. 468–469; Mac-Ruer, *op. cit.*, p. 38; Lietzmann, "Der Prozess Jesu," pp. 313 ff.; Cullmann, *op. cit.*, p. 32; Isaac, *Jésus et Israel*, p. 346; *et al.*

12. Goguel, *op. cit.*, Vol. II, p. 497.

13. Keim, quoted by Goguel, *ibid.*, n. 4. In another context, Keim wrote that the story of Judas is beset with dismay and depression of Christians and the disdain and contempt of their enemies; according to Celsus, the Platonian, "the discipline and piety of a band of robbers would be better than was that of the disciples of Jesus"; and the story gives rise to so much shame and despair that it could not just have been invented (*op. cit.*, p. 297).

14. MacRuer, *op. cit.*, p. 38. For the story that high priests sent their slaves to rural priests' threshing floors and seized their tithes, see note 49, p. 350, *supra*.
15. MacRuer, *op. cit.*, p. 38.
16. Olmstead, *op. cit.*, p. 179.
17. B Pessahim 57a. See notes 52–53, p. 350, *supra*.
18. So Klausner, *op. cit.*, pp. 467–468; Isaac, *op. cit.*, p. 321.
19. B Sanhedrin 78b: Where there is reasonable danger that the blows which the victim of an assault has suffered may prove fatal, the assailant is imprisoned until it becomes evident whether the victim will recover or not; if he recovers, the assailant is discharged and will be liable only to pay damages (Exod. 21:19) ; if he dies, the assailant will be charged with homicide.
20. M Sanhedrin IX 5: A man who caused the death of another, and no witnesses are available, shall be imprisoned on rations of bread and water. B Sanhedrin 81b: The same rule applies where only one witness is available (and not the minimal two: Deut. 19:15) , or where the accused is not criminally responsible because of ignorance of the law, it not being proved that he had been explicitly warned beforehand that, if he committed murder, he would be liable to the death penalty.
21. Powell, *op. cit.*, pp. 50 ff.
22. M Sanhedrin IX 5; B Sanhedrin 81b.
23. Winter, *op. cit.*, p. 47.
24. Blinzler, *Der Prozess Jesu*, p. 69, maintains that Pilate had no previous notice that Jesus would be brought before him for trial, but he fails to give any reasonable explanation how it was that the governor was available for the trial so early in the morning—a matter which evidently calls for an explanation.
25. Wellhausen, *Das Evangelium Johannis*, p. 105; Winter, *op. cit.*, p. 171.
26. Cf. Winter, *op. cit.*, pp. 42–43, 146–147.
27. *Ibid.*
28. Goguel, *op. cit.*, Vol. II, p. 481.
29. Wellhausen, *op. cit.*, p. 106.
30. The view has been expressed that there might have been a lockup or some prison cells in the "cabins" of the high priest's house, similar to what is reported to have existed in the house of Jonathan the scribe (Jer. 37:15–16) ; or that Jesus was, according to John, brought into the house of Annas, because only there, and not in the house of Kaiaphas, were prison cells available (Klausner, *op. cit.*, p. 470). But there is absolutely nothing in the Gospel texts or in any other sources to suggest that there were any prison cells in the house of any high priest.
31. Schweitzer, *op. cit.*, p. 392: "Is it not almost unintelligible that his disciples were not involved in his fate? Not even the disciple who smote with the sword was arrested along with him!"

32. Cf. Strauss, *Das Leben Jesu*, pp. 124–125; Goguel, *op. cit.*, Vol. II, p. 499.

33. Brandon, *Jesus and the Zealots*, pp. 306 ff.; Carmichael, *op. cit.*, pp. 118 ff., and others, accept the historicity of the tradition as an indication that Jesus' followers offered armed resistance to his arrest, and hence would have been zealots (cf. Luke 22:36: "He that hath no sword, let him sell his garment, and buy one"). Even if this theory is correct, it provides no explanation for the lack of reaction on the part of the police—on the contrary, it renders it all the more difficult to understand that the Roman officer and his troops would remain passive in the face of unmistakable zealot activity.

5. IN THE HOUSE OF THE HIGH PRIEST

1. Franz Meyer, *op. cit.*, at p. 546, rightly says that an investigation into the reasons which prompted Luke and John to deviate from the Marcan account is overdue, and that Blinzler's view (*Der Prozess Jesu*, pp. 120 ff.) that they did so only because their readers knew that story already from Mark and Matthew is manifestly untenable.

2. Cf. Winter, *op. cit.*, pp. 21 ff.

3. E.g., Stauffer, *Jesus—Gestalt und Geschichte*, pp. 92 ff.

4. Among the foremost protagonists of the unhistoricity of any trial before the Sanhedrin are Lietzmann ("Der Prozess Jesu," pp. 313 ff.), Goguel (*op. cit.*, Vol. II, p. 512), Winter (*op. cit.*, pp. 24–25), Dibelius ("Das historische Problem der Leidensgeschichte," at p. 200), and, preceding them all, Salvador (*Jésus-Christ et sa Doctrine*, pp. 520–570).

    The historicity of the trial before the Sanhedrin is maintained by Blinzler and most legal (MacRuer, Powell, Lord Shaw, Taylor Innes) and Catholic writers. The protagonists of the Jewish Trial Theory have recently been joined by Schneider, "Gab es eine Szene 'Jesus vor dem Synedrium'?," at pp. 24 ff.

5. See Chap. 2, *supra;* Jaeger, *Il Processo di Gesù*, pp. 31 ff.

6. See Chapter 8, *infra.*

7. Blinzler, *Der Prozess Jesu*, p. 12: "This approach is common to almost all authors who have written on the subject in later years and whose books deserve any attention" (my translation from the German).

8. See note 4, *supra.*

9. The Great Sanhedrin sat in the Hall of Hewn Stones (*Lishkat Ha-Gazith*), and from there "the law went out to all Israel": M Sanhedrin XI 2. "If there arise a matter too hard for thee in judgment . . . then shalt thou arise, and get thee up into the

place which the Lord thy God shall choose" (Deut. 17:8) : the temple is the place which the Lord had chosen, and that is where the Sanhedrin is required (or allowed) to sit and adjudicate. The tradition is that there were three courts sitting within the temple precincts, one at the entrance to the Temple Mount, one at the entrance to the temple lobby (*Azarah*), and one in the Hall of Hewn Stones (Sifrei Shoftim, 152) ; but while the other courts would adjudicate generally in criminal and civil matters, the Great Council of ultimate jurisdiction (as to which see Chap. 2, *supra*) was empowered to review the judgments of those other courts and lay down the binding law. The next following verse, "And thou shalt do according to the sentence, which they of that place which the Lord shall choose shall show thee" (Deut. 17:10) , in which the stress on that particular chosen place is repeated, was interpreted to mean that it was only when sitting in that place, that is, the temple, and not in any other place, that the Sanhedrin was competent to exercise any jurisdiction at all, and that only if made and issued at that particular place were its decrees and judgments binding and enforceable (B Avodah Zarah 8b; B Sanhedrin 41b; B Shabbat 15a; *et al.*) .

10. The following is the text of the Mishna: "Civil cases are tried during the day and may be completed at night; criminal cases are tried during the day and must be completed during daytime. If the accused is acquitted, the criminal trial may be completed on one and the same day; but if not, it is adjourned to the next following day, on which judgment will then be pronounced. Therefore no criminal trials are held either on the eve of a sabbath day or on the eve of a festival day" (M Sanhedrin IV 1) .

11. *Ibid.*

12. "At the mouth of two witnesses, or three witnesses, shall he that is worthy of death be put to death; but at the mouth of one witness he shall not be put to death" (Deut. 17:6) . "One witness shall not rise up against a man for any iniquity or for any sin . . . at the mouth of two witnesses, or at the mouth of three witnesses, shall the matter be established" (Deut. 19:15) . "No person accused of a capital offense can be convicted otherwise than on the strength of the testimony of witnesses": T Sanhedrin XI 1. Among the differences between civil and criminal cases we find that, while in civil matters a person is bound by his own admission, in criminal cases he will not be so bound, and any confession, whether made in or out of court, is inadmissible in evidence against him: T Shevu'ot III 8.

13. *Ibid.*

14. No person accused of a capital offense may be put to death otherwise than after conviction by a court of twenty-three, passed on the strength of testimony of competent witnesses both as to the commission of the offense and as to the offender having been warned

beforehand that if he committed the act, he would incur the death penalty (B Sanhedrin 8b and 80b; T Sanhedrin XI 1). Some hold that he must have been warned beforehand also as to what kind of death penalty he would incur if he committed the offense (*ibid.*). Ignorance of the law was not only a good defense to any criminal charge in Jewish law, but was presumed in favor of the accused until his knowledge of the law was positively proven.

15. "Whosoever curseth his God shall bear his sin. And he that blasphemeth the name of the Lord, he shall surely be put to death, and all the congregation shall certainly stone him: as well the stranger, as he that is born in the land, when he blasphemeth the name of the Lord, shall be put to death" (Lev. 24:15–16). The difference between the blasphemer (curser) who only "bears his sin" and the blasphemer who is put to death is that the latter blasphemes the Name, in addition to the cursing (cf. the more accurate Bible translation of the Jewish Publication Society of America [Philadelphia, 1962]: "Anyone who blasphemes his God, shall bear his guilt; but if he pronounces the name LORD, he shall be put to death"). The law was accordingly laid down to be that a "blasphemer is not liable to the death penalty, unless he has pronounced the Name": M Sanhedrin VII 5. Cursing or blaspheming God without pronouncing the Name, by using any of God's many descriptive or circumscriptive epithets, is punishable by flogging only (B Sanhedrin 56a).

16. Several other inconsistencies with, and deviations from, Jewish law were detected by various writers—most of them based on misconceptions of Jewish law. Mention is, for instance, made of a rule that prosecutors were not to act as judges (the—wholly unwarranted—assumption being that the members of the Sanhedrin were Jesus' prosecutors and judges at the same time) : but no such rule in fact exists, if only for the simple reason that there were no prosecutors in criminal trials at all. Blood-avengers (Num. 35:24–25) who might have initiated proceedings as complainants could not be heard at the trial except as witnesses. The rule is, indeed, that a *witness* may not become a judge in a cause in which he is about to testify (B Rosh Hashanah 25b-26a, B Bava Kama 90b) — including, of course, a prosecutor or complainant who qualifies as a witness. The question arose (about a century after Jesus' death) whether a court was allowed to adjudicate upon a crime which was committed before its very eyes, such as homicide committed in open court; the majority held that it was disqualified, the judges being required to testify as witnesses; but there was a dissenting opinion to the effect that the court could try the case then and there (*ibid.*). It was this dissenting opinion, which never had become law, which prompted some writers to maintain that the members of the Sanhedrin, though themselves witnesses to the blasphemy

uttered by Jesus, were still competent to try and condemn him
then and there (Stauffer, *Jesus—Gestalt und Geschichte,* p. 95) .

Or, mention is often made of a rule according to which the accused had to be acquitted whenever the verdict against him was
unanimous—such unanimity being suspected of originating in some
prejudice or conspiracy against him. Now there is a dictum reported of a third-century scholar to the effect that where the Sanhedrin was unanimous in convicting, the accused would be "dismissed" forthwith (B Sanhedrin 17a) . The reason there given is
that in view of such unanimity it would be useless to adjourn
the case until the next day, as was required in all capital cases
(M Sanhedrin V 5) . I am afraid the "dismissal" has been widely
misinterpreted: what was meant surely was not that in the face of
a unanimous verdict the accused was to be discharged and set free,
but that he could be dismissed from court and executed at once,
without any further adjournment for further deliberations being
required. We find the same "dismissal," in the sense of an adverse
adjudication, in the case of a litigant who is by law required to take
the oath and refuses to do so—whereupon he is to be "dismissed,"
that is, summarily condemned (B Shevu'ot 39a) . There is no valid
reason to assume that, though the technical term used is the same,
the "dismissal" should have a different meaning in criminal procedure from that it undoubtedly has in civil procedure. But even
if there should be some substance in the traditional Jewish interpretation of "dismissal," in the case of the unanimous verdict,
as an acquittal of the accused, I would submit that the dictum of
a third-century scholar cannot be relied upon as accurately describing a rule of law which in actual practice must have been obsolete
already for more than two hundred years—the less so as the dictum
is based not on any historical tradition, but rather on the purely
logical consideration there expressed, that the unanimity would
render an adjournment unnecessary. And there is no authority
other than this dictum for holding that the reported unanimity of
the Sanhedrin in the case of Jesus could have vitiated his condemnation.

17. Cf. Craveri, *op. cit.,* pp. 380 ff., and the references given on pp.
    462–463.
18. *Ibid.,* p. 52. To the same effect: Taylor Innes, *The Trial of Jesus
    Christ,* p. 23; Powell, *op. cit.,* pp. 87–88.
19. Carmichael, *op. cit.,* p. 41, writes that the "texts have of course been
    studied from a legal point of view any number of times; the most
    these quasi-juridical studies have produced is the unintelligible
    claim that every form of justice was violated and that Jesus was the
    victim of a judicial murder."
20. Powell, *op. cit.,* p. 88.
21. Some authors do not hesitate, notwithstanding all the available in-
    formation to the contrary, to maintain not only that a trial was

conducted before the Sanhedrin, but that it was conducted in conformity with all rules of law and procedure. Stauffer (*Jesus—Gestalt und Geschichte*, p. 96) writes: "The conduct of the trial by Kaiaphas was a legalistic masterpiece. In innumerable large and small points, which cannot here be dealt with, he strictly and with demonstrative pedantry adhered to the rules of procedure" (my translation from the German; and see note 59, p. 351, *supra*). It is rather a pity that all the many large and small points in which the rules of procedure were so pedantically adhered to remain undisclosed. In fact, there was none. Earlier in the same context, Jesus is credited with being a "thorough expert of the rules of criminal procedure and superb courtroom dialectician" (p. 92) —for which surprising proposition John 18:23 is quoted as authority (at p. 159). While Jesus' expert knowledge of all branches of the law is in no way doubted, it certainly cannot, on the strength of the Gospel reports, be said of him that, either before the Sanhedrin or before the Roman governor, he used any courtroom dialectics to advantage!

22. Jaubert, *La Date de la Cène, passim.*
23. "There is no earlier and no later in Scripture": B Pessahim 6b.
24. Blinzler, "Das Synedrium von Jerusalem und die Strafprozessordnung der Mischna," *passim,* and *Der Prozess Jesu,* pp. 86 ff.; Powell, *op. cit.,* pp. 75 and 86; Klausner, *op. cit.,* p. 471; *et al.*
25. For a full description of Sadducean doctrine, see Finkelstein, *op. cit.,* Vol. II, pp. 636–753.
26. See Chap. 2, *supra.*
27. There is a discussion in the Talmud, even among Pharisaic scholars, as to whether sentences pronounced may be executed on the Sabbath: B Sanhedrin 56a.
28. B Sanhedrin 34b.
29. Opinions on this are divided. From the exposition in T Shevu'ot III 8, it would appear that it is a matter of written rather than oral law. Maimonides (Mishneh Torah, Hilkhot Sanhedrin 18,6) describes the rule as laid down by Scripture, regarding it as a necessary implication from the two-witnesses rule.
30. Blinzler, "Das Synedrium von Jerusalem," at p. 60, mentions the two-witnesses rule as Sadducean law, but fails to offer an explanation for the absence of trustworthy and competent witnesses to provide the necessary basis for the conviction of Jesus even in a trial under Sadducean law.
31. M Sanhedrin VI 2: After conviction, and before execution, the convicted man is told to confess, "because it is the normal thing for a man to confess before his death, and he who confessess has a share in the world to come; and so we find in the case of Achan, that Joshua said unto him, My son, give, I pray thee, glory to the Lord God of Israel, and make confession unto him; and tell me now what thou hast done; hide it not from me. And Achan

answered Joshua, and said, Indeed I have sinned against the Lord God of Israel, and thus and thus have I done (Josh. 7:19-20). And whence do we know that this confession did indeed expiate his sin? From what is written, And Joshua said, Why hast thou troubled us? The Lord shall trouble thee this day (Josh. 7:25) — *this day* you are troubled, but in the days of the world to come you will not be troubled."

However ancient this mishnaic tradition may have been, the biblical text would suggest that Achan was asked to confess upon being caught by lot (Josh. 7:18), possibly with the prohibited chattels in his possession, and that there had been no other evidence forthcoming against him. Indeed, Maimonides, in his Commentary on the Mishna, observes that Joshua's execution of Achan was an emergency action ordained by God Himself, and not the result of any regular judicial proceedings, and that, had Achan been tried according to law, he would have been acquitted for lack of evidence.

32. Another confession is recorded in I Sam. 14:43: "Saul said to Jonathan, Tell me what thou hast done. And Jonathan told him, and said, I did but taste a little honey with the end of the rod that was in mine hand, and, lo, I must die." But "the people rescued Jonathan, that he died not" (I Sam. 14:45). The "rescue" may have had for its sole cause the popularity of Jonathan, or have been prompted also by the insignificance of the offense or the lack of evidence.

33. The King James Version renders the word "pronounces" (*nokeiv*) as "blasphemeth," an inaccuracy justifiable only by the consideration that all blasphemy—as distinguished from "cursing"—indeed presupposes the pronunciation of the Name. And see note 15, *supra.*

34. Num. 15:30: "The soul that does aught presumptuously, shall be cut off from among his people." This "cutting off" (*kareth*) is done by God himself in His own time; but the later jurists introduced the reform—perhaps because the threat of being "cut off" by God was regarded by them as too severe and too indeterminate a punishment—that all offenders threatened with divine cutting off were liable, on judicial conviction, to be flogged, and, having undergone the punishment of flogging, would no longer be liable to be cut off by God (M Makkot III 15)—the presumption being that God would not punish anybody twice, or a second time, for an offense for which he had already been punished (Maimonides, Commentary *ad loc.*). And see my "The Penology of the Talmud," at pp. 72 ff.

35. That the execution of Stephen was a judicial one, and not lynching, has been demonstrated by Horvath, "Why Was Jesus Brought to Pilate?" at p. 178. Scholars who held that Stephen had been lynched sought to justify the lynching by another mishnaic rule,

namely, that zealots may strike down persons caught *in flagrante delicto* committing certain grave offenses, including blasphemy (M Sanhedrin IX 6). To this effect, e.g., Klausner, *From Jesus to Paul*, Vol. I, p. 273; and cf. Kilpatrick, *op. cit.,* p. 18. But the rule applied only to cases, like that of the biblical Phinehas (Num. 25:7–8), in which the sight of the offense provoked an "impassioned" eyewitness to immediate action: those in which a court could be first assembled and consulted were expressly excluded from the rule (B Sanhedrin 82a). Therefore, no lynching could be justified in the case of Stephen, as judicial proceedings preceded the "lynching" (Acts 6:12–7:54).

36. Chap. 3, *supra*.
37. B Sanhedrin 52b.
38. M Sanhedrin XI 1. Stoning is a mode of execution applied only where expressly provided for in Scripture, e.g., for blasphemy with pronunciation of the Name (Lev. 24:16); but in the case of adultery, no particular mode of execution is prescribed in the Bible, the law being that the adulterer and the adulteress shall be put to death (Lev. 20:10). In all cases in which no particular mode of execution is prescribed in the Bible, the execution is to be by strangulation—this being considered not only the most humane but also the one most resembling the divine method: for as God brings death without leaving outward signs on the human body, so the court should inflict death in such a way that no outward signs are left on the body (B Sanhedrin 52b). And see my "The Penology of the Talmud," at pp. 60 ff.
39. For the legal implications of this passage, see Noerr, "Rechtsgeschichtliche Probleme in den Evangelien," p. 100.
40. B Sanhedrin 52b.
41. Allon, *Mehkarim Betoledot Yisrael*, Vol. I, p. 41. And cf. Josephus, *Antiquities*, 20,9,6.
42. Instances recorded in the Talmud can be found in M Sanhedrin VI 4 and 6; Rashi (Shlomo Yitzhaki) *ad* B Sanhedrin 45b.
43. Stauffer, *Jerusalem und Rom im Zeitalter Jesu Christi,* p. 63, 118.
44. Stauffer, *Jesus—Gestalt und Geschichte,* p. 96.
45. M Sanhedrin VI 4: After some discussion whether only men or also women must be hanged after execution (Deut. 21:22), one of the scholars is reported to have asked: But Simon ben Shetah did hang women at Askalon! Whereupon he was told: He hanged eighty women, though no more than one accused may be tried on any one day. In other words: the hangings of Simon ben Shetah were illegal anyway, and no rule can be deduced therefrom.
46. Chap. 7, *infra*.
47. Courts were expressly warned that "no law is to be deduced from emergency measures": Maimonides, Commentary *ad* M Sanhedrin VI 4 and 6; Rashi (Shlomo Yitzhaki) *ad* B Sanhedrin 45b.
48. Blinzler, *Der Prozess Jesu,* p. 146.

49. Josephus, *Antiquities,* 18,1,4. And see Chap. 2, *supra.*
50. Bienert, *op. cit.,* p. 43.
51. Allon, *Mehkarim Betoledot Yisrael,* Vol. I, p. 105.
52. M Sanhedrin V 5: "If [after the day's hearings] they found him not guilty, they shall discharge him; in any other case they shall adjourn the hearing until the next day; they shall abstain from much eating and drinking and shall, in groups of two, consult with each other all night long, and return to court early the next morning."
53. Schalit, "Kritische Randbemerkungen zu Paul Winters On the Trial of Jesus," p. 93. This view has already been refuted by Baer, *op. cit.,* at p. 144.
54. Winter, *op. cit.,* p. 29.
55. So Schalit, *op. cit.,* p. 94; Flusser, *Jesus,* p. 120, and "Mishpat Yeshu," p. 113.
56. Stauffer, *Jesus—Gestalt und Geschichte,* pp. 95–96. The learned author entirely misconceived the mishnaic rules for the trial of a "rebellious elder." In M Sanhedrin XI 2, we read of three different courts before which the accused is to be brought: the first, sitting at the entrance of the Temple Mount, is to hear what the rebellious elder had taught; if it considers his teachings in order, he is discharged; if not, he is brought before the second court, sitting at the temple entrance (*Azarah*), where the procedure is repeated; if this court considers the teachings to be in order, he is discharged; if not, he is brought before the court sitting in the Hall of Hewn Stones within the temple, whence "the law goes out unto all Israel." The first two courts are not, as Stauffer thinks, holding preliminary inquiries at all; but the law is that until an elder can be held to be "rebellious" and be convicted of teaching illegal doctrine, three courts must, independently of one another, have found the doctrine to be indefensible.
57. Mommsen, *op. cit.,* pp. 323 ff.
58. *Ibid.,* pp. 490 ff.
59. In an earlier part of his book, Mommsen maintains that in Roman law there was a preliminary inquiry known as *anquisitio,* which was held before a magistrate prior to the regular trial (p. 164). This view appears to be mistaken: the *anquisitio* was a trial, held before a *magistratus,* and always resulted in a *judicium,* that is, a judgment. It is true that this judgment was not final, but subject to appeal by way of *provocatio* before the people's assembly; and it may be that historians like Mommsen did not properly distinguish between an order of committal for trial and a judgment subject to review by a higher court. In its earliest form, the *anquisitio* was conducted by the magistrate in the presence of an informal assembly of citizens (*contio*), who attended the whole proceedings in order to be able to pass final judgment on the spot, in case the accused appealed against his condemnation by the magistrate. See Berger, *Encyclopedic Dictionary of Roman Law, q.v.* "Anquisitio," p. 363.

60. Thus, e.g., Kilpatrick, *op. cit.*, p. 20.
61. Digesta 47,23,2: Si plures simul agant populari actione, praetor eligat idoneiorem.
62. Mommsen, *op. cit.*, p. 491.
63. Codex Theodosius IX 1,9–14; Codex Justinianus IX 12,7 and 46,7.
64. Codex Theodosius IX 36,1; Mommsen, *op. cit.*, pp. 492 ff.
65. Digesta 47,15,1–2.
66. Similarly: Katz, *Jesus und das Judentum*, p. 6 and *passim;* and more recently, Dimont, *Jews, God, and History*, who writes (p. 139): "Does it not seem more probable that Jesus was arrested by the Jews to *protect* him from the Romans, who had never any compunction about crucifying one Jew more or less, that this protective arrest was to no avail, and that the Romans demanded that the Jews turn Jesus over to them for punishment?"
67. Where a man is pursued by another to be killed, the pursued must be saved even by killing the pursuer: M Sanhedrin VIII 7; B Sanhedrin 73a–74a.
68. See Allon, *Toledot Hayehudin Beeretz Yisrael Bitekufat Hamishna Vehatalmud,* Vol. I, p. 28.
69. See Chap. 3, *supra.*
70. The saving of a life is more important than, and hence ousts, the duty to observe the Sabbath or festival: B Shabbat 132a; B Yoma 85a-b.
71. Strauss, *op. cit.*, p. 126.
72. And cf. Matt. 24:2; Mark 13:2; Luke 21:6.
73. The biblical injunction, "Thou shalt inquire, and make search, and ask diligently" (Deut. 13:14), was literally interpreted to require witnesses to be subjected to three different kinds of examination: inquiry (*Hakirah*), search (*Derishah*), and interrogation (*Bedikah*): B Sanhedrin 40a. The rule applied in criminal and in civil cases alike (M Sanhedrin IV 1). *Hakirah* is the examination relating to the time and place at which the event in issue has occurred (M Sanhedrin V 1; B Sanhedrin 40b); *Derishah* is the examination relating to the substance of the facts in issue: who did it, what did he do, how did he do it, did you warn him beforehand, etc. (M Sanhedrin V 1; B Sanhedrin 40b); and *Bedikah* is a sort of cross-examination relating to accompanying and surrounding circumstances and not directly touching upon the facts in issue; and the more the court indulges in cross-examinations of this kind, the better (M Sanhedrin V 2). Any inconsistency or contradiction in the testimonies of the several witnesses, insofar as they related to matters directly touching upon the facts in issue, that is, inconsistencies or contradictions arising in the course of either *Hakirah* or *Derishah*, rendered the evidence of them all inadmissible (B Sanhedrin 30b). Thus witnesses found "not consistent," or whose evidence "agreed not together," could prove nothing, however

credible each of them might personally appear to be; but if they were "consistent" and "agreed together," their evidence had to be accepted and acted upon, provided they were competent witnesses (that is, not disqualified by reason of any personal interest or moral turpitude), however doubtful the recollection of any of them might appear to be (B Sanhedrin 41a).

74. A judge who suspected a witness of being untruthful, notwithstanding the failure of cross-examination to yield any contradictions or inconsistencies, was advised to disqualify himself and let another judge take his place (B Shevu'ot 31a; B Sanhedrin 32b).

75. See notes 14 and 15, *supra.*

76. Mommsen, *op. cit.,* pp. 437–438.

77. To a similar effect: Schalit, *op. cit.,* p. 93.

78. Lietzmann, *Der Prozess Jesu,* p. 6.

79. The divine descent of Jesus is, of course, already mentioned in the Gospels (Matt. 1:20; Luke 1:35; *et al.*), but was laid down as a binding dogma as late as 325 at the Council of Nicaea. See Bainton, *Early Christianity,* p. 166.

80. E.g., Fritz Bauer, Der Prozess Jesu, p. 1716.

81. As to the dicta of Jesus alleged in John 10:30–31, see Chap. 3, *supra.* The authors of the Gospels According to Luke and to John must have felt that it was, indeed, not conclusive enough for Jesus to claim only that he would sit on the right hand of power and come in the clouds of heaven; so Luke puts into his mouth, in reply to an explicit question, "Art thou then the Son of God?," an explicit statement, "Ye say that I am" (22:70); while John lets "the Jews" allege that "he made himself the son of God" (19:7) — which, for the readers of John, was, of course, nothing new. The admission put by Luke into the mouth of Jesus, at the crucial moment of the proceedings against him, must—if only by reason of its isolation—be regarded as a later in erpolation.

Aicher, *Der Prozess Jesu,* pp. 58–75, even interprets Jesus' reply to the high priest as a denial, negativing any messianic pretenses.

82. Exod. 28:41; Lev. 8:12; 16:32; Num. 3:3; *et al.*

83. Judg. 9:15; I Sam. 9:16; 10:1; 15:1; 16:12; II Sam. 2:4; 3:39; II Kings 11:12; Ps. 99:21; *et al.*

84. I Kings 19:17; Isa. 61:1; *et al.*

85. Gen. 31:13; Exod. 30:26–29; Num. 7:1; *et al.*

86. See Goguel, *op. cit.,* Vol. II, pp. 574–575.

87. Dalman, *The Words of Jesus,* pp. 234 ff., 250.

88. *Ibid.,* pp. 252–253.

89. *Ibid.,* p. 265.

90. B Hagigah 14a; B Sanhedrin 38b; and see Baer, *op. cit.,* p. 142.

91. Goguel, *op. cit.,* Vol. II, p. 509, writes that this messianic declaration of Jesus is "absolutely authentic. It cannot have been invented either by Jews or by Christians. The former would have been the last to place in the mouth of Jesus words which would justify the

claims made by his disciples. The latter, if they had wished to express their faith in a declaration attributed to their master, would not have simply affirmed their expectation of the *parousia,* but would also have expressed their faith in the certainty of the resurrection, which was its guarantee." In a rather more cautious tone, Klausner, *Jesus von Nazareth,* p. 474, says that Jesus' messianic declaration is "not at all impossible." At the other end of the line stands Craveri, *op. cit.,* p. 383, who writes that "it is impossible that Jesus himself would have so announced his own glorification at the right hand of Yahweh and his coming in the clouds of heaven."

92. Bickermann, quoted by Winter, *op. cit.,* p. 25, contends that the word *blasphemia* in Mark 14:64 "does not carry the meaning of 'blasphemy' in the technical sense of Jewish law, but was used by our writer in the sense of énormité, outrage, gross impropriety." This interpretation seems to find support in Luke 22:65, where the word "blasphemously" occurs in the meaning of impertinently or aggressively.

93. M Sanhedrin VII 5: "The courtroom is cleared of the public, and then the first witness is asked what exactly he has heard, and when he has repeated it, all the judges stand up and rend their garments; and then the second witness says, I have heard the same, and the third says, I have heard the same."

94. There is no support whatever for the view of Stauffer, *Jesus—Gestalt und Geschichte,* p. 94, that all the members of the Sanhedrin present did, as "a matter of course," as the high priest did, and rent their garments.

95. See note 33, *supra,* and text.

96. Strack and Billerbeck, *op. cit.,* Vol. I, p. 1018; Eduard Meyer, *op. cit.,* Vol. II, p. 20; Wellhausen, *Das Evangelium Marci,* p. 132; *et al.*

97. The appellation "Power" (*Gevurah*) for God occurs many times in the Talmud: e.g., B Shabbat 88b; B Makkot 24a; B Babba Metzia 58b; B Yevamot 72b and 105b.

98. Stauffer, *Jesus—Gestalt und Geschichte,* p. 94, writes as follows: "*Ani Hu* is the holiest formula of theophany, originating in Isaiah 43:10, and playing a great role in the liturgy of Jewish festivals. For having used it in respect of himself at the Feast of Tabernacles, Jesus was to be stoned (John 8:58); he had repeated it only a short while before at the Passover table (John 13:19). And now he takes this taboo-like formula of revelation again into his mouth, not just in the circle of his disciples, but before the highest religious tribunal of his people. Kaiaphas perceives at once the enormous claim inherent in this I-formula . . ." (my translation from the German). But according to John 8:58, what is said to have enraged the people was not Jesus' saying that he was, but his saying that he was before Abraham was. And his saying to his disciples, "Ye may believe that I am he" (John 13:19), may refer to his messianic

vocation and to his mastership and need not at all refer to his divinity. Be that as it may, the *Ani Hu* (I am he) is no part at all of Jewish theophany, and never has been; and any-liturgical use made of this combination of personal pronouns was entirely fortuitous and had no particular sacrosanctity attached to it.

For further material and elaborations on *"Ani Hu,"* see Strack and Billerbeck, *op. cit.,* Vol. II, p. 797; and Dodd, *The Interpretation of the Fourth Gospel,* pp. 93–96.

99. See Chap. 3 (at note 42).
100. Finkelstein, *Akiba—Scholar, Saint, and Martyr,* pp. 9–10.
101. Blinzler, *Der Prozess Jesu,* p. 101; Jost, *Geschichte des Judentums und seiner Sekten,* Vol. I, p. 408.
102. For examples of contradictory views being recognized as the words of the One Living God, see also B Eruvin 13b; B Gittin 6b.
103. For biblical examples, see Gen. 37:29, 34; Num. 14:6; Josh. 7:6; Judg. 11:35; II Sam. 1:11; 3:31; I Kings 21:27; Job 1:20; 2:12; Esther 4:1; *et al.*
104. B Mo'ed Kattan 26a.
105. As distinguished from the rule in M Sanhedrin VII 5: see note 93, *supra.*
106. Husband, *op. cit.,* p. 201.
107. B Sanhedrin 45a. The *ratio legis* appears to be that so long as your neighbor lives an active life, your love for him will naturally be based on an expectation of mutuality, and hence not be devoid of utilitarian motivation; it is only the "neighbor" who has been convicted of a capital offense and is about to be executed for whom your love will be entirely unselfish, and hence pure obedience to God's command.
108. B Sanhedrin 58b.
109. Schalit, *op. cit.,* p. 91, regards even the Marcan text as indicating not a formal condemnation but rather an informal exclamation. Dalman, quoted by Winter, *op. cit.,* p. 165, n. 24, regards the words "guilty of death" as an inaccurate rendering of the Hebrew formula *"hayav mitat beth din,"* meaning "liable to capital punishment" (cf. J Yevamot 6b; B Ketubot 36a; B Sanhedrin 55a and 73a–b; *et al.*) ; the "condemnation" would then be an exclamation of what may be in future in store for Jesus, rather than "the formal passing of a death sentence" (Winter, *op. cit.,* p. 27).

According to Brandon, *The Trial of Jesus of Nazareth,* p. 188, n. 58, "it seems more likely that Mark was concerned to show that the Sanhedrin had really condemned Jesus to death."
110. Winter, "The Trial of Jesus," in *Trivium* (1967), p. 143, and in *The Tablet* (1961), p. 519.
111. See, e.g., Baer, *op. cit.,* p. 139.
112. Isaak Heinemann, *Philos juedische und griechische Bildung,* pp. 211, 534.

113. *Epistulae* X 96. And see Winter, "Tacitus and Pliny: The Early Christians," pp. 36 ff.

114. Mommsen, *op. cit.,* p. 404, n. 4, and p. 147, n. 3; Codex Theodosius IX 3,1.

115. Noerr, *op. cit.,* p. 104.

116. Mommsen, *op. cit.,* pp. 938–939.

117. Stauffer, *Jesus—Gestalt und Geschichte,* p. 95.

118. B Sanhedrin 88b.

119. B Sanhedrin 46b.

120. In the view of Brandon, *The Trial of Jesus of Nazareth,* p. 92, the fact that the Sanhedrin did not execute Jesus by stoning, nor ask the Roman governor for the confirmation of its sentence, proves that there could not have been any formal trial before the Sanhedrin.

121. In a recent article, Horvath (*op. cit.,* pp. 182–184) propounds the theory that the Sanhedrin decided to deliver Jesus unto Pilate, not after trial and condemnation, but in order to give him the ultimate opportunity to establish his messianic claims. As we have seen (Chap. 3, at note 42) , the men of that age would always ask for "signs" before accepting any pretender to divine inspiration; and the one conclusive proof of true messiahship would lie in the supremacy over the Roman governor: if, indeed, Jesus was the Messiah, then his confrontation with the governor would result in his victory and the governor's defeat; if, on the other hand, Jesus would be sentenced and executed, then it would have been established that he could not be the true Messiah. This very ingenuous theory takes, I am afraid, no account of uncontrovertible psychological data: as I have tried to show, the Jewish authorities of that time never would or could have delivered a Jew into the hands of the Romans, least of all for experimental (or ordeal) purposes. Furthermore, there is no record of any "sign" ever having been chosen by the questioner and superimposed upon the pretender: "signs" are always asked from Heaven, or from the pretender himself, to be chosen by them at their discretion. No pretender to messiahship (and there were many of them) was ever subjected to an ordeal of a Roman trial so that his divine mission might be proven; and there is nothing to show why Jesus should have been subjected to any such ordeal. (For similar theories of Kamelsky, see note 45 to Chap. 3, *supra,* and of de Vries, see Chap. 6, at note 42, *infra.*)

The theory presented in this book is dismissed by Horvath (*ibid.,* p. 181) for two reasons, namely, that no real rebel would give up a fight, and no religious man would accept unjust accusation and die for it; and that, if Jesus was as popular as all that, "it is hard to believe that there was no one in the whole of Jerusalem who would have witnessed in favor of him, especially if it was known that the leaders themselves wanted to save him from the Romans." Jesus had, of course, his reasons for not putting up a fight, and these reasons held good in a Roman-initiated trial no less than in any Jewish-initiated ordeal: if Jesus' acquiescence in his fate provides an argument against my theory, it must provide the same argument against Horvath's theory—but it does not, in fact, provide any argument at all, because the attitude of Jesus, as it eventually transpired, could not have been taken into account beforehand when the decision on the course to be taken was made. My theory starts from the premise that the decision was taken in the hope and expectation that the attitude of Jesus would be one of cooperation and of readiness "to put up a fight," and that the attitude of Jesus, as it actually came to pass, was a source of bitter disappointment and frustration. And as for the witnesses, I have tried to show that the number of witnesses available to testify for Jesus was virtually unlimited; that such witnesses as testified to dicta of Jesus from which any rebellious intent or zealot activity could possibly be inferred had been branded as false and inconsistent, so that their evidence had to be rejected; but that neither the availability of witnesses in his favor nor the elimination of witnesses against him could be of any use in view of Jesus' own insistence on his messiahship. The Sanhedrin was faced with the alternative either to accept Jesus as the Messiah and bow to his authority or to maintain its own authority and demand his loyalty and submission; and it is hardly surprising that it chose the latter course.

6. THE TRIAL

1. Goguel, *op. cit.*, Vol. II, p. 513.
2. Berger, *op. cit.*, *q.v.* "Praetorium," p. 648.
3. Mommsen, *op. cit.*, pp. 149, 362.
4. Entering the council chamber where a provincial governor held court was considered a grave offense: Novellae Theodosii 15,2,1. The *apparitores* were, it seems, clerks learned in the law and held permanent tenure, while their superiors were mostly politicians who held office for short terms; they were, therefore, largely dependent on the *apparitores* for legal and technical assistance when holding court (Berger, *op. cit.*, *q.v.* "Apparitores," p. 364) . When *apparitores* brought before their superiors for trial matters which ought not to have been brought before them, it was said that the apparitores wrongly entered the council chamber where court was to be held: Codex Theodosius II 1,8,3.
5. Berger, *op. cit.*, *q.v.* "Secretarium," p. 693. And cf. Ammianus Marcellinus XV 7,5; Symmachus, *Epistulae* X 23,4.
6. Codex Theodosius I 16,7: "lifting the velum," or chamber curtain, meant giving admittance to litigants; and *apparitores* who extorted bribes for lifting it were guilty of a crime. And see Mommsen, "Die Pilatus-Acten," pp. 201–202.

7. Berger, *op. cit., q.v.* "Imperium Merum," p. 494.

8. Amos, *History and Principles of the Civil Law of Rome,* p. 355; Schuerer, *op. cit.,* Vol. I, pp. 470–471, n. 85.

9. Codex Theodosius I 16,6 (Pharr trans., p. 28).

10. Codex Theodosius I 16,9 (Pharr trans., p. 29).

11. *Roemisches Strafrecht,* p. 359.

12. Schuerer, *op. cit.,* Vol. I, p. 457, n. 32.

13. *Ibid.,* p. 458.

14. See also Klausner, *Jesus von Nazareth,* p. 478; Goguel, *op. cit.,* Vol. II, p. 513; Guignebert, *op. cit.,* p. 555. The fact that excavations uncovered a thickly paved courtyard in the Tower of Antonia north of the temple has led some scholars to believe that the *praetorium* where Pilate held court was there (cf. John 19:13) and not in the palace: Craveri, *op. cit.,* pp. 384–385; Flusser, *Jesus,* pp. 125, 129.

15. Num. 19:14: "This is the law: when a man dies in a tent, all that come into the tent, and all that is in the tent, shall be unclean seven days." The "tent" includes any roofed edifice: B Berakhot 19b *et al.*

16. The touch of idols, and other implements of idolatry, renders a person impure; but while one may not sit in the shade of a place of idolatry, one does not become impure only by entering and sitting there: M Avodah Zarah III 8. A house built for the sole purpose of idolatry may not be entered, as distinguished from houses built for other purposes, even though idolatry may take place there: M Avodah Zarah III 7. The story is told of the famous Gamliel (who was a contemporary of Jesus) frequenting a bathing house in Acre which was dedicated to the goddess Aphrodite; when asked how he could do that, he replied, I did not go to her—she came to me; the bathing house was not a gift of worship to Aphrodite, but Aphrodite was a gift of beauty to the bathing house: M Avodah Zarah III 4.

    For a codification of the rules relating to impurity by idolatry, see Maimonides, Mishneh Torah, Hilkhot She'ar Avot Ha-Tum'ah, Chap. 6.

17. M Pessahim VII 4 and IX 4; B Pessahim 75b and 95b.

18. Cf. Maimonides, Mishneh Torah, Hilkhot Korban Pessah, 7,1: Single individuals who were impure on the first day of Passover shall keep the Passover on the fourteenth day of the next following month (Num. 9:9–12); but if the majority of the people, or any priests or any sacrificial implements, were impure, their impurity shall not affect Passover sacrifices and rituals on the appointed day, but impure and pure together shall offer the sacrifices and perform the ritual.

19. Cf. Eduard Meyer, *op. cit.,* Vol. I, p. 200; Michlin, quoted by Klausner, *Jesus von Nazareth,* p. 479, n. 81.

20. Josephus, *Wars,* 2,14,8.

21. See, for example, the English Official Secrets Act, 1920, Section 8. And compare the United Nations Draft Covenant of Civil and Political Rights (1966), Article 14 (1).
22. Blinzler, *Der Prozess Jesu*, p. 228.
23. MacRuer, *op. cit.*, p. 96.
24. See Chap. 2, *supra*.
25. Lea, *The Inquisition of the Middle Ages*, pp. 250 ff.; Coulton, *Inquisition and Liberty*, pp. 168 ff.
26. Cf. Corpus Juris Canonici, 984,5.
27. B Sanhedrin 48b.
28. Goguel, *op. cit.*, Vol. II, pp. 468, 523.
29. "Quod homines credere volunt, id facile credunt."
30. To a similar effect: Kautsky, *op. cit.*, p. 426; Winter, *On the Trial of Jesus*, p. 57; *et al.*
31. Marcianus, Digesta, 48,8,1.
32. Mommsen, *op. cit.*, p. 632.
33. Digesta, 48,11; Codex Justinianus IX 27.
34. Berger, *op. cit.*, *q.v.* "Lex Julia Repetundarum," pp. 555; Mommsen, *op. cit.*, pp. 921–922.
35. For examples, see Mommsen, *op. cit.*, p. 634, n. 2.
36. Blinzler, *Der Prozess Jesu*, p. 228. See note 22, *supra*.
37. Codex Justinianus IX 47,12.
38. Mommsen, *op. cit.*, pp. 41 ff.
39. See note 36, *supra*.
40. Koch, *op. cit.*, p. 147. And see note 120 to Chap. 5, *supra*.
41. Brandon, *Jesus and the Zealots*, p. 177.
42. De Vries, *De Dood van Jesus van Nazareth*. The quotations are from letters of the author to myself.
43. See text over notes 60 ff. in Chap. 5, *supra*.
44. E.g., Jost, *op. cit.*, Vol. I, p. 408.
45. Winter, *op. cit.*, p. 57.
46. See note 37, *supra*.
47. Eduard Meyer, *op. cit.*, Vol. I, p. 195, n. 2.
48. Flusser, "Mishpat Yeshu," p. 117, and *Jesus*, p. 125.
49. Cullman, *op. cit.*, pp. 29, 34; Carmichael, *op. cit.*, pp. 131, 164.
50. Brandon, *Jesus and the Zealots*, p. 262.
51. De Vries, *loc. cit.* in note 42, *supra*.
52. Brandon, *Jesus and the Zealots*, p. 259.
53. Winter, *op. cit.*, p. 94.
54. M Pessahim VIII 6.
55. Flusser, "Mishpat Yeshu," p. 117, n. 41; Stauffer, *Jerusalem und Rom im Zeitalter Jesu Christi*, p. 110.
56. B Pessahim 91a.
57. M Mo'ed Kattan III 1–2: prisoners released during the week of the feast may have their hair cut and beard shaved and laundry washed —though all this is forbidden during that week to other people (so as to have them attend to it before the feast).

58. Codex Theodosius IX, 38,3 (Pharr trans., p. 253).
59. Codex Theodosius IX 38,4 (Pharr trans., p. 253).
60. Codex Theodosius IX 38,8 (Pharr trans., p. 254).
61. Schweppe, *Roemische Rechtsgeschichte*, p. 562.
62. Digesta, 48,8,4. And see Mommsen, *op. cit.*, p. 558.
63. Schuerer, *op. cit.*, Vol. I, p. 469.
64. Cf. Brandon, *Jesus and the Zealots*, p. 263; Goguel, *op. cit.*, Vol. II, p. 250; Klausner, *Jesus von Nazareth*, p. 481; Winter, *op. cit.*, p. 95; Craveri, *op. cit.*, pp. 389–390; *et al.*
65. See Chap. 1, *supra*.
66. Brandon, *Jesus and the Zealots*, pp. 261–262. At another place at the beginning of his book, Brandon puts the matter thus: "The crowd, prompted by the chief priests, ask for Barabbas and demand the crucifixion of Jesus. The account of the incident thus greatly magnifies the culpability of the Jews, both leaders and people, for the death of Jesus—they are depicted as preferring a bloodstained revolutionary to Jesus, whom they condemn innocently to bear the penalty that Barabbas justly deserved. But, to obtain this effect, Mark presents Pilate, a Roman governor, not only as criminally weak in his failure to do justice, but as a fool beyond belief. For, if he had truly sought to save Jesus, he could surely have done nothing worse to defeat his purpose than to offer the Jewish crowd a choice between Jesus and Barabbas. To them Barabbas was a patriot who had risked his life against their hated Roman rulers, whereas Jesus, according to Mark, had advised them to pay tribute to these Romans. To have offered the people such a choice, with the intention of saving Jesus, was the act of an idiot. The result was a foregone conclusion: inevitably Barabbas was preferred" (*ibid.*, pp. 3–4).
67. Suetonius, *Domitianus*, 10,1. And see Winter, *op. cit.*, p. 109; Goguel, *op. cit.*, Vol. II, p. 521, n. 2. In Greece, judgments passed against traitors and apostates were, by way of aggravation of the punishment, inscribed on stone pillars for all to see: Lipsius, *Das Attische Recht und Rechtsverfahren*, Vol. III, p. 942.
68. Suetonius, *Caius Caligula*, 32.
69. Eusebius, *Historia Ecclesiae*, V 1,44.
70. Berger, *op. cit., q.v.* "Crimen Maiestatis," p. 418.
71. Digesta, 48,4, 1 and 11.
72. Suetonius, *Domitianus*, 10,3.
73. Tacitus, *Annales*, 3,38.
74. *Ibid.*, 3,24.
75. Codex Theodosius IX, 5,1.
76. Ammianus Marcellinus, 28,1,11 and 31,14,5.
77. Mommsen, *op. cit.*, p. 542.
78. *Ibid.*, p. 557.
79. *Ibid.*
80. *Ulpian*, 1,18,6,8: qui provincias regunt, ius gladii habent.

81. Mommsen, *op. cit.*, p. 244,n. 3.
82. *Digesta*, 1,16,6; 1,21,1; 50,17,70.
83. Cf. Dio Cassius, 53,14.
84. Hunter, *Introduction to Roman Law*, pp. 58–59; Mommsen, *op. cit.*, pp. 423 ff., Berger, *op. cit.*, *q.v.* "Ampliatio," p. 361.
85. Mommsen, *op. cit.*, p. 406; Blinzler, *Der Prozess Jesu*, p. 237.
86. Mommsen, *op. cit.*, p. 437.
87. E.g., Goguel, *op. cit.*, Vol. II, p. 514.
88. E.g., Koch, *op. cit.*, p. 101.
89. E.g., Klausner, *Jesus von Nazareth*, p. 479. That Jesus' answer was not premeditated but given on the spur of the moment might perhaps appear from the advice which Jesus is said to have given his disciples: "When they deliver you up, take no thought how or what ye shall speak, for it shall be given you in that same hour what ye shall speak" (Matt. 10:19) ; "When they shall lead you and deliver you up, take no thought beforehand what ye shall speak, neither do ye premeditate, but whatsoever shall be given you in that hour, that speak ye, for it is not ye that speak, but the Holy Ghost" (Mark 13:11). If that was indeed Jesus' prescription it may well be that his "Thou sayest it" was what occurred to him at the moment, and that he said it without any preconceived intent. Even so, he would not have disavowed the meaning which his words would have conveyed.
90. For examples, see J Kilayim IX 4; T Keilim I 1 and 6; B Ketubot 104a. Dodd, *Historical Tradition in the Fourth Gospel*, p. 99, who says that he has not found sufficient support for this proposition in actual examples, then proceeds to prove the contrary meaning of "thou sayest it" by a quotation from one of Sir Walter Scott's novels.
91. Cf. Powell, *op. cit.*, p. 115.
92. Cf. Gesta Senatus Urbis Romae, A.D. 438, para. 2 (to be found in English trans. in Pharr [ed.], *The Theodosian Code*, p. 3).
93. Mommsen, *op. cit.*, pp. 769–771.
94. Tacitus, *Annales*, 2,50: si qua de Augusto irreligiose dixisset.
95. Paulus, 5,29,1: Verba impia.
96. Cicero, *De Legibus*, 2,8,19 and 2,10,25: non iudex sed deus ipse vindex erit.
97. Powell, *op. cit.*, p. 123.
98. Strauss, *op. cit.*, p. 132 (my translation from the German).
99. See Chap. 10 *infra*.
100. Dibelius, "Herodes und Pilatus," pp. 113–126; Lietzmann, "Der Prozess Jesu," p. 4; Eduard Meyer, *op. cit.*, Vol. I, pp. 201–202; Strauss, *op. cit.*, p. 133; Goguel, *op. cit.*, Vol. II, p. 515, n. 1; Guignebert, *op. cit.*, pp. 571–572; Brandon, *Jesus and the Zealots*, p. 317, n. 5 (but cf. Brandon, *The Trial of Jesus of Nazareth*, pp. 120–124 and 195, n. 107, where the question of historicity is left

open) ; Craveri, *op. cit.*, p. 386; Klein and Winter, *Zum Prozess Jesu*, pp. 30 and 32.

101. See note 82 and text, *supra*.
102. Cf. Buechsel, "Zur Blutgerichtsbarkeit des Synedrions," pp. 87, 206.
103. Josephus, *Antiquities*, 18,2,3 and 18,4,5.
104. Koch, *op. cit.*, pp. 133–134.
105. Cf. Blinzler, *Der Prozess Jesu*, p. 249.
106. Winter, in *Jewish Quarterly*, at p. 34; Flusser, *Jesus*, p. 126.
107. Blinzler, *Der Prozess Jesu*, p. 253.
108. Goguel, *op. cit.*, Vol. II, p. 521.
109. Thus: Vogt, "Augustus und Tiberius," at p. 11. Craveri, *op. cit.*, p. 392, writes that "one very cogent reason to doubt that the trial before Pilate ever took place is the utter lack of any report of it by him in the imperial archives in Rome, though an event of this kind would have required him to make one, and of any reference to it by later historians. The Christians have tried to fill the gap with a forgery: it was easily proved that the so-called Acts of Pilate (*Acta Pilati*) was an apocryphal document of the fourth century A.D." For the *Acta Pilati*, see Goguel, *op. cit.*, Vol. I, pp. 99–104, and Chap. 11, *infra*.

7 . THE SCOURGING

1. Mommsen, *op. cit.*, p. 938. And see Titus Livius, 34,26; Josephus, *Wars*, 2,14,9 and 5,11,1; *et al.*
2. Klausner, *Jesus von Nazareth*, p. 486; Brandon, *The Trial of Jesus of Nazareth*, p. 191, n. 124; Goguel, *op. cit.*, Vol. II, p. 527; Winter, *Zum Prozess Jesu* (ed. Koch) , p. 38; *et al.*
3. Koch, *op. cit.*, pp. 154–156; Blinzler, *Der Prozess Jesu*, pp. 242–243.
4. Strauss, *op. cit.*, p. 133; Olmstead, *op. cit.*, pp. 235–236.
5. Husband, *op. cit.*, p. 268.
6. Blinzler, *Der Prozess Jesu*, p. 238, and *Zum Prozess Jesu*, p. 39.
7. Goguel, *op. cit.*, Vol. II, p. 527.
8. Mommsen, *op. cit.*, p. 407; Wenger, *Quellen des roemischen Rechts*, p. 288.
9. Digesta, 48,18,15 and 22,5,21.
10. Cf. Codex Theodosius IX 35.
11. Berger, *op. cit.*, *q.v.* "Tormentum," p. 738.
12. Mommsen, *op. cit.*, pp. 47, 983. The view apparently taken by Blinzler, *Der Prozess Jesu*, p. 287, that the *fustuarium* constituted the penalty of flogging, is erroneous: *fustuarium* was a mode of execution in which death was caused by continuous flogging. See Berger, *op. cit.*, *q.v.* "Fustuarium Supplicium," p. 481. The theory was also propounded that Jesus was actually executed by *fustuarium*,

that is, his death was caused by the flagellations which he suffered on the cross: see Radin, *op. cit.,* pp. 255 ff.

13. Justin Martyr, quoted by Eusebius, *Historia Ecclesiae,* IV 17,6.
14. *Epistulae* X 96. English trans. by Winter, "Tacitus and Pliny: The Early Christians," at pp. 36–37.
15. Tertullian, *Apologeticus,* 2.
16. Plinius, *Epistulae,* X 96 (trans. by Winter, "Tacitus and Pliny," at p. 40).
17. Winter, "Tacitus and Pliny," p. 37.
18. Ernst Meyer, *Roemischer Staat und Staatsgedanke,* pp. 404 ff.
19. Mommsen, *op. cit.,* pp. 406–407.
20. The mode of torture most commonly employed was the *eculeius* (also spelled *equuleius*), a wooden horse to which the head and hands of the man were bound with ropes *(fidiculis)* on the one side and his feet on the other; the horse was then raised from the ground, with the man hanging thereon; and then screws *(cochleae)* were applied to all parts of his body, until joints and bones were dislocated and started from their sockets *(ut ossium compago resolveretur)*. If it was desired to aggravate and prolong the torture, plates of glowing metal were then laid on the skin *(laminae candentes)*, or boiling pitch was poured over the body, and were taken down after such degrees of burning had been attained as were short of fatal. See: Seneca, *Epistulae,* 8; Adam, *op. cit.,* Vol. I, p. 471; Schweppe, *op. cit.,* p. 554; Scott, *History of Torture Throughout the Ages,* pp. 169 ff. Some emperors excelled in devising ever new and ever crueler methods of torture of their own: see Suetonius, *Tiberius,* 62; *Caligula,* 32–33; *Domitianus,* 10; *Claudius,* 34; *Nero,* 37–38.
21. Scott, *op. cit.,* pp. 169 ff.
22. Codex Theodosius VIII 1,4.
23. Codex Theodosius XIV 7,6.
24. Codex Theodosius IX 16,6: "If he should be convicted of his crime, and by denial should oppose those who reveal it, he shall be delivered to the torture horse, iron claws shall tear his sides, and he shall suffer punishment worthy of his crime" (Pharr trans., p. 238).
25. The scourging accompanying capital punishment was not uniform. In cases of execution other than by crucifixion, the convict was flagellated on all parts of his body, both on the way to and after having arrived at the place of execution; there was originally a difference in the treatment meted out to convicts between slaves and free-born, for slaves were scourged with leather whips *(flagellae)* and free citizens with rods or clubs *(virga* or *fustis)*, but these differences seem to have later disappeared, and natives in the provinces overseas were anyway treated like slaves. In cases of crucifixion, however, the scourging was particularly elaborate: the convict was first undressed, then his head was covered, then a forked instrument with two prongs *(furca)* was placed on his back and his two hands bound to it, each hand to one of the prongs—and thus the convict

had to drag the *furca* to the place of crucifixion; once arrived there, he was flaggellated while remaining bound to the *furca*. A milder form of castigation was for the convict to carry his own gallows to the place of execution: the vertical stake of the cross was a permanent fixture, or already installed beforehand for each particular execution, while the transverse bar (*patibulum*) was loaded on the back of the convict, for him to drag to the place of execution; in some instances he was already bound or nailed to the *patibulum* on his way there, in others he was allowed to carry the *patibulum* freely on his back and would be bound or nailed to it only there.

See: Mommsen, *op. cit.,* pp. 919, 983; Hentig, *Die Strafe,* Vol. I, p. 254; Scott, *op. cit.,* pp. 169 ff.; Berger, *op. cit., q.v.* "Castigatio," p. 382; Seneca, *Ad Marciam,* 20,3; *Lactantius,* 6,17,28; Plutarchus, *De Sera Numinis Vindicta,* 9; Plautus, *Miles Gloriosus,* 359.

26. Not unlike the popular executions under biblical law; see Lev. 24:16; Num. 15:35; Deut. 17:7; 21:21; 22:21.

27. Particulars in note 25, *supra.*

28. This is the view of Blinzler, *Der Prozess Jesu,* p. 239.

29. This is the view of Klausner, *Jesus von Nazareth,* p. 487.

30. Goguel, *op. cit.,* Vol. II, p. 527.

31. Koch, *op. cit.,* p. 154.

32. Keim, *op. cit.,* p. 334.

33. Olmstead, *op. cit.,* p. 235, identifies the scourging reported in John 19:1 with the mockery reported in Mark 15:16–19 and Matt. 27:27–30, observing that "the brutal Roman soldiery" imitated their commander, "and their mockery was not so much at the expense of the innocent victim as that of the hierarchy," whom Pilate had "deliberately insulted." If this were so, it would indeed follow that the scourging was trifling—the soldiers would hardly beat the poor victim only to displease the hierarchy, the less so since any such beating could only please the hierarchy as depicted. The better view seems to be that propounded by Craveri, *op. cit.,* at p. 388, namely that the whole account of the Roman soldiers' brutality was perhaps "inserted into the New Testament only in order to meet this need of making the life of Jesus conform to the Old Testament's Messianic prophecies"—"the catalogue of these outrages ascribed to the Roman soldiery" repeating almost verbatim passages like Isaiah 50:6 or Micah 5:1; and "one begins to suspect that the entire episode is a sheer invention." For the adaptation of the Passion story to messianic prophecies in the Bible, see also Chap. 8, *infra.*

34. Stauffer, *Jesus—Gestalt und Geschichte,* p. 160, n. 47, writes that the scourging of Jesus was not (or not only?) carried out by Roman soldiers, but by "levite police," and that it constituted the flogging to which under Jewish law (M Makkot III 15) the blasphemer is liable who had not pronounced the sacred Name (Lev. 24:15), or to which Jesus may have become liable for some other offense. For this purpose, Stauffer writes, the convict is bound to a pillar, and

pilgrims from Bordeaux in the year 333 saw the pillar in the palace of Kaiaphas in Jerusalem to which Jesus had been bound for scourging. The legend of this pillar (or any such "pillars of shame") has long been conclusively refuted: see Blinzler, *Der Prozess Jesu,* p. 240. And as for a flogging under Jewish law, if it had indeed been administered, Jesus would then have been discharged, in the same way in which Peter and the apostles were upon having been flogged (Acts 5:40), and would not have been delivered to Pilate for any further punishment.

35. See note 25, *supra.*
36. See note 25, *supra.*
37. Goguel, *op. cit.,* Vol. II, p. 530.
38. Solomon Reinach, quoted by Goguel, *ibid.*
39. Craveri, *op. cit.,* p. 395; Lietzmann, *History of the Early Church,* Vol. I, p. 284; Keim, *op. cit.,* p. 337.
40. Lietzmann, *op. cit.,* p. 280; Goguel, *op. cit.,* Vol. II, p. 531.
41. Strauss, *op. cit.,* p. 135.
42. *Ibid.*
43. Eduard Meyer, *op. cit.,* Vol. I, p. 118.
44. Pessikta Rabbati 31; Midrash Bereshit Rabba 561; Midrash Seihel Tov *ad* Genesis 22,6 (ed. Buber, p. 61) ; *et al.*
45. Goguel, *op. cit.,* Vol. II, p. 532.

8. THE CRUCIFIXION

1. Thus most modern translations. See, for instance, *The New Testament in Today's English Version,* published by the American Bible Society, New York (2d ed., 1966), pp. 73, 126. And cf. Brandon, *Jesus and the Zealots,* p. 238, n. 3, and p. 351, n. 1.
2. *Ibid.*
3. Brandon, *op. cit.,* p. 351. And see Winter, *op. cit.,* p. 148.
4. Stauffer, *Jerusalem und Rom im Zeitalter Jesu Christi,* pp. 123, 125 ff.
5. By Winter, *op. cit.,* pp. 62 ff.
6. E.g., Targumim *ad* Genesis 40:19, 22; *ad* Deuteronomy 21:23; *ad* Joshua 8:29; 10:26; *ad* II Samuel 4:12; 21:12; *ad* Esther 2:23; 5:14; 7:10; 9:13.
7. The root *shelov* occurs in Exod. 26:17 ("boards set one against another") ; I Kings 7:28; J Ta'anit IV 7.
   That *shelov* is the true source of the Hebrew *tselov,* as distinguished from the Aramaic *tselov,* is submitted on the authority of Ben Yehuda, *Thesaurus Totius Hebraitatis,* Vol. XI, p. 5482.
8. Bezold, *Babylonisch-Assyrisches Glossar,* p. 106b.
9. *Zaqapu* and *Suqalulu: ibid.,* pp. 115a and 284b.

10. E.g., *Zaqaf* for "hang," and *Zaqifa* for "stake": B Babba Metzia 59b and 83b; B. Avodah Zarah 18b; B Megillah 16b.

11. Kittel, "Gekreuzigt Werden," p. 284.

12. B Sanhedrin 46b; Sifrei Devarim 221; Midrash Tanna'im, Devarim 21,22 (ed. Hoffmann, p. 132). The midrashic version is: "He is hanged alive in the way practiced by the government," while the talmudic version leaves out the word "alive."

13. E.g., Gaster, *The Dead Sea Scriptures,* p. 243; Dupont-Sommer, *The Essene Writings from Qumran* (English trans. by Vermes), p. 269.

14. "Affront to God" is the paraphrase used by the translators of the Bible for the Jewish Publication Society of America (Philadelphia, 1962, p. 364). The King James version is, "for he that is hanged is accursed of God," which is the more literal translation.

15. Josephus, *Antiquities,* 13,4,2; and *Wars,* 1,4,6.

16. I Macc. 7:15.

17. Buechler, "Die Todesstrafen der Bibel und der nachbiblischen Zeit," p. 703; Dupont-Sommer, *op. cit.,* p. 269, n. 2; Daniel-Rops, *op. cit.,* p. 177.

18. M Sanhedrin VII 1.

19. The King James version is inaccurate, rendering the words given in the text as "and he be to be put to death." The correct translation is in the past tense, not in the future.

20. B Sanhedrin 46b: proceedings in court are to be protracted until shortly before sunset, so that execution is to follow sentence immediately. And see note 118, p. 369, *supra.*

21. M Sanhedrin VI 4.

22. Stauffer, *Jerusalem und Rom im Zeitalter Jesu Christi,* p. 123.

23. Yonathan ben Uziel, Deut. 21:23.

24. M Sanhedrin VI 4; Sifrei Devarim 221. And cf. Gal. 3:13.

25. There is, however, a strong dissent to the effect that we have here an express biblical injunction to execute certain criminals (to wit, idolaters) by hanging them alive: Rav Hissda, in B Sanhedrin 34b. If this were the correct view, then Phinehas would, at any rate, have disobeyed the divine command, by taking a javelin and thrusting it through the bodies of the offenders (Num. 25:7–8), instead of hanging them, and he would hardly have deserved the praise that God showered on him for his valiant deed (25:11–13). Be that as it may, the fact that, by a legitimate and grammatical interpretation, there is to be found some biblical authority for hanging alive has led some scholars to assume that such hangings may have been known and practiced in ancient Israel; but so far no evidence whatever has come to light to support any such theory.

26. That the word *hoqa* stands for "hanging" was sought to be proved by the occurrence of the same word in II Sam. 21:9. The talmudic tradition is that the Gibeonites did hang the sons of Saul: B Sanhedrin 34b; but they may well have hanged their victims according

to their own laws and customs, and the fact that they did has no
bearing on the laws and customs of the Israelites.

27. See notes 3 and 22, *supra.*

28. Hentig, *op. cit.,* Vol. I, p. 254; Herodotus III, 125 and 159.

29. The exact dates of these translations are unknown: they appear to
be first mentioned and referred to in the eleventh century. For
particulars, see Zuntz, *Die gottesdienstlichen Vortraege der Juden,*
Chap. 5.

30. Midrash Ruth Rabba 1.

31. M Sanhedrin VII 3: strangulation is effected by two men (the two
witnesses) pulling ties wrapped around the convict's neck, each to
opposite sides, until suffocation ensues. See my "The Penology of
the Talmud," Chap. II.

32. It is to be observed, though, that there is no resemblance, in operation, between hanging and the mishnaic strangling described in the
previous note. The view has recently been proffered that, in substituting hanging for strangling, the translators relied on a pre-
mishnaic tradition: see Joseph Heinemann, "Targum Shemot
22,4 Vehahalakha Hakedumah," p. 296—a hypothesis which can be
neither proved nor disproved; but it is strange that a tradition of
such long standing should have left no trace or clue other than in
this late translation.

33. M Sanhedrin VI 4. And see note 44, p. 363.

34. J Hagigah II 8; Rashi (Shlomo Yitzhaki) *ad* Sanhedrin 44b.

35. Graetz, *op. cit.,* Vol. III, p. 152; Dubnow, *op. cit.,* Vol. II, p. 117;
et al.

36. M Sanhedrin VI 4; B Sanhedrin 46a.

37. It was the same Simon ben Shetah who acquitted a murderer
caught *in flagrante delicto* by one witness, only because there had
been no second witness present: B Sanhedrin 37b. In another case,
he ruled that circumstantial evidence, however strong and conclusive it may seem, as, e.g., finding a corpse and seeing a bloodstained man fleeing from the scene with a knife in his hand, was
never sufficient to support a conviction: *ibid.,* and B Shevu'ot 34a.
Where a court had convicted one of two false witnesses of perjury
and executed him without having tried and convicted the other, he
denounced the execution as judicial murder: T Sanhedrin VI
6. While insisting on careful and probing cross-examinations
of witnesses, he warned of pitfalls, lest the witness might, by con-
fusing questioning, be induced to lie: M Avot I 9. And it was
Simon ben Shetah who, presiding over the Sanhedrin, upheld the
dignity and power of the court even as against the king's majesty,
by successfully insisting that the king should appear and defend
himself in court against a claim brought against him: B Sanhedrin
19a.

38. Witches and sorcerers are liable to stoning: M Sanhedrin VII 4.

39. Maimonides, Commentary *ad* M Sanhedrin VI 6; Rashi (Shlomo Yitzhaki) *ad* B Sanhedrin 45b.
40. M Sanhedrin VII 11.
41. B Sanhedrin 67b.
42. Baron, *Social and Religious History of the Jews,* Vol. I, p. 211, writes that at that time "Jewish women, generally more illiterate and superstitious than men, were irresistibly attracted to the magic arts. The Talmud repeatedly speaks of 'the majority of women being witches' (J Sanhedrin VII 19 and 25, B Sanhedrin 67a) and says that the most pious of women is engaged in sorcery (Soferim 15). Official Judaism protested vainly. Not even Simon ben Shetah's fanatical execution of eighty women in Ascalon, evidently carried out with great difficulty because of Ascalon's independence, could stop a practice rooted in the conditions of the age."
43. Cf. Hansen, *Zauberwahn, Inquisition und Hexenprozess im Mittelalter,* p. 13.
44. M Sanhedrin IX 6. And see note 34, p. 362.
45. B Sanhedrin 8b and 80b. And see Allon, *Mehkarim Betoledot Yisrael,* Vol. I, p. 103.
46. B Sanhedrin 82a. And see note 25, p. 379.
47. *De Legibus Specialibus,* I 55.
48. Winter, *op. cit.,* pp. 74 ff., has put forward the theory that the particular mode of strangulation prescribed in the Mishna was contrived as a means of execution in secret: with the cessation of criminal jurisdiction in the year 70 (see note 43, p. 346), the Jewish courts in Roman-occupied Judaea exercised criminal jurisdiction clandestinely and had to avoid modes of execution which had to be carried out in public. "The methods formerly in use—burning, stoning, beheading—would have been a flagrant contravention of Imperial rule. Strangling and the similar procedure that went under the name of 'burning' provided convenient ways of escaping detection. Such was the reason why the rabbis, otherwise so meticulous in their compliance with the letter of the Torah, resorted to the expedient of execution by strangling, thereby bringing into their statute book a new form of inflicting capital punishment of which the Old Testament had known nothing" (Winter, *ibid.*). This theory presupposes that the cessation of criminal jurisdiction was the result of a Roman decree, and that the continuation of the exercise of such jurisdiction would have been contrary to Roman law; while under Jewish law nothing prevented the continuation of such jurisdiction. This is a misconception of both Roman and Jewish law: we have no information of any Roman decree to the effect that the criminal jurisdiction of local Jewish courts was to cease in the year 70; but, on the other hand, there is ample material in the Jewish sources to indicate that it was precisely under Jewish law that criminal jurisdiction ceased with, and because of, the destruction of the temple in that year: B Sanhedrin 52b; B

Ketubot 30a; *et al.* Apart from the emergency measures already mentioned, the Jewish courts would no longer impose capital punishment—not because any Roman decree forbade it, but because their competence under their own law had ceased; they had nothing to hide from the Romans, because they would not unlawfully assume any jurisdiction from which they had been ousted by the only law they recognized as binding upon them. And see my "The Penology of the Talmud," at p. 61.

49. For a detailed description of the consequences of crucifixion from the medical point of view, and the possible causes of death thereby induced, see Blinzler, *Der Prozess Jesu*, pp. 185 ff.

50. B Sanhedrin 43a. This charitable custom reported of the "dear women of Jerusalem" has grown into law: Maimonides ruled that, when being led to his execution, the convict is to be given a drink of wine with incense, so that he may get intoxicated and insensible —and only then is he to be executed (Mishneh Torah, Hilkhot Sanhedrin 13,2).

51. Justinus, 22,7.

52. Mommsen, *op. cit.,* p. 918.

53. Suetonius, *Claudius,* 34.

54. Mommsen, *op. cit.,* p. 919.

55. *Apologiae,* 1,35; *Dialogus,* 97,3.

56. Hentig, *op. cit.,* Vol. I, pp. 255–256.

57. This theory attracted such novelists as George Moore (*The Brook Kerith*) and D. H. Lawrence (*The Man Who Died*).

58. Schonfield, *op. cit.,* pp. 155 ff.

59. *Autobiography,* 75.

60. Since the blood of a living person is pure, but the blood of the dead is impure and may not be touched by anyone who must, for sacrificial or other ritual purposes, keep himself pure, the question arose as to when the blood of the convict on the cross becomes impure—the exact time of his death on the cross not always being readily ascertainable: M Ohalot III 5. Maimonides, in his Commentary *ad loc.,* maintains that death would normally result from the loss of the blood that is dripping from the man on the cross; but the dripping might continue even after death. The same rule is found in T Ohalot IV 10 without express reference to crucifixion; and the question may, indeed, arise not only in the case of a man dying on the cross, but also in cases of stoning or slaying and other executions or deaths entailing the loss of blood.

61. M Shabbat VI 10.

62. B Shabbat 67a.

63. J Shabbat VI 9.

64. Maimonides, Mishneh Torah, Hilkhot Shabbat 6,10.

65. Maimonides, Commentary *ad* M Shabbat VI 10.

66. Plinius, *Historia Naturalis,* 28,36.

67. Hentig, *op. cit.,* Vol. I, p. 257.

68. B Sanhedrin 46b. And see note 12, p. 379.
69. Josephus, *Antiquities*, 17,10,10; *Wars*, 2,5,2.
70. Josephus, *Antiquities*, 20,5,2.
71. Josephus, *Wars*, 2,12,6.
72. *Ibid.*, 2,13,2.
73. *Ibid.*, 2,14,9.
74. *Ibid.*, 5,11,1.
75. M Yevamot XVI 3.
76. J Yevamot XVI 3.
77. B Yevamot 120b. And see Maimonides, Mishneh Torah, Hilkhot Geirushin 13,18.
78. Hentig, *op. cit.*, Vol. I, p. 257, n. 1.
79. Rashi (Shlomo Yitzhaki) *ad* B Yevamot 120a.
80. Tossaffot *ad* Yevamot 120a (*q.v.* "Ve'ein Me'idin").
81. T Gittin VII 1; B Gittin 70b.
82. B Gittin 70b.
83. Strauss, *op. cit.*, pp. 136–137; Craveri, *op. cit.*, pp. 395 ff.
84. Paulus, 3,5,8 and 5,21,4.
85. Mommsen, *op. cit.*, p. 918.
86. *Ibid.*, pp. 918 ff.
87. *Annales*, 14,48.
88. Hentig, *op. cit.*, Vol. I, p. 254.
89. *In Verrem*, 5,64.
90. Goguel, *op. cit.*, Vol. II, p. 535.
91. *Ibid.*, p. 539.
92. Winter, *op. cit.*, p. 106.
93. Olmstead, *op. cit.*, p. 241, relying on John 19:35.
94. Goguel, *op. cit.*, Vol. II, p. 535.
95. Nicholas de Lyra (fourteenth century), quoted by Goguel, *ibid.*, p. 543: "Talis enim potatio aceti mortem accelerat, ut dicunt aliqui."
96. B Keritot 18b.
97. Renan, *op. cit.*, p. 439.
98. Strauss, *op. cit.*, p. 136; Klausner, *Jesus von Nazareth*, p. 490. In the words of Craveri (*op. cit.*, p. 396): "We may dismiss Matthew's statement that the wine was mixed with gall and vinegar. Once again the insistence on fulfilling a Biblical prophecy produced nonsense."
99. Cf. Jer. 7:33 and 16:4: "Their carcasses shall be meat for the fowls of heaven and for the beasts of the earth." Or Ps. 79:2: "The dead bodies of thy servants have they given to be meat unto the fowls of the heaven, the flesh of thy saints unto the beasts of the earth."
100. For a talmudic tradition that the "pierced" one is indeed the Messiah, see B Sukkah 52a.
101. Strauss, *op. cit.*, pp. 143–144.
102. Goguel, *op. cit.*, Vol. II, p. 462.
103. *Ibid.*, p. 545, n. 1.
104. Suetonius, *Augustus*, 67.

105. Suetonius, *Tiberius*, 44.
106. Firmicus Maternus, 8,6; Victor, *Caesares*, 41. For further sources see Mommsen, *op. cit.*, p. 920, n. 6.
107. Eusebius, *Historia Ecclesiae*, V 21.
108. Keim, *op. cit.*, p. 347.
109. A person condemned to death was stripped of what he had on himself before execution, and his executioner had the right to claim it as his property: see Berger, *op. cit.*, *q.v.* "Spolia," p. 712. Craveri (*op. cit.*, p. 398) writes that "the sharing out of his clothes among the soldiers on guard followed a Roman custom: the *lex de bonis damnatorum* required this division of the *spolia*." To the same effect, see Strauss, *op. cit.*, p. 136; Goguel, *op. cit.*, Vol. II, p. 536; *et al.*
110. E.g., Blinzler, *Der Prozess Jesu*, p. 52.
111. Schonfield, *op. cit.*, pp. 165 ff. and *passim*.
112. Digesta, 48,24,1; Tacitus, *Annales*, 6,29.
113. Cicero, *Pro Rabirio Perduellionis Reo*, 5,16; Hentig; *op. cit.*, Vol. I, p. 254.
114. Mommsen, *op. cit.*, p. 989.
115. Ulpian, Digesta, 48,24,1; Paulus, Digesta, 48,24,3.
116. *Wars*, 4,5,2.
117. M Sanhedrin VI 5.
118. Semahot II 7 and 11.
119. J Kilayim IX 4; J Terumot VIII 10; M Shabbat XXIII 4; M Sanhedrin VI 5.

9 . PETER AND PAUL

1. See Chap. 2, *supra*.
2. See Chap. 3, *supra*.
3. M Makkot III 15. And see note 34, p. 377, and note 33, p. 362.
4. Gamliel was *Nassee*, meaning president: B Shabbat 15a; B Sanhedrin 11a; T Sanhedrin II 5. His office was in the Hall of Hewn Stones, the seat of the Sanhedrin (see note 9, p. 357) : M Pei'ah II 6. And cf. Mantel, *op. cit.*, pp. 1-28.
5. Klausner, *From Jesus to Paul*, Vol. I, p. 266.
6. Josephus, *Antiquities*, 20,5,1.
7. Eduard Meyer, *op. cit.*, Vol. II, p. 404; Schuerer, *op. cit.*, Vol. I, p. 543.
8. Josephus, *Antiquities*, 20,5,2.
9. *Ibid.*, 18,1,1.
10. This appears to be the view of Eduard Meyer, *op. cit.*, Vol. II, p. 403.
11. Klausner, *From Jesus to Paul*, Vol. I, pp. 211-212, 264-266.
12. Brandon, *Jesus and the Zealots*, p. 101.

13. See Chap. 5, *supra*.
14. See note 34, p. 377.
15. See note 3, *supra*.
16. B Shabbat 88b.
17. M Sanhedrin VI 1: On the close of the proceedings, execution shall take place. And see Maimonides, Mishneh Torah, Hilkhot Sanhedrin 14,2: Any capital punishment prescribed by law is in the nature of a (divine) command upon the court to have any person found liable to undergo it duly executed.
18. Eduard Meyer, *op. cit.*, Vol. III, p. 226.
19. *Ibid.*, p. 227; Brandon, *Jesus and the Zealots*, pp. 167–168.
20. *Antiquities*, 20,9,1. According to Eusebius, *Historia Ecclesiae*, II 23, James was convicted for declaring that Jesus was the Son of God; but this is surely a later interpretation.
21. Eduard Meyer, *op. cit.*, Vol. III, p. 227, n. 2; Eusebius, *ibid.*, II 23–24 and 25,3.
22. Goguel, *op. cit.*, Vol. I, p. 105, n. 1.
23. Lietzmann, *History of the Early Church*, Vol. II, pp. 94 ff.
24. Various efforts made at adjusting the contradictory texts proved unsuccessful, as, for instance, the attempt to incorporate the four Gospels into one: *ibid.*, at p. 99.
25. Blinzler (in: *Zum Prozess Jesu*, pp. 50–51) takes the verse in I Thess. 2:15 as a clear indication of Jewish as distinguished from Roman responsibility: "So haette sich der Apostel und ehemalige Christenfeind nie und nimmer ausdruecken koennen, wenn er der Ansicht gewesen waere, dass Jesus einzig und allein auf Grund eines roemischen Urteils hingerichtet wurde. Wohl aber konnte er so schreiben, wenn er mit Markus und den anderen Evangelisten der Auffassung war, dass zuerst die juedischen Fuehrer ein Todesurteil gefaellt und dann von Pilatus die Verurteilung und Hinrichtung Jesu nach roemischem Recht erzwungen haben. Ich muss gestehen, dass es mir schon immer unverstaendlich war, wie man angesichts dieses aeltesten Zeugnisses ueber den Tod Jesu die evangelischen Berichte von der Synedrialverhandlung ueberhaupt ernsthaft hat in Zweifel ziehen koennen." For the reasons given in the text, I would submit that this Pauline utterance cannot be reasonably regarded as "evidence" (*Zeugnis*) at all, nor was it intended to constitute a statement of facts. For an interpretation of the term "Jews" in this context as godless people, not necessarily of Jewish descent, see Michel, "Fragen zu 1 Thessaloniker 2, 14–16: Antijuedische Polemik bei Paulus," pp. 53 ff.
26. Bachmann, *Der erste Brief an die Korinther*, p. 123.
27. Goguel, *op. cit.*, Vol. I, pp. 112–113.
28. Dibelius, *Die Geisterwelt im Glauben des Paulus*, pp. 89 ff.; Lietzmann, *An die Korinther*, pp. 11 ff.
29. The discharge from responsibility is almost explicit in Verse 8: "For had they known it, they would not have crucified the Lord of glory"

—whoever they were, they acted from ignorance and mistake rather than from enmity and malice. And see Isaac, *op. cit.*, p. 413.

30. To the same effect: Isaac, *op. cit.*, pp. 414–416.
31. Ehrlich, "Paulus und das Schuldproblem," pp. 45 ff.
32. Parkes, *op. cit.*, pp. 64 ff.; Thieme, *op. cit.*, pp. 52–59.

10. HIS BLOOD BE UPON US
AND OUR CHILDREN

1. Eusebius, *Historia Ecclesiae,* III 5,5.
2. *Wars,* 2,18,8.
3. Flannery, *The Anguish of the Jews,* p. 28.
4. Schelkle, "Die Selbstverfluchung Israels nach Matthaeus 27, 23–25," p. 149.
5. M Sanhedrin IV 5.
6. H. M. Cohn, "Sein Blut komme ueber uns," pp. 82 ff.
7. Bienert, *op. cit.*, p. 27.
8. Klausner, *Jesus von Nazareth*, p. 481; *et al.*
9. Bultmann, *Geschichte der synoptischen Tradition,* p. 305; Dibelius, *Formgeschichte des Evangeliums,* p. 137; Bienert, *op. cit.*, pp. 30–31; Isaac, *op. cit.*, pp. 410 ff.; Brandon, *The Trial of Jesus of Nazareth,* p. 115; Winter, *op. cit.*, pp. 55–56.
10. To the contrary effect: Blinzler, *Der Prozess Jesu,* pp. 230–232; Stauffer, *Jesus—Gestalt und Geschichte,* p. 101; Schelkle, *op. cit.*, p. 153; MacRuer, *op. cit.*, pp. 71–72; *et al.*
11. Maurer, in *New Testament Apocrypha* (ed. Wilson) , p. 179.
12. *New Testament Apocrypha* (ed. Wilson) , p. 183.
13. See Brandon, *Jesus and the Zealots,* p. 303, n. 2.
14. Bienert, *op. cit.*, pp. 23, 31.
15. *Contra Judaeos,* Cap. 8.
16. St. Augustine, Commentary to Psalm 50, and *Contra Faustus* 13,10; and in a letter written by Pope Innocent III, we read: "The Lord made Cain a wanderer and a fugitive over the earth, but set a mark upon him, making his head to shake, lest anyone finding him should slay him. Thus the Jews, against whom the blood of Jesus Christ calls out, although they ought not to be killed . . . yet as wanderers must they remain upon the earth, until their countenance be filled with shame and they seek the name of Jesus Christ, the Lord" (Flannery, *op. cit.*, p. 102) .
17. Sulpicius Severus (fourth century), quoted in Flannery, *op. cit.*, p. 51.
18. St. Augustine, *Contra Judaeos,* 15 (trans. by Flannery, *op. cit.*, p. 50) .
19. St. John Chrysostom (344–407), *Homilies against the Jews,* 6,2 (Flannery, *op. cit.*, pp. 47–49) .

20. *Ibid.*, 1, 4–6.
21. *Ibid.*, 7,1.
22. Isaac, *op. cit.*, p. 411, quotes a book by Abbé Louis Richard, entitled *Israel et la Foi Chrétienne,* in which the very pertinent question is put whether God actually chose those vehemently hostile elements which clamored before Pilate as the accredited representatives of His people—or, if God did not, who did?
23. Flannery, *op. cit.*, pp. 62–63, speaking not of "believers" but of "misguided men."
24. Schelkle, *op. cit.*, p. 155.

11. THE ACTS OF PILATE

1. Prologue to the Acts of Pilate. The translation of this and all following quotations in this chapter are taken from *New Testament Apocrypha* (ed. Wilson), pp. 449 ff. (F. Scheidweiler).
2. For the different views as to the dating of the Acts, see Scheidweiler, *ibid.*, p. 444.
3. Mommsen, *Die Pilatus-Acten*, p. 198.
4. Goguel, *op. cit.*, Vol. I, p. 158.
5. Von Dobschuetz, "Der Prozess Jesu nach den Acten Pilati," pp. 89 ff.
6. Mommsen, *Die Pilatus-Acten*, at p. 205.
7. Lev. 19:12: "Ye shall not swear by my name *falsely*"; Exod. 20:7: "Thou shalt not take the name of thy Lord *in vain*"; both indicating that taking a secular oath, not by the name of God, as well as swearing to the truth in a matter of substance, is perfectly lawful. Cf. Mekhilta Yitro 7.
8. B Sanhedrin 67a; B Shabbat 104b. And see Chap. 12, *infra.*
9. Mommsen, *Die Pilatus-Acten*, at p. 202.
10. Scheidweiler, *op. cit.*, at p. 458, n. 1.
11. See Chap. 10, *supra*, text over notes 3–6.
12. See note 10, *supra.*
13. See Chap. 10, *supra*, text over note 21.

12. NON-CHRISTIAN SOURCES

1. For a concise statement of the origin, compass, contents, and datings of talmudic and midrashic literature, see Strack, *Introduction to the Talmud and Midrash.*
2. Klausner, *Jesus von Nazareth*, pp. 18–54, maintains that the deficiency of the talmudic sources in this respect is not surprising. He points out that we would scarcely know anything about the Maccabean revolt, for instance, had we been restricted to accounts in the

Talmud for our information. According to Klausner, Jesus lived in that stormy period when attention was concentrated on other, more important, events, and thus passed through Jewish history almost unnoticed.

3. Baraitha (literally: the extraneous) is the generic name of teachings and dicta of the mishnaic period which were not included in the Mishna: see Strack, *op. cit.,* p. 4.
4. B Sanhedrin 43a.
5. Justin, *Dialogus cum Triphone Judaicus,* Chap. 69.
6. B Shabbat 104b; T Shabbat XI 15.
7. M Sanhedrin VII 10.
8. B Sanhedrin 67a.
9. M Sanhedrin VII 6.
10. Goguel, *op. cit.,* Vol. I, p. 72.
11. Buechler, "Die Todesstrafen der Bibel und der nachbiblischen Zeit," pp. 701–702.
12. M Sanhedrin VI 4.
13. Buechler, "Die Todesstrafen," pp. 701–702; Jost, *op. cit.,* Vol. I, p. 403, n. 1.
14. M Sanhedrin VI 1.
15. B Sanhedrin 46b.
16. R. Yehudah, in M Sanhedrin XI 4.
17. B Sanhedrin 89a.
18. Goguel, *op. cit.,* Vol. I, pp. 72–73.
19. B Sanhedrin 33b.
20. B Sanhedrin 67a.
21. M Sanhedrin VII 10.
22. Maimonides, Mishneh Torah, Hilkhot Sanhedrin 11,5.
23. B Sanhedrin 67a; B Shabbat 104b.
24. Kohut, *Arukh Hashalem,* Vol. II, p. 119.
25. T Sanhedrin X 11; J Sanhedrin VII 25.
26. Such identification is first traceable to R. Hisda (3d century): B Shabbat 104b, and is refuted already by medieval commentators: see Tossaffot *ad loc., q.v.* "Ben Stada."
27. Cf. M Avot I 6.
28. B Sotah 46a; B Sanhedrin 107b.
29. Most of the censored passages are reprinted in Rabbinowicz, *Dikdukei Sofrim,* and are here quoted from that work.
30. Strack, *op. cit.,* p. 78.
31. *Ibid.,* p. 274, n. 17.
32. Parkes, *op. cit.,* p. 110. And cf. T Sanhedrin XIII 5; B Shabbat 116a.
33. *Antiquities,* 18,3,3.
34. *Ibid.,* 20,9,1.
35. Brandon, *Jesus and the Zealots,* p. 361.
36. *Contra Celsum* 1, 47.
37. Walter Bauer, "The Works and Sufferings of Jesus," p. 436.

38. Goguel, *op. cit.*, Vol. I, pp. 78–81; Klausner, *Jesus von Nazareth,* pp. 55–56.
39. Thomas Reinach, "Josèphe sur Jésus," p. 13.
40. Schuerer, *op. cit.*, Vol. I, pp. 547 ff.; Winter, "Josephus on Jesus," *passim;* Zeitlin, "The Christ Passage in Josephus," *passim; et al.*

    Goguel, *op. cit.*, Vol. I, p. 82, writes that since Josephus "felt it impossible to mention Christianity shorn of its Messianic element, he preferred to be silent, in order that he might not expose Judaism to the accusation of a compromising connexion with a movement which was already hateful in the eyes of the ruling classes." In a note he adds (*ibid.*) that, for the same reason, Justus of Tiberias, author of a *Chronicle* and a *History of the Jewish War*, "written at the same time and in the same spirit as the works of Josephus, does not mention Jesus or Christianity either. So far as Philo is concerned, the fact that he makes no mention of the Gospel is sufficiently explained when we recall that most probably he died very soon after the year 40 of our era, and there is nothing to prove that Christianity had been taken to Alexandria before that date."
41. Brandon, *Jesus and the Zealots*, pp. 362–363; Eisler, *Iesus Basileus u Basileusas*, Vol. I, pp. 873 ff.; Norden, "Josephus und Tacitus ueber Jesus Christus und eine messianische Prophetie," pp. 244–253.
42. Or "indictment": Brandon, *Jesus and the Zealots*, p. 363, n. 3.
43. *Historia Ecclesiae*, I 11; *Demonstratio Evangelica*, III 3.
44. Lietzmann, *History of the Early Church*, Vol. III, p. 44.
45. *Ibid.*
46. *Historia Ecclesiae*, I 9. These memoranda appear to be identical with the memoirs of Pilate published in 311 by the Emperor Maximin: see Brandon, *The Trial of Jesus of Nazareth*, p. 153.
47. Brandon, *Jesus and the Zealots*, p. 359.
48. *Wars*, 2,174—as translated by me from the French text of Pascal, *La Prise de Jérusalem de Josèphe le Juif*, Vol. I, pp. 149–150, quoted by Brandon, *Jesus and the Zealots*, pp. 366–367.
49. *Wars*, 5,195. Translation taken from Goguel, *op. cit.*, Vol. I, p. 86 (by Olive Wyon).
50. Berendts and Grass, *Flavius Josephus vom juedischen Kriege nach der slavischen Uebersetzung, passim.*
51. Zeitlin, "The Hoax of the Slavonic Josephus," pp. 177 ff.; Williamson, *The World of Josephus*, pp. 309–310; Goguel *op. cit.*, Vol. I, pp. 90–91.
52. Eisler, *The Messiah Jesus and John the Baptist*, pp. 383 ff.; Thackeray, *Josephus: The Man and the Historian*, pp. 34 ff.
53. Brandon, *Jesus and the Zealots*, p. 367.
54. Cf. Goguel, *op. cit.*, Vol. I, p. 84, n. 1.
55. *Ibid.*, p. 87.
56. Some translators replace "notwithstanding" by "according to" or "in accordance with"—see Goguel, *op. cit.*, Vol. I, p. 85—which is surely erroneous.

57. We find the inscription described here interpreted also as an "inscription in the Temple said to have commemorated the crucifixion of Jesus": cf. Goguel, *op. cit.*, Vol. I, p. 90—the Jewish authorities having regarded the inscription on the cross "as an insult to their nation," they now replied by an inscription of their own in the temple (Eisler).

58. Goguel, *op. cit.*, Vol. I, pp. 89–90.

59. Suetonius, *Claudius*, 25,4.

60. Suetonius, *Nero*, 16.

61. Cf. Goguel, *op. cit.*, Vol. I, pp. 97–98.

62. Tacitus, *Annales*, XV 44.

63. Hochart, *De l'Authenticité des Annales et des Histoires de Tacite*, and *Nouvelles Considérations au Sujet des Annales et des Histoires de Tacite, passim;* Drews, *Die Christusmythe*, Vol. I, p. 179.

64. Mr. Abraham Tulin, a private scholar, of New York, writes in a letter to me: "The fact is that Pliny and the other learned Romans of the time wrote about nearly everything under the sun, but none of them have a single word to say about either Jesus or Pontius Pilatus. This would seem to militate against the guess that Pliny told Tacitus privately about Jesus and his execution by Pontius Pilatus. It is, moreover, the fact that the name of Pontius Pilatus is not mentioned anywhere in *heathen* Latin literature, except in this one passage in Tacitus. . . ."

65. Harnack, *Der juedische Geschichtsschreiber Josephus und Jesus Christus,* extensively quoted by Norden, *op. cit.*

66. Norden, *op. cit.*, pp. 256 ff.

67. Eduard Meyer, *op. cit.*, Vol. I, p. 209, and Vol. III, p. 505.

68. Plinius, *Epistulae*, X 96. See Chap. 6, *supra.*

69. Cichorius, quoted by Norden, *op. cit.*, p. 258.

70. Cf. Gibbon, *The Decline and Fall of the Roman Empire*, Chap. XVI.

71. Brandon, *Jesus and the Zealots*, p. 226.

13 . THE PERVERSION OF JUSTICE

1. T Menahot XIII 22; B Yoma 9a; *et al.* And see Strack and Billerbeck, *op. cit.*, Vol. I, pp. 195 ff., 366 ff., 937 ff., and Vol. II, pp. 253 ff.

2. See note 43, p. 346, *supra.*

3. R. Tarphon: B Shabbat 116a. The view that these books must be burned appears not to have been endorsed by any other scholar, and has not become law.

4. For this and further similar material, see the list of "Martyrdoms of the First Century Ascribed to Jews," appended to Parkes, *op. cit.*, at pp. 402–404.

5. Trachtenberg, *The Devil and the Jews*, pp. 101 ff.; Flannery, *op. cit.*, pp. 109–110.

6. Lea, *The Inquisition of the Middle Ages,* p. 448, n. 1.
7. Trachtenberg, *op. cit.,* pp. 140 ff.
8. *Ibid.,* p. 144.
9. Some of the published records of ecumenical and interfaith meetings make impressive and encouraging reading. See, for instance, Gollwitzer and Sterling (ed.), *Das gespaltene Gottesvolk,* and particularly the contribution of Zimmerli, "Die Schuld am Kreuz," pp. 32–43.
10. It is not now, of course, for the first time that the collective responsibility of all later generations of Jews for the death of Jesus is being doubted. With the advent of the "liberal" schools of biographers of Jesus in the nineteenth century, the sentiment denying and rejecting such responsibility became rather popular. But the prejudice and animosity persisted nonetheless—and not for the reason only that the story of Jewish guilt for the crucifixion was, even by the liberals, adopted and reiterated. One of the leading and most popular exponents of the liberal school, Ernest Renan, has this to say: "According to our modern ideas, there is no transmission of moral culpability from father to son: nobody has to render account, either to human or to divine justice, for what he has not himself done or omitted. Consequently, every Jew who today still suffers for the murder of Jesus has a right to complain: for perhaps was he Simon of Cyrene; perhaps was not he among the crowds which shouted, Crucify him! But nations have their responsibility like individuals. And if ever a crime was that of a nation, it was the murder of Jesus. It was a 'legal' murder, in the sense that its primary cause was the law which was the very soul of the nation. The mosaic law pronounced the death penalty for any attempt to change the established cult. Jesus, no doubt, attacked that cult and aspired to destroy it. . . . That law was detestable; but it was the law of ferocity of ancient times; and the hero who volunteered to abrogate it had first of all to submit to it. Alas! it took more than eighteen hundred years for the blood then shed to bear its fruits. In his name, throughout the centuries, tortures would be inflicted and lives taken, and the victims would be thinkers as noble as he. Even today, in countries calling themselves Christian, punishments are imposed for religious offenses. . . . Christianity has been intolerant; but intolerance is not essentially Christian. It is Jewish, in this sense that Judaism was the first to vest religion with a theory of the absolute, postulating that every reformer—even though supporting his doctrine with miracles—must be dragged to the gallows and stoned by all and sundry" (pp. 411–412; my translation from the French).

The moralist will have difficulty in determining what is worse—to make the sons responsible for the sins of their fathers or to make later generations responsible for the bad laws of their ancestors: "modern ideas" appear to shrink from the one no less than from the other. The underlying *ratio* of this particular brand of "national" responsibility is, of course, wholly theological, and, even though men like Renan would not care to admit it, in fact they are the unwitting mouthpiece of classical scholastic theology. The Jews are reproached (and persecuted) not so much for what they or their forefathers have actually done to Jesus, but for sticking to their ancient law; not for anything done or omitted by their ancestors, but rather for their own wicked obstinacy. The conversion of Jews to the new faith is a Christian mission quite independent of the death of Jesus; but the Jewish law under which Jesus allegedly found his death became a symbol, a flag, by which his murderers could easily and unmistakably be identified.

For many other theories of Jewish guilt, see, e.g., Parkes, *The Conflict of the Church and the Synagogue* and *The Foundations of Judaism and Christianity, passim;* Flannery, *The Anguish of the Jews, passim;* and the vast literature on the history of anti-Semitism.

11. Von Hippel, *Die Perversion von Rechtsordnungen,* pp. 187 ff.

12. Schonfield, *The Passover Plot, passim,* maintains that Jesus desired to be sentenced and executed, and conducted himself accordingly throughout. This view is taken by many theologians and novelists alike, and can hardly be disproved.

13. By Brandon in his books *Jesus and the Zealots* and *The Trial of Jesus of Nazareth,* respectively.

BIBLIOGRAPHY

SOURCES

OLD AND NEW TESTAMENTS. Quotations are from the King James Version unless otherwise noted.

OLD TESTAMENT APOCRYPHA. Translations are the author's unless otherwise stated.

NEW TESTAMENT APOCRYPHA. Quotations are from Hennecke, *New Testament Apocrypha* (Vol. I: *Gospels and Related Writings*). English translation edited by Wilson (1963).

TALMUD AND MIDRASH. All quotations are translations of the author unless otherwise stated.

The following abbreviations are used in the Notes:

    B—Babylonian Talmud

    J—Jerusalemite Talmud

    M—Mishna;

    T—Tossefta.

    (For the explanation of these terms, see Strack, *Introduction to the Talmud and Midrash,* paperback edition, 1959).

Standard editions of the Talmudim have been used, and in addition the following:

Tossefta, ed. Zuckermandel (2d ed., 1937).

Mekhilta, ed. Friedmann (1870).

Sifre, ed. Friedmann (1864).

Sifra, ed. Schlossberg (1862).

Midrash Rabba, ed. Theodor and Albeck (1912–36).

Midrash Tanhuma, ed. Buber (1885).

Midrash Tanna'im, ed. Hoffmann (1908).

Midrash Tehillim, ed. Buber (1891).

Pessikta Rabbati, ed. Friedmann (1885).

Megillat Ta'anit, ed. Lurie (1964).

Avot de-Rabbi Nathan, ed. Schechter (1887).

Mekhilta de-Rabbi Shimon bar Yohai, ed. Hoffmann (1905).

English translations are available of:

The Babylonian Talmud, under the editorship of Epstein (Soncino edition, 1935–52).

The Mishna, by Danby (1933).

The Mekhilta, by Lauterbach (1933–35).

Midrash Rabba (Soncino edition).

DEAD SEA SCRIPTURES

The standard English translations are:

Burrows, *The Dead Sea Scrolls* (1955).

Dupont-Sommer, *The Essene Writings from Qumran*, translated by
Vermes (1962).

Gaster, *The Dead Sea Scriptures* (1956).

Allegro, *The Dead Sea Scrolls* (1956).

OTHER JEWISH SOURCES

Josephus, Flavius, *De Bello Judaico* (quoted as *Wars*). English translation in Loeb Classical Library (1926).

———, *Antiquitates Judaicae* (quoted as *Antiquities*). English translation in Loeb Classical Library (1963–65).

———, *Vita* (quoted as *Autobiography*). English translation in Loeb
Classical Library (1928).

———, *Contra Apionem*. English translation in Loeb Classical Library
(1928).

———, Slavonic Version of Josephus: Berendts and Grass, *Flavius
Josephus vom juedischen Krieg nach der slavischen Uebersetzung
deutsch herausgegeben* (1924–27).

Philo Alexandrinus, *Legatio ad Gaium*. English translation by Smallwood (1961).

———, *De Legibus Specialibus*. English translation in Loeb Classical
Library (*Works*, 9 vols., 1929 ff.).

OTHER CHRISTIAN SOURCES

Augustinus, *Contra Judaeos*.

———, *Contra Faustus*.

———, *Commentarium in Psalmos*.

———, *De Consensu Evangelistarum*.

Chrysostom, *Homiliae Contra Juaeos*.

Eusebius, *Historia Ecclesiastica*. English translation in Loeb Classical Library (1926) and by Williamson (Penguin Classics, 1965).

———, *Demonstratio Evangelica*.

Hieronymus, *Commentarium in Evangelium Mattheum*.

Justinus (Martyr), *Dialogus cum Triphone Judaicus*.

Origen, *Contra Celsum.*

———, *Commentarium in Evangelium Mattheum.*

Sulpicius Severus, *Chronica.*

Tertullianus, *Adversus Judaeos.*

———, *Apologeticus.* English translation in Loeb Classical Library (1931).

ROMAN SOURCES

Ammianus Marcellinus, *Historiae.* English translation in Loeb Classical Library (1951–52).

Cicero, Marcus Tullius, *In Verrem.*

———, *Pro Rabirio Perduellionis Reo.* English translations in Loeb Classical Library.

Codex Justinianus and *Digesta.* English translation (*Corpus Juris Civilis*) by Scott (1931).

Codex Theodosius. English translation by Pharr (1952).

Dio Cassius, *Historia Romana.* English translation in Loeb Classical Library (1924).

Firmicus Maternus, *De Errore Profanarum Religionum.*

Gellius, Aulus, *Noctes Atticae.* English translation in Loeb Classical Library (1927–28).

Justinus, Marcus Junianius, *Historiae Philippicae.*

Lactantius, *Divinae Institutiones.*

Livius, Titus, *Ab Urbe Condita Libri.* English translation in Loeb Classical Library (1951–59).

Paulus, Julius, *Digesta.* English translation (*Corpus Juris Civilis*) by Scott (1931).

Plautus, Titus Maccius, *Miles Gloriosus.* English translation in Loeb Classical Library (1928).

Plinius (the Elder), Gaius Secundus, *Naturalis Historia.* English translation in Loeb Classical Library.

Plinius (the Younger), Caecilius Secundus, *Epistulae.* English translation in Loeb Classical Library (1921).

Plutarch, *De Sera Numinis Vindicta.* English translation in Loeb Classical Library (1927).

Seneca, Lucius Annaeus, *Ad Marcian Consolationes.*

———, *Epistulae.*

Suetonius, Gaius, *De Vita Caesarum.* English translations by Graves (Penguin Classics, 1957), and in Loeb Classical Library (1914).

Symmachus, Quintus Aurelius, *Epistulae.*

Tacitus, Cornelius, *Annales.* English translations in Loeb Classical Library (1931) and in Penguin Classics (1962).

———, *Historiae.* English translations in Loeb Classical Library (1925–31) and in Penguin Classics (1964).

Ulpianus, Domitius, *Digesta.* English translation (*Corpus Juris Civilis*) by Scott (1931).

Victorinus, Gaius Marius, *Caesares.*

BOOKS AND ARTICLES

Books are listed in the language in which they were consulted. Where translations into English are available, they are indicated in parentheses as ET.

Abrahams, I.: *Studies in Pharisaism and the Gospels,* 2 vols., New York, Ktav Publishing House, 1967 (reprint of 1924 edition) .

Adam, A.: *Handbuch der roemischen Altertuemer,* 2 vols., Erlangen, 1794–1796.

Adam, K.: *Jesus Christus,* Augsburg, 1931 (ET: *The Son of God,* New York, Sheed & Ward, 1934) .

Aicher, G.: *Der Prozess Jesu,* Bonn, 1929.

Albright, F. W.: *From the Stone Age to Christianity,* 2nd ed., New York, Doubleday Anchor Books, 1957.

Allegro, J.: *The Dead Sea Scrolls,* London, Penguin Books, 1956.

Allon, G.: *Mehkarim Betoledot Yisrael,* 2 vols., Tel Aviv, 1957.

————: *Toledot Hayehudim Be'eretz Yisrael Bitekufat Hamishna Vehatalmud,* 2 vols., 3rd ed., Tel Aviv, 1959.

Amos, S.: *The History and Principles of the Civil Law of Rome,* London, Kegan Paul, 1883.

Arnold, W.: *Kultur und Recht der Roemer,* Aalen, 1964 (reprint of 1868 edition) .

Bachmann, W.: *Der erste Brief an die Korinther,* Goettingen, 1905.

Baer, F.: "Judaism in the Synoptic Gospels" (Hebrew) , in *Zion,* Vol. 31 (1966) .

Bainton, F.: *Early Christianity,* New York, Anvil Books, Van Nostrand & Reinhold, 1960.

Barclay, W.: *Jesus As They Saw Him,* London, 1962.

Baron, S. W.: *A Social and Religious History of the Jews,* 3 vols., 2nd ed., New York, Columbia University Press, 1957.

Bauer, Fritz: "Der Prozess Jesu," in *Tribuene,* Vol. 4 (1965) .

Bauer, Walter: *Das Leben Jesu im Zeitalter der neutestamentlichen Apokryphen,* 2nd ed., Tuebingen, 1909.

————: "The Alleged Testimony of Josephus," in *New Testament Apocrypha,* ed. R. McL. Wilson, London, Lutterworth Press, 1963.

Baumann, R. A.: *The Crimen Maiestatis in the Roman Republic and Augustan Principate,* Johannesburg, Witwatersrand University Press, 1967.

Beare, F. W.: *The Earliest Records of Jesus,* Oxford, Blackwell, 1962.

Belkin, S.: *Philo and the Oral Law,* Harvard University Press, 1942.

Ben Chorin, S.: *Bruder Jesus—der Nazarener in juedischer Sicht,* Muenchen, 1967.

Bentwich, N.: "Philo as Jurist," in *Jewish Quarterly Review*, Vol. 21 (1930).

Berendts, A., and Grass, K.: *Flavius Josephus vom juedischen Kriege nach der slavischen Uebersetzung deutsch herausgegeben und mit dem griechischen Text verglichen*, Dorpat, 1927.

Bezold, C.: *Babylonisch-Assyrisches Glossar*, Heidelberg, 1926.

Bienert, W.: "Von der Kollektivschuld am Tode Jesu," in *Das Christentum und die Juden*, Arbeiten der Melanchton-Akademie, Koeln, 1966.

Bikerman, E. J.: "Al Hasanhedrin," in *Zion*, Vol. 3 (1938).

Billerbeck, P.: see Strack and Billerbeck.

Bin Gorion, M. J.: *Yeshu Ben Hanan*, Tel Aviv, 1959.

Blinzler, J.: *Der Prozess Jesu*, 3rd ed., Regensburg, 1960 (ET: *The Trial of Jesus*, Cork, 1959).

————: "Das Synedrium von Jerusalem und die Strafprozessordnung der Mischna," in *Zeitschrift fuer Neutestamentliche Wissenschaft*, Vol. 52 (1961).

————: *Zum Prozess Jesu*, ed. Koch, Weiden, 1967.

Boman, Th.: *Die Jesus-Ueberlieferung im Lichte der neueren Volkskunde*, Goettingen, 1967.

Bonsirven, J.: *Palestinian Judaism in the Time of Christ*, New York, McGraw-Hill Paperback, 1965.

Bornkamm, G.: *Jesus von Nazareth*, 7th ed., Stuttgart, 1965 (ET: *Jesus of Nazareth*, New York, Harper & Row, 1960).

Bousset, D. W.: *Kyrios Christos*, 2 vols., 2nd ed., Goettingen, 1921.

————: *Die Religion des Judentums im spaethellenistischen Zeitalter*, 4th ed., Tuebingen, 1966.

Brandon, S. G. F.: *Jesus and the Zealots*, Manchester University Press, 1967.

————: *The Trial of Jesus of Nazareth*, London, Batsford, 1968.

————: "The Trial of Jesus," in *History Today*, Vol. 16 (1966).

Bruce, F. F.: *The New Testament Documents*, 5th ed., London, Inter-Varsity Fellowship, 1960.

Bruckberger, R. L.: *L'Histoire de Jésus-Christ*, Paris, 1965.

Buechler, A.: *Das Synedrion in Jerusalem und das grosse Beth-Din in der Quaderkammer des jerusalemischen Tempels*, Wien, 1902.

————: "Die Todesstrafen der Bibel und der nachbiblischen Zeit," in *Monatsschrift fuer Geschichte und Wissenschaft des Judentums*, Vol. 50 (1906).

Buechsel, F.: "Zur Blutgerichtsbarkeit des Synedrions," in *Zeitschrift fuer Neutestamentliche Wissenschaft*, Vols. 30 (1931) and 33 (1934).

Bultmann, R.: *Die Erforschung der synoptischen Evangelien*, Goettingen, 1925.

———: *Die Geschichte der synoptischen Tradition*, 5th ed., Goettingen, 1961 (ET: *The History of Synoptic Tradition*, New York, Harper & Row, 1963) .

———: *Jesus*, 3rd ed., Siebenstern Taschenbuch, 1967 (ET: *Jesus and the Word*, London, 1935) .

———: "Das Verhaeltnis der urchristlichen Christusbotschaft zum historischen Jesus," in *Sitzungsberichte der Heidelberger Akademie der Wissenschaften, Philosophisch-Historische Klasse*, 1960, Vol. III.

Burkill, T. A.: "The Competence of the Sanhedrin," in *Vigilae Christianae*, Vol. 10 (1956) .

———: "The Trial of Jesus," in *Vigilae Christianae*, Vol. 12 (1958) .

Burkitt, F. C.: *The Gospel History and Its Transmission*, Edinburgh, Clark, 1906.

Burrows, M.: *The Dead Sea Scrolls*, New York, Viking Press, 1955.

———: *More Light on the Dead Sea Scrolls*, New York, Viking Press, 1958.

Busolt, G.: *Griechische Staatskunde*, 3rd ed., Muenchen, 1926.

Caillois, R.: *Pontius Pilate*, New York, Macmillan, 1963.

Carmichael, J.: *The Death of Jesus*, London, Pelican Books, 1966.

Chandler, W. M.: *The Trial of Jesus from a Lawyer's Standpoint*, 2 vols., New York, 1908.

Chewer, H. M.: "The Legal Aspects of the Trial of Christ," in *Biblioteca Sacra*, Vol. 60 (1903) .

Chwolson, D. A.: *Das letzte Passamahl Christi und der Tag seines Todes*, 2nd ed., Leipzig, 1908.

Cohen, Boaz: *Jewish and Roman Law*, 2 vols., New York, Jewish Theological Seminary, 1966.

———: "The Rabbinic Law Presupposed by Matthew 12:1 and Luke 6:1," in *Harvard Theological Review*, Vol. 23 (1930) .

———: *Law and Tradition in Judaism*, New York, Ktav Publishing House, 1969.

Cohn, Haim: *Al Onesh Hassekilah*, Ramatgar, Bar-Ilan University, 1962.

———: "Prolegomena to the Theory and History of Jewish Law," in *Essays in Jurisprudence in Honor of Roscoe Pound*, Indianapolis, Bobbs-Merrill, 1962.

———: "The Penology of the Talmud," in *Israel Law Review*, Vol. 5 (1970) .

Cohn, H. M.: "Sein Blut komme ueber uns," in *Jahrbuch fuer juedische Geschichte und Litteratur*, Vol. 6 (1903) .

Couchoud, P. L.: *The Enigma of Jesus,* London, Watts, 1924.

Craveri, M.: *The Life of Jesus,* London, Panther Books, 1969.

Cullmann, O.: *Der Staat im Neuen Testament,* 2nd ed., Tuebingen, 1961 (ET: *The State in the New Testament,* London, 1957).

Dalman, G. H.: *Aramaeisch-Neuhebraeisches Woerterbuch zu Targum, Talmud und Midrasch,* Frankfurt, 1901.

————: *Orte und Wege Jesu,* 3rd ed., Guetersloh, 1924 (ET: *Sacred Sites and Ways,* London, Society for Promoting Christian Knowledge, 1935).

————: *Die Worte Jesu,* Leipzig, 1898 (ET: *The Words of Jesus,* Edinburgh, Clark, 1902).

————: *Jesus-Jeschua: Studies in the Gospels,* New York, Macmillan, 1929.

Danby, H.: "The Bearing of the Rabbinical Criminal Code on the Jewish Trial Narratives in the Gospels," in *Journal of Theological Studies,* Vol. 21 (1919–1920).

Daniel-Rops, H. (Henry Petiot): *Daily Life in the Time of Jesus,* New York, Mentor-Omega Books, 1964.

————: *Jesus in His Time,* London, Spottiswoode, 1955.

Daniélou, J.: *The Dead Sea Scrolls and Primitive Christianity,* Baltimore, Helicon Press, 1958.

Daube, D.: *Collaboration with Tyranny in Rabbinic Law,* Oxford University Press, 1965.

————: *The New Testament and Rabbinic Judaism,* London, Athlone Press, 1956.

Davey, F. N.: see Hoskyns and Davey.

Davies, W. D.: *Christian Origins and Judaism,* Philadelphia, Westminster Press, 1962.

Dibelius, M.: *Die Formgeschichte des Evangeliums,* 4th ed., Tuebingen, 1961.

————: *Die Geisterwelt im Glauben des Paulus,* Tuebingen, 1909.

————: "Herodes und Pilatus," in *Zeitschrift fuer Neutestamentliche Wissenschaft,* Vol. 16 (1915).

————: *Jesus,* Berlin, 1949.

Dimont, M. I.: *Jews, God and History,* New York, Signet Books, 1962.

Dobschuetz, E. von, "Der Prozess Jesus nach den Akten Pilati," in *Zeitschrift fuer Neutestamentliche Wissenschaft,* Vol. 3 (1902).

Dodd, C. H.: *The Authority of the Bible,* New York, Harper Torchbooks, 1960.

————: *Historical Tradition in the Fourth Gospel,* Cambridge University Press, 1963.

————: *The Interpretation of the Fourth Gospel,* Cambridge University Press, 1958.

Doerr, F.: *Der Prozess Jesu in rechtsgeschichtlicher Beleuchtung,* 2nd ed., Berlin, 1920.

Drews, A.: *Die Christusmythe,* Jena, 1910 (ET: *The Christ Myth,* Chicago, Open Court Publishing Co., 1911).

———: *Das Markusevangelium,* 2nd ed., Jena, 1928.

Driver, G. R.: *The Judaean Scrolls,* Oxford, Blackwell, 1965.

Dubnow, S.: *Divrei Yemei Am Olam,* 2nd ed., Tel Aviv, 1936.

Dunkerley, R.: *Beyond the Gospels,* London, Penguin Books, 1957.

Dupin, M.: see Salvador, J.

Dupont-Sommer, A.: *The Essene Writings from Qumran,* New York, Meridian Books, 1962.

———: *The Jewish Sect of Qumran and the Essenes,* New York, Macmillan, 1954.

Ehrhardt, A.: *The Framework of the New Testament Stories,* Manchester University Press, 1964.

Ehrlich, E. L.: "Paulus und das Schuldproblem; erklaert an Roemer 5 und 8," in *Antijudaismus im Neuen Testament?,* Muenchen, 1967.

Eisler, R.: *The Enigma of the Fourth Gospel,* London, Methuen, 1938.

———: *Jesus Basileus u Basileusas,* 2 vols., Heidelberg, 1929–1930.

———: *The Messiah Jesus and John the Baptist,* London, Methuen, 1931.

———: "Flavius Josephus on Jesus Called the Christ," in *Jewish Quarterly Review,* Vol. 31 (1930–1931).

Enslin, M.: *The Prophet from Nazareth,* New York, Schocken Books, 1968.

Eppstein, V.: "The Historicity of the Gospel Account of the Cleansing of the Temple," in *Zeitschrift fuer Neutestamentliche Wissenschaft,* Vol. 55 (1964).

Epstein, A.: "Ordination et Autorisation," in *Revue des Etudes Juives,* Vol. 46 (1903).

Felten, J.: *Neutestamentliche Zeitgeschichte: Judentum und Heidentum zur Zeit Christi und der Apostel,* 2 vols., Regensburg, 1910.

Filson, F. V.: *A New Testament History,* London, SCM Press, 1965.

Finegan, J.: *Light from the Ancient Past,* Princeton University Press, 1946.

Finkelstein, L.: *Akiba—Scholar, Saint and Martyr,* New York, Meridian Books, 1962.

———: *The Pharisees,* 2 vols., 3rd ed., Philadelphia, Jewish Publication Society of America, 1962.

Flannery, E. H.: *The Anguish of the Jews,* New York, Macmillan, 1965.

Flusser, D.: *Jesus,* Rowohlt Taschenbuch, 1968 (ET: *Jesus,* New York, Herder & Herder, 1970).

————: "Mishpat Yeshu," in *Tarbitz*, Vol. 31 (1960).

Foerster, W.: *Palestinian Judaism in New Testament Times*, Edinburgh, Oliver & Boyd, 1964.

Frankel, Z.: *Der gerichtliche Beweis nach mosaisch-talmudischem Rechte*, Berlin, 1846.

Friedlaender, M.: *Geschichte der juedischen Apologetik*, Zurich, 1903.

Gaster, T. H.: *The Dead Sea Scriptures*, New York, Doubleday Anchor Books, 1956.

Geib, K. G.: *Geschichte des roemischen Kriminalprozesses bis zum Tode Justinians*, Aalen, 1969 (reprint of 1842 edition).

Gibbon, E.: *The Decline and Fall of the Roman Empire*, 1776–1788 (quotations are from Modern Library Edition, Penguin Books, London, no date).

Glover, T. R.: *The Jesus of History*, New York, Association Press, 1917.

Goguel, M.: *Jesus and the Origins of Christianity*, Vol. I: *Prolegomena to the Life of Jesus;* Vol. II: *The Life of Jesus*, New York, Harper Torchbooks, 1960.

Goldin, H. E.: *The Case of the Nazarene Reopened*, New York, Exposition Press, 1948.

Goldstein, M.: *Jesus in the Jewish Tradition*, New York, Macmillan, 1950.

Graetz, H.: "Die absetzbaren Hohepriester waehrend des zweiten Tempels," in *Monatsschrift fuer Geschichte und Wissenschaft des Judentums*, Vol. 1 (1851–1852).

————: *Geschichte der Juden*, Vol. 3, Leipzig, 1856 (ET: *History of the Jews*, London 1891).

Grant, F. C.: *Ancient Judaism and the New Testament*, New York, Macmillan, 1959.

————: *The Gospels, Their Origin and Their Growth*, 2nd ed., New York, Harper & Row, 1965.

Grass, K.: see Berendts and Grass.

Graves, R., and Podro, J.: *The Nazarene Gospel Restored*, New York, Doubleday, 1954.

————: "The Pharisees and Jesus," in *History Today*, Vol. 2 (1952).

Greenwald, L.: *Letoledot Hasanhedrin Beyisrael*, New York, 1950.

Gressmann, H.: *Der Messias*, Goettingen, 1929.

Guignebert, Ch.: *Jésus*, Paris, 1933 (ET: *Jesus*, New York, University Books, 1956).

————: *The Jewish World in the Time of Jesus*, London, Kegan Paul, 1939.

Guitton, J.: *The Problem of Jesus*, New York, P. J. Kenedy & Sons, 1955.

Gulak, A.: "Lesseider Hamissim Haroma'im Ba'aretz," in *Sefer Magnes*, Jerusalem, 1938.

Hamilton, N. Q.: "Temple Cleansing and Temple Bank," in *Journal of Biblical Literature*, Vol. 88 (1964).

Hansen, J.: *Zauberwahn, Inquisition und Hexenprozess im Mittelalter*, Aalen, 1964 (reprint of 1900 edition).

Harnack, A. von: *The Expansion of Christianity in the First Three Centuries*, New York, Putnam's, 1905.

———: *The Sayings of Jesus*, New York, Putnam's, 1908.

Heinemann, Isaak: *Philos juedische und griechische Bildung*, Breslau, 1932.

Heinemann, Joseph: "Targum Shemot 22,4 Vehahalakha Hakedumah," in *Tarbitz*, Vol. 38 (1969).

Hengel, M.: *Die Zeloten*, Leyden, 1961.

Hentig, H. von: *Die Strafe*, 2 vols., Berlin, 1954 (ET: *Punishment*, London, 1935).

Herford, R. T.: *Christianity in Talmud and Midrash*, London, Williams & Norgate, 1903.

———: *Judaism in the New Testament Period*, London, Lindsey Press, 1928.

———: *Pharisaism, Its Aim and Method*, New York, Putnam's, 1912 (quotations are from the German, *Das pharisaeische Judentum*, Leipzig, 1913).

———: *The Pharisees*, Boston, Beacon Press, 1962.

Hippel, F. von: *Die Perversion von Rechtsordnungen*, Tuebingen, 1955.

Hirsch, E. G.: *The Crucifixion from the Jewish Point of View*, Chicago, 1892.

Hochart, H.: *De l'Authenticité des Annales et des Histoires de Tacite*, Paris, 1890.

———: *Nouvelles Considérations au Sujet des Annales et des Histoires de Tacite*, Paris, 1894.

Hoenig, S. B.: *The Great Sanhedrin*, Philadelphia, Dropsie College, 1953.

Hoffmann, D.: *Der oberste Gerichtshof in der Stadt des Heiligthums*, Berlin, 1878.

———: "Die Praesidentur im Synedrium," in *Magazin fuer die Wissenschaft des Judentums*, Vol. 5 (1878).

Holtzmann, O.: *Das Leben Jesu*, Tuebingen, 1901 (ET: *The Life of Jesus*, London, 1904).

Horvath, T.: "Why was Jesus Brought to Pilate?," in *Novum Testamentum*, Vol. 11 (1969).

Hoskyns, Sir E., and Davey, F. N.: *The Riddle of the New Testament*, London, 1931.

Hunter, W. A.: *Introduction to Roman Law*, 9th ed., London, Sweet & Maxwell, 1934.

Husband, R. W.: *The Prosecution of Jesus,* Princeton University Press, 1916.

Innes, A. Taylor: *The Trial of Jesus Christ,* Edinburgh, Clark, 1899.

Isaac, J.: *Jésus et Israel,* Paris, 1948 (new edition, 1959) (quotations are from the German, *Jesus und Israel,* Wien, 1968).

Isorin, J.: *Le vrai Procès de Jésus,* Paris, 1967.

Jacobs, J.: *Jesus As Others Saw Him,* Boston, Houghton, 1895.

Jaeger, N.: *Il Processo di Gesù,* Turino, 1962.

James, E. H.: *The Trial Before Pilate,* 2 vols. Concord, Massachusetts, 1909.

Jaubert, A.: *La Date de la Cène: Calendrier Biblique et Liturgie Chrétienne,* Paris, 1957.

————: "Les Séances du Sanhedrin et les Récits de la Passion," in *Revue de l'Histoire des Réligions,* Vols. 166 (1964) and 167 (1965).

Jelski, I.: *Die innere Einrichtung des grossen Synedrions zu Jerusalem,* Breslau, 1894.

Jeremias, J.: *Jerusalem zur Zeit Jesu,* 3rd ed., Goettingen, 1962 (ET: *Jerusalem in the Time of Jesus,* London, SCM Press, 1969).

————: "Zur Geschichtlichkeit des Verhoers Jesu vor dem Hohen Rat," in *Zeitschrift fuer Neutestamentliche Wissenschaft,* Vol. 41 (1950).

Jolowicz, H. F.: *Historical Introduction to the Study of Roman Law,* 2nd ed., Cambridge University Press, 1952.

Jost, J. M.: *Geschichte des Judentums und seiner Sekten,* 3 vols., Leipzig, 1859.

Juster, J.: *Les Juifs dans l'Empire Romain,* 2 vols., Paris, 1914.

Kalthoff, A.: *Die Entstehung des Christentums,* Leipzig, 1904.

Kastner, K.: *Jesus vor Pilatus,* Muenster, 1912.

Katz, K.: *Jesu und das Judentum,* Prag, 1926.

Kaufmann, Y.: *Golah Veneikhar,* Tel Aviv, 1929–1932.

Kautsky, K.: *Der Ursprung des Christentums,* Stuttgart, 1908 (ET: *The Foundations of Christianity,* London, 1953).

Kee, H. C.: "The Question About Fasting," in *Novum Testamentum,* Vol. 11 (1969).

Keim, Th.: *Die Geschichte Jesu,* 3rd ed., Zurich, 1893.

————: *Geschichte Jesu von Nazareth,* 3 vols., 2nd ed., Zurich, 1873 (ET: *The History of Jesus of Nazareth: Considered in Its Connection with the National Life of Israel and Related in Detail,* 6 vols., London, Williams & Norgate, 1873–1883).

Kilpatrick, G. D.: *The Trial of Jesus,* Oxford University Press, 1953.

Kittel, G.: "Gekreuzigt Werden," in *Zeitschrift fuer Neutestamentliche Wissenschaft,* Vol. 35 (1936).

Klausner, J.: *Yeshu Ha-Notzri,* 6th ed., Tel Aviv, 1954 (ET: *Jesus of*

Nazareth, New York, Macmillan, 1925) (quotations are from the German, *Jesus von Nazareth,* 3rd ed., Jerusalem, 1952) .

———: *Mi-Yeshu ad Paulus,* Tel Aviv, 1939 (ET: *From Jesus to Paul,* New York, 1943) .

———: *Historia shel Habayit Hasheni,* 5 vols., 3rd ed., Jerusalem, 1952.

Klein, G.: *Zum Prozess Jesu,* ed. Koch, Weiden, 1967.

Koch, W.: *Der Prozess Jesu,* Koeln, 1966.

——— (ed.) : *Zum Prozess Jesu,* Weiden, 1967.

Kohut, A.: *Sefer Arukh Hashalem,* 4 vols., Wien, 1878.

Konvitz, M.: *Expanding Liberties,* New York, Viking Press, 1966.

Krauss, S.: *Das Leben Jesu nach juedischen Quellen,* Berlin, 1902.

———: *Paras Veromi Batalmud Ubamidrashim,* Jerusalem, 1948.

———: "The Jews in the Works of the Church Fathers," in *Jewish Quarterly Review,* Vols. 5 (1893) and 6 (1894) .

Kuemmel, W. G.: "Die Weherufe ueber die Schriftgelehrten und Pharisaeer (Matthaeus 23:13–36) ," in *Antijudaismus im Neuen Testament?,* Muenchen, 1967.

Kuenen, A.: "Ueber die Zusammensetzung des Sanhedrin," in *Gesammelte Abhandlungen zur Biblischen Wissenschaft,* Leipzig, 1894.

Lacey, T. A.: *The Historic Christ,* London, Williams & Norgate, 1905.

Laible, H.: *Jesus Christus im Thalmud,* 2nd ed., Berlin, 1900 (ET: *Jesus Christ in the Talmud,* Cambridge, 1893) .

Lauterbach, J. Z.: "The Pharisees and their Teachings," in *Hebrew Union College Annual,* Vol. 6 (1929) .

Lea, H. C.: *The Inquisition of the Middle Ages* (abridged by Margaret Nicholson) , New York, Macmillan, 1961.

Lengle, J.: *Roemisches Strafrecht bei Cicero und den Historikern,* Leipzig, 1934.

Levin, S. S.: *Jesus Alias Christ—A Theological Detection,* New York, Philosophical Library, 1969.

Levy, J.: "Die Presidentur im Synedrium," in *Monatsschrift fuer Geschichte und Wissenschaft des Judentums,* Vol. 4 (1855) .

Lieberman, S.: "Roman Legal Institutions in Early Rabbinics and in the Acta Martyrium," in *Jewish Quarterly Review,* Vol. 35 (1944–1945) .

Lietzmann, H.: *An die Korinther,* 2nd ed., Tuebingen, 1923.

———: "Der Prozess Jesu," in *Kleine Schriften,* Vol. 2, 1958.

———: "Bemerkungen zum Prozess Jesu," in *Zeitschrift fuer Neutestamentliche Wissenschaft,* Vols. 30 (1931) and 31 (1932) .

———: *A History of the Early Church,* 4 vols. in 2, New York, Meridian Books, 1961.

Lipsius, J. H.: *Das Attische Recht und Rechtsverfahren,* 3 vols., Leipzig, 1905.

Loewe, H. M. J.: *Render unto Caesar: Religious and Political Loyalty in Palestine,* Cambridge University Press, 1940.

Loofs, F.: *What Is the Truth about Jesus Christ?,* New York, Scribner's, 1913.

Lurie, B. Z.: *Megillat Ta'anit,* Jerusalem, 1964.

MacRuer, J. C.: *The Trial of Jesus,* Toronto, Clarke, Irwin & Co., 1964.

Mantel, H.: *Studies in the History of the Sanhedrin,* Harvard University Press, 1965.

Mauriac, F.: *The Life of Jesus,* New York, Longmans Green, 1937.

Mayr, R. von, "Der Prozess Jesu," in *Archiv fuer Kriminal-Anthropologie und Kriminalistik,* Vol. 21 (1906).

Merkel, J.: "Die Begnadigung am Passahfeste," in *Zeitschrift fuer Neutestamentliche Wissenschaft,* Vol. 6 (1905).

Meyer, Eduard: *Ursprung und Anfaenge des Christentums,* 3 vols., 5th ed., Stuttgart, 1924 (reprint, 1962).

Meyer, Ernst: *Roemischer Staat und Staatsgedanke,* 2nd ed., Zurich, 1961.

Meyer, Franz: "Einige Bemerkungen zur Bedeutung des Terminus Synhedrion in den Schriften des Neuen Testaments," in *New Testament Studies,* Vol. 14 (1968).

Michel, O.: "Fragen zu 1 Thessalonicher 2:14–16: Antijuedische Polemik bei Paulus," in *Antijudaismus im Neuen Testament?,* Muenchen, 1967.

Miscio, G. di: *Il Processo di Cristo,* Milano, 1967.

Mommsen, Th.: "Die Pilatus-Acten," in *Zeitschrift fuer Neutestamentliche Wissenschaft,* Vol. 3 (1902).

——: "Die Religionsfrevel nach roemischem Recht," in *Historische Zeitschrift,* Vol. 44 (1890).

——: *Roemisches Staatsrecht,* 3 vols., Leipzig, 1887–1888.

——: *Roemisches Strafrecht,* Graz, 1955 (reprint of 1899 edition).

——: *Das Weltreich der Caesaren,* 2nd ed., Wien, 1933.

Montefiore, C. G.: *The Synoptic Gospels,* New York, Ktav Publishing House, 1968 (reprint of 1927 edition).

——: *Rabbinical Literature and Gospel Teachings,* London, Macmillan, 1930.

Montefiore, H. W.: *Josephus and the New Testament,* London, Mowbray, 1962.

Moore, G. F.: *Judaism in the First Centuries of the Christian Era,* 3 vols., Harvard University Press, 1927–1930.

Morrison, W. D.: *The Jews under Roman Rule,* 3rd ed., New York, Putnam's, 1893.

Nardi, C.: *Il Processo di Gesù, re dei Guidei,* Bari, 1966.

Noerr, D.: "Rechtsgeschichtliche Probleme in den Evangelien," in *Kontexte*, Vol. 3, *Die Zeit Jesu*, Stuttgart, 1966.

Norden, E.: "Josephus und Tacitus ueber Jesus Christus und eine messianische Prophetie," in *Kleine Schriften zum Klassischen Altertum*, 1966.

Noth, M.: *A History of Israel*, 2nd ed., London, Black, 1965.

Olmstead, A. J.: *Jesus in the Light of History*, New York, 1942.

Papini, G.: *The Life of Christ*, New York, Blue Ribbon Books, 1923.

Parkes, J.: *The Conflict of the Church and Synagogue*, New York, Meridian Books, 1964.

————: *The Foundations of Judaism and Christianity*, London, Mitchell, 1960.

————: *A History of the Jewish People*, London, Pelican Books, 1964.

Pedersen, J.: *Israel, Its Life and Culture*, 2nd ed., Oxford University Press, 1959.

Peter, J.: *Finding the Historical Jesus*, London, Collins, 1965.

Petiot, H.: see Daniel-Rops, H.

Pfeiffer, R. H.: *History of New Testament Times with an Introduction to the Apocrypha*, New York, Harper & Bros., 1949.

Pickl, J.: *Messiaskoenig Jesus in der Auffassung seiner Zeitgenossen*, 2nd ed., Muenchen, 1935 (ET: *The Messias*, St. Louis, 1946).

Pin, B.: *Jérusalem contre Rome*, Paris, 1938.

Podro, J.: see Graves and Podro.

Powell, F. J.: *The Trial of Jesus Christ*, London, Paternoster Press, 1949.

Rabbinowicz, R. N.: *Dikdukei Sofrim*, 13 vols., Muenchen, 1867–1897.

Rabin, Ch.: *Qumran Studies*, Oxford University Press, 1957.

Radin, M.: *The Trial of Jesus of Nazareth*, University of Chicago Press, 1931.

Reimarus, H. S.: *Geschichte der Leben Jesu Forschung*, 2nd ed., Tuebingen, 1906.

Rein, W.: *Das Kriminalrecht der Roemer von Romulus bis auf Justinian*, Aalen, 1962 (reprint of 1844 edition).

Reinach, S.: *Orpheus—A History of Religions*, New York, Liveright, 1942.

Reinach, Th.: "Josèphe sur Jésus," in *Revue des Etudes Juives*, Vol. 35 (1897).

Renan, E.: *La Vie de Jésus*, 8th ed., Paris, 1863 (ET: *The Life of Jesus*, New York, Modern Library, 1927).

Ricciotti, G.: *The Life of Christ*, Milwaukee, Bruce Publishing Co., 1952.

Riddle, D. W.: *Jesus and the Pharisees*, University of Chicago Press, 1928.

Riessler, P.: *Altjuedisches Schrifttum ausserhalb der Bibel,* 2nd ed., Heidelberg, 1966.

Robertson, A. T.: *Commentary on the Gospel According to St. Matthew,* New York, Macmillan, 1911.

————: *The Pharisees and Jesus,* New York, Macmillan, 1920.

Robertson, J. M.: *The Historical Jesus—A Survey of Positions,* London, Watts, 1916.

————: *Jesus and Judas—A Textual and Historical Investigation,* London, Watts, 1927.

Rosadi, G.: *The Trial of Jesus,* New York, Dodd Mead, 1905.

Roth, C.: "The Cleansing of the Temple and Zechariah 14:21," in *Novum Testamentum,* Vol. 4 (1960).

————: *The Historical Background of the Dead Sea Scrolls,* Oxford, Blackwell, 1958.

Rousseau, J. J.: *Émile—Profession de Foi,* Paris 1846 (ET: *Emile,* Everyman's Library, 1911).

Sadler, G. T.: *Has Jesus Christ Lived on Earth?,* London, Daniel, 1914.

————: *Behind the New Testament,* London, Daniel, 1921.

Salvador, J.: *Histoire de la Naissance de l'Église, de son Organisation et de ses Progrès pendant le Premier Siècle,* Paris, 1938.

————: *Histoire des Institutions de Moise et du Peuple Hébreu* (with Appendix: Dupin, M.: *Jésus devant Caiphe et Pilate*), 3 vols., 2nd ed., Bruxelles, 1830.

————: *Jésus-Christ et Sa Doctrine,* 2 vols., Paris, 1838.

Sandmel, S.: *A Jewish Understanding of the New Testament,* Cincinnati, Hebrew Union College, 1957.

Schalit, A.: "Kritische Randbemerkungen zu Paul Winters On the Trial of Jesus," in *Annual of the Swedish Theological Institute,* Jerusalem, Vol. 2 (1963).

Scheidweiler, F.: "The Gospel of Nicodemus, Acts of Pilate, and Christ's Descent into Hell," in *New Testament Apocrypha,* ed. R. McL. Wilson, Vol. I, London, Lutterworth Press, 1963.

Schelkle, K. H.: "Die Selbstverfluchung Israels nach Matthaeus 27:23–25," in *Antijudaismus in Neuen Testament?,* Muenchen, 1967.

Schisas, F. M.: *Offences against the State in Roman Law,* London, University Press, 1926.

Schlatter, D. A.: *Die Geschichte Israels von Alexander dem Grossen bis Hadrian,* Stuttgart, 1925.

Schleiermacher, F. E. D.: *Das Leben Jesu,* in *Saemtliche Werke,* Vol. 6, Berlin, 1864.

Schmidt, P. W.: *Die Geschichte Jesu,* Vol. 1, Freiburg, 1899, Vol. 2, Tuebingen, 1904.

Schmithals, W.: "Paul und der historische Jesus," in *Zeitschrift fuer neutestamentliche Wissenschaft,* Vol. 53 (1962).

Schneider, G.: "Gab es eine Szene 'Jesus vor dem Synedrium'?" in *Novum Testamentum,* Vol. 12 (1970).

Schoeps, H. J.: *Die grossen Religionsstifter,* Erlangen, 1950.

Schonfield, H. J.: *The Passover Plot,* New York, Bantam Books, 1967.

Schuerer, E.: *Die Geschichte des juedischen Volkes im Zeitalter Jesu Christi,* 3 vols., 3rd ed., Leipzig, 1901 (ET: *A History of the Jewish People in the Time of Jesus Christ,* 3 vols., Edinburgh, Clark, 2nd ed., 1891).

Schuhmann, H.: "Bemerkungen zum Prozess Jesu vor dem Synedrium," in *Zeitschrift der Savigny-Stiftung fuer Rechtsgeschichte,* Vol. 82 (1965).

Schweitzer, A.: *The Quest of the Historical Jesus,* New York, Macmillan Paperback, 1961.

Schweppe, A.: *Roemische Rechtsgeschichte,* Goettingen, 1822.

Scott, W.: *History of Torture Throughout the Ages,* 3rd ed., Edinburgh, 1943.

Shaw, Lord of Dunfermline, *The Trial of Jesus Christ,* London, Newnes, 1928.

Sherwin-White, A. N.: *Roman Society and Roman Law in the New Testament,* Oxford, Clarendon Press, 1963.

Silver, A. H.: *A History of Messianic Speculation in Israel,* New York, Macmillan, 1927.

Sjoeborg, E.: *Der verborgene Menschensohn in den Evangelien,* Lund, 1955.

Smallwood, E. M.: "High Priests and Politics in Roman Palestine," in *Journal of Theological Studies,* Vol. 13 (1962).

Smith, G. A.: *Jerusalem,* London, Hodder, 1907.

Smith, W. B.: *Der vorchristliche Jesus,* Giessen, 1906 (ET: *The Pre-Christian Jesus,* London, 1906).

Stalker, J.: *The Life of Jesus Christ,* 4th ed., Edinburgh, Clark, 1891.
———: *Das Verhoer und der Tod Jesu,* 2nd ed., Leipzig, 1908.

Stapfer, E. L.: *The Death and Resurrection of Jesus Christ,* New York, Scribner's, 1905.
———: *Palestine in the Time of Christ,* New York, Armstrong, 1885.

Stauffer, E.: *Christus und die Caesaren,* Hamburg, 1952.
———: *Jerusalem und Rom im Zeitalter Jesu Christi,* Bern, 1957.
———: *Jesus—Gestalt und Geschichte,* Bern 1957 (ET: *Jesus and His Story,* New York, Knopf, 1960).

Stendahl, K. (ed.): *The Scrolls and the New Testament,* New York, Harper & Bros., 1957.

Stevenson, G. H.: *Roman Provincial Administration*, Oxford, Blackwell, 1949.

Strachan-Davidson, J. L.: *Problems of the Roman Criminal Law*, 2 vols., Oxford, Clarendon Press, 1912.

Strack, H. L.: *Introduction to Talmud and Midrash*, New York, Meridian Books, 1959.

———— and Billerbeck, P.: *Kommentar zum Neuen Testament aus Talmud und Midrasch*, 4 vols., Muenchen, 1922–1928.

Strauss, D. F.: *Das Leben Jesu*, rev. ed., Tuebingen, 1864 (ET: *The Life of Jesus Critically Examined*, New York, Blanchard, 1855).

Taubes, Z.: *Hanassi Basanhedrin Hagedolah*, Wien, 1925.

Taylor, V.: *The Formation of the Gospel Tradition*, 2nd ed., London, Macmillan, 1949.

————: *The Gospel According to St. Mark*, London, Macmillan, 1952.

————: *The Life and Ministry of Jesus*, London, Macmillan, 1954.

Tchernowitz, Ch. (Rav Tza'ir) : *Toledot Hahalakha*, 4 vols., New York, 1934–1950.

Thackeray, H. St. John, *Josephus—The Man and the Historian*, New York, Ktav Publishing House, 1967 (reprint of the 1929 edition).

Thieme, K.: "Die religioes motivierte Judenfeindschaft," in Thieme, K. (ed.), *Judenfeindschaft*, Frankfurt, 1963.

Trachtenberg, J.: *The Devil and the Jews*, Meridian Books, New York, 1961.

Trocmé, E.: "Jésus-Christ et le Temple: Eloge d'un Naïf," in *Revue d'Histoire et Philosophie Réligieuses*, Vol. 44 (1964).

Trotter, F. T.: *Jesus and the Historian*, Philadelphia, Westminster Press, 1968.

Urbach, E. E.: *Class-Status and Leadership in the World of the Palestinian Sages*, Jerusalem, 1966.

Van Buren, P.: *The Secular Meaning of the Gospel*, London, Pelican Books, 1968.

Vawter, A.: "Are the Gospels Anti-Semitic?," in *Journal of Ecumenical Studies*, 1968.

Villa Fausto, *Il Processo di Gesù*, Turino, 1925.

Vogt, J.: "Augustus und Tiberius," in *Kontexte*, Vol. 3: *Die Zeit Jesu*, Stuttgart, 1966.

Walther, A. B. von, *Juristisch-historische Betrachtungen ueber die Geschichte vom Leiden und Sterben Jesu Christi*, Breslau, 1777.

Walther, J. A.: "The Chronology of Passion Week," in *Journal of Biblical Literature*, Vol. 72 (1958).

Weber, M.: *Ancient Judaism*, New York, Free Press, 1952 (paperback ed., 1967).

Weiss, B.: *The Life of Christ*, 3 vols., Edinburgh, Clark, 1883–1884.

Weiss, J.: *Earliest Christianity*, 2 vols., New York, Harper Torchbooks, 1959.

Wellhausen, J.: *Einleitung in die drei ersten Evangelien*, 2nd ed., Berlin, 1911.

——: *Das Evangelium Johannis*, Berlin, 1908.

——: *Das Evangelium Marci*, Berlin, 1903.

——: *Die Pharisaeer und die Sadduzaeer: eine Untersuchung zur inneren juedischen Geschichte*, 2nd ed., Hanover, 1924.

——: *Prolegomena to the History of Ancient Israel*, New York, Meridian Books, 1957.

Wendland, P.: *Die hellenistisch-roemische Kultur in ihren Beziehungen zu Judentum und Christentum*, 2nd ed., Tuebingen, 1912.

Wenger, L.: *Die Quellen des roemischen Rechts*, Wien, 1953.

Willam, F. M.: *Das Leben Jesu im Lande und Volke Israel*, Freiburg, 1934.

Williamson, G. A.: *The World of Josephus*, Boston, Little Brown, 1964.

Wilson, E.: *The Scrolls from the Dead Sea*, New York, Meridian Books, 1964.

Winter, P.: "Josephus on Jesus," in *Journal of Historical Studies*, 1969.

——: *On the Trial of Jesus*, Berlin, 1961.

——: "Sadduzaeer und Pharisaeer," in *Kontexte*, Vol. 3, *Die Zeit Jesu*, Stuttgart, 1966.

——: "Tacitus and Pliny: The Early Christians," in *Journal of Historical Studies*, 1967.

——: "The Trial of Jesus," in *Trivium*, 1967.

——: *Zum Prozess Jesu*, ed. Koch, Weiden, 1967.

——: "Zum Prozess Jesu," in *Altertum*, Vol. 9 (1963).

——: "Zum Prozess Jesu," in *Antijudaismus im Neuen Testament?*, Muenchen, 1967.

Wolff, H. J.: *Roman Law: A Historical Introduction*, University of Oklahoma Press, 1951.

Wolfson, H. A.: "How the Jews Will Reclaim Jesus," in *Menorah Journal*, Vol. 49, 1962.

——: *Philo: Foundations of Religious Philosophy in Judaism, Christianity and Islam*, 2 vols., Harvard University Press, 1947.

Zahrnt, H.: *The Historical Jesus*, London, Collins, 1963.

Zeitlin, S.: "The Christ Passage in Josephus," in *Jewish Quarterly Review*, Vol. 19 (1928).

——: "The Crucifixion—A Libellous Accusation against the Jews," in *Jewish Quarterly Review*, Vol. 55 (1964).

——: "The Crucifixion of Jesus Re-examined," in *Jewish Quarterly Review*, Vols. 31 (1940–1941) and 32 (1941–1942).

——: "The Halakha in the Gospels and Its Relation to the Jewish

Law at the Time of Jesus," in *Hebrew Union College Annual,* Vol. 1 (1924).

————: "The Hoax of the Slavonic Josephus," in *Jewish Quarterly Review,* Vol. 39 (1948).

————: *Who Crucified Jesus?,* 2nd ed., New York, Bloch Publishing Co., 1947.

Zimmerli, W.: "Die Schuld am Kreuz," in *Das gespaltene Gottesvolk,* Stuttgart, 1966.

Zucker, H.: *Studien zur juedischen Selbstverwaltung im Altertum,* Berlin, 1936.

Zumpt, A. W.: *Der Kriminalprozess der roemischen Republik,* Leipzig, 1871.

Zuntz, L.: *Die gottesdienstlichen Vortraege der Juden historisch entwickelt,* 2nd ed., Berlin, 1892 (quotations follow the Hebrew translation, Jerusalem, 1954).

Zuri, J. S.: *Toledot Hamishpat Hatziburi Ha'ivri,* Vol. 1. Paris, 1931, Vol. 2, London, 1934.

INDEX

ABOUT THE AUTHOR

Mr. Justice Haim H. Cohn was born in Luebeck, Germany, in 1911. He graduated from the Heinrich Hertz Realgymnasium in Hamburg in 1929 and until 1930 studied humanities (philosophy and Semitic languages) at the University of Munich. In 1930 he came to Palestine and took up rabbinical studies at the Yeshivat Merkaz Harav as well as Judaistic studies at the Hebrew University in Jerusalem. In 1932 he returned to Germany to study law, and with the advent of the Hitler regime in 1933 he returned again to Palestine. In 1937 he graduated from the Palestine Government Law School and was called to the Bar of Palestine. Until 1948 he practiced as an attorney in Jerusalem. Upon the establishment of the State of Israel in 1948 he was appointed State Attorney and shortly thereafter Director-General of the Ministry of Justice. In 1950 he was made the Attorney-General of Israel. In 1952 he joined the Cabinet as Minister of Justice and in 1953 resumed the Attorney-Generalship until his appointment in 1960 as a Justice of the Supreme Court of Israel, an office he still holds.

Mr. Justice Cohn represented the State of Israel on the United Nations Commission on Human Rights and on various *ad hoc* United Nations committees. He is the Chairman of the Israel National Sections of the International Commission of Jurists and of the Association Internationale de Droit Pénal. He was formerly Chairman of the Executive Council of the Hebrew University of Jerusalem and is Deputy Chairman of the State Council of Higher Education. He is a member of the Permanent Court of Arbitration at The Hague and has recently been elected to the Board of Governors of the International Institute of Human Rights in Strasbourg, France. He lectures on the History of Penal Law, Penal Philosophy and Jurisprudence at the Hebrew University of Jerusalem and at the University of Tel-Aviv.